AMERICA'S NATIONAL CEMETERIES

WAR, MEMORY, AND CULTURE

Series published in cooperation with

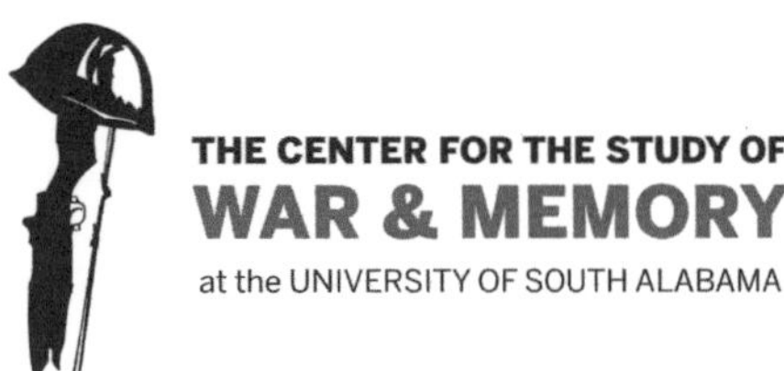

AMERICA'S NATIONAL CEMETERIES

A Meditation on History, Memory, and Place

Timothy B. Spears

Foreword by Roderick Gainer, Curator, US Army

Published in Cooperation with George F. Thompson Publishing

THE UNIVERSITY OF ALABAMA PRESS | *Tuscaloosa*

The University of Alabama Press
Tuscaloosa, Alabama 35487–0380
uapress.ua.edu

All photographs courtesy of Timothy B. Spears

Typeface: Adobe Jenson Pro

Cover image: Fort Rosecrans National Cemetery (2018); photograph courtesy of Timothy B. Spears
Cover design: Lori Lynch

Cataloging-in-Publication data is available from the Library of Congress.
ISBN: 978-0-8173-2240-3 (cloth)
E-ISBN: 978-0-8173-9568-1

"National cemeteries are established as national shrines in tribute to the gallant dead who have served in the Armed Forces of the United States. Such areas are protected, managed, and administered as suitable and dignified burial grounds and as significant cultural resources."

—Code of Federal Regulations, 36 C.F.R. § 12.2 (June 5, 1970)

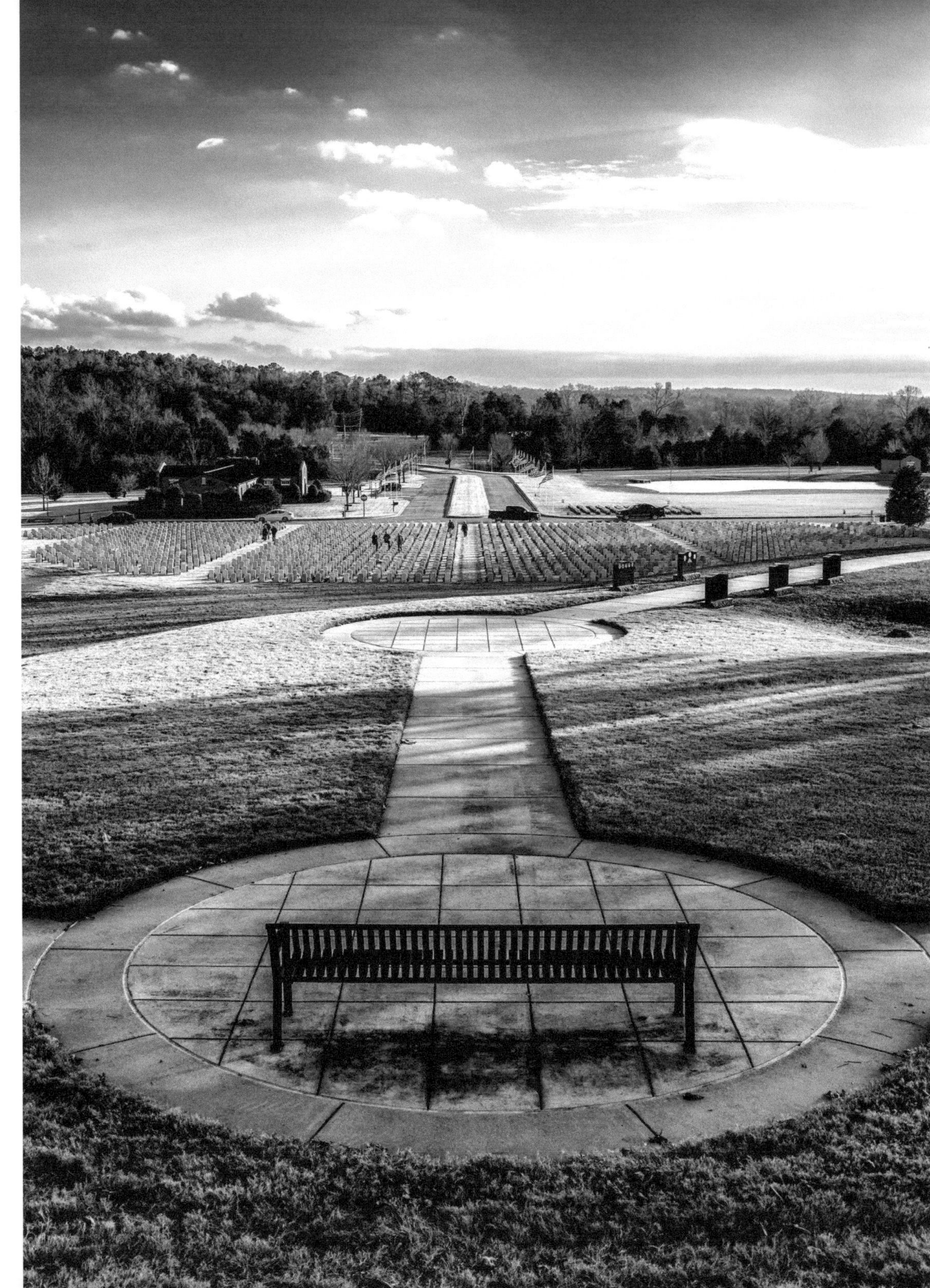

Alabama National Cemetery (established in 2007), Montevallo, Alabama, 2019.

Contents

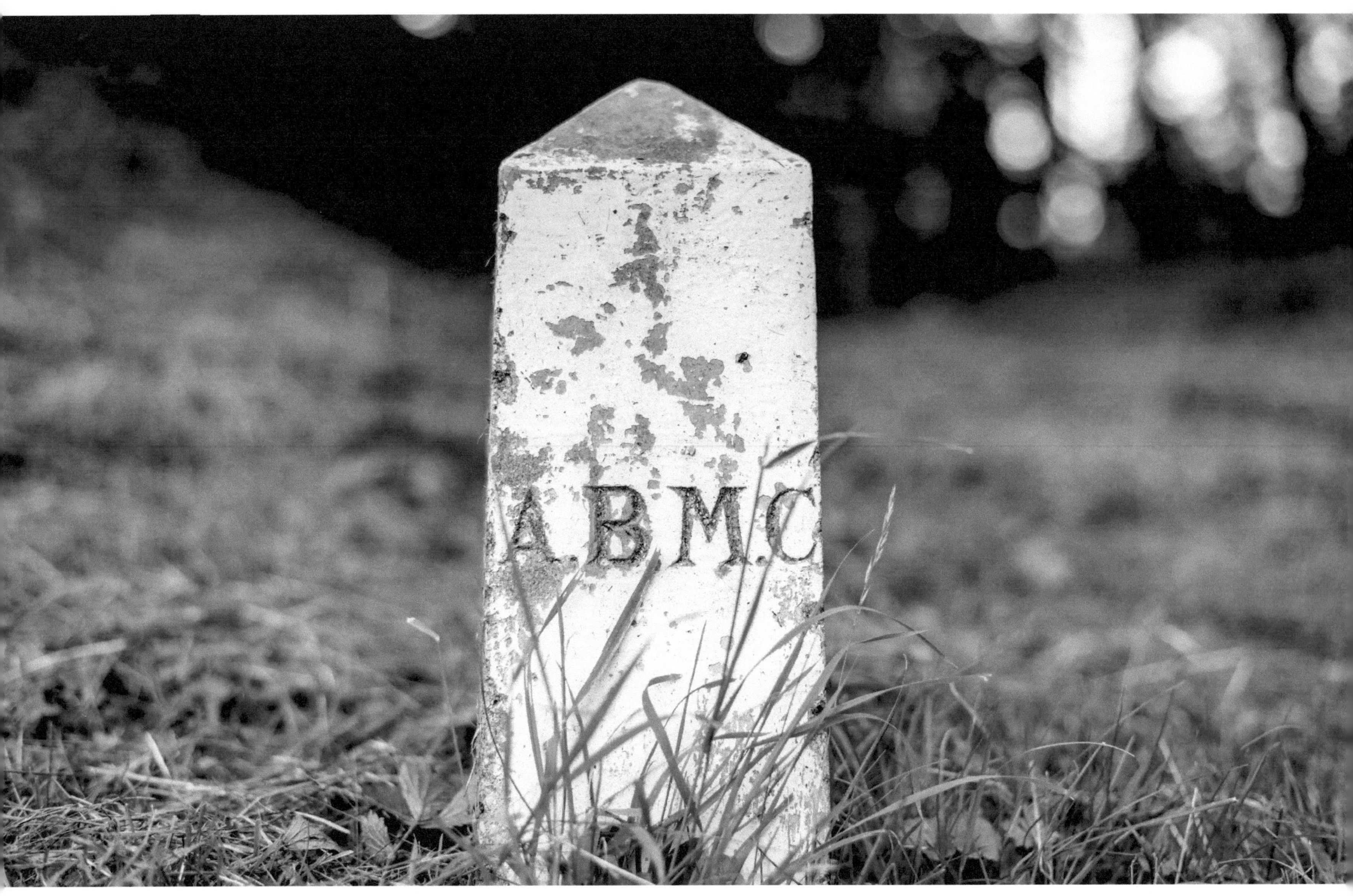

A boundary marker of the ABMC (American Battle Monuments Commission) near Montfaucon American Monument (dedicated in 1937), Montfaucon-en-Argonne, France, 2016.

Foreword

Roderick Gainer

Military landscapes play a key role in how Americans interpret their shared—and diverse—views of history. Despite the much-ballyhooed "decline of history" trumpeted by the chattering classes, history remains a vibrant and popular discipline and subject of general interest. Every year innumerable books dealing with often-obscure military topics are released, and the Internet channels hundreds, if not thousands, of podcasts and locally made historical documentaries that often feature highly regarded experts and are of the highest quality.

There is an old joke, long revered by battlefield interpreters and historians, about an enthusiastic visitor who, awed by the weight of a site's history, gushes, "You need to move these battlefield parks closer to the big cities where more people can enjoy them!" Military actions and the cemeteries they invariably produce are often in out-of-the-way places. Access to them often takes careful planning and study and furthermore requires extensive travel. Timothy B. Spears knows this better than anyone. His visits took him at first to the great battlefields of World War I in Europe, where he visited many of its haunting cemeteries that still bear mute witness to the carnage of that world conflict. Upon his return, Spears next began visiting US National Cemeteries, and his stories about visiting and experiencing all but a few of America's 155 national cemeteries are highlights of his inspirational book. He deftly integrates the roles of scholar and citizen and weaves a tale of national heartbreak as well as national reconciliation, especially regarding the fallen from the American Civil War, the nation's most shattering event. No town, village, city, or state escaped the carnage of that war, and the national cemeteries reflect this.

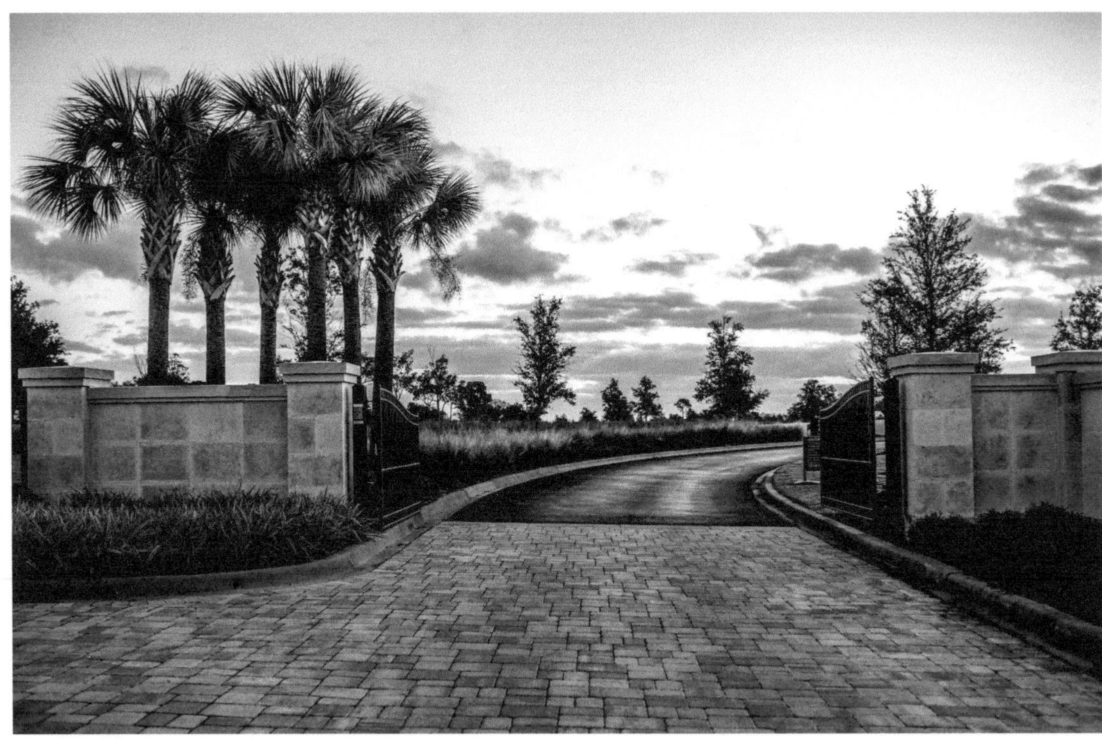

Cape Canaveral National Cemetery (established in 2015), Mims, Florida, 2019.

Spears's travels took him far and wide: from the bloody fields of Gettysburg, Shiloh, and Antietam to less-renowned cemeteries in places like Elmira, New York, and Keokuk, Iowa. The military situations may have differed—the latter two examples are, respectively, a Union prisoner-of-war camp and a hospital—but the meaning of these landmarks remains the same: they are places where a nation commemorates and mourns Americans who answered war's klaxon, many of whom never returned to their home. Spears also notes how these sacred sites are maintained: some, sadly, are neglected while others are carefully manicured and maintained. Throughout his account, Spears evokes a sense of place we can embrace, of what it is like to wander through a cemetery, as each site in kind evokes its own sense of place by way of its design and scale, topography and location, time of day and year, and, yes, the weather conditions that can impact one's visit.

The Civil War unleashed a seismic shift in American culture, as the bane of slavery legally ended and the country came out of the divisive fire with a new purpose. Feelings ran harsh,

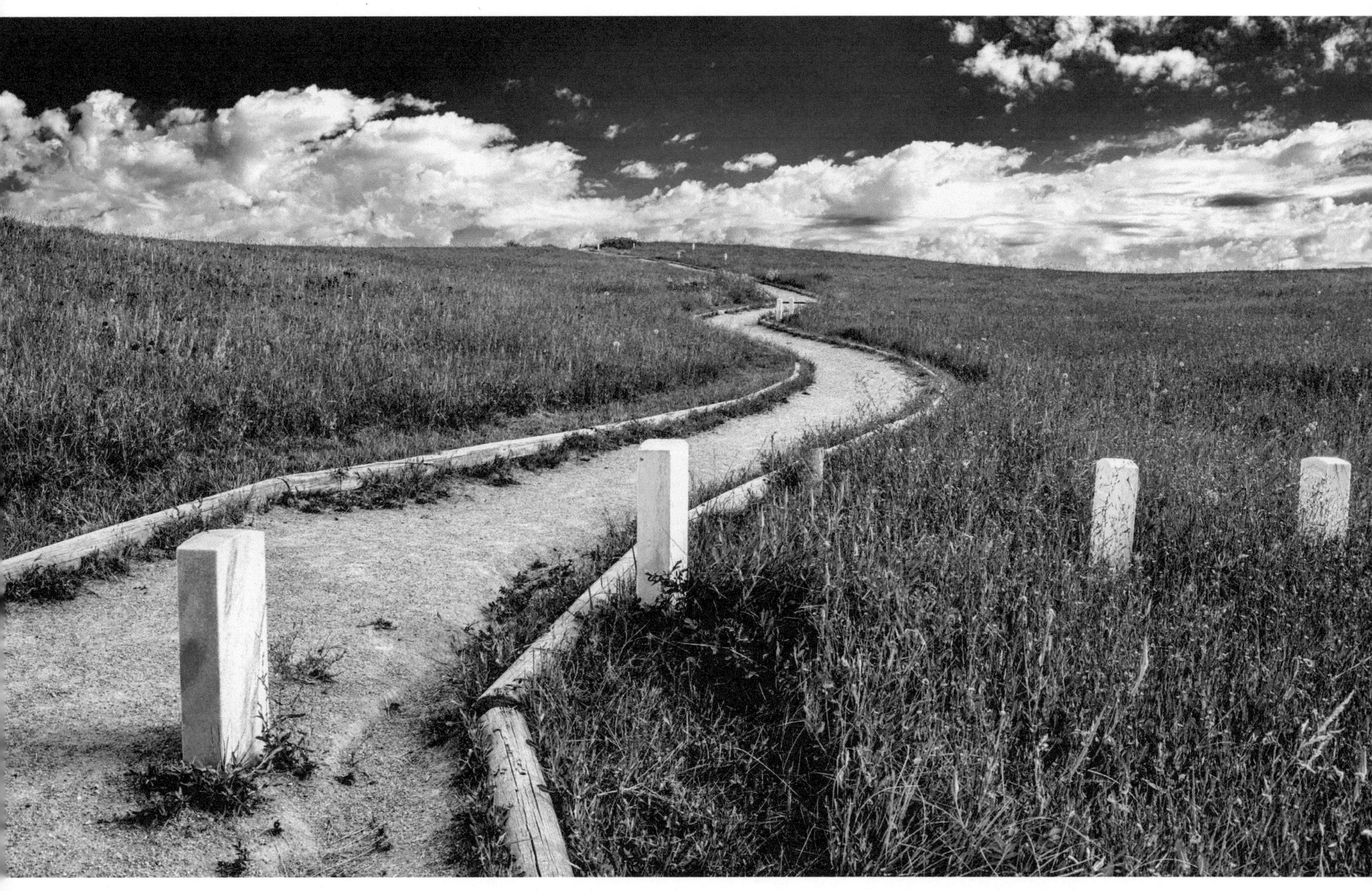

Little Bighorn Battlefield National Monument (established in 1879), Crow Agency, Montana, 2018. The headstones mark the places where US soldiers died in the Battle of the Greasy Grass/Little Bighorn on June 25, 1876. Their remains were later reinterred in a mass grave located near the battlefield on Last Stand Hill or moved to other cemeteries such as Fort Leavenworth. Elsewhere on the battlefield, stone markers designate the places where Lakota and North Cheyenne combatants fell.

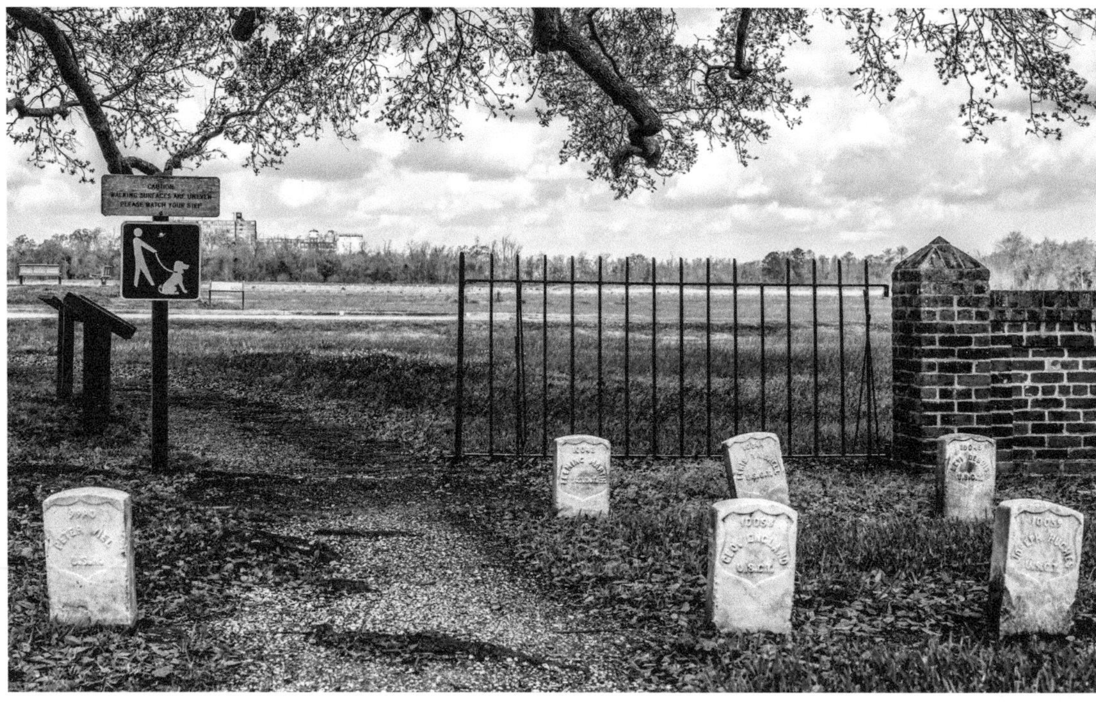

Chalmette National Cemetery (established in 1864), Chalmette, Louisiana, 2018.

especially in the defeated South, where Union graves were looked upon with scorn. How could a nation—one that had recently split into two nations and waged a bloody conflict in which more than six hundred thousand lives were lost—find common ground in commemoration? The two sides, of course, initially clashed in bitter recrimination. Unrepentant southerners disliked Yankee graves on their soil, and Union veterans railed against any Confederate memorialization, much less burials, in national battlefields or parks. In one well-known altercation in 1868 at Arlington National Cemetery, veterans of the GAR (Grand Army of the Republic) posted guards to prevent the decoration of Confederate graves![1]

Of interest to most visitors, regardless of the cemetery, is the actual design of these sacred spaces. Often field expedients, with the dead lying near where they fell or buried in an otherwise hasty manner, these cemeteries soon took distinct shapes, either in remembrance of lost loved ones or in facilitating ceremonies for the living. The rise of Decoration Days, and especially Memorial Day, gave birth to carefully manicured "fields of the dead" so that the survivors of the ghastly Civil War could better come to grips with the massive and lingering human cost of the conflict.

By the latter part of the nineteenth century, attitudes in America changed. National reconciliation became the order of the day, and segregation once again became the order of the nation. Despite the pleas of some aging Union veterans, Confederate service became valorized, and monuments to the Lost Cause were built throughout the nation. These conflicts became especially prevalent in the commemoration of the remains of fallen African American soldiers, who, even in death, remained in segregated sections often placed away from the "main" (that is, white) burial area. No less a personage than Frederick Douglass decried this postmortem segregation, arguing that those who saved the Union should be buried together.[2] Spears's examination of this dichotomy is among the most interesting aspects of his work. He also details the changing nature of commemoration at these Civil War fields of battle, from ones of victorious reunion to one of national reconciliation and, regrettably, the rise of Jim Crow. At the end of chapter 6, Spears's side journey to and examination of the National Memorial for Peace and Justice in Montgomery, Alabama, offers a stark reminder of this American failing.

Other affecting sections of Spears's "meditation" involve his previously mentioned visits to overseas military cemeteries. From the grand cities of the dead of World War I to the more Art Deco cemeteries of World War II, Spears traveled far and wide in his search for how the United States—with the help of its overseas allies—honored its dead who fell overseas. His journeys to the killing fields of the Somme and Verdun, places where the very flower of much of Europe's youth fell, are especially poignant. The much smaller US cemeteries, overseen since 1923 by the American Battlefields and Monuments Commission, are also thoughtfully examined in moving detail. One wonders what the fate of many of these cemeteries will eventually be, as memory and time can dull the grief from the twin cataclysms of World Wars I and II.

Spears concludes his book with one of his most compelling accounts: a somber catalog of individual graves in a Gallery of Honor. Here, he focuses on the individual, rather than on national mores, commemoration, or shared grief. It is here that the focus of one's visitation to the national cemeteries should remain, on those who served, without regard to race or class, gender or creed, who made up the nation's armed forces throughout its history. This is, to many, the most significant contribution of America's military cemeteries, for each grave has a story to tell of a life lived and, in many cases a story lost. The memory of those who served will continue as long as their experiences can be retrieved or recalled. Spears readily illustrates this in a perfect blend of artful photographs and captivating text.

America's National Cemeteries: A Meditation on History, Memory, and Place is a much-needed book in which the author narrates the evolving story about the creation, purpose, and maintenance of these national treasures. From the lonely plots scattered on nearly forgotten neighborhoods or frontier forts to the massive new cemeteries like Abraham Lincoln south of Chicago that can accommodate up to four hundred thousand burial spaces, from the majestic American Battlefield Military cemeteries to the stark grandeur of Arlington National Cemetery, every grave has a story. And behind every story lies an important narrative of our shared national identity.

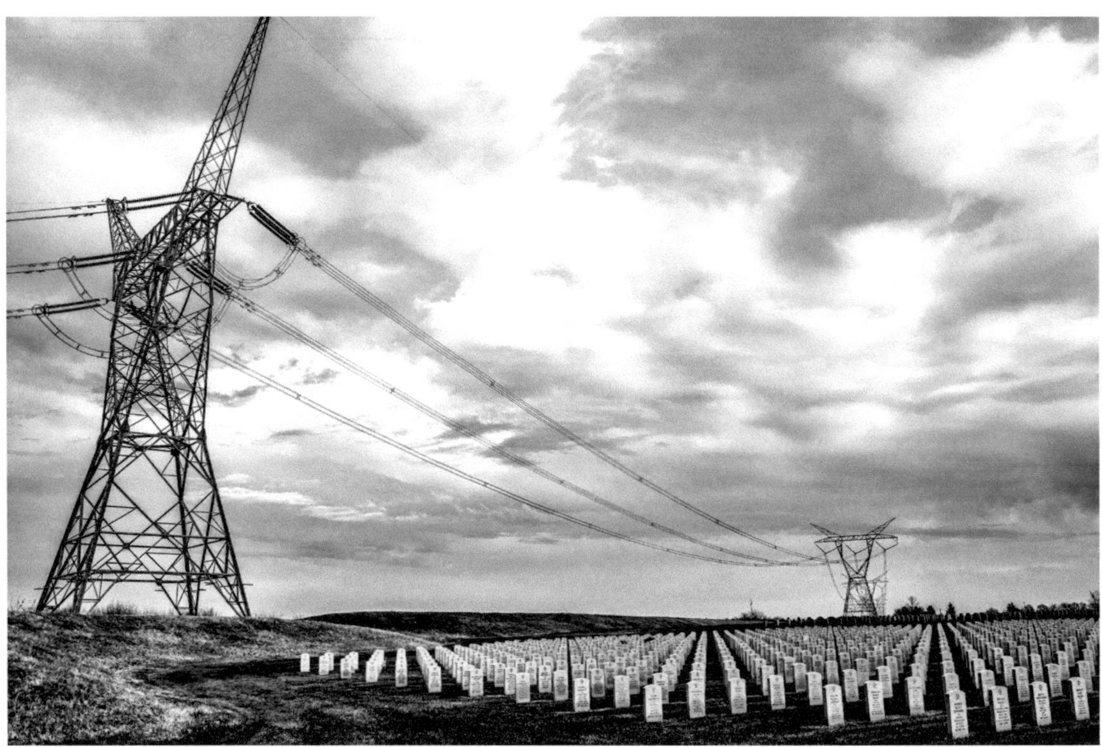

Abraham Lincoln National Cemetery (established in 1996), Elwood, Illinois, 2017.

Introduction

In June 2015, I traveled with my wife and son for a week of sightseeing in northeastern France, the area of the country most altered by World War I. We wanted to walk the land and see history from the ground up—memorials in town squares, trenches dug alongside forest paths, and other tangible signs of a civilization gone sideways. As tourists often do—though less frequently now because of the smartphone revolution—I brought a camera with me. A few days into the trip we visited the Meuse-Argonne American Cemetery, a US government burial ground located near the village of Romagne-sous-Montfaucon that is the resting place of 14,246 American soldiers who died in the Great War, including some of the Black Americans in the 369th Infantry Regiment, known as the Harlem Hellfighters.[1]

After exiting the highway, we drove several kilometers through the French countryside until we turned into the cemetery gates and followed the driveway toward the classically designed landscape with immaculately groomed lawns, flower beds, a chapel, and thousands of marble headstones, perfectly aligned and shimmering in the summer sun. It seemed like a world unto itself, in the middle of what a Frenchman told me was the country's "deep interior": rural, provincial, and economically depressed. Except for a group of schoolchildren on a field trip, we were alone. We strolled the grounds, and when I pulled out my Nikon and began to take pictures, I did not want to stop.

After I returned home to Vermont, I was preoccupied with the idea of turning the encounter into some kind of project. Instinctively, I wanted to go back and take more pictures, but I felt I had to explain myself—to others and to myself. For the moment I was happy to say I had taken a few photography classes in college and was rekindling an old interest. When I told a photographer friend about my plan and haltingly confided that I felt there was something about these landscapes that could only be portrayed with a camera, he just raised his eyebrows and nodded. Photographs can express truths that words fail to convey.

I soon realized that I did not need to return to Europe to take pictures of military cemeteries. The national cemetery system was closer to home and offered plenty of opportunities for exploring this corner of history. And as I learned more about the national cemeteries, I decided I was not fleeing the archive but rather augmenting traditional forms of research through split-screen views of American culture.

Within a year of our trip to France, I visited the cemeteries at Gettysburg, Shiloh, and Andersonville, memorial sites established for the Union dead toward the end of the Civil War that are now part of the national cemetery system. In the fall of 2017, I decided I would try to visit and photograph all 155 of the national cemeteries. I doubted I would get to every single one, but I was at a point in my life when this sort of commitment seemed to make a strange kind of sense. Over the next four years, working off a list of cemeteries on the National Cemetery Administration's website, I planned dozens of itineraries and traveled throughout the country, driving where I could from my home in Vermont and flying to other locations, where I would spend two or three days in a rental car going from one cemetery to the next to take pictures and experience the distinctive features of each cemetery.

The photographs presented here are the result of those trips and portray scenes from military cemeteries located throughout the continental United States, Alaska, and Hawaii. Inspired by my tour of Meuse-Argonne, I eventually returned to Europe to photograph other World War I cemeteries, and I have documented that travel as well. Conceived as a photo-essay, this book also includes reflections on the cemeteries' histories and designs, their places in the broader American landscape, the politics that continue to shape their identities and, perhaps most important, the intangible qualities we bring to our encounters with the dead—as mourners, citizens, and curious visitors. I say "our" because the cemeteries' memorial functions are inseparable from their unifying purpose as national landscapes. In describing these spaces, I write from a first-person perspective to explain their effect on me and, by implication, their capacity to move other people as well.

This experiential orientation filters into how I discuss the photographic aspects of this project. Although I like to think the images stand on their own as evidence of the cemeteries' historical significance and expressive power as a place, I occasionally highlight the ways in which

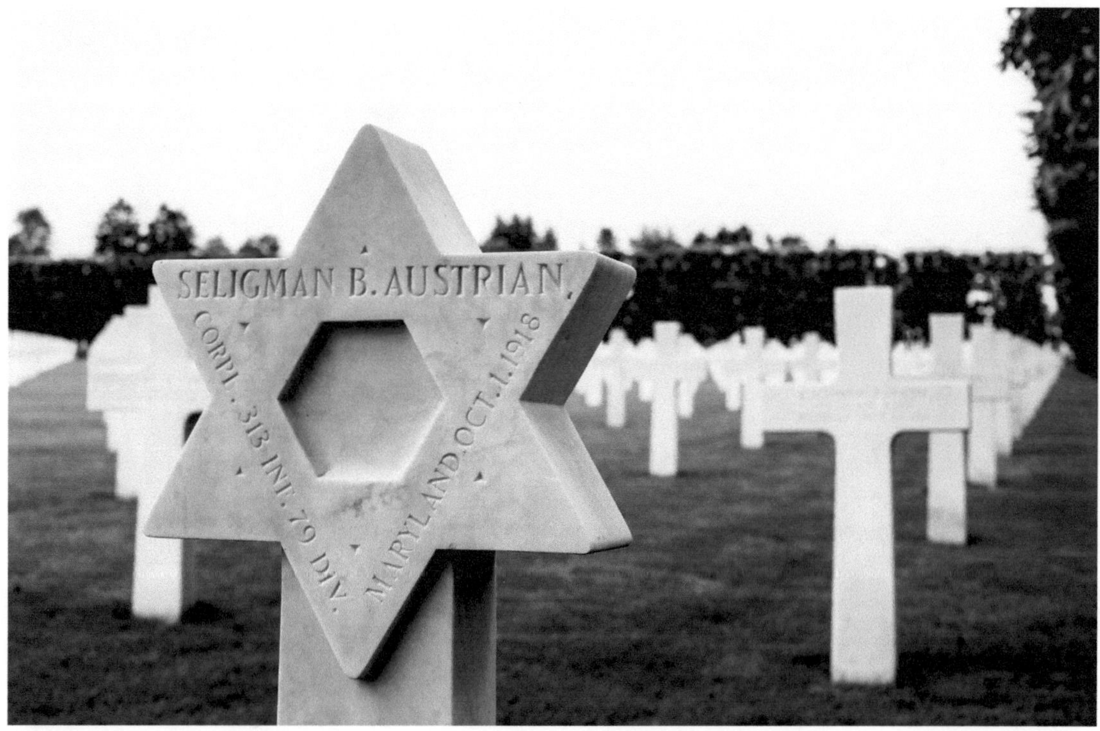

Meuse-Argonne American Cemetery (established in 1918; dedicated in 1937), near Romagne-sous-Montfaucon, France, 2016.

my picture taking—my visual exploration of the grounds and the headstones, trees, and gates—informs how I have come to understand these landscapes. Being there matters. And it can be liberating.

To a certain extent, the scope of this project is best understood in terms of the federal infrastructure that supports the national cemeteries. Currently, the National Cemetery Administration, which sits within the Department of Veterans Affairs, oversees the 155 cemeteries in 42 states and Puerto Rico. It is the primary custodian of memorial spaces managed by the US government.[2] The National Park Service, under the purview of the Department of Interior, maintains fourteen of these cemeteries, nearly all linked to Civil War battlefield sites. Meanwhile, the Department of the Army, reporting through the Department of Defense, manages Arlington National Cemetery, the largest (in terms of interments) and most prominent of the cemeteries, as well as US Soldiers' and Airmen's Home National Cemetery in Washington, DC. For

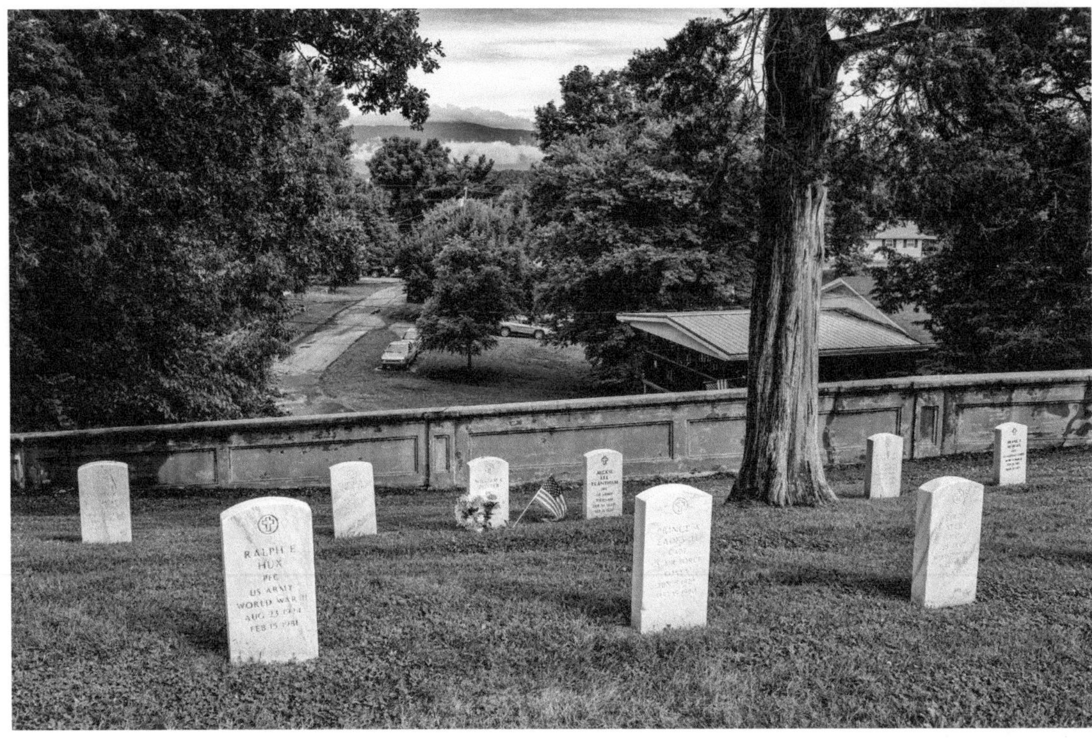

Andrew Johnson National Cemetery (established in 1906), Greeneville, Tennessee, 2019.

decades, the US Army also administered ten cemeteries affiliated with forts, for example, Fort Devens in Massachusetts. Then in 2020, as part of a reorganization effort initiated in 2018, the National Cemetery Administration assumed responsibility for most of them, and the army cemeteries became national cemeteries. The National Cemetery Administration also shares the cost of maintaining the Soldiers' Lots established after the Civil War, small enclaves of Union soldier graves located in private cemeteries, and it provides support to the dozens of veteran cemeteries administered at the state level as well as several located on tribal lands.[3]

Although the cemeteries honor the service and sacrifice of American military personnel, they are part of Veterans Affairs, an organization focused on civilian interests. Yet it is difficult to separate the memorial benefits available to veterans from the military history that drove the cemeteries' growth. All honorably discharged members of the military, including their spouses and even some dependents, are eligible for interment in a national cemetery. This history began with the bloody trauma of the Civil War, which created an urgent need for burial space and continues today with the professionalized role that the military plays on the global stage. The cemeteries are critically and (you might say) naturally linked to the military history of the United States. According to the latest government figures (posted in 2022), more than four million men and women are interred on their grounds.[4] But, like the Lincoln Memorial and similar commemorative sites, they were designed to exemplify democratic ideals.

Here, it is important to note that these memorial landscapes are called national cemeteries not military cemeteries. For while the cemeteries were, and are still, founded "as national shrines in tribute to the gallant dead who have served in the Armed Forces" (as per the code quoted at the front of the book), their status as places of tribute depends on their connection to the nation and the principles that informed the reestablishment of the Union after the Civil War. In other words, the intended purpose of the cemeteries is to build allegiance to the Republic, a mission supported by the ongoing interment of American citizens. How this purpose affects one's experience of these spaces is a question that prompts much of the reflection in this book.

I came to understand the cemeteries' place in history over time, drawn by the visual power of these landscapes. As I traveled and visited more and more cemeteries, I began to compile a digital trove of photographs, which I reviewed and processed in Adobe Lightroom. Soon after my first trip to France, I went to the National Archives in College Park, Maryland, to learn more about the American Battle Monuments Commission, the governmental agency charged with developing World War I cemeteries and memorials in Europe. I also spent time in the National Archives in Washington, DC, examining the records of the national cemeteries, to gain a better understanding of how the architects of the system envisioned their future role. As a historian trained in American studies who has spent a lot of time in the archives, I was accustomed to this work and I also benefited enormously from the books and articles written by scholars who have studied cemeteries, the culture of death and dying, mortuary practices, nationalism, war and remembrance, and Civil War commemoration. At the same time, I was persuaded, as I moved forward with this project, that the book I wanted to create would be different from any of the others I had read.

References to the national cemeteries run throughout the scholarly literature on American war and remembrance. And more than one hundred national cemeteries—most dating to the Civil War era—appear in the National Register of Historic Places, the official list of culturally significant sites, buildings, landscapes, and other physical resources that the government is committed to preserving.[5] There is no book, however, that brings the cemeteries and their history into a single volume with images that illuminate their distinctive character as built landscapes. My hope is that *America's National Cemeteries* will fill this gap and appeal to students and teachers of commemorative culture, military history, landscape history, and photography. Beyond these more specialized audiences, I also hope it will appeal to general readers interested in how the nation honors the sacrifice of its citizens, people who, after reading these reflections or just looking at the pictures, may decide to visit national cemeteries wherever they live or their travels take them.

I see more clearly now than I did at the start of this project why I want to note the expressive power of these uniquely configured landscapes. I use the word "note"—a benignly neutral term—to signal the discomfort I feel about formulating anything resembling an argument based on the remains of so many dead people, whose impact on us, however sure, is also ineffable. In

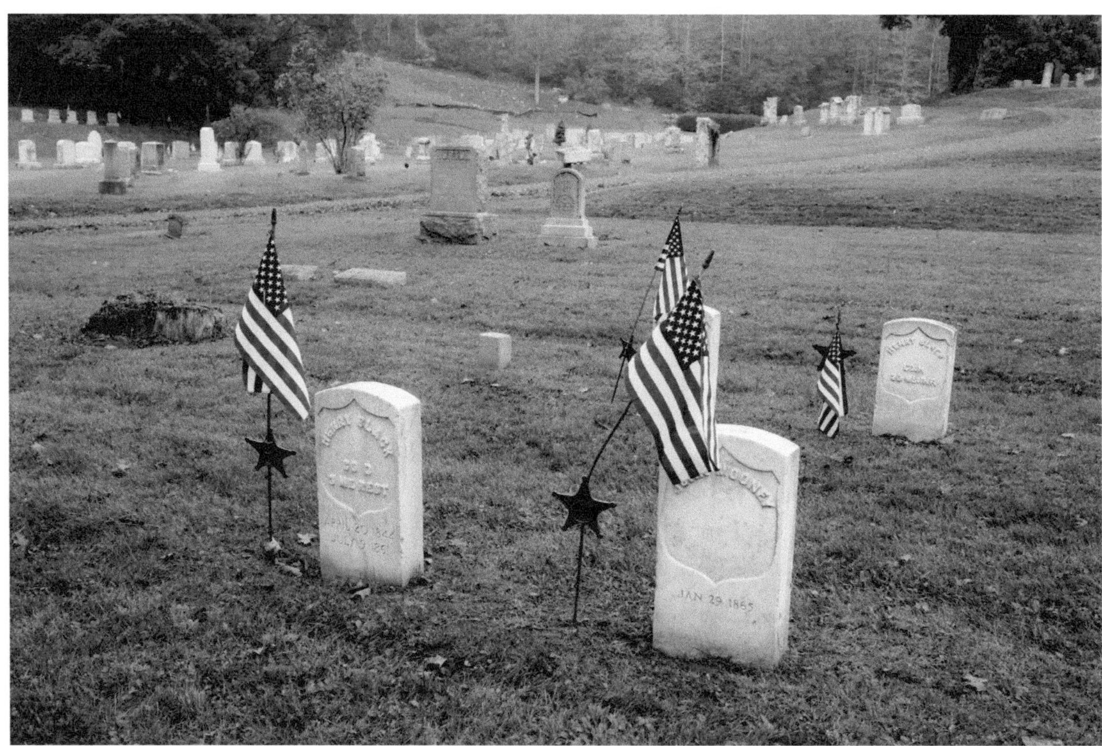

Soldiers' Lot in Green Mount Cemetery (lot established in 1866), Montpelier, Vermont, 2017.

this respect, the passionate if naive faith I have placed in taking photographs of these memorial spaces stems from my belief that sometimes it should be enough just to bear witness: to death, sacrifice, remembrance, individual accomplishment, nationalism, regional difference, and a distinctive American landscape that continues to grow. With so much human history before me, it seems arrogant and insensitive to pronounce upon it all.

If those are my inclinations, then the reality is something different. Indeed, after visiting nearly all 155 national cemeteries during the past five years, I found it impossible to stand on the sidelines and not offer some opinions about the role these landscapes play, or should play, in the larger culture. To be sure, the current political climate and the disruptive calls to "make America great again" have galvanized my thinking. Just as affecting has been my experience of engaging the national cemeteries not simply as individual memorial sites but as a series of interconnected landscapes that together illuminate the aspirations and realities of American culture. And together, I propose, the cemeteries tell a story about the nation that is more hopeful than their status as graveyards might suggest.

Finally, some thoughts about the book's focus and organization. I could not have learned what I know about national cemeteries without leaving home to visit them. Consequently, much of my account takes place on the road and unfolds as a travelogue. This format allows me—as a pilgrim, scholar, US citizen, and would-be guide—to approach the cemeteries as specially constructed landscapes within the larger American environment and to ask questions about their general representativeness. Also, though many cemeteries follow similar patterns of design, they were built at different times and on different sites and in different regions of the country, and these distinctions animate my geographically based narrative.

For the most part, the chapters follow the chronology of my travels. In chapter 1, I describe visits made to California and Florida in the spring of 2018, and in chapter 10, I focus on trips taken in 2020, following the outbreak of COVID-19. I occasionally deviate from this order to underscore key details—indeed, in chapter 1, I open with a description of Hot Springs National Cemetery, which I visited in the summer of 2018—and address the history of the national cemeteries. To accomplish this last objective, I explore the origins of the cemeteries during the Civil War in chapters 2 and 3 and follow the system's expansion in subsequent chapters. For instance, in chapter 8, which I call "Good Wars," I discuss the impact of World War II and describe my visit to the National Memorial Cemetery of the Pacific (the "Punchbowl") in Honolulu, Hawaii, in the fall of 2020. Thus, while the narrative spreads out across much of the United States, it also tracks the history of the national cemeteries.

This history is likewise reflected in the photo captions, where I note the date that the cemetery in view was established. This information comes from governmental sources, mainly the National Cemetery Administration website, but the originating date can be misleading since some of the cemeteries served as military burial grounds before they became "national" cemeteries. Further details about the cemeteries' evolving status may be found online.[6]

That said, this book is not a comprehensive history of the national cemetery system but, rather, a meditation on how these landscapes function as sites of memory, which means I am particularly interested in how the past leaves its imprint on the land and how the presence of the dead informs our sense of place. In taking this approach, I engage the cemeteries in an episodic fashion, sometimes concentrating on the physical landscape and sometimes exploring historical and philosophical themes that extend their significance. Because I want to accentuate the cemeteries' relevance as open, civic spaces, I minimize analyses that might seem overly academic or theoretical. At the same time, I draw from the scholarly literature on memorial culture to illuminate the distinctive characteristics of the American system—the largest of its kind in the Western world—while also trying to avoid seeming narrow or insular in perspective. This goal may be hard to achieve since this book is, at its core, a study of American memorial landscapes. Nonetheless, it is important to acknowledge (however obviously) that death is a topic of universal interest about which no one has the final word.

Whatever political commentary I offer derives from my search for common ground, a figurative space that is hard to find these days. With that in mind and despite the history of conquest, violence, and racism that has shaped too much of this nation's evolution since the arrival of enslaved Africans at Jamestown, Virginia, in 1619, I turn repeatedly to the fact that national cemeteries were created to bring American citizens of varying opinions and walks of life into shared territory, a prospect of national unity that inspires and can still be glimpsed and felt in these landscapes.[7] A number of historians have argued that American commemorative sites—like battlefields or monuments—are sites of "contested discourse," places where ordinary citizens can formulate their own understanding of what the nation should remember and honor. This insight applies in a very particular way to national cemeteries, since, as landscapes designed to encourage mourning and reflection, they provide ample space for varying forms of seeing, feeling, and thought.[8] Some readers may be put off by the notion that such a vision of democracy can exist on grounds that commemorate military service, sacrifice, war, and national identity. Still, it is my hope they will find in these pages and in these special places reason to think differently.

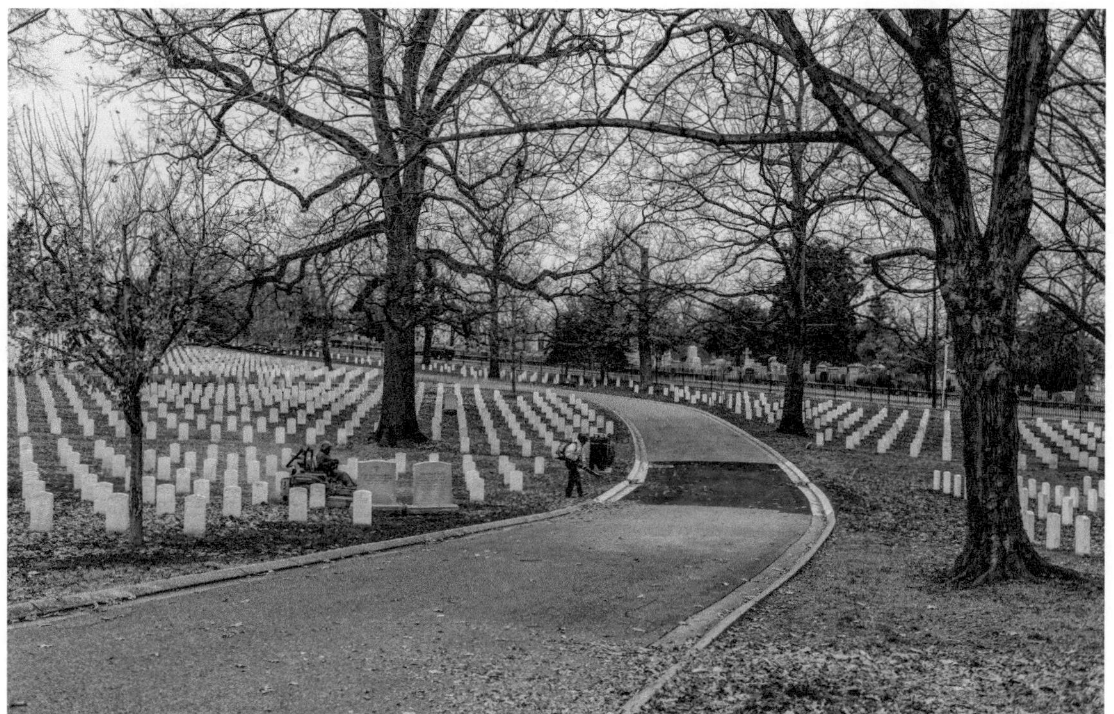

United States Soldiers' and Airmen's Home National Cemetery (established in 1862), Washington, DC, 2017.

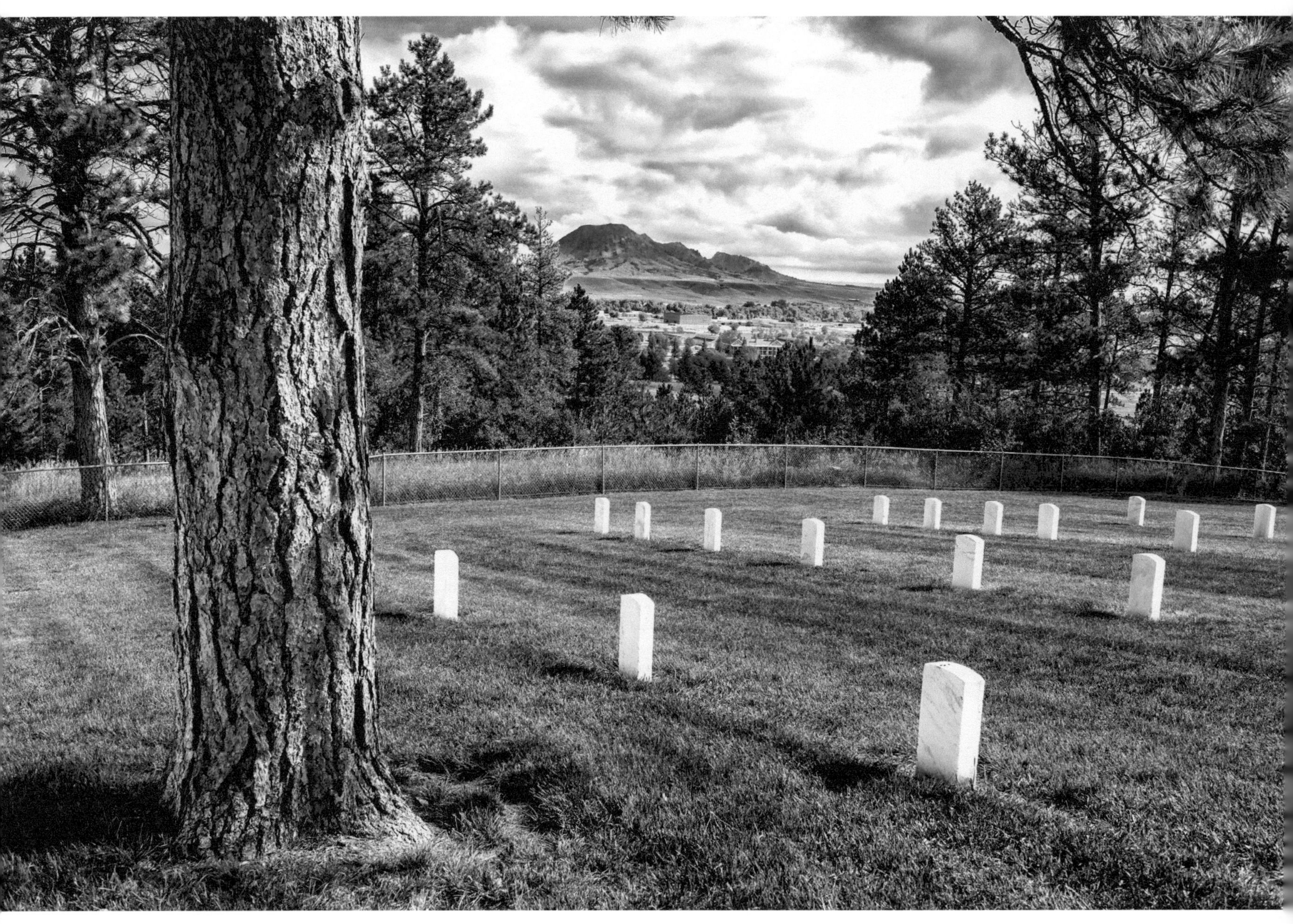

Fort Meade National Cemetery (established in 1947), Sturgis, South Dakota, 2018.

AMERICA'S NATIONAL CEMETERIES

1

Under a Big Sky

National cemeteries reveal the challenges of holding on to sacred ground. Some of the cemeteries have aged past the time of remembering and are silent and empty, except perhaps on Memorial Day or Veterans Day or during the Christmas holidays when squadrons of volunteers sweep in to lay wreaths on the graves. Others are surrounded by dilapidated neighborhoods, strip malls, and car dealerships, the carefully maintained grounds and finely wrought stonework framed by the ebb and flow of American life.

Despite a fairly uniform aesthetic—symmetrical rows of marble markers and standardized headstones—each national cemetery, by virtue of its location, argues for its own distinct sense of place. At Hot Springs National Cemetery in South Dakota are red sandstone buildings erected during the 1870s to address the health needs of Civil War veterans and take advantage of the local waters' healing powers. In Sturgis there are two burial sites: Fort Meade National Cemetery, officially established in 1947 (but with an older story to tell), and Black Hills National Cemetery, founded in 1948. To get to Fort Meade, you follow a gravel road up into the hills until you arrive at a square, two-acre plot bordered by a chain-link fence and hiking trails. With only 235 gravesites—most holding the remains of US cavalrymen and, in some cases, their wives and even children—the cemetery feels like a wilderness outpost standing watch over distant buttes and rock formations.

Black Hills National Cemetery is easier to find. Located just off Interstate 90, it sits on a rolling landscape, offering views of rail lines and highway traffic along the base of the Black Hills, which, during early August, is dominated by motorcycles heading to and from the Sturgis Motorcycle Rally. At one hundred acres, Black Hills is fifty times bigger than Fort Meade, includes more than twenty thousand graves, all with polished marble markers, as opposed to the weathered stone faces at the older cemetery. Black Hills is open to interments and positioned for future growth.

Four hundred miles to the south, in Colorado, Fort Logan National Cemetery is larger still and also denser. Across the 214 acres of tree-shaded lawns, monuments, and two well-tended lakes, the 122,000 interments constitute a small city or, perhaps more accurately, a suburb, since the Denver skyline spans the northwest horizon. Named for the frontier fort that once occupied the site, the cemetery is divided into multiple fields of gravestones and also features two sets of columbaria, the modern, space-efficient venues for holding cremated remains.

Names bring order, if not meaning, to the national cemeteries. They mark the headstones, line the columbaria, and fill the electronic database that visitors consult to locate an individual grave. In principle, they hallow the ground. But to recognize the dead, even to etch the word "unknown" on a headstone, is to assert a connection between individual sacrifice and national purpose that does not happen just by declaration or design. Landscapes themselves also frame questions that people bring to these spaces, quandaries shaped by grief, love, patriotism, and a desire for common ground. Transcendence can be a man-made thing.

I started visiting national cemeteries in a systematic way during the summer of 2017. The trips were steady but ad hoc, taken during gaps in my work schedule. Then, in the spring of 2018, I had a partial leave from my academic job that allowed me to accelerate my travel. At first, I only wanted to take pictures—writing would have nothing to do with it—a desire that I privately designated as artistic in nature. Even confessing that ambition evokes the self-consciousness that I tried to avoid by just heading out on the road with my camera, in a kind of romantic embrace of the documentary tradition. Now I realize in prose that there is more to be said about these spaces, more to be learned about what these cemeteries have meant—to me and others—than I am capable of conveying in images.

Hovering around this project, no doubt, are my attitudes about death. Many of us may be uncertain or unresolved on the issue—until we are not—and studies show that Americans, in particular, are reluctant to talk about death.[1] By spending time in cemeteries, I would not necessarily say I was bucking this trend. After all, memorializing death, or representing that effort, is several steps removed from the real thing. But neither would I say that my interests were solely aesthetic or chiefly historical in nature. The cemeteries are mysterious in ways that other places are not; they roll out like an inland sea and pull visitors toward some undiscovered territory.

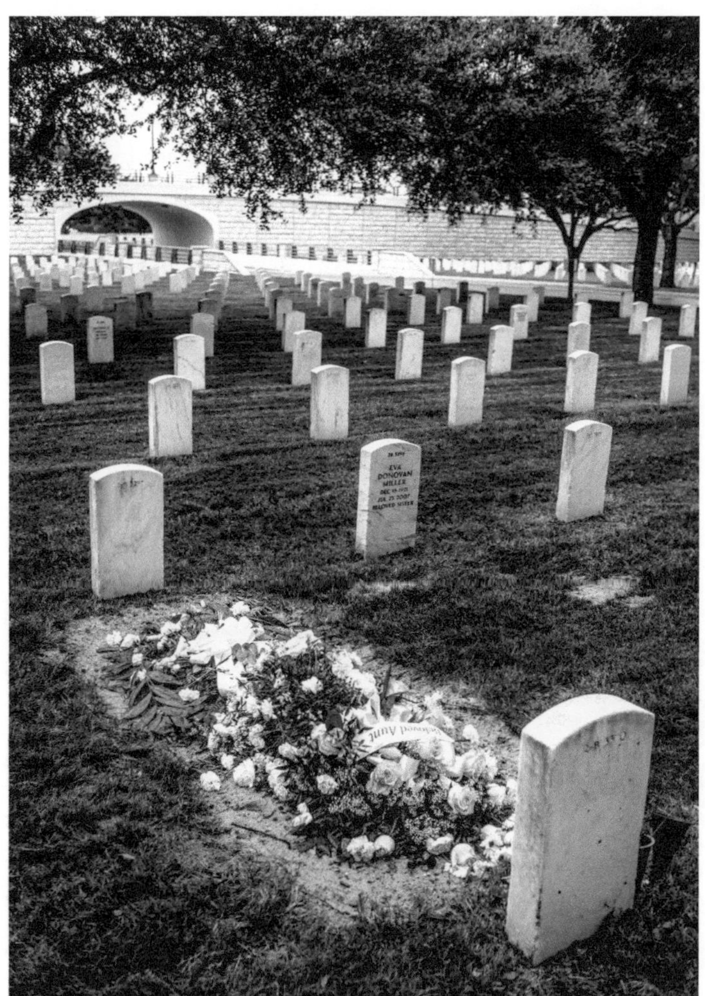

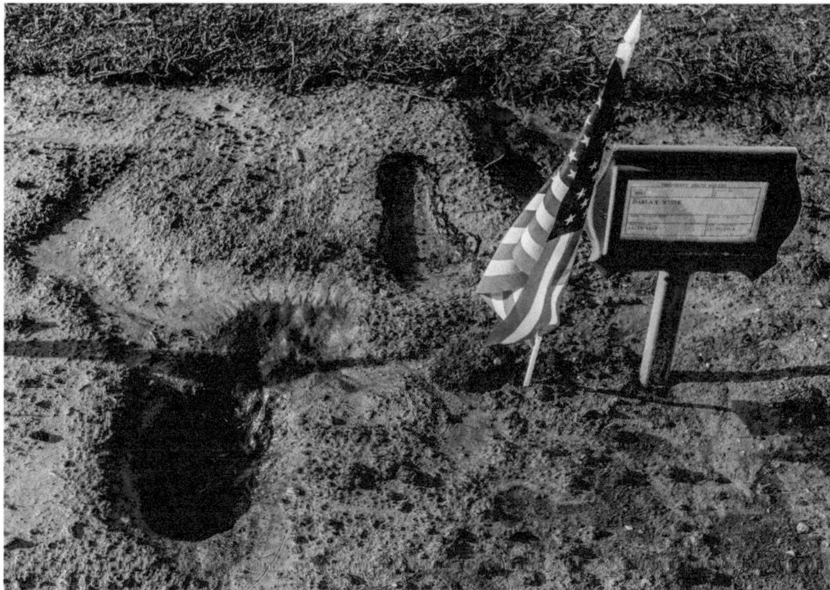

(*Above*) A fresh grave at Louisiana National Cemetery (established in 2012), Zachary, Louisiana, 2018.

(*Left*) Fort Sam Houston National Cemetery (established in 1937), San Antonio, Texas, 2018.

When I decided to explore the national cemeteries in a comprehensive way, I was unsure where to start. My instinct as a historian was to start at the beginning, with cemeteries established during the Civil War. But death in the military tradition resists chronological order; there is no hierarchy among fallen soldiers. Moreover, my sabbatical started in February, and I had to consider how the weather might affect my travel. So I made the sensible choice and booked tickets for California and Florida.

Burial in a national cemetery is a significant benefit. Although the deceased's family is responsible for all mortuary services and the cost of the funeral, the federal government pays to open and close the grave. It supplies a burial liner to protect the coffin or urn from decomposition. It provides a headstone, lawn-level marker, or name plate if the cremains are placed in columbaria. Perhaps most important of all, the government offers "perpetual (ongoing) care of the gravesite"—a guarantee that it will maintain the cemetery for as long as the United States exists.[2]

In its 2018–24 strategic plan, the Department of Veterans Affairs affirmed its commitment to making sure that 95 percent of all veterans live within a seventy-five-mile drive of a national cemetery or a state or tribal veterans cemetery. In absolute terms, the system's expansion has largely mirrored the growth of the veteran population. California has nine national cemeteries, as does Florida, while Texas has six. Only Virginia has more—fifteen—but most of its cemeteries were established during the Civil War era and are closed to future burials. The exception is Arlington

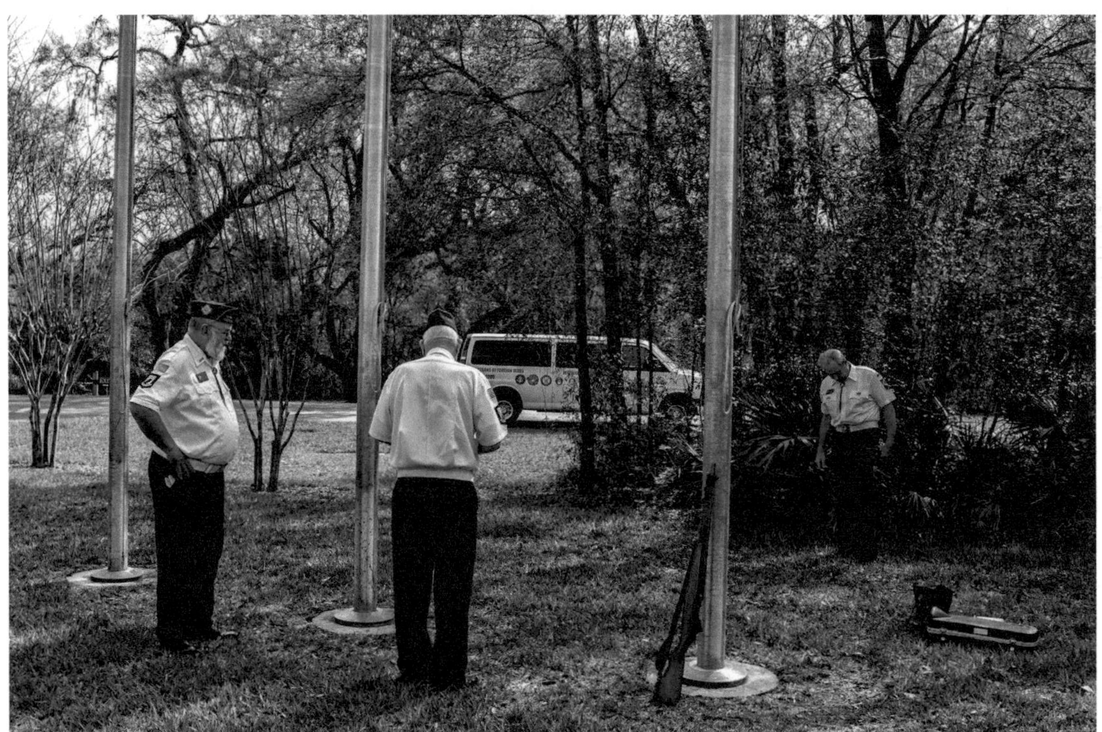

Florida National Cemetery (established in 1983), Bushnell, Florida, 2018. An Honor Guard, representing the Veterans of Foreign Wars, carries out its duties.

National Cemetery, the nation's flagship cemetery (dedicated in 1866) and also the largest, with some four hundred thousand gravesites.[3] Arlington is not on the list of Virginia cemeteries because it is managed by the US Army not the National Cemetery Administration. Arlington is still open to interments, though it is running out of room and recently added a large columbarium complex on the southeast side of the cemetery.

To drive across the length and breadth of California and Florida was not feasible, so I organized my travel in phases, planning to see most of the cemeteries during an initial visit and the rest during subsequent trips. Driving in California was primarily a north–south affair, following the freeway from beach to desert to mountains. The cemeteries in Florida, on the other hand, took me in several directions—to the east and west coasts, along the pine-wooded Panhandle, and across or around the watery expanse of the Everglades.

Landscapes draw us in toward ourselves as much as they pull us out toward their physical characteristics, and, in making these trips, I was retracing familiar routes. My first exposure to Florida came from visiting my grandparents during the late 1960s. My father's parents lived in Jupiter on the East Coast, and I remember driving there from Cleveland, Ohio, Dad pushing through the southern night, my siblings and I stretched out in back of the station wagon, waking intermittently to perfumed air and soft-voiced exchanges with gas station attendants. Decades later, my parents retired to Florida, and I carried these memories with me when I took my own kids to visit their grandparents, supplemented by trips to Walt Disney World.

I did not set foot in California until I was a senior in college, when I interviewed for a job teaching high school English in Los Angeles. After getting the job, I drove cross-country with a friend in my new used Karmann Ghia, not quite starstruck but smitten by the rugged—and, to me, exotic—landscape that rose up out of the Great Plains once we entered Mountain Time. I knew the West I was now seeing was not just physical space but also a mash-up of images absorbed from years of reading, watching television and movies, and listening to popular music. In fact, those impressions are part of what drew me to California in the first place. Now, I would be living at the edge of the continent, where all things begin and end.

My schedule for the California trip was ambitious. I planned to spend the first couple days in the Bay Area, visiting Golden Gate National Cemetery and San Francisco National Cemetery. Then I would fly to San Diego and drive north to Bakersfield National Cemetery, stopping at Miramar and Riverside National Cemeteries along the way. On my return drive, I wanted to

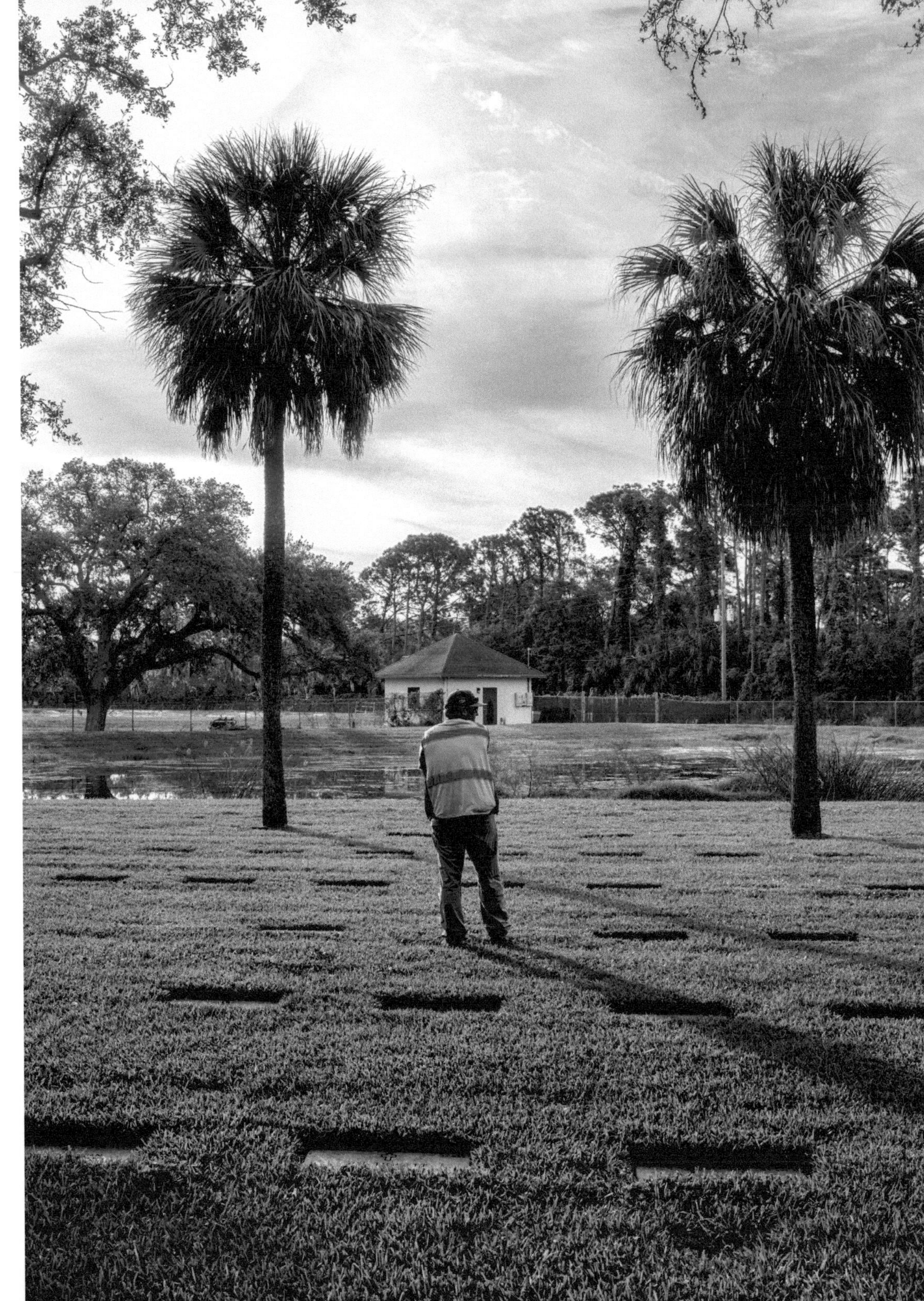

Lawn-level markers, rather than headstones, are a feature at Bay Pines National Cemetery (established in 1933), Bay Pines, Florida, 2019.

see Los Angeles National Cemetery before continuing on to Fort Rosecrans National Cemetery, which sits on a peninsula in San Diego, offering views of the city on one side and the Pacific Ocean on the other. This second leg of the trip would take four more days. I saved the other two cemeteries in the state—San Joaquin Valley National Cemetery and Sacramento National Cemetery—for another visit.

I had some worries about the trip, not just the driving from place to place on busy freeways and the challenges of sticking to my itinerary. I was nagged by the seeming incongruity between the tropical environment and the memorial landscapes I had come to visit. What would a meaningful picture of these spaces look like? Should its "beauty" reflect the sunlit palm trees that surrounded me? How could I avoid making postcard pictures of hallowed ground, soil I was determined to respect? Was there an ethical code I ought to follow? The government has rules for how one should behave in the national cemeteries, but the guidelines are (mostly) silent on the use of cameras.

Of course, photographers and critics have long argued about the morality of pointing the camera one way or another. As Susie Linfield notes in her trenchant defense of photography's humanistic importance, postmodern critics have all but dismissed photography's transcendent status.[4] Gone is the shared belief in the picture's capacity to reveal some kind of truth. Photographs that, in an earlier time, might have been taken to expose the cruelties of war or poverty—and perhaps correct them—now traffic in a global network of images that showcases these spectacles without altering the structures of power that enable them.

It would be naive to deny the pervasive influence of digital culture or to return to early forms of trust since any image can now be photoshopped. Still, I am compelled by Linfield's contention that photography "brings us close" to "experiences of suffering in ways that no other form of art or journalism can."[5] This argument matters to me because it identifies a link between empirical reality and human emotion that I wanted to illuminate in my pictures of cemeteries. I was a lifetime away from taking pictures in the field of battle but somewhere on the continuum of suffering and grieving, engaging a reality—a truth—founded on the permanence of death and seen and felt through the silent arrangement of graves, stones, and names.

Whether the emotions I felt in these spaces could be translated to photographs, I was not sure, though my stop at Golden Gate National Cemetery was instructive. Located in San Bruno, twelve miles south of San Francisco, Golden Gate spans 160 acres and includes almost 140,000

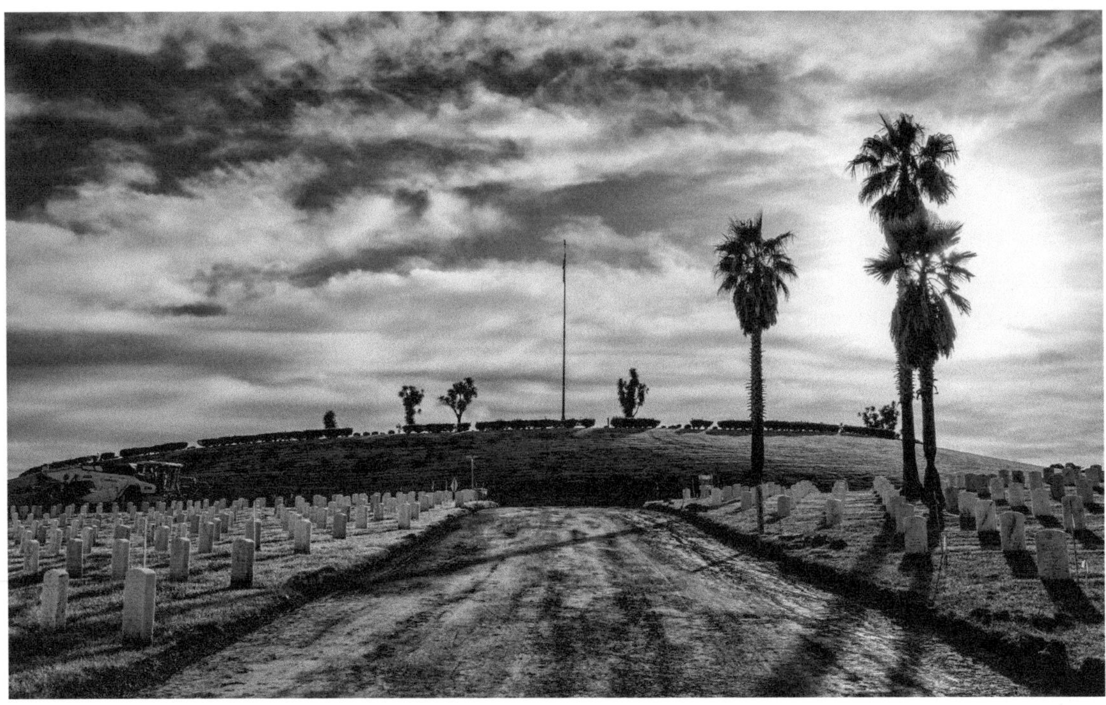

Golden Gate National Cemetery (established in 1938), San Bruno, California, 2018.

interments, more than three times the number of people who live in the municipality. This scale is matched by the scenery within: long views of the hills, freeway, and city; tree-lined boulevards and small bridges; and a hilltop flag installation and ring road just inside the entry gate.

When you stand in the middle of this memorial landscape, the everyday world recedes and Golden Gate begins to resemble Elysian Fields, the mythical resting place of Greek gods that inspired the creation of the first modern cemeteries in Britain and Europe during the early 1800s. But this internal logic dissolves around the edges, where backyard pools and Weber grills push into view, and you can almost reach through the cemetery's outer fence and push the "walk" button at the corner of Sneath Lane and El Camino Real.

Before walking the perimeter of Golden Gate, I did a windshield survey. If I were an individual mourner, I would probably drive straight to a specific gravesite and never mind the whole. But here, as at other cemeteries, I wanted to understand the general layout as well as anything else the landscape had to show me, so I covered as much ground as possible.

What I did not see as I drove through the cemetery were many other people. This makes sense because Golden Gate, which was dedicated in 1942, is now closed to future burials. The most recently interred veteran fought in the Korean War, which ended in 1953. In a way, Golden Gate has become less a destination for family and friends to honor their dead and more an artifact of history.

National cemeteries that are open to interments such as Miramar can be active places, with funerals happening on a daily basis, family members visiting burial sites, and workers preparing the ground for burials. At the other end of the spectrum are cemeteries that have been full for decades and receive few visitors. Golden Gate is somewhere in the middle, in transition, yet insisting through beauty and grandeur that its landscape still matters. That insistence is also confusing. For while national cemeteries are designed to illuminate American ideals, only some of them—like Gettysburg or Antietam—are explicitly linked to well-known historical narratives

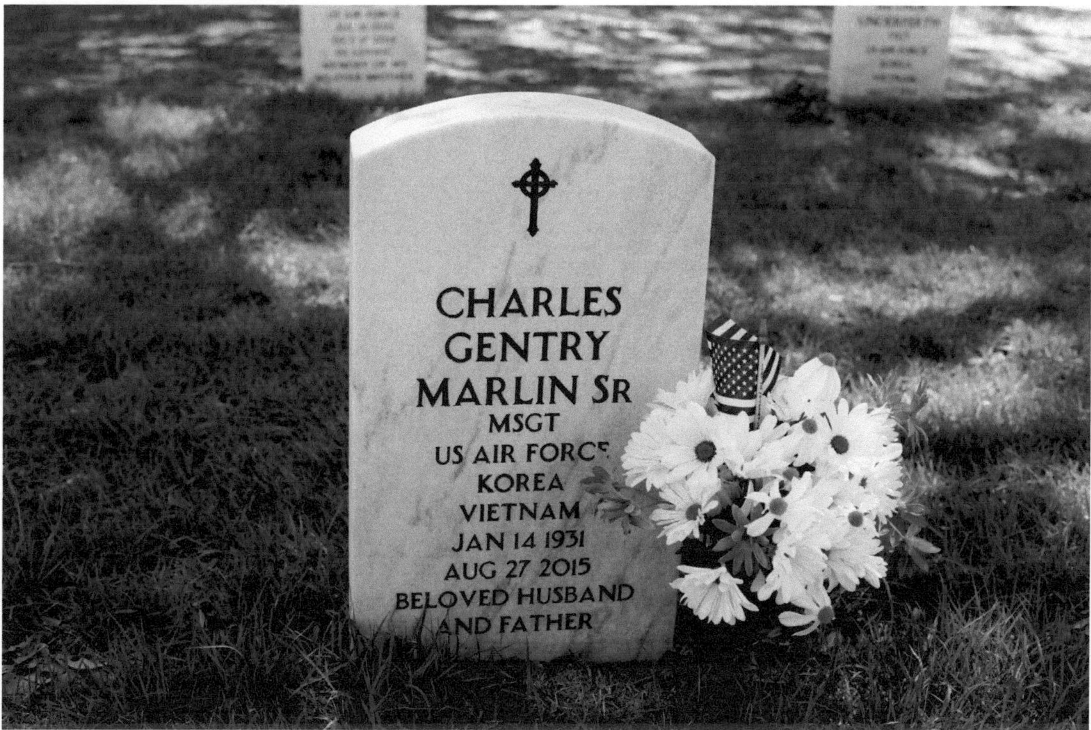

Andersonville National Cemetery (established in 1865), Andersonville, Georgia, 2017.

and events. At most national cemeteries, history seems more personal and takes place through the commemoration of individual sacrifice on headstones or columbarium walls.

I felt this tension between big and small history when I visited Andersonville National Cemetery in Georgia, almost a year after my first trip to France. The cemetery is about half a mile from where the infamous prison once stood and is filled with the graves of thirteen thousand Union soldiers who died while incarcerated. A section on the east side is still open for burials, and I headed that way during my stroll through the grounds, toward red soil and fresh graves, yet not ready to take pictures because there was an older woman, standing in front of a headstone. We said hello, and I asked what brought her here, and she said her husband, who died a couple of years earlier, and that she drove down from Macon every few months to visit his grave. Our exchange settled into silence, and I said goodbye, walking back under the tree canopy to my car.

At Golden Gate, I saw how history molds these spaces in ways that have little to do with the

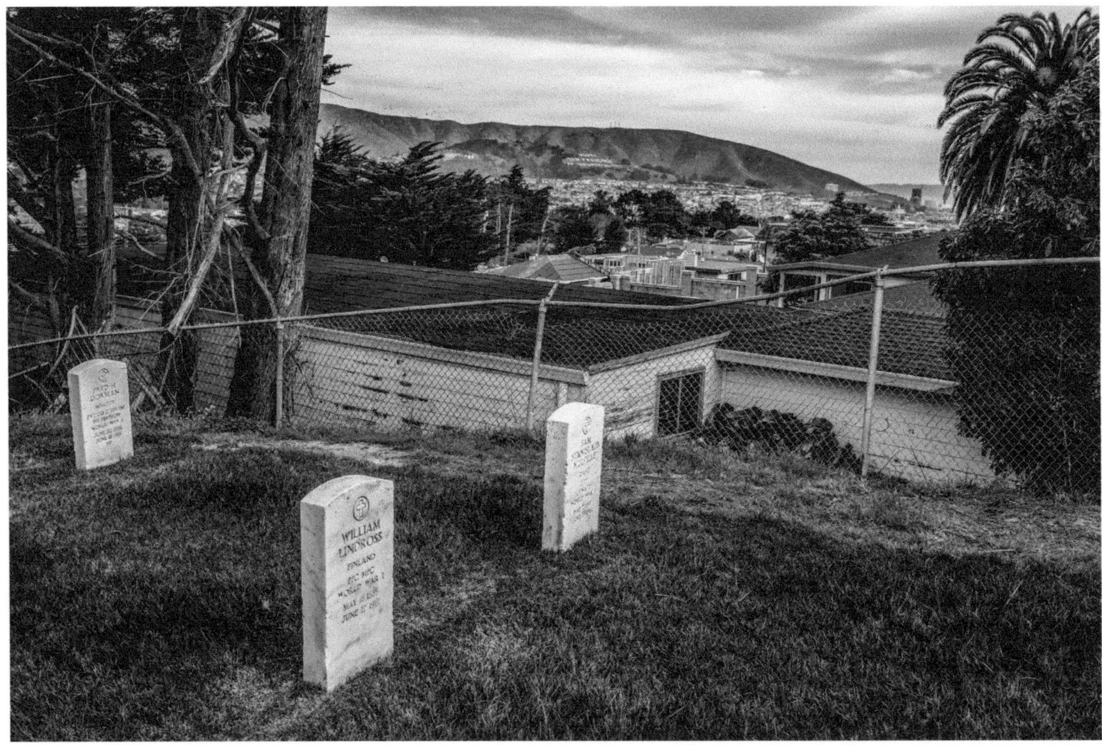

Golden Gate National Cemetery, 2018.

past that we seek to remember. When I followed the lot line up into one of the corners of the cemetery, I looked north toward San Francisco and saw houses and trees stacked up against each other, leading in syncopated rhythm to the hills and a giant, earth born sign that reads SOUTH SAN FRANCISCO INDUSTRIAL CITY. In front of me was the final row of headstones. Just beyond were patches of dirt next to a partially torn chain-link fence and then someone's yard and a pile of cut wood pushed up against what looked to be a garage.

I could not resist seeing the world outside the cemetery boundaries any more than the stones and roads and ground could resist the regular wear and tear of time. It was part of the bigger picture I experienced and wanted to share at Golden Gate. Moreover, the democratic design prompted me to point my camera beyond the perimeter. At national cemeteries, everyone is buried the same way—the headstone of Admiral Chester W. Nimitz is identical in shape to every other individual marker in the cemetery—and the arrangement begs the question of what this civic space has do with the everyday landscape that sprawls beyond the burial ground.

This is an abstract query that national cemeteries answer in concrete, visual terms. On the northern edge of the city, at San Francisco National Cemetery, space and time are also compressed. Sited within the Presidio, the cemetery is confined to nine acres and includes more than twenty-six thousand interments, roughly three times the number of graves per acre than at Golden Gate. The site is picturesque, not simply because it is built on a hillside, shaded by eucalyptus trees with glimpses of the Golden Gate Bridge. The views are layered in such a way that history seems ever present. As I walked down the hill toward the gate, I shot through the nineteenth-century monuments to reveal the traffic on Lincoln Boulevard to show how the scene was constructed.

I wonder if this dramatic scenery blurs the fact that thousands of military personnel are buried here, a sleight of hand encouraged by the location of a jogging trail on the backside of the cemetery. San Francisco National Cemetery is not a park, and recreation is forbidden in national cemeteries; in fact, I once saw a security guard at Arlington tell two runners they had to leave. Yet the cemeteries are not meant to be static, unreceptive spaces. Quiet reflection is part of their mission and has been since the first military cemeteries were established during the early 1860s, following an act passed by the US Congress on July 17, 1862, giving the president the authority "to purchase cemetery grounds, and cause them to be securely enclosed, to be used as a national cemetery for the soldiers who shall die in the service of the country."[6] All cemeteries are places of mourning and contemplation, though some private cemeteries allow activities like jogging, bicycling, and dog walking.

What reflection means in the context of the national cemetery is another question. When I arrived at Los Angeles National Cemetery, I discovered an oasis just off the freeway in the middle of the busy Westwood neighborhood. I easily parked in the cemetery, though I would have struggled to find a spot on the street. I saw a handful of people, maybe UCLA students, walking the grounds and seated on benches. They did not appear be visiting any burial sites, just enjoying the peace and quiet.

I like to think that when I photograph these places I am engaged in a kind of mindful reflection, though I realize that my movements—a man with a camera, searching for the right view—may send a different message. During my travels, I was sometimes questioned for taking pictures. One encounter took place at the Gerald B. Solomon Saratoga National Cemetery in

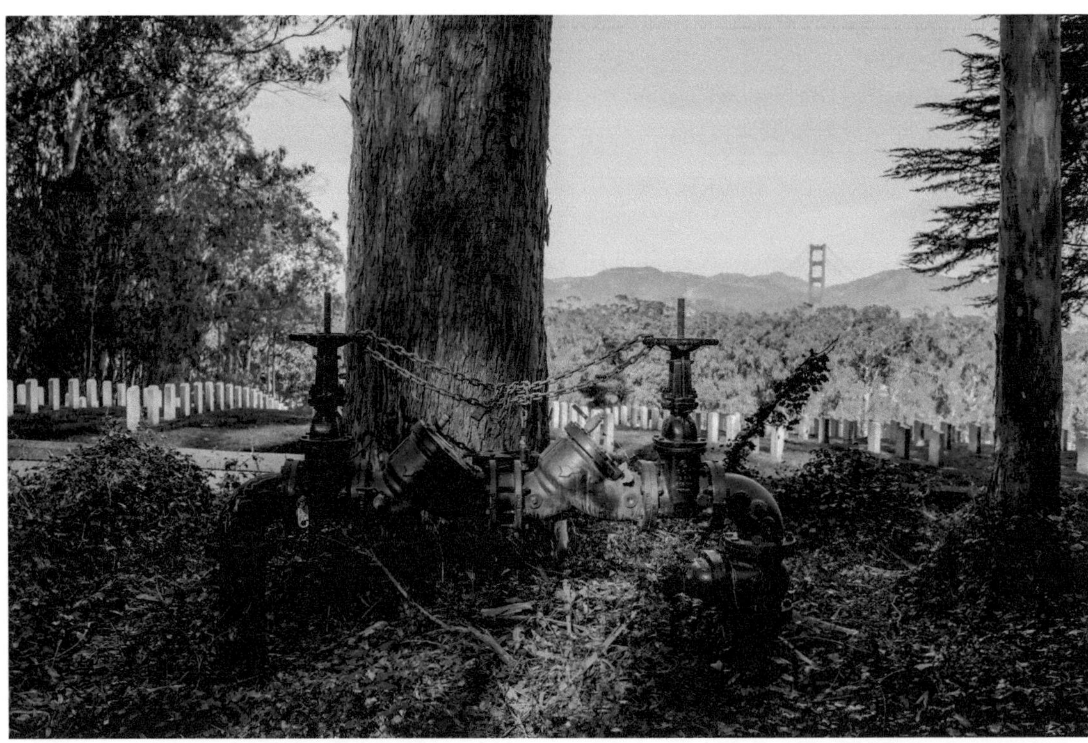

San Francisco National Cemetery (established in 1884), with a view of the Golden Gate Bridge in the right background, San Francisco, California, 2018.

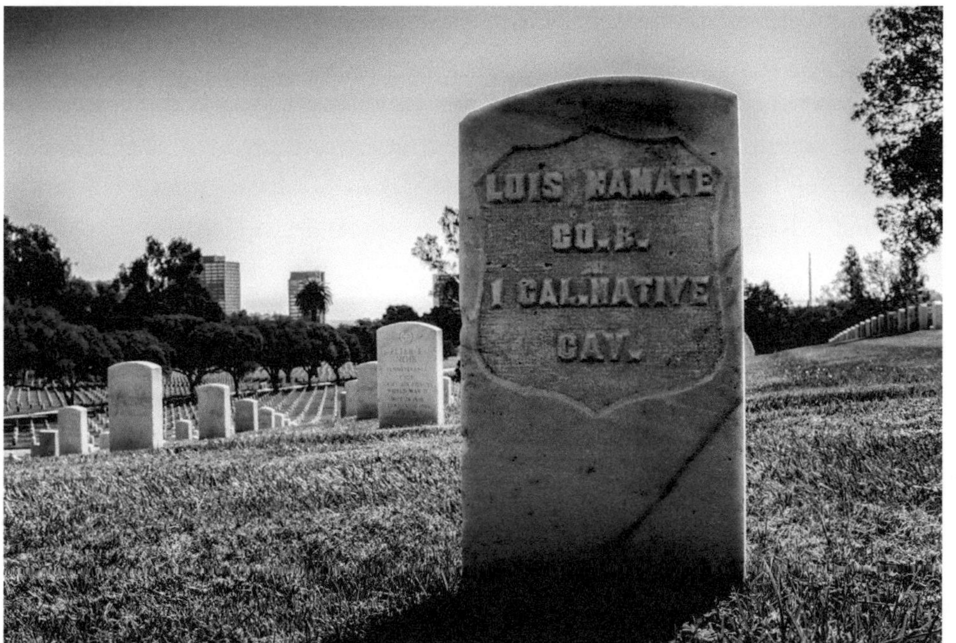

Los Angeles National Cemetery (established in 1889), Los Angeles, California, 2018.

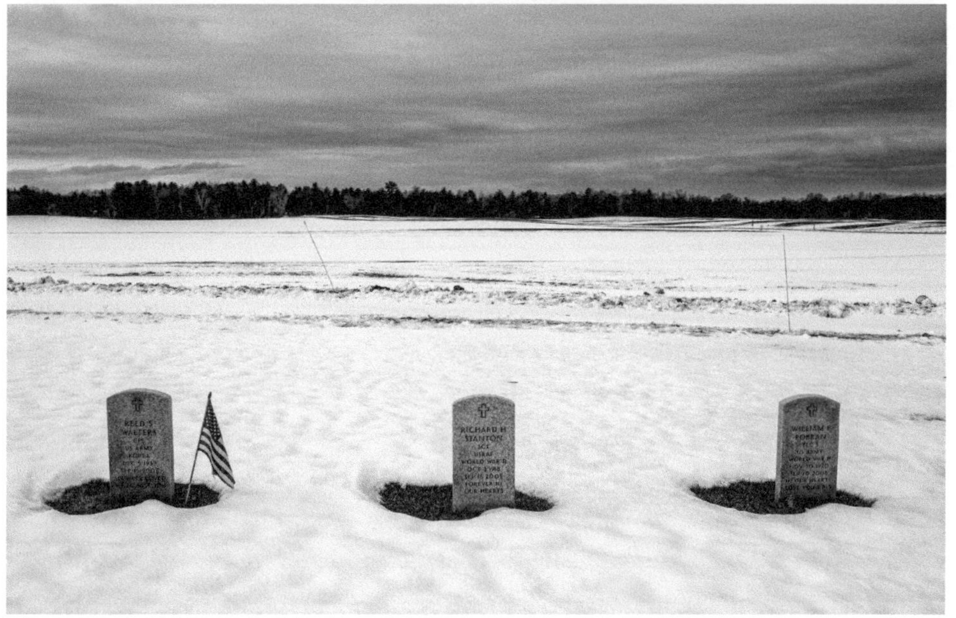

Gerald B. H. Solomon Saratoga National Cemetery (established in 1994), Schuylerville, New York, 2018.

Schuylerville, New York. It was early spring, a wet snow had just fallen, and I was walking between sections when a pickup truck pulled up alongside of me and stopped.

The driver identified himself as a cemetery volunteer and said, "You know, you really aren't supposed to take pictures here." I expressed surprise, tempted to say, "No, that is wrong," but instead explained that I was unfamiliar with that rule. "There is a lot they don't tell you," he responded. "My buddy is buried there," and he pointed to a snow-draped block of headstones. "He was killed in Vietnam. People should get permission to take pictures." I told him I was sorry about his friend, that I was doing research on national cemeteries, and that I always try to be respectful when taking pictures. He nodded, smiled, and moved his truck forward but not before telling me that he has friends in Vermont and really likes the state. I did not tell him where I was from, so this seemed to be his way of letting me know he had seen my car with Vermont plates and knew where to find me.

And who would grant permission if such a protocol existed? Family members? Friends? The military? The cemetery administration? From a practical perspective, especially given the ubiquity of smartphone cameras and social media, the policy would be impossible to enforce. Then there are the politics of representation and my presumed right to take photographs on shared space. Still, I cannot shake the important question of what these landscapes have to do with collective memory and how that memory should be upheld.

The encounter stuck, and I ask myself whether people should obtain permission to take pictures. Yet "should" is probably not the answer. I realize this every time I visit a national cemetery and a member of the grounds crew nods or smiles or ignores me. I could be visiting the grave of my grandfather or aunt or next-door neighbor. Or I might be a history buff searching for a Medal of Honor recipient. Or somebody just passing through the area and interested in seeing something new. It does not matter. Although these landscapes are designed to remind Americans of their ties to the nation and the sacrifices so many fellow citizens have made, they do not compel allegiance. I am free to explore the grounds.

My sense of freedom picked up as I drove through southern California and not just because I was hurtling from place to place on four-line freeways with the windows down. Miramar, Riverside, and Bakersfield are all relatively new cemeteries—still open for interments—and inclusive of new burial practices, like flat stone markers and columbaria. They are big desert or high desert landscapes revealed by translucent western light and open to the world.

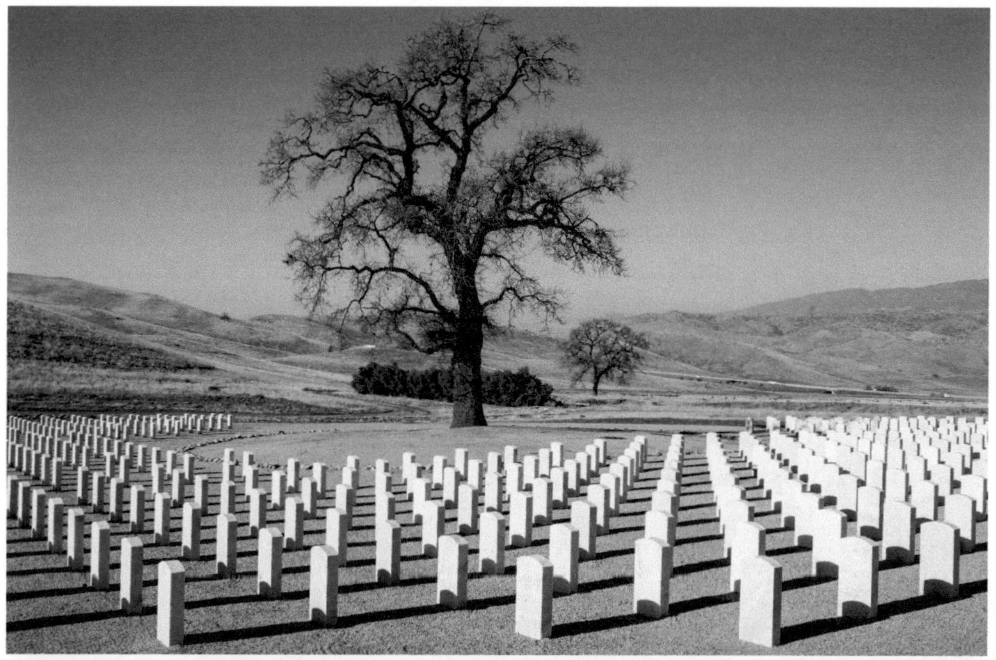

Bakersfield National Cemetery (established in 2008), Arvin, California, 2018.

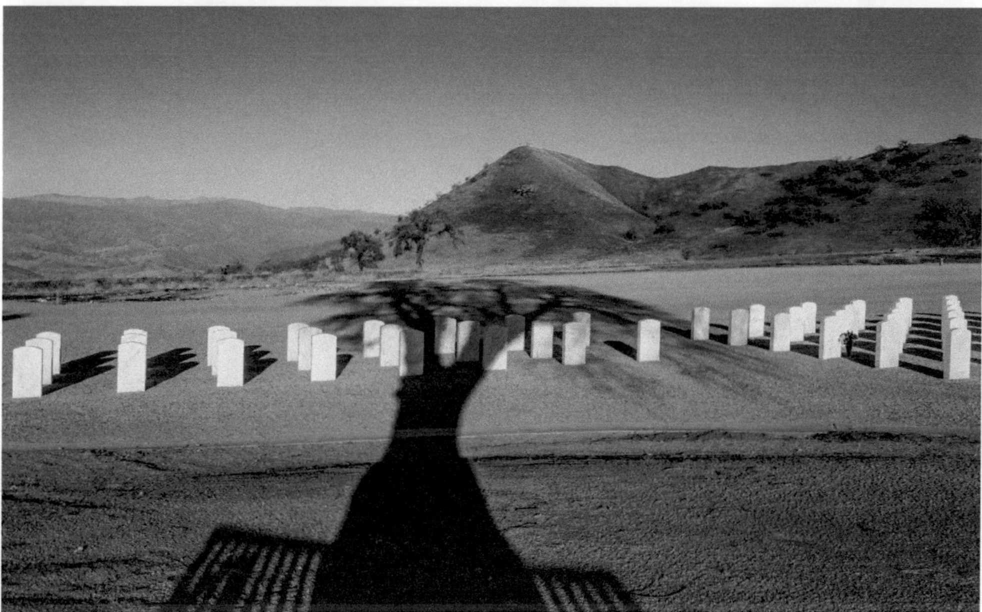

Bakersfield National Cemetery, 2018.

I got to Riverside at midday and stepped out from the car into the all-consuming sunlight and looked out over the neatly trimmed lawns. This was my first exposure to a cemetery dominated by ground flush memorial plaques, and while it was disconcerting not to see rows of headstones spanning the horizon, the reflection of sun off the metal plates and the shadows that framed the columbaria, benches, and planted trees brought another dimension to the place. So did the gaggle of geese that paraded up from the artificial lake and fountain.

Bakersfield National Cemetery also seemed to merge with the surrounding landscape without much regard for official boundaries. Actually located in Arvin, Bakersfield sits on mountainous terrain that peaks at a flag stand placed on a hill overlooking the site. I walked through the hills and dry grass, with hawks overhead, minding the posted warnings about snakes, looking for the best perspective on the headstones that stand around an enormous, desiccated tree with the freeway in the distance, winding though mountain passes.

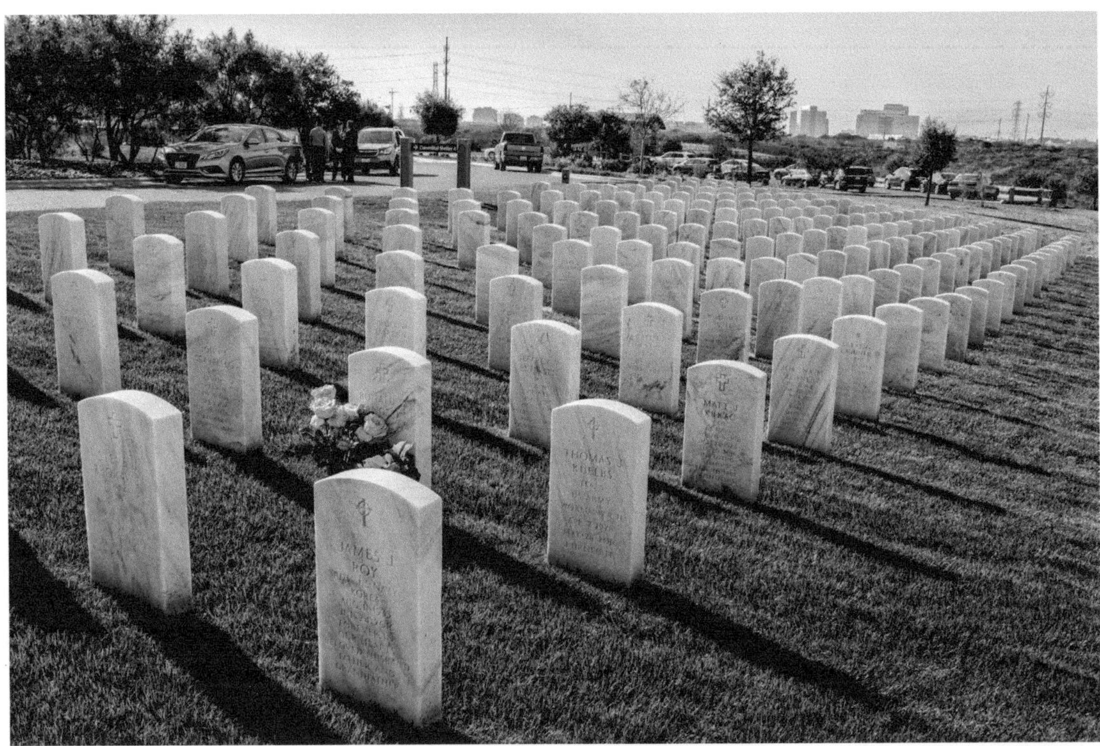

A funeral at Miramar National Cemetery (established in 2010), San Diego, California, 2018.

As much I tried to focus on the distinctive features of the cemetery—the white marble headstones posed against the golden hills and the two or three metal roofed committal shelters set back from the road—I could not escape the feeling of being in several places at the same time. Whether it was the Old West, Golden California, or Death Valley, I was navigating the allusive—and elusive—pull of several iconic landscapes. As writer Walker Percy said of encountering the Grand Canyon, it is difficult to see the place "for what it is" because its meaning "has already been formed in the sightseer's mind."[7]

The fact that these cemeteries are working landscapes helped me reframe their status. I saw this when I looked out at the cattle grazing in the hills and again, at San Joaquin, when I visited that cemetery several months later. Like Bakersfield, San Joaquin is set in the high desert with views of the San Luis Reservoir. It is larger than Bakersfield, and the fencing only nominally separates the flush ground markers from the ranch next door. There are electrical generators and water pumping stations distributed throughout the cemetery, lines of cypress trees separating the burial sections, rows of flags unfurled along the roads leading through the cemetery, and tiered seating built into the amphitheater near the visitor center. Beside the seats, I found open wire cages, habitats for the squirrels in the area. This is not just the new West but also a new memorial space, designed with environmental needs in mind.

Design follows practice, which is to say that the newer national cemeteries provide more flexibility and a wider array of gathering spaces than cemeteries founded during the nineteenth century. When I visited Miramar, just outside San Diego, a funeral was concluding at the committal shelter in one section of the cemetery, while, close by, several people were visiting a grave, one of them sitting under an umbrella to stay out of the heat. Meanwhile, a crew was preparing to install a new headstone in a nearby gravesite. If death is the great leveler, the national cemetery meets this reality with a democratic embrace.

Further south, at the tip of the peninsula that comprises Fort Rosecrans National Cemetery, light and water bring this dynamic into dramatic relief. In the evening, the setting draws visitors to either side of the cemetery to see the waning light bathe San Diego in a warm glow and then to the northside to watch the sun set on the Pacific. With a history that dates to California's early days as a state, Fort Rosecrans is closed to interments, which helped to explain the tourist-like atmosphere, though the visitors—whether families, couples, or groups of young people—dispersed into the elongated burial spaces on either side of the road with quiet expectancy. When I returned

Fort Rosecrans National Cemetery (established in 1934), San Diego, California, 2018.

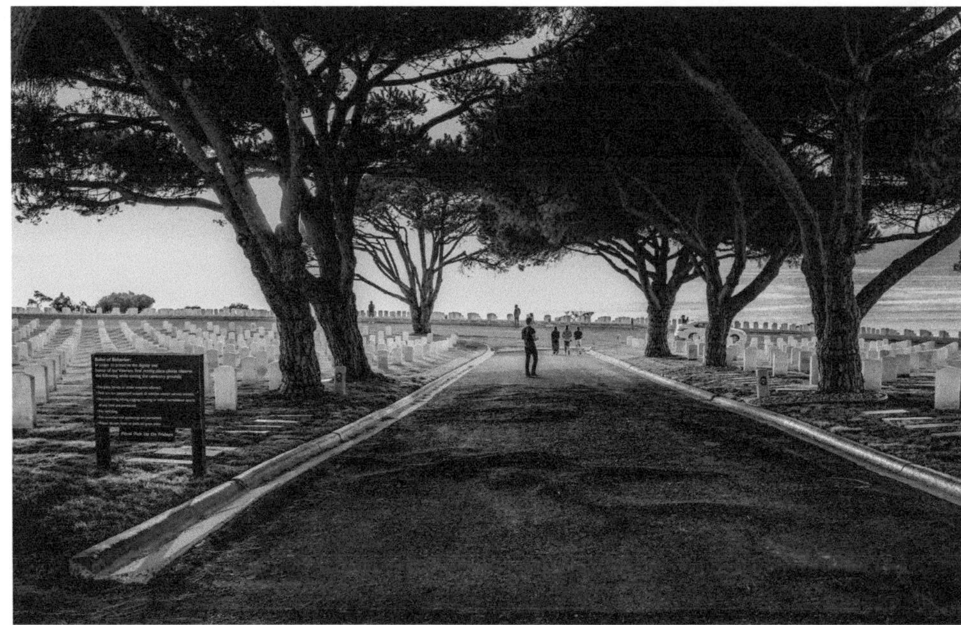

Fort Rosecrans National Cemetery, 2018.

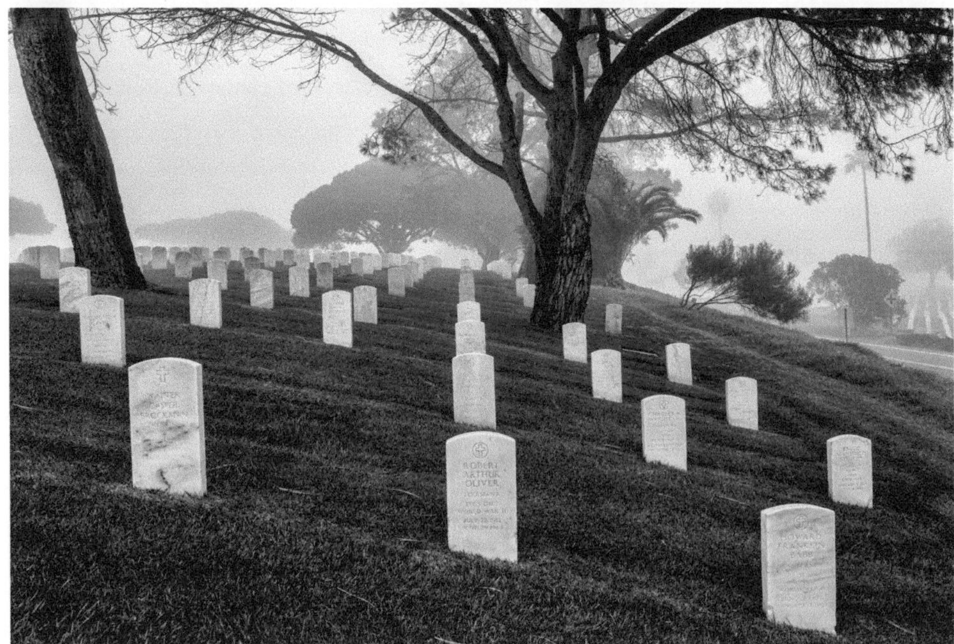

early the next morning to take pictures, the peninsula was socked in with fog, and I passed cyclists pushing through the gloam on their regular loops. National cemeteries are open from sunrise to dusk, so I parked and waited for the fog to lift and looked out at the groundskeepers who had just started work and were moving through the mist as on a silent newsreel.

I replay that scene now and remember a run I took on the beach in Florida ten years earlier, just after my mother died. I was jogging on the hard sand, trying to avoid the flattening waves and realizing how different everything felt. It was a moment of convergence in which I could almost touch my mother's absence but was at the same time swept along by nature's diurnal power. The moment seemed to continue when I got to the airport to fly home and explained to the TSA agent that the box I was carrying through security contained my mother's ashes.

When I returned to Florida in the spring of 2018, I first went to St. Augustine National Cemetery, then up to Jacksonville National Cemetery, and finally to Florida National Cemetery, in Bushnell, which is fifty miles west of Orlando. The contrast between St. Augustine and the newer sites in Jacksonville and Bushnell mirrors the difference between San Francisco and Miramar and Bakersfield. Established in 1828, St. Augustine sits in a small, walled enclosure within a prosperous section of America's oldest city. The cemetery is historic and picturesque and contains hints of Spanish colonial architecture. Given the pedestrian traffic, which includes military personnel from nearby St. Francis Barracks, a National Guard facility run by the US Army, it appears to function more like a plaza than a graveyard.

The newer cemeteries are transparent about their function, avoiding the identity problem that Walker Percy described. But Percy was more concerned with what happens when this problem affects people and humans are treated as specimens instead of spiritual beings, resulting in what he called "the loss of the creature."[8] This is a challenge posed by all large cemeteries, driven, ironically, by the effort to recognize all the dead. Jacksonville National Cemetery is barely fifteen years old and has only one thousand interments, but it spans more than five hundred acres and its up-to-date, antiseptic design seems to lack the personal touch. Florida National Cemetery is older—it opened in 1988—but its 516 acres were likewise built to scale and now includes 130,000 interments, colocated within the Withlacoochee State Forest. With section after section hewn from scrub pine woods, you really do need a map to find an individual grave.

I hiked the grounds at Florida National Cemetery from one section to the next, the rows of headstones aligned one after the other, 60 to 120 per section, each section separated from the

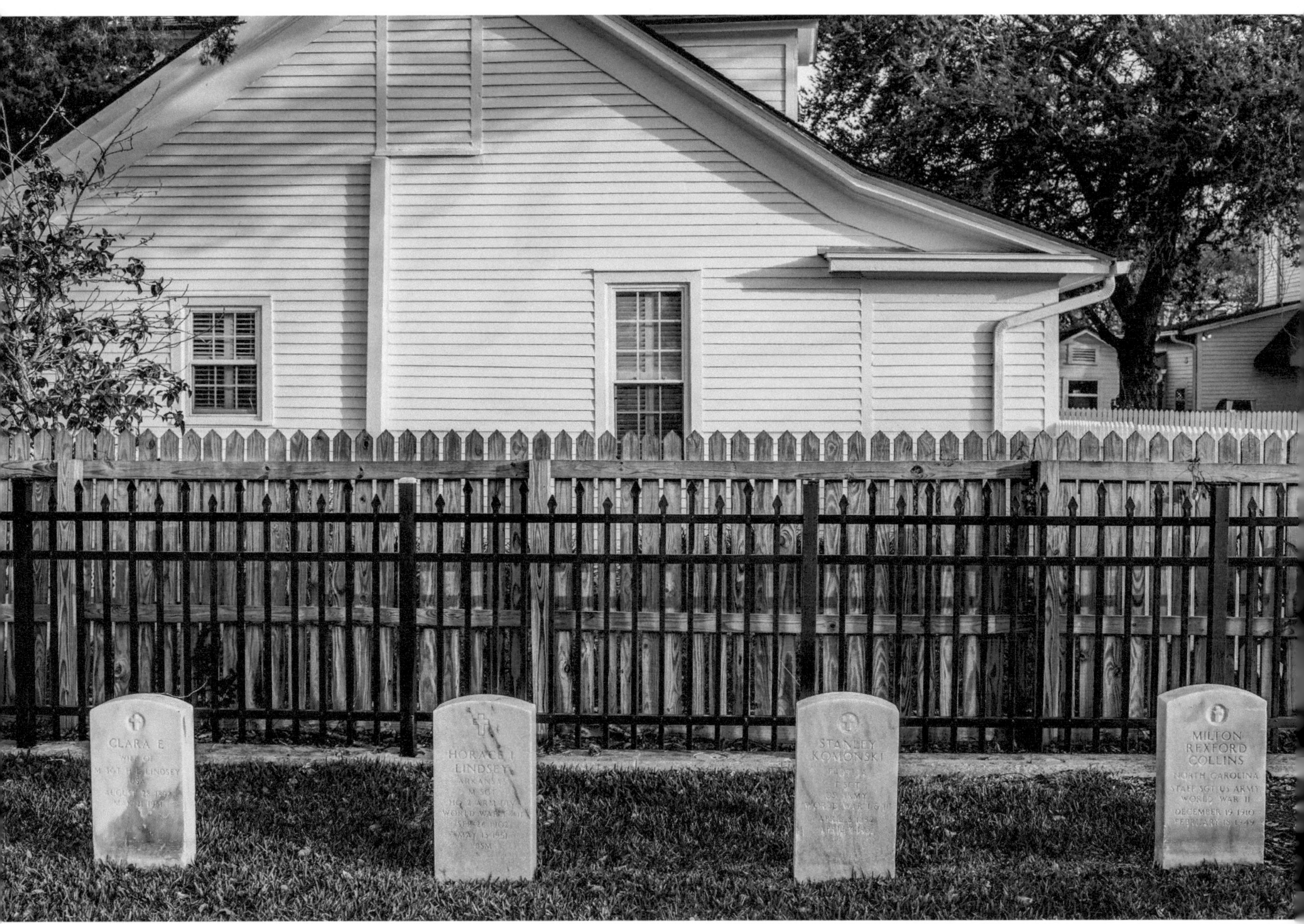

St. Augustine National Cemetery (established in 1881), St. Augustine, Florida, 2018.

next by trees and underbrush, and I was careful to remember where I parked. Like other large cemeteries created during the late twentieth century—Calverton National Cemetery on Long Island is another example—Florida National Cemetery lacks connected through paths and roadways. I doubt I covered a quarter of the acreage during my walk, but, without clear boundaries, it is easy to lose your bearings. No walls or fences divide the landscape, and though I did not see any wild pigs (I read that I might), I felt I was moving into untamed territory.

Yet Florida National Cemetery is not without sculpted beauty. The Cremation Garden includes blooming hedgerows, flower beds surrounded by imitation wrought iron, and several live oak trees, whose branches and moss hang over the gently curving path. Here, design evokes the landscape of the Old South, and I realize that a picture of this space, especially a black-and-white photograph, could carry historical connotations I may not intend.

The natural world is everything and everywhere in the natural cemeteries, and it hardly makes sense to discuss the significance of these landscapes—never mind photograph them—without engaging that fact. In *Specimen Days*, his 1882 account of the Civil War era, Walt Whitman described the war's grievous cost, at one point cataloging the random ways in which nature absorbed the casualties—in "bushes, low gullies, or on the sides of hills" and "secluded spots," where "their skeletons, bleach'd bones, tufts of hair, buttons, fragments of clothing, are occasionally found yet." Whitman welcomed the creation of cemeteries as final resting places for "our dead" and, with characteristic generosity, proposed burying Union and Confederate soldiers together.[9]

During the 1880s, this was too much to ask of either northerners or southerners. But, in the final paragraphs of his book, Whitman gave some sense of the thinking that lay behind his proposal. "Democracy most of all affiliates with the open air, is sunny and hardy and sane only with Nature," he wrote, "just as much as Art is. Something is required to temper both—to check them, restrain them from excess, morbidity."[10] To heal the body politic, all parts of the nation must reunite through the influence of American nature.

Whitman's open-air theory may lack traction today, though I had to reassess this judgment following my visit to Barrancas National Cemetery in Pensacola, months after my initial tour of Florida. There, the combination of sunshine and cultivated nature generate the conditions for democratic involvement that so inspired Whitman.

Barrancas is "on post," which means it is located on a military base—in this case, a US Navy base—and I had to stop at a visitor's center to apply for security clearance in order to visit the

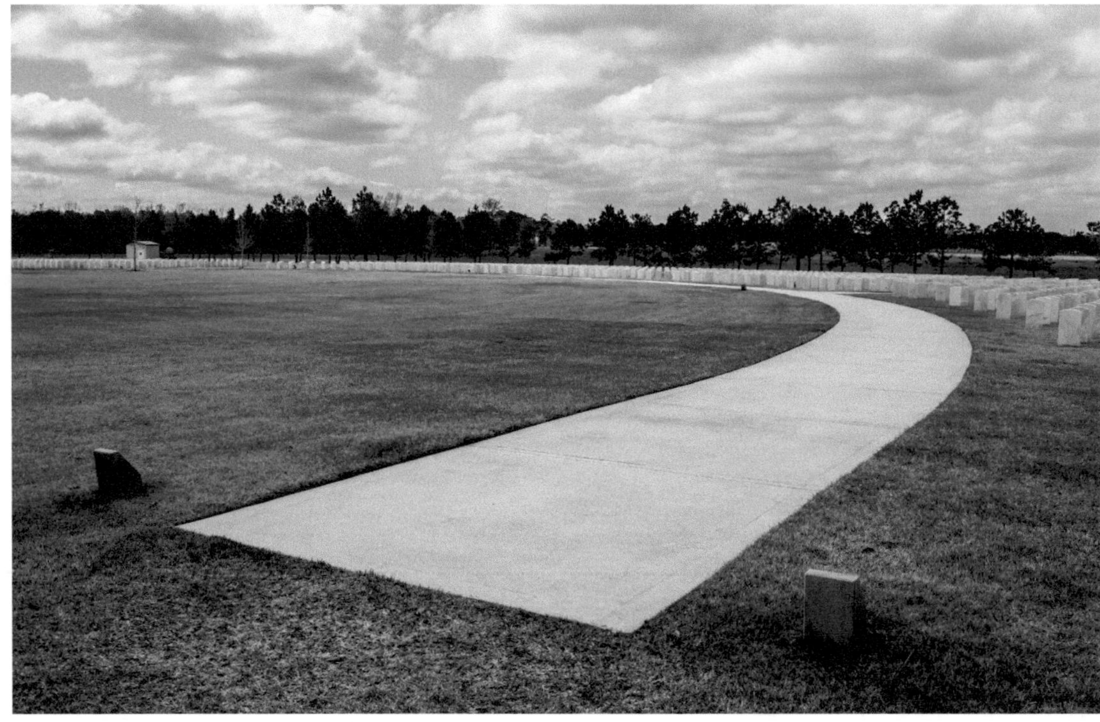

Jacksonville National Cemetery (established in 2008), Jacksonville, Florida, 2018.

cemetery. I showed up at 7:30 a.m. and waited for the center to open, along with two families. From snatches of their conversation I learned that they did not know one another, but their boys were there to attend a ceremony for a youth-training program they took together. And the boys were dressed for the occasion in navy-blue sailor uniforms.

When the officer on duty arrived, he told me I did not have to fill out any paperwork and could simply drive through the gate because today was set aside for "Wreaths Across America" and everyone was welcome. It was December, the holiday season, and I did not realize that my visit would coincide with this popular event, which brings thousands of volunteers to national cemeteries across the nation to lay wreaths on the graves of veterans.

I was scarcely alone that day. Indeed, as I was waved into the makeshift parking lot next to a section of headstones, a crowd had gathered and the atmosphere was festive. Like everyone else, I was there to pay my respects and bear witness, to try and picture what this common landscape feels and looks like.

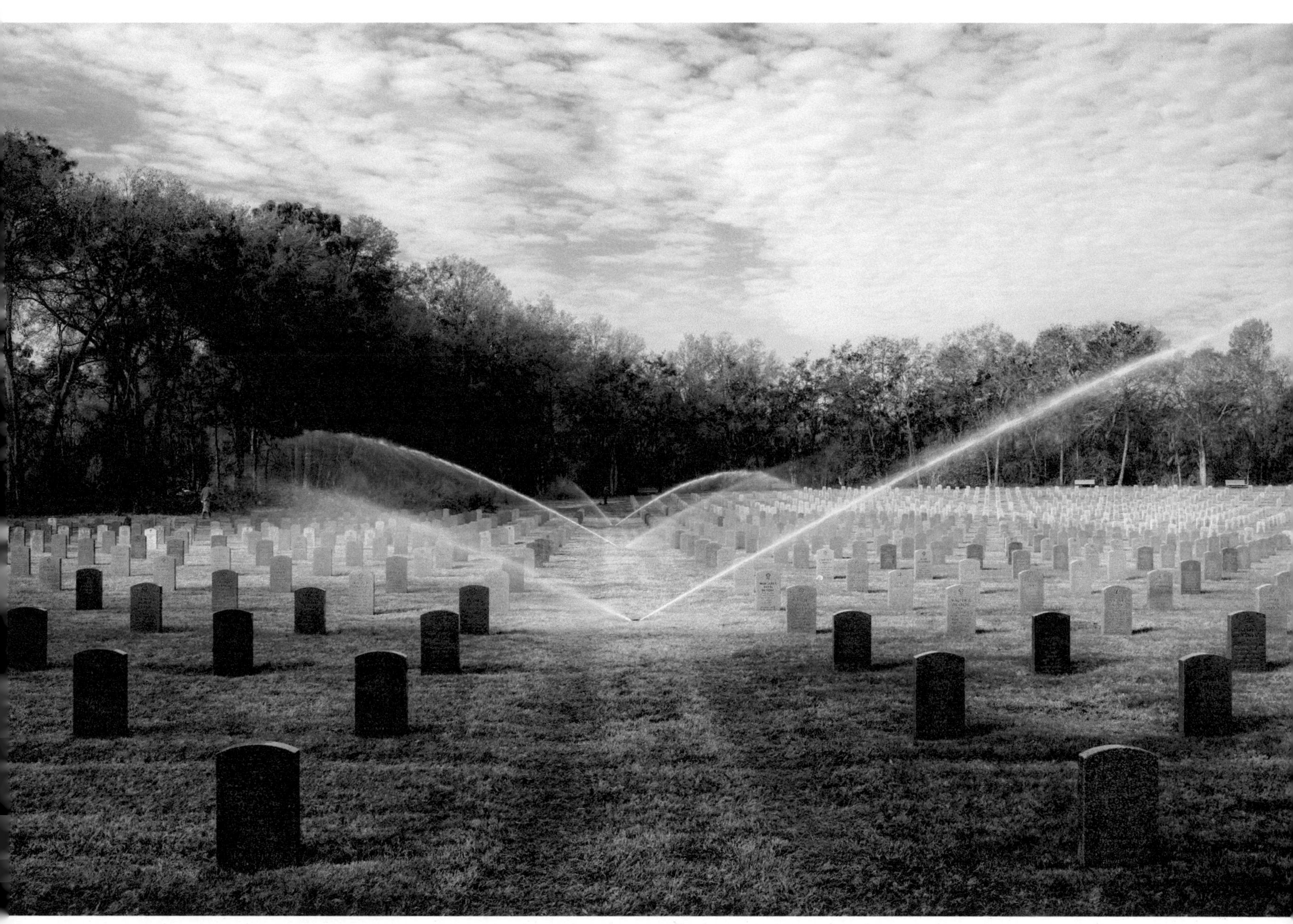

Florida National Cemetery, 2018.

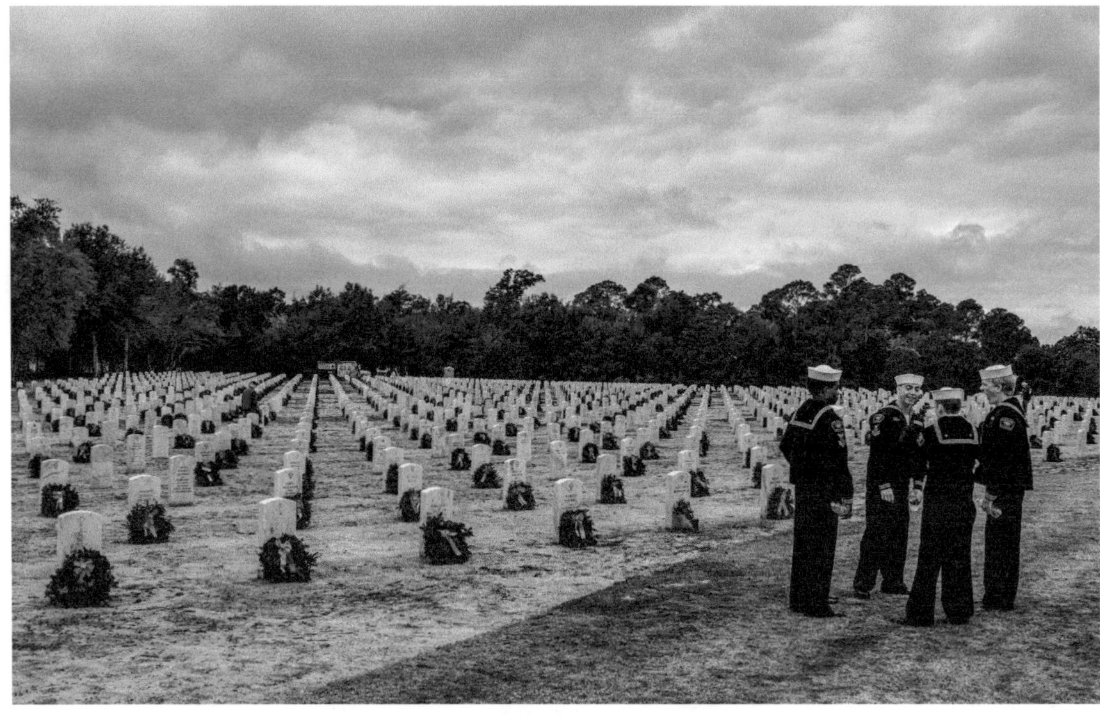

Barrancas National Cemetery (established in 1867), Pensacola, Florida, 2018.

The thousands interred at Barrancas were there not necessarily because the veterans had grown up in the Panhandle or lived in Florida, though many might have, but because they wanted to be laid to rest in a place symbolizing the nation they served. Here, as at Hot Springs, Miramar, and Saratoga, they committed their remains to a landscape founded on aspiration and hope. Maybe some chose a military burial because it is a good deal and the cemeteries are well funded. But beyond this practical reasoning, the ideal still resonates—in the battle hymn I sang in grade school and the vision of a Republic torn asunder and reborn through the moldering of John Brown's body and countless others.

The continental United States is beautiful and unruly, a mass of contradictions. We are all short-timers on this earth, and the national cemeteries are like caesuras in a great tragic poem, places where we pause to remember the dead and what we might be. I go to the cemeteries alone, as many do, but I am not by myself. History lies behind me and in front of me, like an open road. And I drive on.

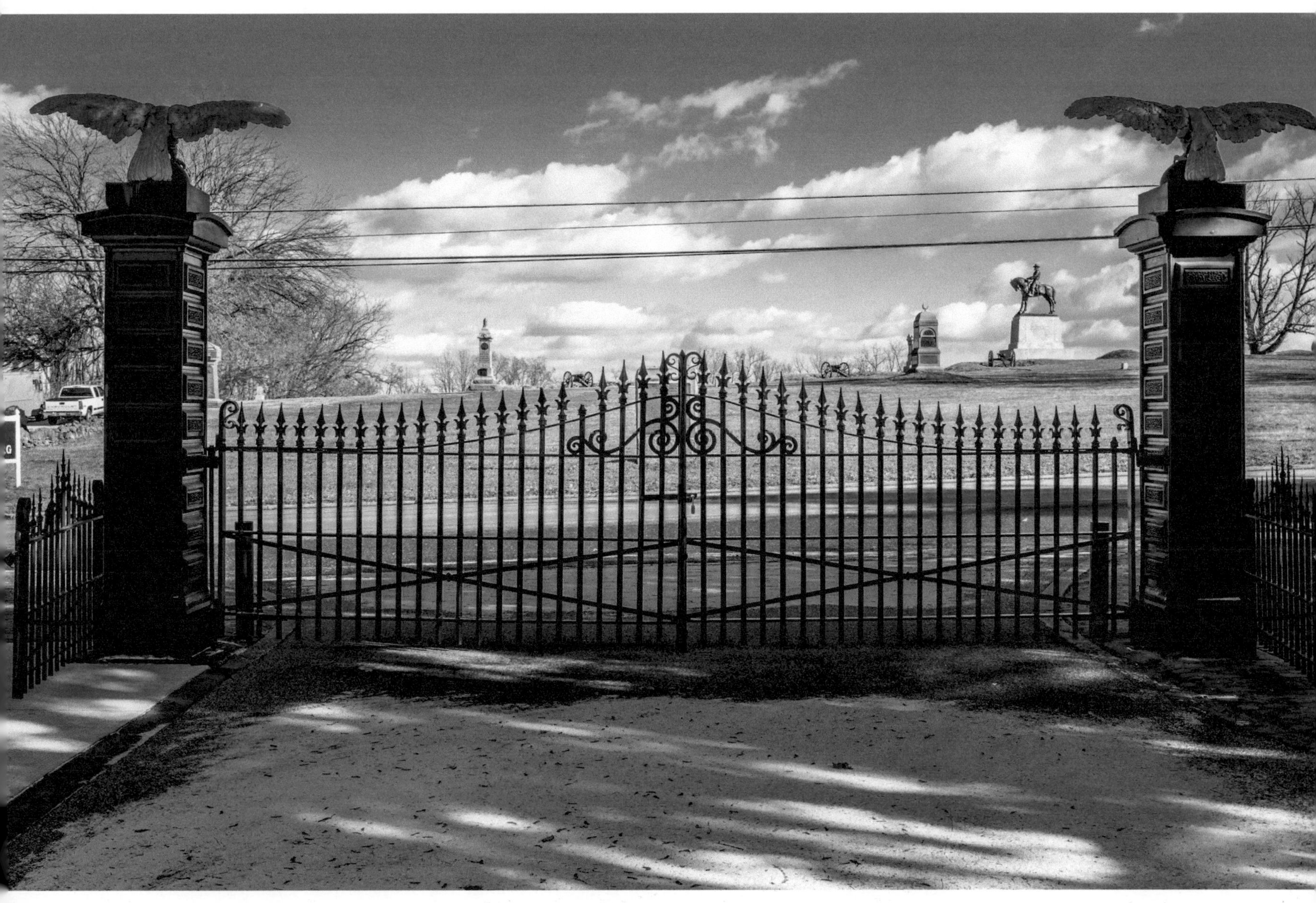

Looking at the field of battle from the entrance to Gettysburg National Cemetery (established in 1863), Gettysburg, Pennsylvania, 2017.

2

Fourscore

THE VISION OF MEMORIAL SPACE GIVING SHAPE TO NATIONALIST ASPIRATION emerged during the Civil War. Though it developed around high-minded principles, the national cemetery system was conceived in trauma and borne of exigency.

In the summer of 1862, faced by rising death counts and no place to put the bodies, Congress enacted the legislation authorizing President Abraham Lincoln to purchase land to establish cemeteries for soldiers "who shall die in the service of the country."[1] The word "shall" shifted the tone from the elegiac note usually associated with death to the imperative needs of the war. If Northerners initially believed the fighting would be over in a manner of weeks or months, the nation's leaders eventually realized that, to save the Union, many more men would have to die.

This sacrifice was the focus of the Gettysburg Address, which Lincoln delivered on November 19, 1863, on the grounds of the Soldiers' National Cemetery after one of the bloodiest battles of the war. The speech is now so much a part of the national ethos that it is easy to lose sight of how important the setting was for the president's eulogy-turned-proclamation. In the early 1900s, to highlight these origins, the government installed displays of the Gettysburg Address in all national cemeteries, in effect returning Lincoln's vision of rebirth and freedom back to the soil from which it sprang.

The sign posting is a bit misleading. While the effort to track and bury the Union dead was, in Drew Gilpin Faust's words, "arguably the most elaborate federal program undertaken in nearly a century of American nationhood," the cemeteries themselves emerged from a mix of practical and idealistic motives. In 1862, the Lincoln administration followed through on the congressional legislation and established a dozen national cemeteries. (For years, government documents indicated that this first group of cemeteries included fourteen sites, but the National Cemetery Administration recently corrected the record and reduced the number by two.) Meanwhile, the War Department created other cemeteries "as emergency circumstance demanded," as Faust puts it, usually near battlefields and hospitals so the army had a place to bury the dead. These burial grounds—for instance, at Chattanooga, Knoxville, and Stones River—eventually became national cemeteries, but the country was at war, and it took time for the landscapes to meet their sacred purpose so that Northerners could properly honor the Union dead.[2] Only in 1867, almost two years after the war ended, did Congress pass the National Cemetery Act, which provided funding and guidance for the growing number of cemeteries.

I consider this history in light of the trip I made to Antietam National Cemetery in the fall of 2017, just months before my tours of national cemeteries in California and Florida. I drove down to Sharpsburg, Maryland, from Gettysburg, Pennsylvania, where I had spent the night at

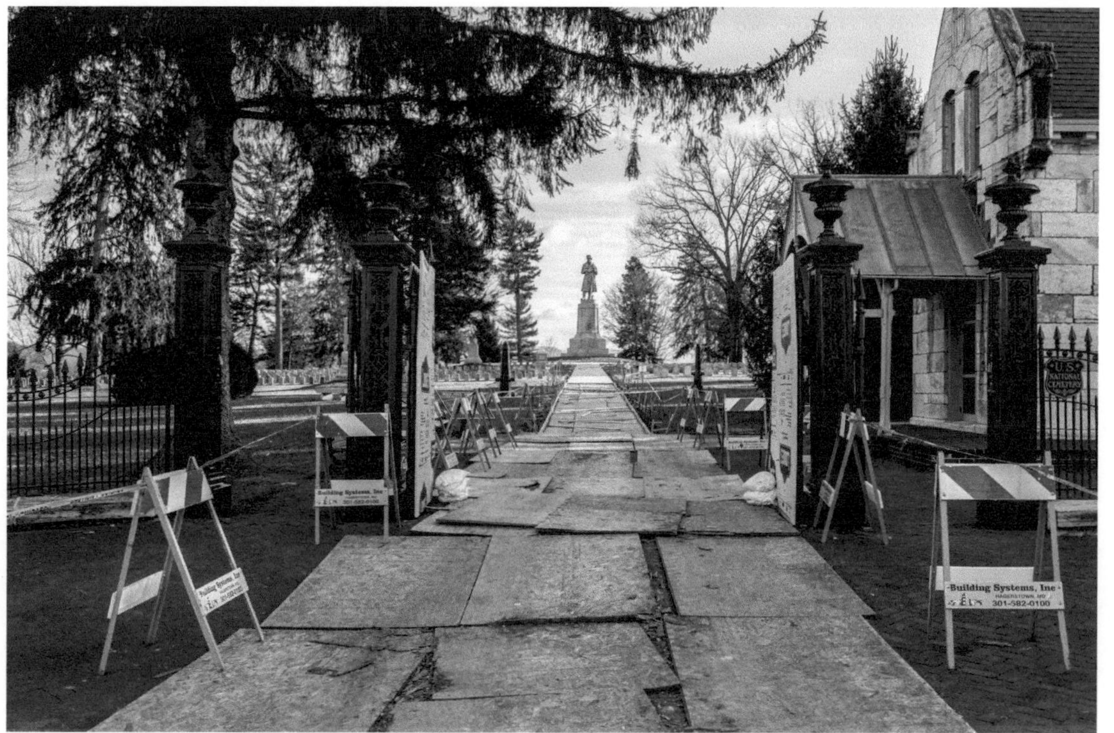

The entrance to Antietam National Cemetery (established in 1865), Sharpsburg, Maryland, 2017. The path leads to the Private Soldier Monument, a forty-four-foot-tall statue of a Union soldier standing with a rifle "in place of rest" and facing north toward "home."

an overdecorated Wyndham Motel, with portraits of Dwight Eisenhower and Jefferson Davis hanging by the elevators. I was in Sharpsburg out of season, and the town—modest by comparison to Gettysburg—was free of traffic. Finding the cemetery was a matter of driving east on Main Street, past several blocks of clapboard and stone houses, some dating to the nineteenth century, and then turning left into a parking lot where the road becomes Shepherdstown Pike. The cemetery is on the other side of the street, and, on the day I visited, the ceremonial gate and walkways were under construction, but no one was working.

Though the cemetery is on the edge of Sharpsburg's commercial district, it is also part of the battlefield park that stretches north and south of the burial grounds. After the horrifying violence at Antietam—twenty-three thousand killed, wounded, or missing on one day in 1862, the deadliest in US military history—the dead were buried wherever space could be found, mostly in graves hastily dug on farm fields. Two years later, the state of Maryland purchased land for a cemetery, aided by contributions from other Northern states. The federal government did not take ownership of the cemetery until 1877, but the War Department carried out the harrowing task of exhuming—and consolidating—the scattered remains. Some 4,700 Union bodies were reinterred in the new cemetery, and when it was dedicated in 1867—by President Andrew Johnson—it included a wall, gates, walkways, a superintendent's lodge, and the Private Soldier Monument at the center of the site.

We can see how some of the cemetery was built from the expenses detailed by the Antietam National Cemetery Association:[3]

Estimated Amount Required to Complete the Antietam
National Cemetery
Prepared for the Board by General Superintendent
Augustin A. Biggs, M.D., December 13, 1865

Cost of Grounds	$1,164.75
2,663 perches stone, delivered at $1.20 per perch[4]	3,163.20
173 perches stone, delivered for keeper's lodge at $1.20 per perch	207.60
Expense of laying 2,636 perch at $1.50 per perch	3,954.60
Expense of excavating 820 yards of foundation at 40 cents per yard	328.00

Expense of 18,161 yards of foundation at 40 cents per yard	5,484.30
Expense of 6,560 bushels sand, at 4 cents per bus	262.40
Expense of 2,500 bushels lime, at 25 cents per bus	625.00
For labor	7,000.00
For survey	25.00
For keeper's lodge	1,500.00
For entrance gate	500.00
For powder and fuse	60.00
For 1,915 linear feet coping, at $3.25 per foot	6,223.75
For removal, boxing, and burial of 6,000 dead, at $5 each	30,000.00
For tools and implements	230.00
For 6,000 headstones for inscriptions, at $3 each	18,000.00
For carriage ways and drainage	1,000
For 797 feet iron fence, on front line, at $3 per ft	3,391
For blacksmithing	500.00
For iron clamps and lead for coping (on enclosing wall)	420.00
For pointing wall, outside and inside, at 12 cents per perch	316.22
For contingent expenses	2,500.00
Total estimated cost	$85,852.32

The formal design of cemeteries like Antietam offers a partial counterbalance to the violent, seemingly random nature of death. Here, the Private Soldier Monument—or "standing soldier"—commemorates the role that ordinary citizens played in the war. But the real innovation are the graves themselves. The government's decision to identify each casualty in turn was the first time since the fifth century BCE—when the Greeks honored the men who perished in the Attic War—that a nation recognized the military dead with individual, named burial spaces. Historian Thomas Laqueur calls this form of commemoration, which accelerated during World War I, "necronominalism." And he attributes its emergence to the traumatic effects of modern warfare and the state's desire to reconnect with the public, heal the grieving, and build a national community—of the living and the dead.[5]

At Antietam, it is difficult to see modernity in the darkened, mildewed stone markers that

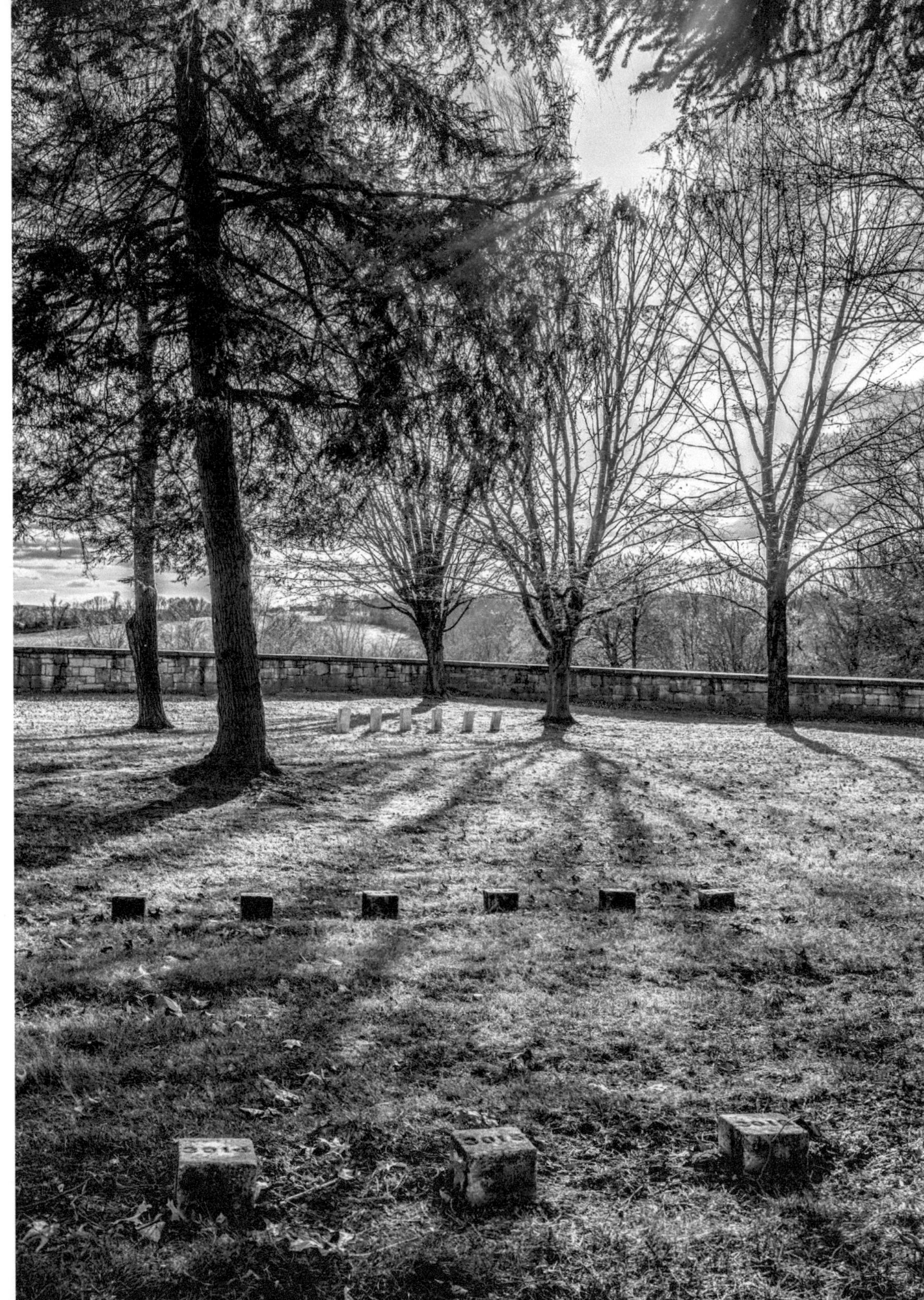

Looking at the southwest corner of Antietam National Cemetery, 2017. The square markers represent unknown Union dead who fell at the Battle of Antietam.

extend across the grounds in irregularly placed rows. Some are full-sized headstones, while others are blocks with numbers on top. The numbers represent unknown soldiers, the tally enumerated stone by stone, a method of accounting that has no meaning outside the battle itself or government ledgers. At other Civil War cemeteries, unidentified bodies are designated by regular headstones simply labeled "unknown."

At older national cemeteries, such as Richmond National Cemetery, headstones occasionally extend from tree trunks like snaggle teeth because nothing was done to curtail the growth of the tree. There is a tension in these spaces between the formal act of commemoration and the steady force of nature.

The day was cold and bright when I walked the Antietam site, and shadows slanted through the trees and across the stones, adding another layer of order. Sunlight illuminated the whole, holding it in place, and, as I approached the back wall, the view opened up to the battlefield park, the fields still green though it was mid-December. If a battle had not been fought on this spot, this expanse might still be farmland. Had fewer men died (one section of the battlefield was called "bloody lane"), a cemetery might not have been built on this hill so close to this town whose sympathies stretched to North and South.

While Antietam is one of the first cemeteries established through an 1862 congressional act, not all graveyards were near the field of battle. Several are in places that seem beyond the range of conflict, for instance, Brooklyn (New York), Philadelphia (Pennsylvania), Springfield (Illinois), and Keokuk (Iowa). But out of range is not out of context, and these locations indicate the war's scope and the effort to transport equipment and troops over conflicted territory and find spaces for the wounded, who were treated in hospitals throughout the North.

A few days before my visit to Antietam, I traveled to Keokuk, crossing the Mississippi River from the Illinois side and driving through town toward the cemetery. The national burial site occupies two sections of the hilly terrain that runs through Oakland Cemetery, a one-hundred-acre public burial ground that was founded during the 1850s. The town's strategic importance during the war stemmed from its location on the river, which gave Union forces access to the war's western theater and made it a logical hub for training centers and hospitals. Initially, the dead were buried at Oakland, but, as the numbers mounted, the town donated land to the federal government. Almost a century later, the new cemetery—Keokuk National Cemetery—expanded to include a second parcel, on a ridge above the Civil War section.

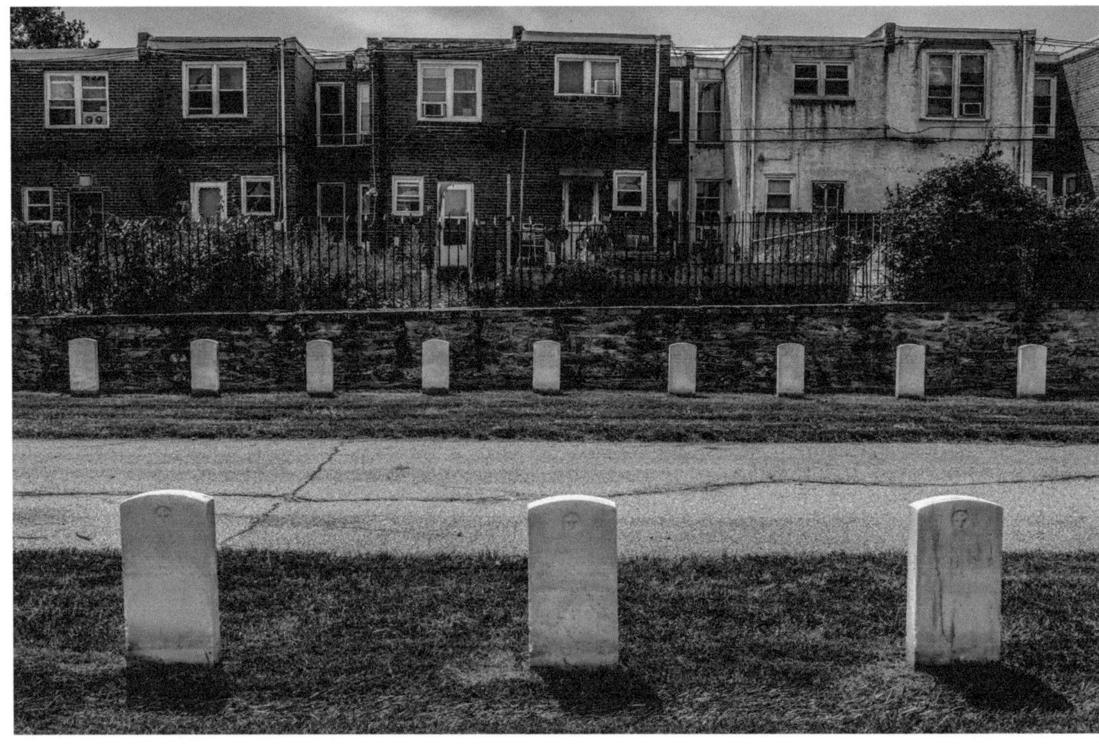

Philadelphia National Cemetery (established in 1885), Philadelphia, Pennsylvania, 2018.

A similar mix of motives guided the development of other national cemeteries. Cypress Hills National Cemetery began as an enclave within a private cemetery in Brooklyn and then expanded to another larger section during the 1880s. In Philadelphia, the dead were moved from city hospitals to several cemeteries, only to be reinterred at Philadelphia National Cemetery. The aggregation of remains was a natural extension of the process that began during the war. But while many of the Union dead ended up in national cemeteries, some stayed in Soldiers' Lots such as the one in Green Mount Cemetery in Vermont, plots within private cemeteries that the National Cemetery Administration likewise maintains. These are small landscapes, twenty-two in all, that quietly fold military service into more traditional burial spaces.

In 1870, General Quartermaster Montgomery C. Meigs—the soldier-engineer who oversaw the creation of the national cemetery system—asked landscape architect Frederick Law Olmsted for advice on how best to design the cemetery grounds. Olmsted recommended that the

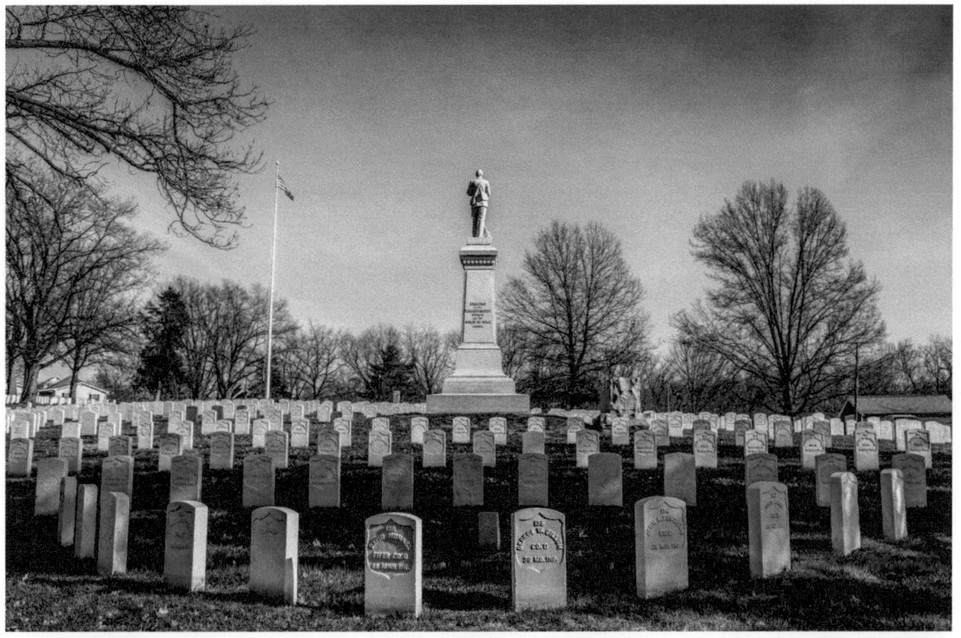

Keokuk National Cemetery (established in 1862), Keokuk, Iowa, 2017.

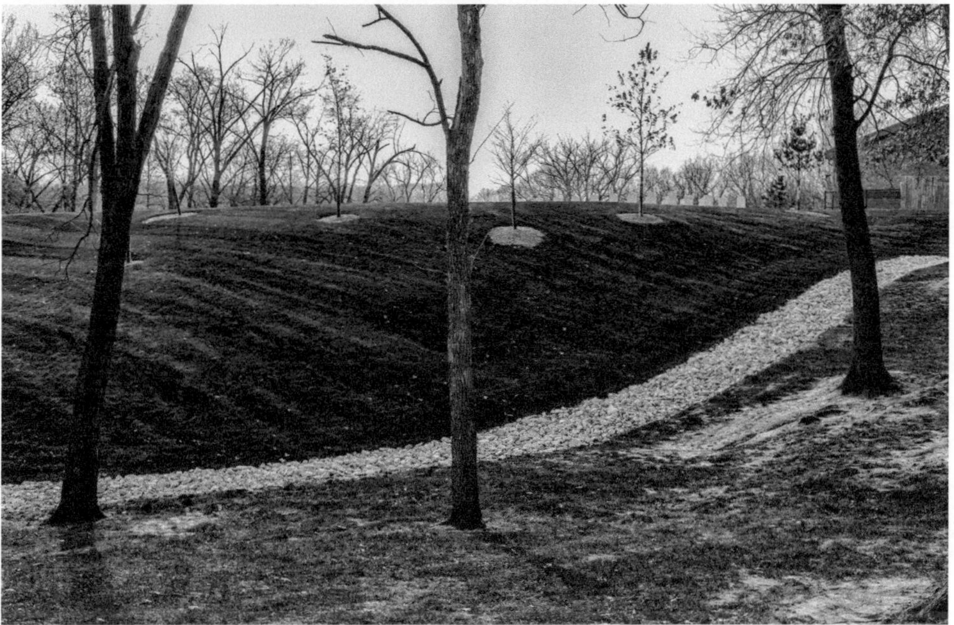

A view of the newer section at Keokuk National Cemetery, 2017.

cemeteries be "studiously simple" and that plantings emphasize indigenous species. The goal, he said, was to create a "sacred grove" within "the enclosing wall and in the perfect tranquility of the trees." Like Lincoln, Olmsted was acutely aware of the spiritual values that many Americans associated with pastoral landscapes, and his recommendation reflected the influence of the mid-nineteenth-century rural cemetery movement, which was aimed at providing more artful, bucolic settings for middle- and upper-class burials.[6]

Seen from a distance, Keokuk National Cemetery looks anything but tranquil. The sightlines at the gate run over the cleanly set Union headstones, hop the wrought iron fence that borders the cemetery, and expand out toward the irregular array of monuments in Oakland Cemetery. Olmsted's vision is more evident in Keokuk's newer section, a park-like glen that includes older trees as well as recent plantings sparingly placed on the hills in a manner evocative of Japanese landscape design. A 1970s-era committal shelter with a concrete pad stands at the center, empty now of visitors—save me—but strangely expectant. Keokuk is still open to interments.

I followed the gravel path back to my parking spot and paused at the top to look at a wire-meshed enclosure, much like a vegetable garden, which included a single headstone, surrounded by dead leaves. The headstone was blank, and I realized I was looking at a demonstration site, though I could not figure out why anyone would dump leaves in the fencing. If Olmsted's intention was to create a naturalistic setting for solemn reflection, the recent trend has been to personalize memorials. So the headstones at Keokuk include customized language as well as the listing of name, rank, branch of service, and date of birth and death: "Love you," "Known as Rocky," "Loving Husband Father and Grandfather," and "Gone Fishing." Similar inscriptions can be found at all the newer burial sites.

A quarter mile away, the six hundred headstones that fill in around the monument to the Unknown Dead (a standing soldier statue) present as a unified whole that is visible from the ridge above. The Civil War section at Keokuk does not literally sit on higher ground, but it dominates the landscape. It feels like a public space, while the newer section is relatively secluded and more private.

Another way of reading this landscape is to say that the Civil War and its legacy are closer than we might think. Although Civil War cemeteries barely qualify as outdoor museums—they are less visited by tourists than historic battlefields—they once played an important role in American civic life. Their original commemorative purpose lives on in all the national cemeteries. They are history hiding in plain sight. And when we peel back the surfaces we see more of ourselves.

This is provisional thinking, a self-guiding prompt as I moved from cemetery to cemetery or stood in the bright sunlight at Keokuk and photographed the scene: ceremonial gate, iron fence, superintendent's cottage, section markers, pathways, instructional plaques, monument, and headstones. The national cemeteries are neither urban or rural or suburban. As a constellation of similarly designed places located throughout the country, they form a metamemorial landscape that calls to mind American ideals yet also provokes memories and emotions that have little to do with nationalism or even grief.

One benefit of traveling this landscape by myself was that I could experience these trips without explanation. The visits were mine alone, and the pictures, I hope, speak for themselves, maybe express something of the anticipation I felt being drawn through the anonymous, utterly familiar, but mysterious American landscape. This feeling edged toward liberation but never achieved the expansive letting go that travel sometimes provides, in part because my trips were usually a tightly organized sequence of airplane flights, car rentals, and motel stays. And the destination was always the same: established patterns of commemoration, a forthright recognition of death, and a solemn declaration of common purpose. I do not consider myself an especially patriotic or even political person, but I find this enduring sense of order to be reassuring. In this sense, I traveled to discover a larger sense of belonging than what ties me to my home and family in rural Vermont.

The decision to build lodges in cemeteries—which Quartermaster Meigs had designed in the popular Second Empire style—was an acknowledgment that cemeteries should be a national home requiring the kind of oversight often given to churches or universities. While the lodges are now empty or have been turned into administrative offices, they once served as homes for caretakers (and their families) who tended the grounds and provided assistance to visitors.

The War Department also posted guidelines for the public: do not picnic or recreate on the grounds, avoid driving carriages on the grass, and so on. The regulations were later replaced by other instructions—for instance, explaining the use of floral arrangements—though you can find the original signs in some of the older cemeteries. With direction from Meigs, the department installed additional signs displaying lines from the poem, "Bivouac of the Dead," by Theodore O'Hara. O'Hara was a career army officer from Kentucky, who, ironically, served with the Confederates. Although Meigs was no apologist for the South—his son John died fighting for the Union—he believed that the verse, which O'Hara wrote during the Mexican War, sounded the proper elegiac note.

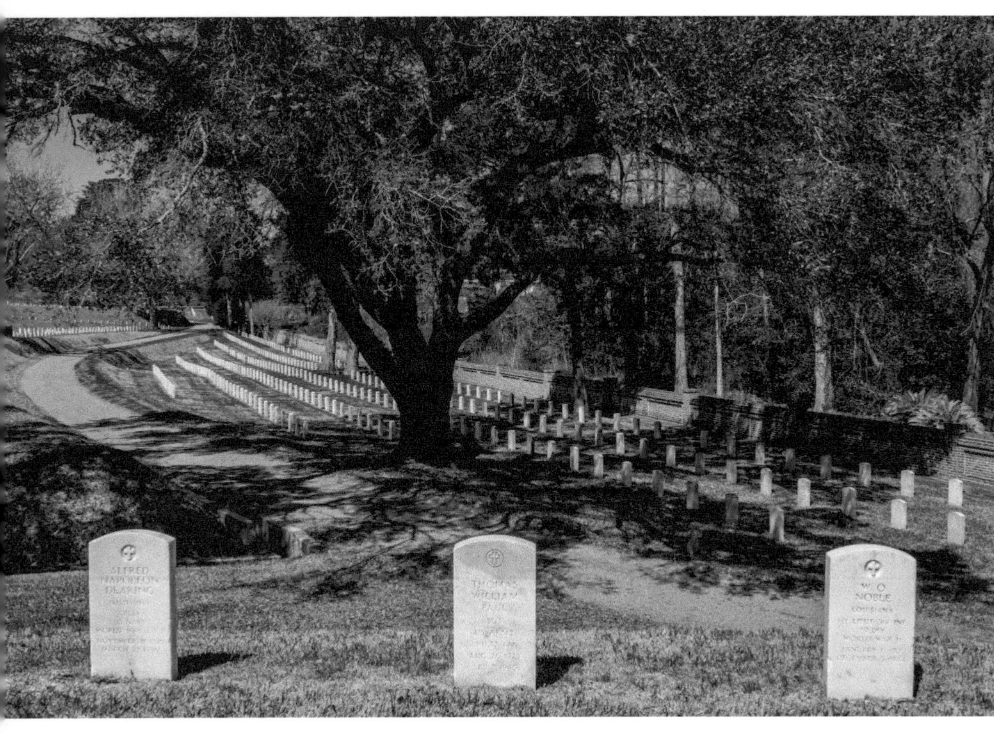

Natchez National Cemetery (established in 1866), Natchez, Mississippi, 2018.

(*Right*) Natchez National Cemetery, 2018.

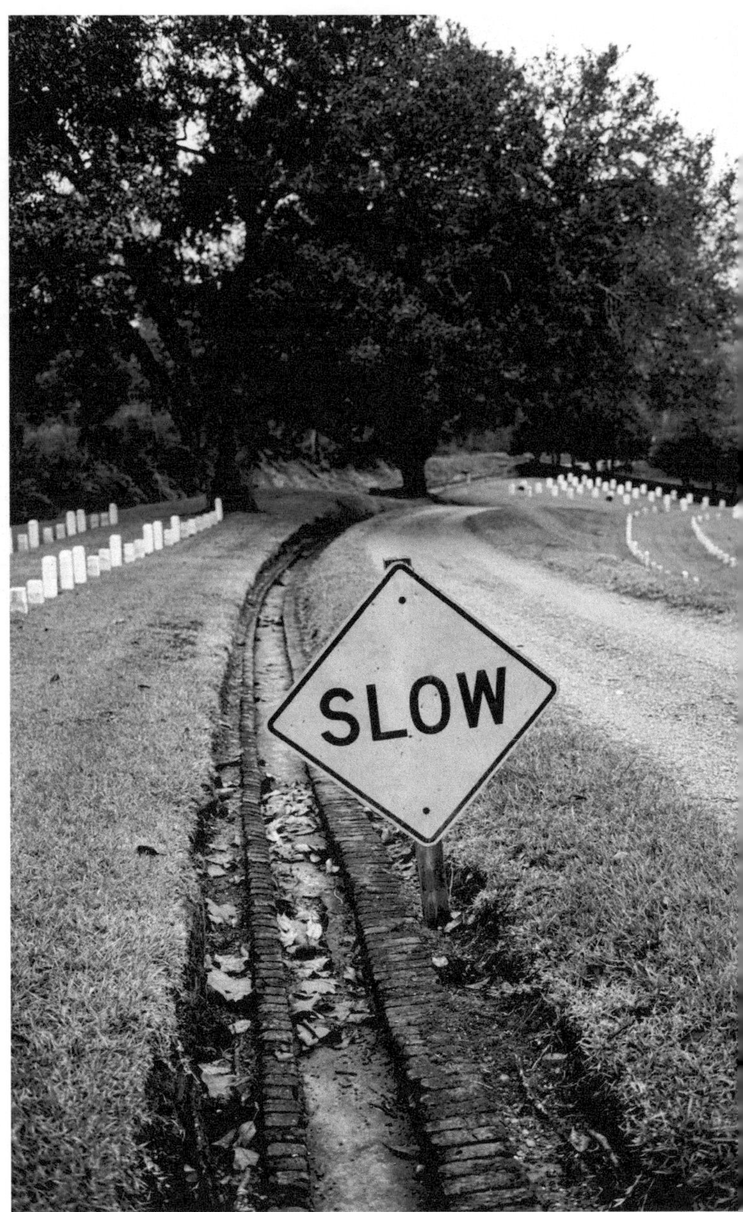

On Fame's eternal camping-ground
Their silent tents are spread.
And Glory guards, with solemn round
The bivouac of the dead.

A bivouac is a temporary encampment, but "to bivouac" also means to stand watch or guard. The Civil War graves at Keokuk suggest both uses of the term, as many of the headstones encircle the Unknown Soldier monument like tents in a camp, while also seeming to protect the cemetery. Nothing in this layout indicates anything is guarding the dead, except maybe the actual existence of the cemetery. O'Hara says that "Glory guards" the dead, an abstraction that the landscape—or the US government—makes real by memorializing the sacrifice made by the men who died defending the Union. This bivouac is supposed to be eternal, not temporary.

Downhill from the Unknown Soldier monument, the semicircular arrangement of graves at Keokuk is unusual but not unique. There are similar designs at Shiloh and Fort Donelson National Cemeteries in Tennessee, some in clusters of three or four, usually including men from the same unit and state. The groupings reflect a state-based conception of national identity—the Northern and Southern armies were both organized at the local level—and sometimes the contours of the land. At Natchez National Cemetery, narrow drainage channels weave in and out of the steep terrain and headstones form rings around one hill, resulting in a "wedding cake" design.

Many of the men interred at Keokuk came from the Midwest, and a good portion of them were Iowans. In fact, the Unknown Soldier monument was established by the Woman's Relief Corps and the state of Iowa in 1912, the date a reminder that commemoration can be an ongoing process and that what we see today is not necessarily what the cemetery looked like during the 1860s or '70s. Also, the inclusion of eight Confederate graves in the original semicircle is something of a surprise, since, in establishing the cemeteries, the War Department was determined not to mix Rebel combatants with Union soldiers. For practical reasons, however, the War Department made exceptions for men who died in Northern prisons or hospitals.

When I walked back from the circle, I looked for the anomalies, the exceptions, the visual quirks that offset this tightly organized landscape. I did not have far to go to find headstones for veterans who fought in World Wars I and II. They represent the growth of the national cemetery system beyond its Civil War core, a harbinger of Keokuk's eastern expansion. The pressure for additional burial space is clear from the placement of headstones against the black iron fence, which barely separates the cemetery from the split-level ranch house and patio behind it. This is a common feature in national cemeteries—stonework wedged up against walls, driveways, and storage buildings. In Philadelphia, I saw a wrecked car in the backyard of a brownstone straining against the fence and in Togus, Maine, a row of trees redlined for lumber in the woods beside the cemetery. To follow the lot lines is to patrol the boundary between death and life, public and domestic space, and wilderness.

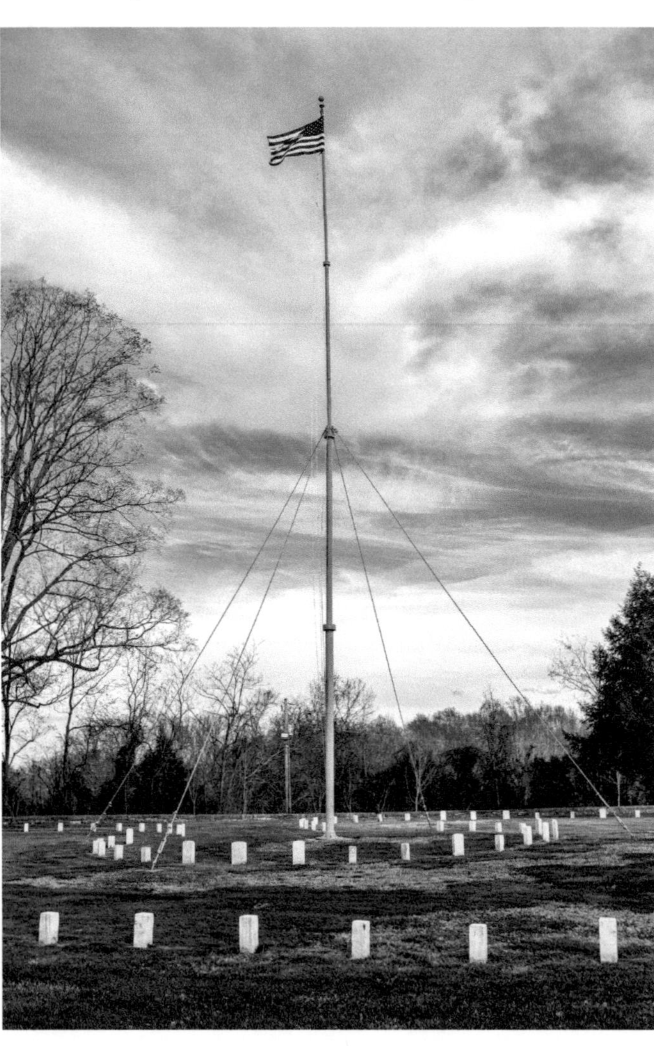

Fort Donelson National Cemetery (established in 1867), Dover, Tennessee, 2018.

The border is prime territory for anthropological and literary reflection. But death is not metaphorical nor are the depressed neighborhoods that surround Keokuk National Cemetery. I drove down the numbered streets to the river, past sturdy homes that had seen better days, and back through the downtown with shuttered stores. It may be clichéd to dwell on the economic crisis that for decades has afflicted the midsection of the country and even worse to drive through without stopping, not talking to anyone. But I did.

3

This Great Sepulture

When I woke up in Murfreesboro at 5:00 a.m., it was raining. A spring rain, soft and steady. Nothing about the forecast had changed from the night before. I got dressed and checked out of the motel, figuring I would wait at the cemetery for the rain to stop.

I had been dodging weather since getting to Louisville two days earlier and driving south to visit cemeteries near the Cumberland River, a route that would take me to Nashville, Chattanooga, Knoxville, and then back up into Kentucky. The first leg of the trip covered some of the key battle sites that comprised the western theater of the Civil War. For a nation still weighted toward the East Coast, Tennessee counted as the West, distinct from Virginia and the territory that the Army of the Potomac sought to control. Tennessee was where Ulysses S. Grant vaulted to prominence in February 1862 with victories at Fort Henry and Fort Donelson. Grant's words to Simon Bolivar Buckner, the commanding Confederate officer at Fort Donelson, endeared him to Lincoln and a Northern public hungry for good news in a war that, up to this point, the South had dominated: "No terms except an unconditional and immediate surrender can be accepted. I propose to move immediately on your works."[1]

I got to Fort Donelson National Cemetery ahead of schedule, arriving in the evening rather than the next morning so as to avoid rain. The cemetery is on high ground, in the town of Dover, less than a mile from the river and about two miles by car from the battlefield park. It was about 7:30 p.m., so I would be walking through a national cemetery after regular business hours. Although national cemeteries are open from dawn to dusk, Fort Donelson, like Antietam, is managed by the National Park Service. That may be why the visitor's center, not just the bathroom, was open when I got there, even though no one else was on the grounds.

Cemeteries are not designed to provide historical information the way battlefields often are. At Fort Donelson, apart from a brief overview at the front gate, there is no account of the battle for Fort Donelson or the rise of "Unconditional Surrender Grant." The cemetery is about the size of a baseball diamond, and the 670 headstones—almost all Civil War dead—are arranged in curved rows with two more tightly drawn circles centered around a flag and cannon head. More recently deceased veterans are on the periphery, as at Keokuk. This quasi-formal design, stones arranged in a field, has a homegrown feel to it. I walked the grounds with my camera, trying to place the circular figures in the rectangular frame. Without an elevated perspective or drone, it was difficult to compose a picture that included the whole.

Located 120 miles to the southeast, off US 24, Murfreesboro was the location of another river fight, which began on New Year's Eve, a year after Grant captured Fort Donelson. There were twenty-three thousand casualties at the Battle of Stones River, more than half of them Northerners. Still, in holding the Union position, General William S. Rosecrans claimed a victory, which Lincoln was happy to accept. About a year later, in the spring of 1864, George H. Thomas, who replaced Rosecrans as the commanding general of the Army of the Cumberland, called for the creation of a cemetery at Murfreesboro to bury the casualties from Stones River. In 1865, the site became the Stones River National Cemetery, and the War Department launched an intensive effort to locate the remains of other Union soldiers who perished on nearby battlefields.

Repeated across central Tennessee and wherever bodies were missing, the search for corpses was a precondition for creating national cemeteries. The man in charge of this work in the Department of the Cumberland, Edward B. Whitman, was a captain in the Quartermaster Division, a New Englander, an abolitionist, and a Harvard graduate. He was passionate about raising the dead, and eloquent in his descriptions of the challenges at hand.

In 1866, almost a year after the war ended, he placed an advertisement in more than three hundred Southern newspapers, asking for information about where Union soldiers were buried.[2] As Whitman noted in his final report—delivered in 1869 to Montgomery Meigs after four years of work—he was responding to, and channeling, a larger chorus of requests: "Here, came an earnest entreaty from a bereaved Father or Mother, that I would find the missing remains of their lost one. There, an appeal from a sorrowing Wife or loving Sister, to tell them where the precious remains of their loved and lost ones were to be found. Others furnished drawings and descriptions designating the precise spot where the body of a friend or comrade had been laid, often so minute and accurate in the details, that any person could process with unerring certainty to the very grave."[3]

He also identified the likely source of this intimately held geography: "Many regiments, especially in the early part of the War, were raised by Townships and Counties, and comprised in their ranks, fathers, sons, brothers, cousins, always neighbors, and friends. In every Regiment there was more or less of a friendly home interest among the numbers, not only to watch over and help each other, but to keep the friends at home informed of all casualties to their relatives. Thus it happened that scarcely a man was killed in battle, or died in a Regimental Hospital, without some friendly and thoughtful spirit near to unite in the last sad rites, drop a tear over the grave, and then to mark the spot and send to the friends at home, a careful and minute description of the last resting place."

And Whitman confirmed how this information aided his work: "By classification and arrangement the information they contained formed a convenient and valuable guide book on the routes of all our Armies, upon every battlefield from one end of the Country to the other: in the woods and groves around Ft. McAlaster [McAllister]; among the rocks and ravines of the Kenesaw [Kennesaw]; along the Banks of the Mississippi; on the mountains of the Cumberland; and through the swamps and canebrakes of Mississippi and Tennessee, everywhere they served as infallible guides to the graves which otherwise might have been overlooked, or in the subsequent removal, been sadly transferred to the new Cemeteries *as Unknown*."

Not all Southerners responded favorably to Whitman's request for information. Those who did earned his gratitude, which he underscored in his report: "Travelling in the midst of a people smarting from defeat and disappointment, and suffering from all the hardships which a devasting war had entailed upon them, I shall not soon forget, either on my own account, or of the dear friends of the dead, many acts of personal courtesy and kindness, and the readiness with which they often furnished us with valuable assistance in the prosecution of our work."

For a military briefing, Whitman's account has an unusually sentimental, even spiritual arc, pulled along as it was by his understanding that he had a sacred duty to bring the dead home, concluding the journey that all soldiers began. The shape of this journey is actually visible at some of the cemeteries. At Shiloh National Cemetery, fallen members from Michigan, Ohio, and Wisconsin regiments—men who may have gone to war as a group—were buried together in

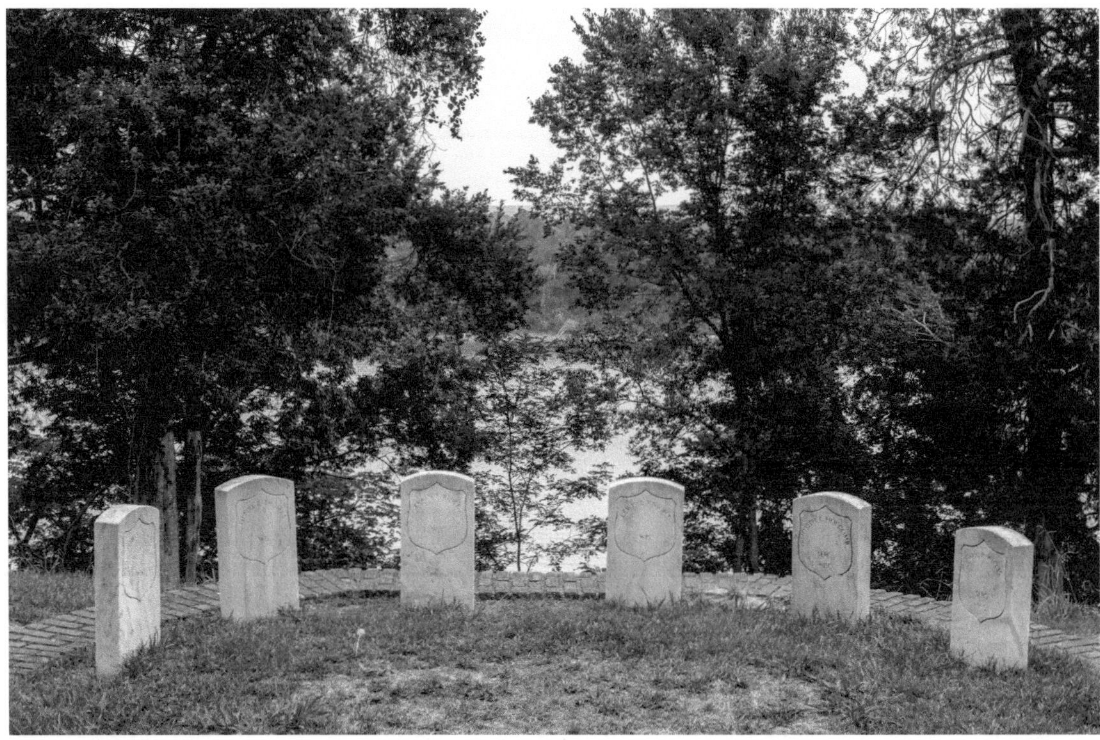

Shiloh National Cemetery (established in 1866), Shiloh, Tennessee, 2017. Beyond the headstones is the Tennessee River.

semicircular plots overlooking the Tennessee River. Whitman believed this arrangement, while unusual, added to the cemetery's "great attraction." During my visit to Shiloh, I walked down from the gate toward the river and the wooded areas that lie beyond the cemetery walls and was struck by how the plots look like ancient markings on some primeval landscape.

However distressing it was that the remains of so many men should be missing, the lag between the battlefield burials and their final disposition gave Whitman and his colleagues time to consider the character of the national cemeteries. In 1866, when Whitman sent Meigs his list of potential cemetery sites, he outlined the principles that informed his recommendations. The cemeteries should be located in places of "great historical interest," where the public could "commemorate the events in which these men had borne a distinguished part and at the same time, bestow, the highest honor upon their memories." They should be sited in "conspicuous" spots near "great thoroughfares" and easily accessed "so that none might be omitted, in this great

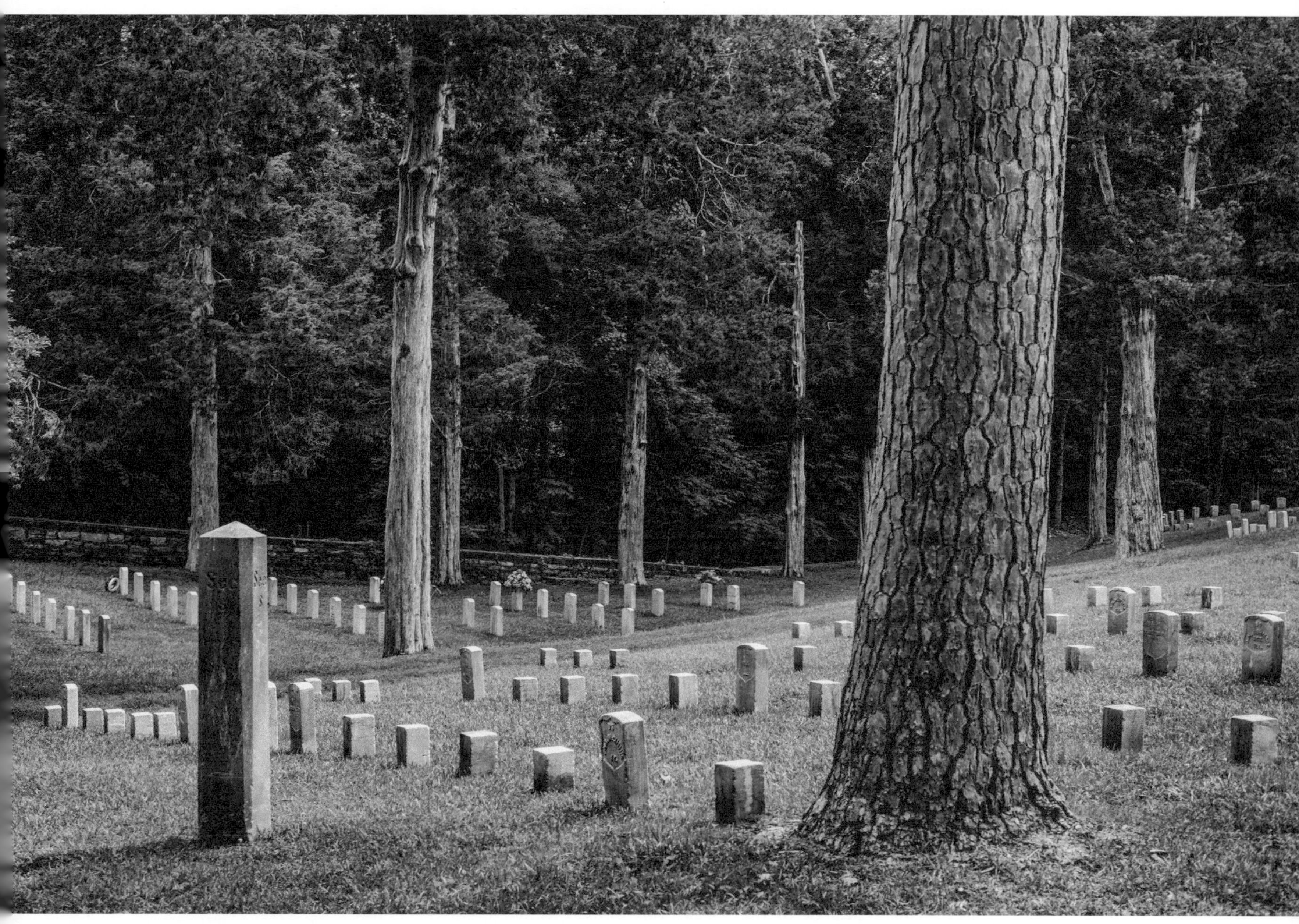

Shiloh National Cemetery, 2017.

sepulture." Finally, the cemetery should provide "favorable conditions for ornamentation, so that surviving comrades, loving friends, and grateful States, might be encouraged to spend liberally of their means for such purposes."

The word "sepulture" refers to the rites of burying the dead, from the ceremonial procession to the cemetery to the act of placing a corpse in the ground. In Whitman's usage, a "great" sepulture is an auspicious ritual that logically includes the broader public. By referring to "this" great sepulture, he seems to designate a memorial process that hardly needed to be identified since it was already happening, right there and right then. The national cemeteries, Whitman believed, would be places where Americans would continue to gather and remember the dead.

While this belief is evident to anyone who visits one of the cemeteries, reading Whitman's report in its original form brought home for me the breathtaking expanse of the vision that sustains these landscapes. Handwritten in precise cursive prose and bound in cracked leather, the report now sits in the National Archives, Record Group 92, Records of the Quartermaster General. One among millions of governmental documents detailing the history of the United States, it not only imagines the community that lives on in the national cemeteries—themselves archives—it also reflects the hopes and dreams that brought men to war.

Of course, this memorial record is imperfect. Not every man who died fighting for the Union was buried in a national cemetery. And the cemeteries also include the remains of soldiers who could not be identified.

At Arlington National Cemetery, not too far from the Tomb of the Unknown Soldier, is the Tomb of the Civil War Unknowns, a rectangular vault with an ornamental top that bears the following inscription:

> Beneath This Stone
> Repose The Bones of Two Thousand One Hundred And Eleven Unknown Soldiers
> Gathered After The War
> From The Fields Of Bull Run, And The Route to Rappahannock.
> Their Remains Could Not Be Identified, But Their Names and Deaths Are
> Recorded In The Archive Of Their Country; And Its Grateful Citizens
> Honor Them As Of Their Noble Army Of Martyrs. May They Rest In Peace.
> September, A.D. 1866.

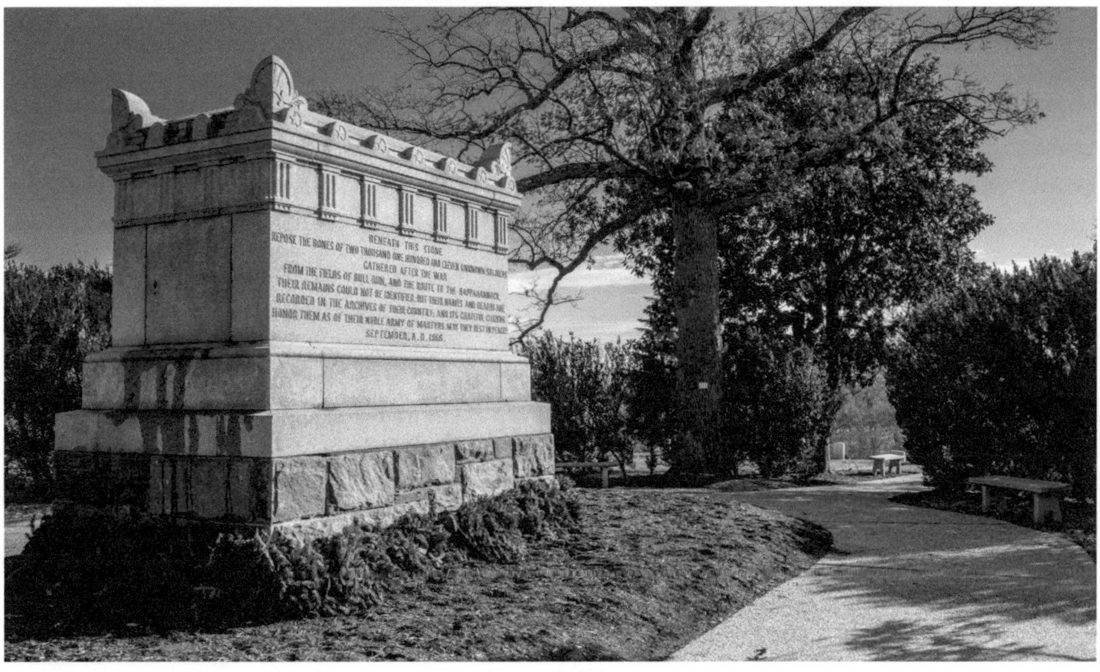

Tomb of the Civil War Unknowns, Arlington National Cemetery (established in 1864), Arlington, Virginia, 2017.

Prior to capping the monument, Colonel M. I. Ludington—who, like Whitman, was responsible for collecting the Union dead in one of the ten designated military districts (his was the Department of Washington)—sent Meigs a progress report. He said he had placed the remains of the "Unknown dead" in the "underground vault" that Meigs designed and that the space "was divided into two large compartments by partition running East and West; which compartments were again sub-divided into small compartments to receive different classes of bones."[4] Ludington put the remains gathered from Bull Run on one side of the vault and the rest on the other.

The first time I saw the Tomb of the Civil War Unknowns I had just watched the ceremony at the Tomb of the Unknown Soldier. I stood with other onlookers behind the rope line, looking out at an army guard cross the parapet in silent recognition of all Americans who have died in battle but whose remains have not been identified. The tomb was established in 1921 to honor the sacrifice of an unidentified soldier who died in World War I, but it now plays a broader, symbolic role and, after the grave of John F. Kennedy, is probably the most popular site in Arlington.

Afterward, I walked over to the older memorial, which is tucked into a garden enclosure with a pathway that runs around the vault. I was alone and stood in front of the tomb to take a picture. Reading the inscription, I wondered if a public memorial established today would include such a frank description of mortal remains. During the 1850s, the life expectancy for a man was less than fifty years, and the Civil War made death a more common occurrence. People were accustomed to talking about death and dying.[5]

My later reading of Ludington's report raised questions about how he—and Meigs—organized the vault. In placing the bones in separate sections, he may have wanted to document the fact that the soldiers died in different locations. Then again, his subdivision of remains into even smaller compartments could have been a way of acknowledging that he was unsure whether the bones he was sifting belonged to Union or Confederate casualties.

The tomb is one of several mass graves located in national Civil War cemeteries. Some are designated by obelisks and others by headstones. For example, Florence National Cemetery (in South Carolina) is across the street from what was a Confederate prison for Union soldiers. Two thousand eight hundred and two men died in Florence, and most of their remains are in trenches beneath a tree-shaded lawn, bounded by several headstones clarifying the number of men buried in that spot, as in "152 Unknown U.S. Soldiers."[6] A similar layout, designed to inter 11,700 bodies, may be found at Salisbury National Cemetery, about forty miles northeast of Charlotte, North Carolina. Here, too, the majority of dead came from a Confederate prison, this one from a complex that was once a cotton mill.

Like the ossuaries established in Europe after World War I, the mass graves reveal a faithful effort to memorialize the horrific effects of mass warfare. No one expected the scale of death generated by the Civil War, and neither the Confederacy nor the federal government devoted adequate resources to the development of prisons; they were simply not a priority. Cemeteries came after the war, and even then Ludington's sifting of bones highlights the difficulties that arose when the military could not name the dead but nonetheless wanted to memorialize their sacrifice.

Sometime after my trip to Arlington, the National Park Service announced that a burial pit had been discovered near Manassas Battlefield Park, along the same route that Ludington had scoured. The makeshift grave, found on a farm field, included the remains of two soldiers, plus eleven other arms and leg bones, which Union Army surgeons had amputated during the heat of battle. As described by a *Washington Post* reporter who viewed the photographs of the

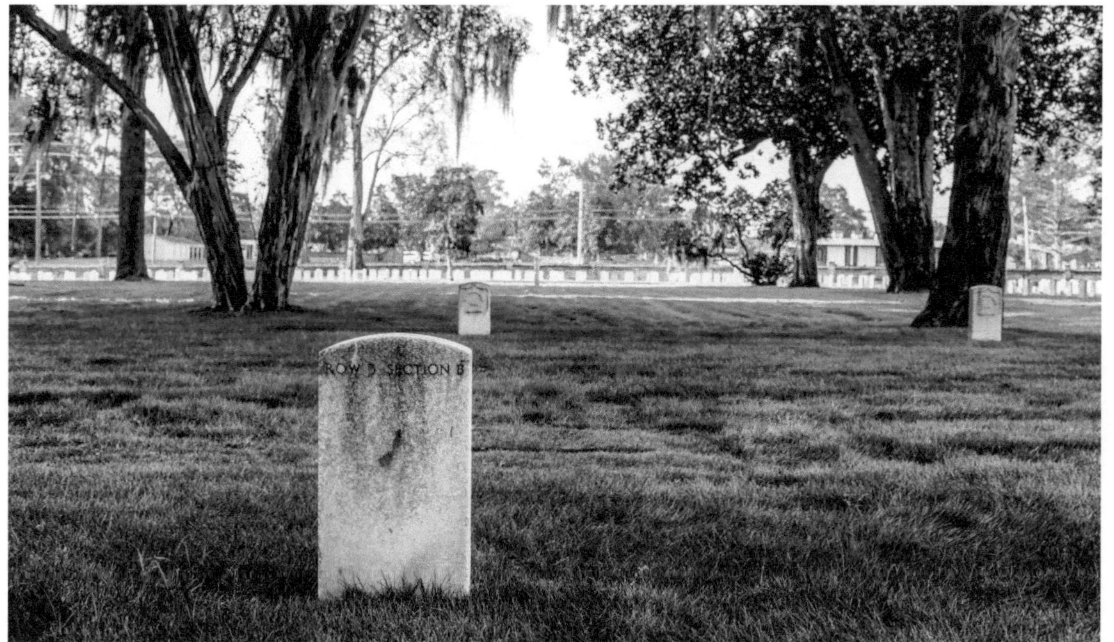

Florence National Cemetery (established in 1865), Florence, South Carolina, 2019.

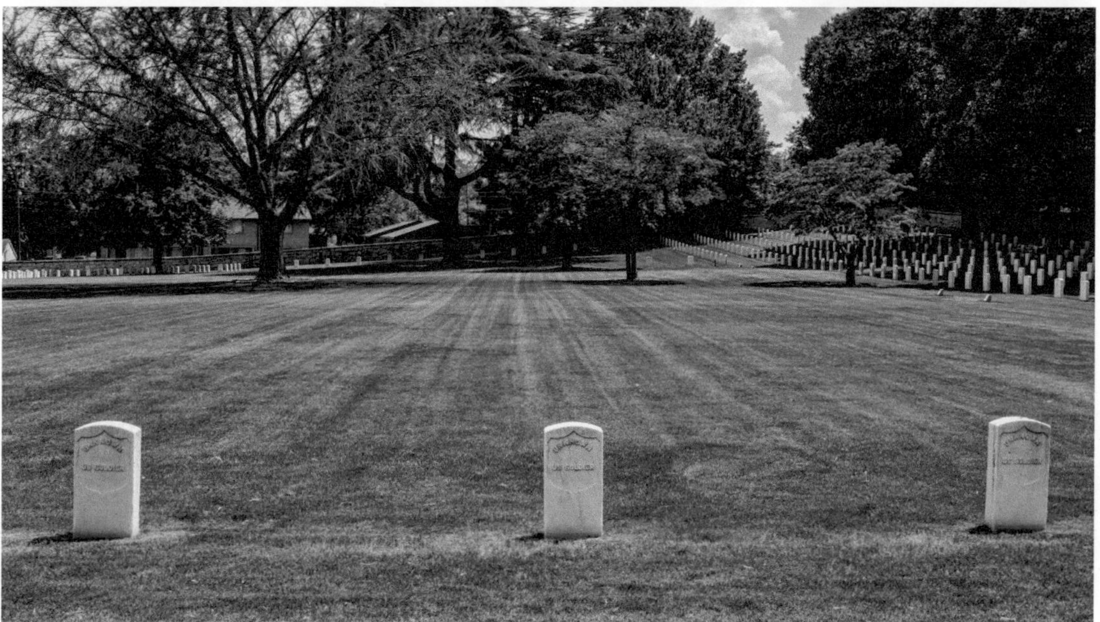

Salisbury National Cemetery (established in 1865), Salisbury, North Carolina, 2018.

pit—the location of which was not revealed to the public—the limbs "were carefully arranged" next to the bodies "like broken tree branches."[7] Despite the grisly sight, the writer's language, like the method of burial, aimed to restore the missing parts to the whole and fend off the loss of the creature, as Walker Percy might say. Meanwhile, the army arranged to have the two unknown soldiers buried at Arlington in coffins made from wood taken from a fallen tree at Manassas.

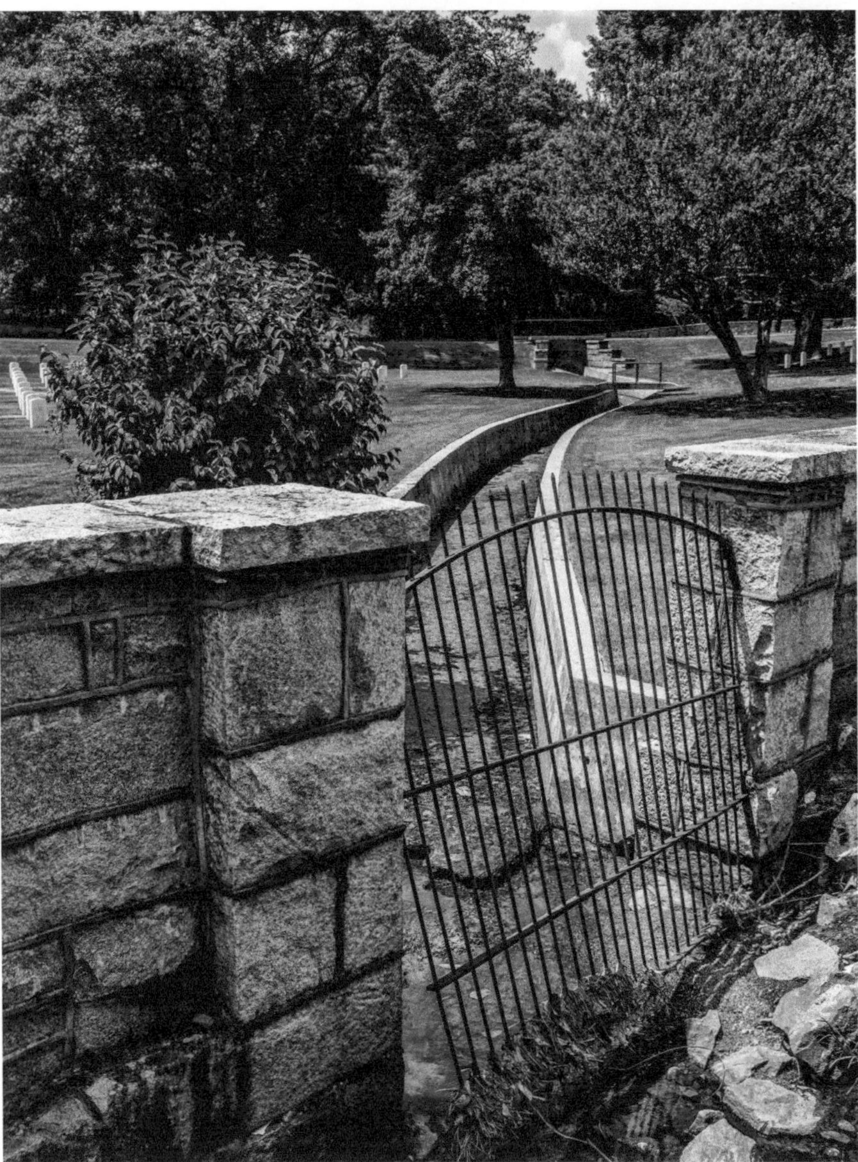

Salisbury National Cemetery, 2018.

The transcendence I sometimes feel when I walk through a national cemetery is related to this tensile link between part and whole, earth and sky, then and now, the living and the dead. As Atul Gawande explains in *Being Mortal: Medicine and What Matters in the End* (2014), ours is the story of aging, falling apart, and dying. Acknowledging the trajectory of this narrative so that physicians and patients can approach the end of life in more compassionate, meaningful ways is perhaps the most important goal of Dr. Gawande's book. Being mortal is not just a synonym for biological finitude. It is, or should be, a matter of consciousness.

Arguably, these ruminations live on in the hard surfaces of headstones and mausoleums, and a decision to walk through any cemetery is an invitation to openness and a different kind of thinking and feeling. But as I sat with

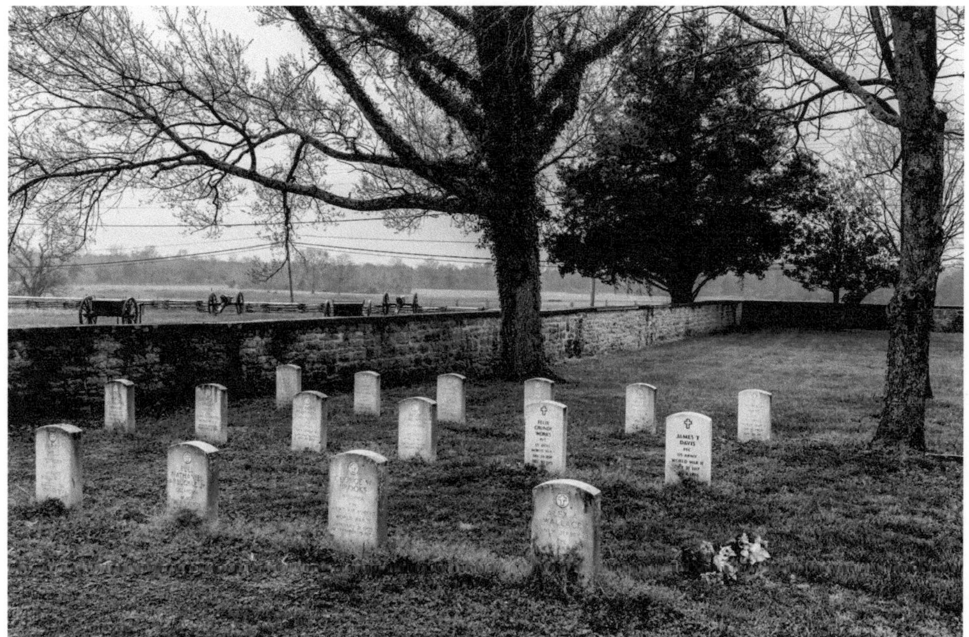

Stones River National Cemetery (established in 1864), Murfreesboro, Tennessee, 2018.

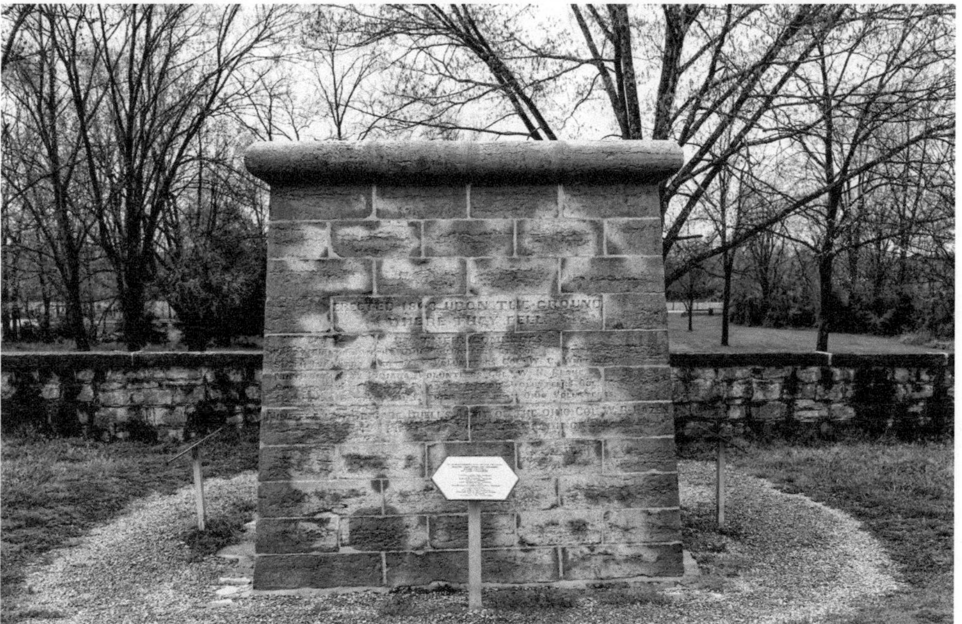

The Hazen Brigade Monument (erected in 1863), Murfreesboro, Tennessee, 2018.

my coffee at Stones River National Cemetery in Murfreesboro, Tennessee, I was mostly nagged by the fact that I had traveled all this way to take pictures and could hardly open the car door without getting soaked. Eventually, the rain did let up, and I walked across the soggy ground, past trees and stone benches, and looked out over the lines of headstones, either toward the Old Nashville Highway or the railroad tracks behind the cemetery. It was all wet grass and trees and stone contained within a three-foot high wall and a leaden sky overhead. I wanted to transfer this sense of saturation to film, a heaviness that seemed to envelope the large, rectangular section of headstones I was trying to photograph. But, later, when I looked at the images on my computer, the headstones sank into the background, as if weighed down by water. In black and white, the gray stones blended into the trees; in color, the image was soaked through with green, the verdant blanketing of spring.

Next to the cemetery, in a small, walled plot back from the road and steps away from the tracks and a concrete mix supplier is the Hazen Brigade Monument. Here, the limestone block reads "Erected 1863—Upon the Ground Where They Fell." Surrounded by fifty-five headstones, the monument is not a vault or grave marker but a memorial that Colonel William B. Hazen's Ohio brigade established in honor of their fellow soldiers who died protecting the Union position between the railroad and the Nashville Pike. Remarkably, along with a group of Indiana soldiers, they managed to erect the monument themselves within six months of the Battle of Stones River, making it "the only American Civil War monument still standing in its original battlefield location," according to the National Park Service.[8] For me, this characterization misses the point or sidesteps the monument's distinctiveness. The memorial is an anomaly because it was created so soon after the soldiers' death, apart from the national cemetery.

More than 160 years later, these differences may seem like academic nits, especially since most of the Civil War cemeteries look like they have been around forever. Stone, the common vernacular in memorial installations, creates an air of permanence. Headstones are old and sunk into earth, but they persist. Brick and granite walls continue to separate the land of the dead from the living. When the landscape gives way to disrepair and walls or stairs crumble, cemeteries can look like ruins, which only enhances their authenticity.

While most of the cemeteries are walled rectangles or squares, some spread out among hills and trees, stretching headstones and monuments toward the horizon. Chattanooga National Cemetery is like this. An expansive park with panoramic views of the cemetery as well as the

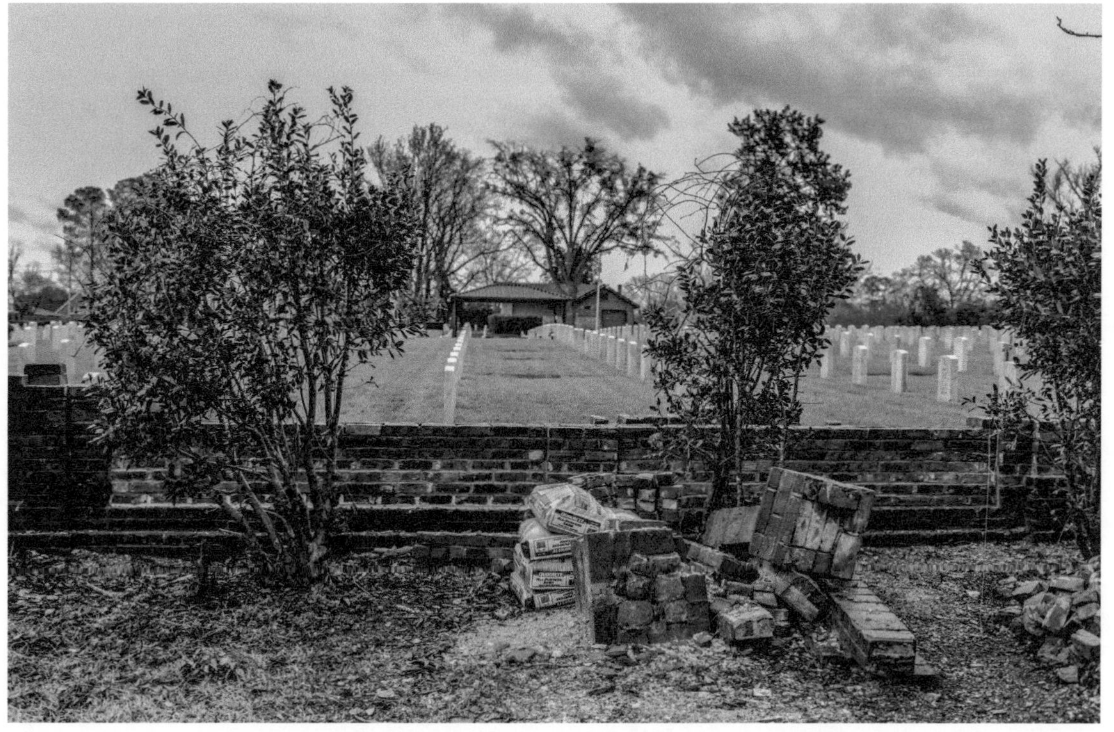

Maintenance is a constant issue for America's national cemeteries. Here, a brick wall is under repair at New Bern National Cemetery (established in 1867), New Bern, North Carolina, 2019.

city and nearby Signal Mountain, it is big enough at 121 acres to contain room for future interments and thus extends history well past the words etched on the monumental archway: "Here rest in peace 12,956 citizens who died for their country in the years 1861–1865."

When I visited Memphis National Cemetery, the site was undergoing extensive renovation, from the administrative offices—which serve as the headquarters for the several cemeteries in the region—to the graffiti-marked walls. The cemetery is in an older part of the city, surrounded by clapboard houses that date to the nineteenth century, backyards and luxuriant vegetation pushing up against the wrought iron fence, car repair shops and convenience stores along the elevated boulevard that skirts the entrance. I arrived early, before the cemetery opened, photographing down from the bridge and then exploring the underpass outside the walls. It was a messy space, as unclaimed urban corridors often are, and the early morning light streaked dumpsters filled with discarded floral arrangements and offered tempting views of the headstones through the

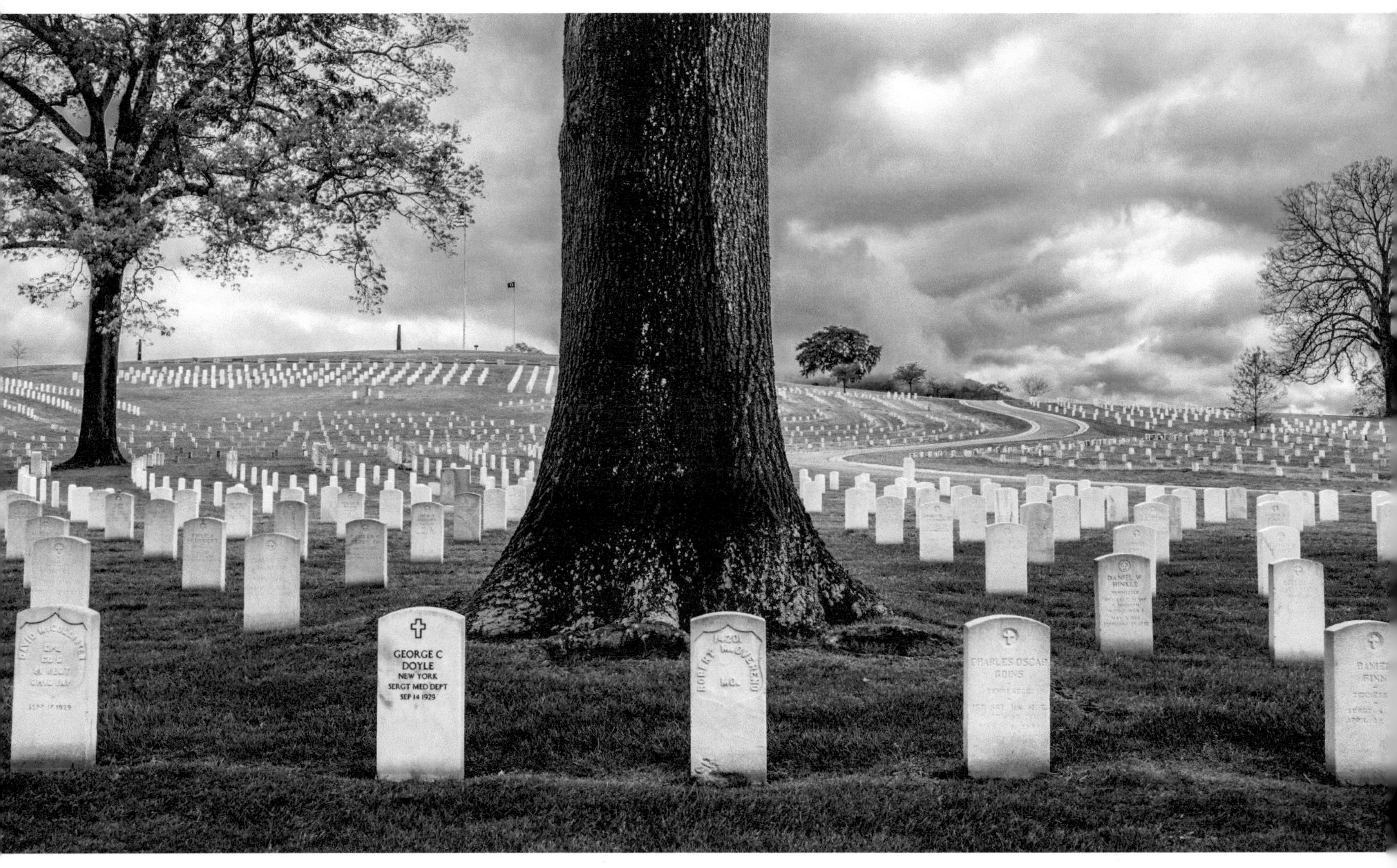

Chattanooga National Cemetery (established in 1863), Chattanooga, Tennessee, 2018.

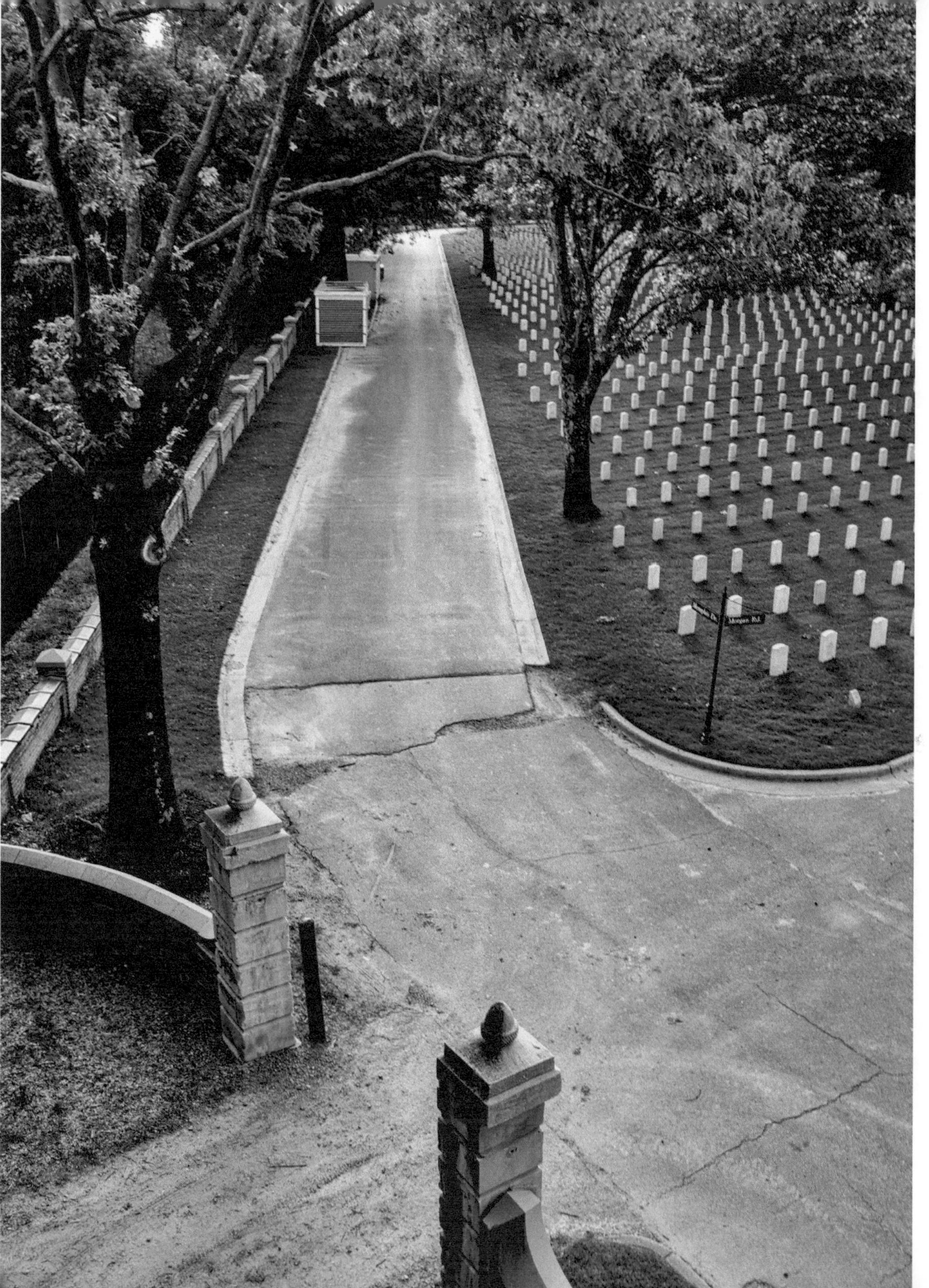

A bird's-eye view of Memphis National Cemetery (established in 1867), Memphis, Tennessee, 2019.

openings in the metal panels that served as yet another border around the cemetery during the construction project.

The first picture I took that morning was of a historical marker that stood just outside the gate, next to the white picket fence of a private residence. Although not an official cemetery sign, it explains that the remains of the 248 Union soldiers who died at Fort Pillow—including 109 US Colored Troops—were buried in the cemetery. In the Battle of Fort Pillow, Confederate forces, led by General Nathan Bedford Forrest, laid siege to a federal garrison on the Mississippi River in the spring of 1864, demanding that the much smaller Union contingent surrender. The Union commander refused, and the Confederates took the fort, killing nearly all the Union troops even though many of them apparently tried to surrender. The Union called it a massacre, with Grant and others claiming that the Confederates deliberately slaughtered the Black troops for taking up arms against the South. The sign, erected by an African American community organization in Memphis and dedicated on June 19, 2018—Juneteenth—summarizes these details, ending with the call that thousands of US Colored Troops would later carry into battle: "Remember Fort Pillow!"

On the plane ride down to Memphis, I was reading a biography of Grant, when the man seated next to me asked if I was a Civil War buff. I said no, not exactly, but I had a special interest in the topic given research I was doing as a faculty member at

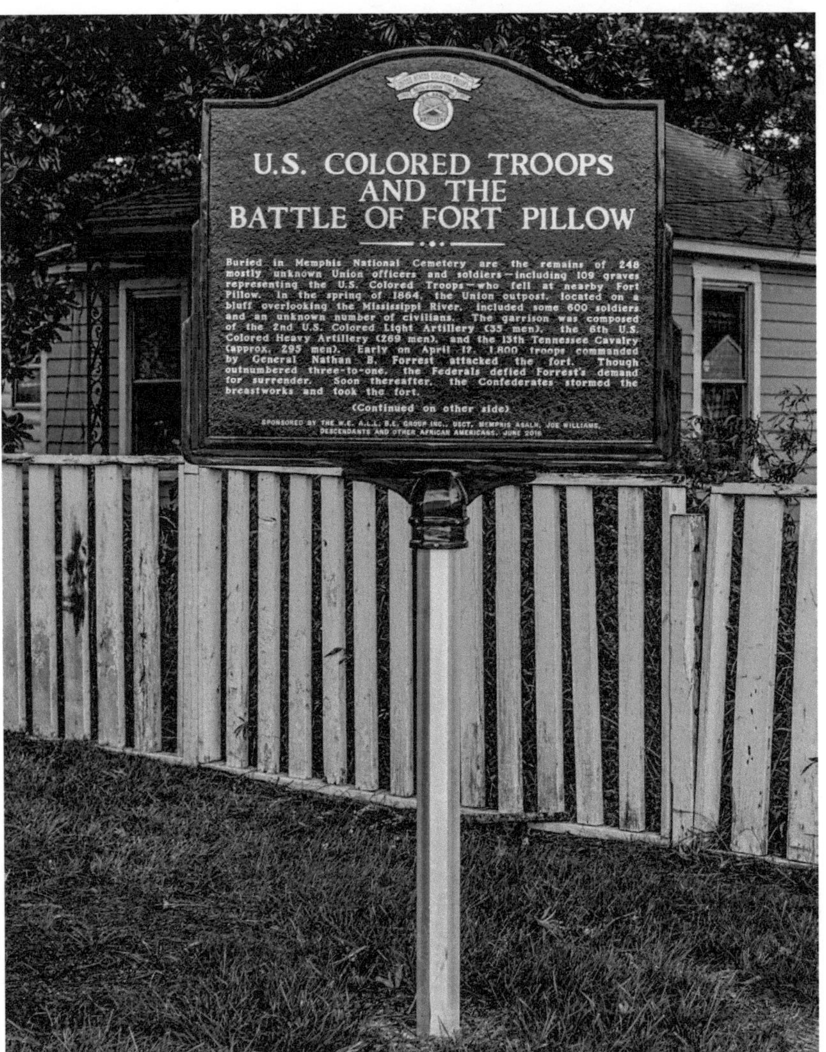

Outside the gates at Memphis National Cemetery, 2019.

a college in Vermont, where I taught American studies, and so on, saying as much as I thought I could without trying his patience. But he asked about my research, and I explained I was headed to Memphis to photograph national cemeteries and then on to Corinth, Mississippi, and Mound City, Illinois, to do the same. He was from Tupelo and was returning from a conference in Philadelphia, but he used to live in Corinth and gave me the names of several restaurants to consider, including a diner that serves the famous "slug burger" made of ground beef, pork, and meal. We talked about the quality of life in Tupelo and the rising cost of college education (he had two children in school) and then returned to the subject of death and remembrance.

And there we stayed for an hour, as he told me how his son, wracked by mental health problems, had taken his life the previous year. He visited his gravesite regularly—it gave him comfort—but he wondered at the same time whether the custom of marking the beginning and end of life missed the bigger picture. He had five children, all so different from each other that he could not believe their personalities were the result of how he and his wife had raised them. Did I believe in the afterlife, he wanted to know. What if their—our—lives originated elsewhere and we are just passing though this world as part of a longer series of lives, one after the other? He was a regular churchgoer and conceded that his thoughts on this topic were unconventional.

We parted with vague assurances to stay in touch, and for weeks afterward I reflected on the turns in our conversation, how an exchange about Civil War cemeteries had led to a discussion of loss, grief, and the terms of existence. The transition happened naturally, and we soon found ourselves on common ground, both grateful, I think, to have the chance, maybe because we were strangers, to discuss questions that lack clear answers and engage a topic that so often feels unapproachable.

Therapists and grief counselors refer to the phenomenon of being "broken open" after a trauma. A person, a family, or community suffers a great loss or things fall apart, and the familiar guideposts disappear only to reveal a new horizon and the possibility of constructing the world anew.[9] To be sure, my encounter on the plane was serendipitous. Still, I did not have to wander too far in my subsequent thinking to imagine my Tupelo friend's vision of reincarnation sketched on the land, one life and death giving way to another, across a quilt work of cemeteries. And if the Civil War broke the nation open, the commemorations that followed—and flourished during the 1870s and '80s—were meant to chart a path forward, toward perpetuity and a new home.

The Civil War cemeteries are mostly empty, as the fulcrum for memorializing the military dead has shifted to newer spaces. Yet they remain powerfully evocative landscapes, places fixed in the amber of history. Historian David Blight calls them "hauntingly beautiful," haunting because many African Americans continue to lack the rights and privileges promised them through the war.[10] In this respect, the nation may still be broken open, though it is not clear what civic space, what call to shared values, might bring people together.

Still, history persists, and the dozen or so national cemeteries that line the state of Virginia seem to bring the memorial process closer to the epicenter of the Civil War. There are eight cemeteries within a twenty-mile radius of Richmond, and I could not help concluding, as I drove south from DC along the Blue Ridge Mountains and then north from Danville toward the Tidewater Trail, that they are in slightly better shape simply because of their proximity to other tourist sites. Of course, the war's impact was widespread, and the Virginia cemeteries are not all dedicated to the Civil War—the interments at Hampton National Cemetery expand well into the twentieth century—nonetheless, this is where Grant encircled Lee during the final months of the war, just before the Virginian surrendered his arms at the town of Appomattox Court House in April 1865.

Some cemeteries, like Poplar Grove in Petersburg, have recently been renovated, the effort to preserve history evident in the restored rostrum I looked out from when I visited one August evening in 2019. Days later, I saw an exhibition at the Valentine Museum in Richmond, featuring twenty-nine plans for redesigning Monument Avenue and defusing the racist Lost Cause ideology represented by the statues of Jefferson Davis, Robert E. Lee, and Stonewall Jackson. (Update: by the fall of 2021, after years of intense protest, every Confederate statue had been removed, the monument to Lee being the last to go.) Then, a few miles away, in Hollywood Cemetery, I visited the newly renovated Jefferson Davis memorial. A life-size figure of Davis—a "martyr to principle" the inscription says—stands over his tomb at the center of Davis Circle, a scenic turnaround offering views of downtown Richmond and the James River.

Hollywood is the most famous of the cemeteries that took in the Confederate dead, but it is not alone. Indeed, up and down Virginia and across Whitman's great sepulture, wherever there is a national cemetery, you can find a Confederate burial ground nearby, usually part of a larger private or town cemetery. In Vicksburg, there is Soldiers' Rest; in Hagerstown, Maryland, there is Washington Cemetery (for the Confederates who died at Sharpsburg or Antietam); and in Fredericksburg, Virginia, the Confederate Cemetery—a municipal cemetery—includes a large,

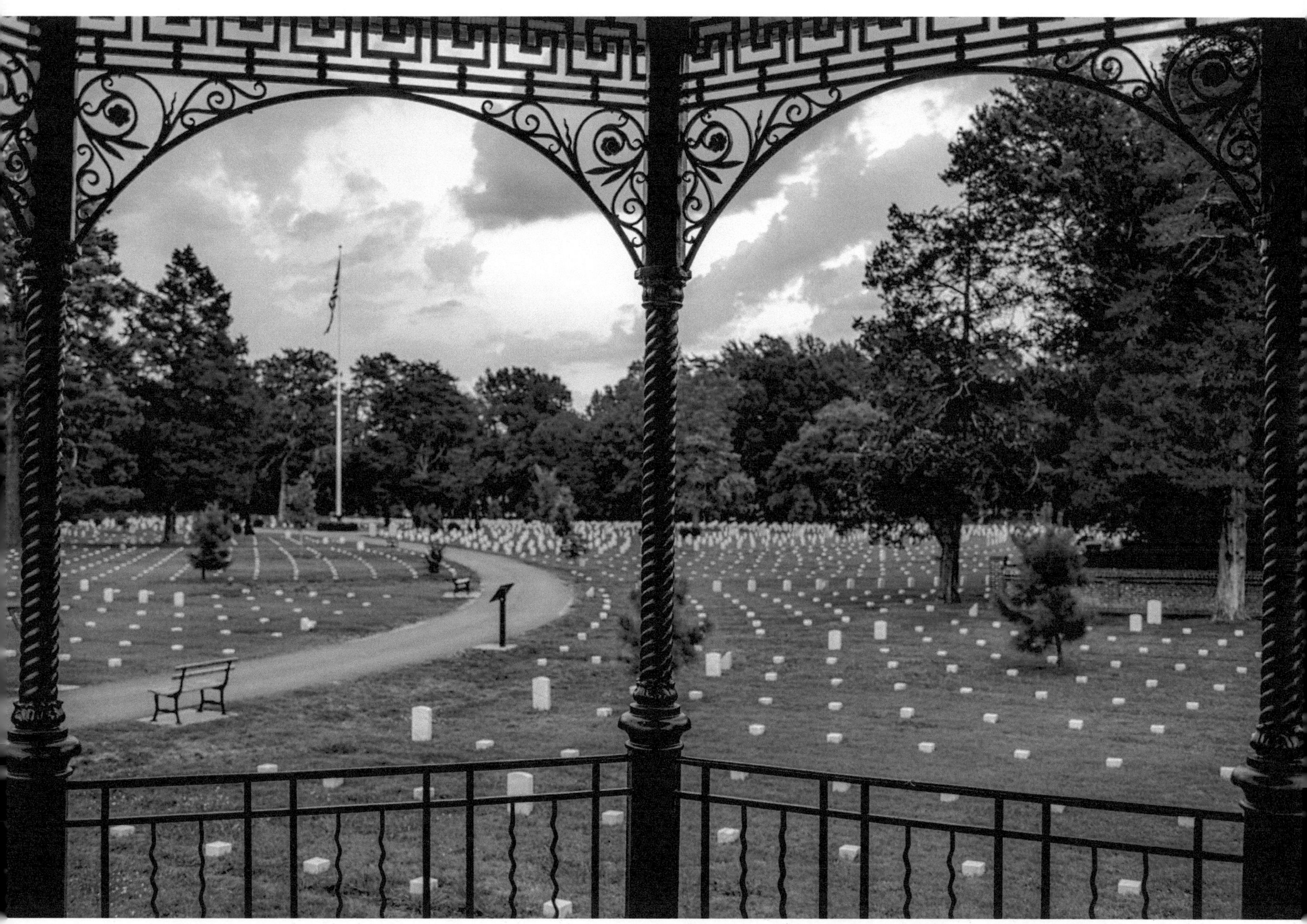

View of the flag stand from the rostrum at Poplar Grove National Cemetery (established in 1866), Petersburg, Virginia, 2019.

standing soldier monument dedicated "To the Confederate Dead" that faces the suburban-style houses just beyond the wall. At Winchester, Virginia, where the federals fought the Southerners on three occasions, the national cemetery is across the street from Stonewall Confederate Cemetery, which occupies a small part of Mount Hebron Cemetery. More than 2,500 Confederate soldiers were buried there, including 829 in a mass grave, the plots divided into sections by small roads like Confederate Lane and Quarles Drive.

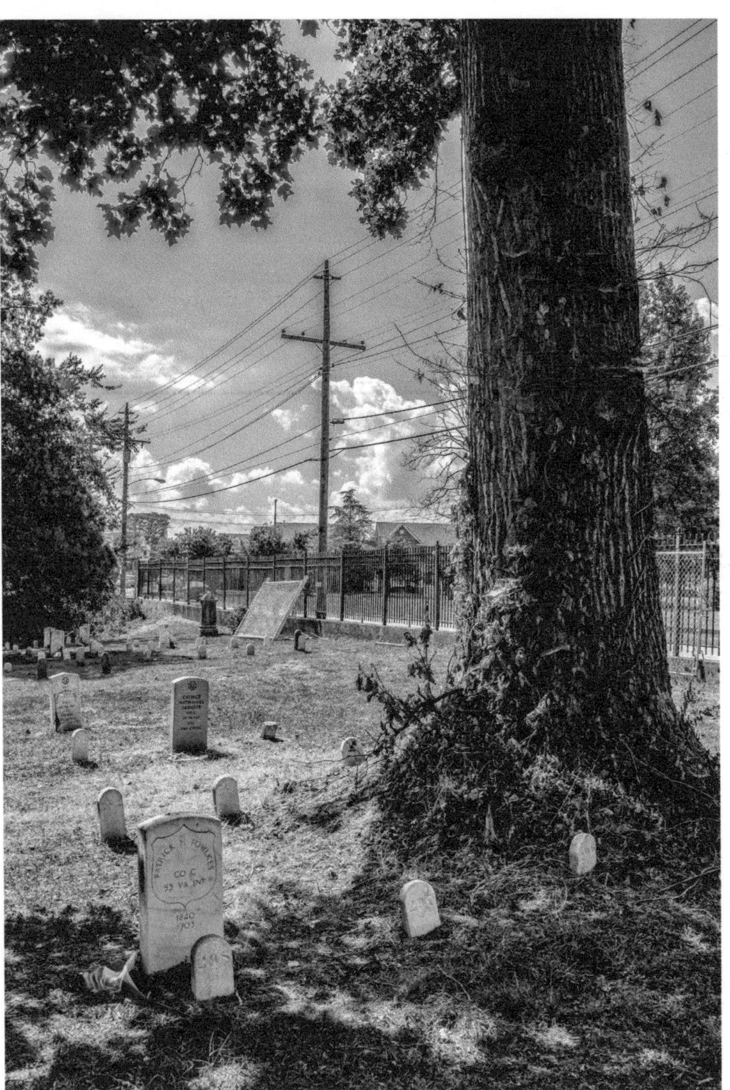

When I got to Danville National Cemetery, the southernmost destination in my tour of Virginia, I discovered that the Confederate burial ground, Green Hill Cemetery, is located next door and that a third site, for African Americans—Freedman's Cemetery—shares a border with them both. Here, as at other cemeteries established during the nineteenth century by Black southerners, the landscape stretches, and the family grave plots are randomly dispersed, often in disrepair. In this modest residential neighborhood, death and the memory of it maps on the social and political terrain that defined the Jim Crow era, separate and hardly equal, the dead quietly accepting the asymmetrical relations.

Or almost quiet. As I crossed the road after trying to photograph something meaningful of this tripartite state, I passed a middle-aged African American man, who pointed back to the national cemetery and said, "My grandfather is buried there." I smiled and nodded my assent, got in my car, and headed north to Richmond.

It is true that I am on a schedule and moving quickly and

Hollywood Cemetery (established in 1847),
Richmond, Virginia, 2019.

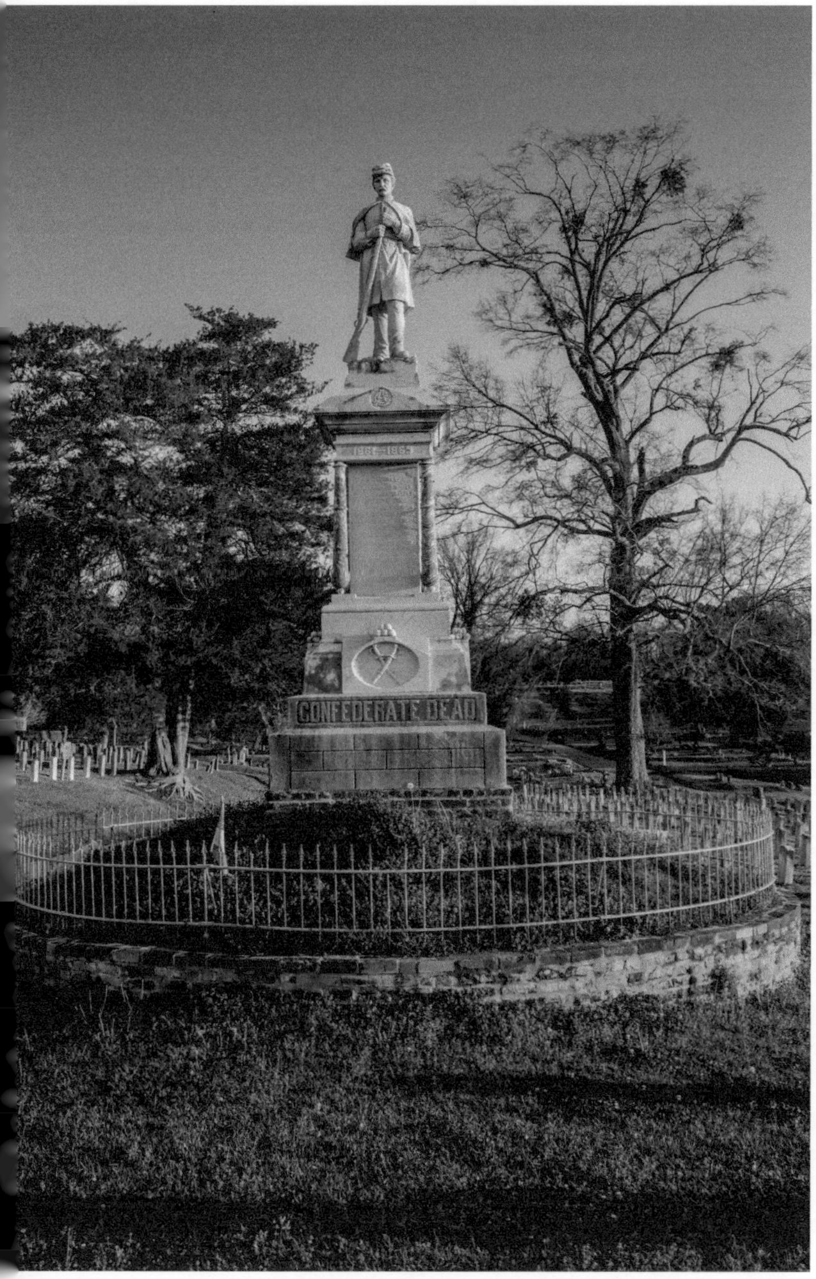

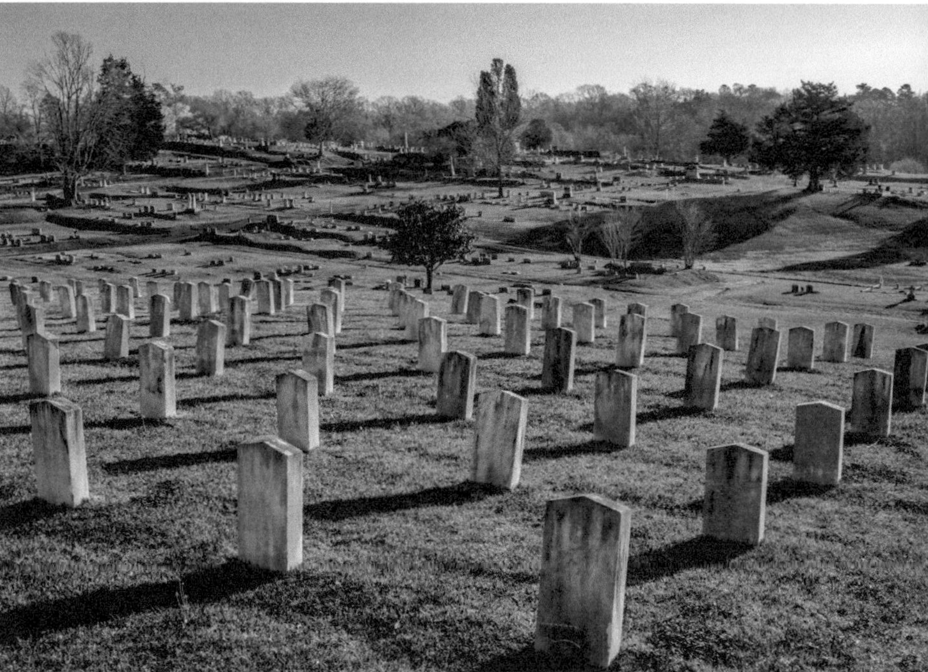

Soldiers' Rest Cemetery (established in 1866) within Cedar Hill Cemetery, Vicksburg, Mississippi, 2018.

(*Left*) The monument at Soldiers' Rest honors the estimated five thousand Confederate soldiers buried here.

Winchester National Cemetery (established in 1866), Winchester, Virginia, 2019. The monument honors the soldiers of the Union Army's Sixth Corps, who died at the Third Battle of Winchester.

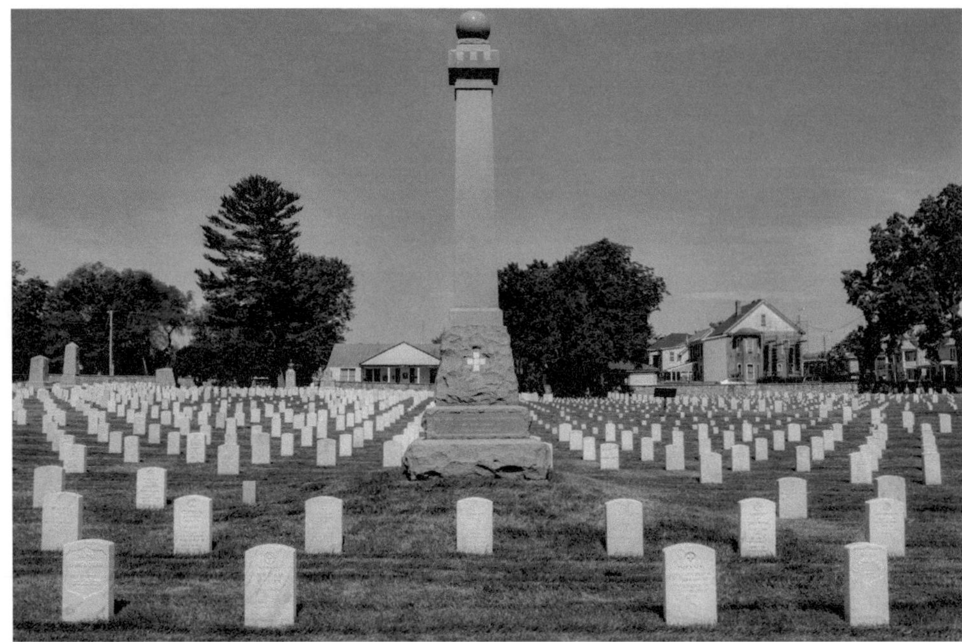

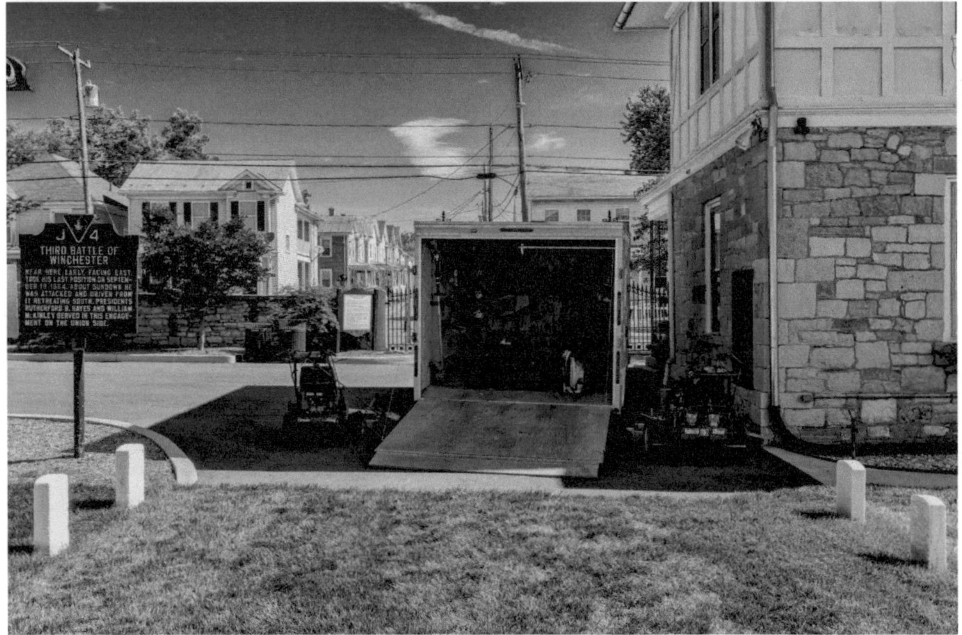

Winchester National Cemetery, 2019.

faster still on these pages than the time I spent on the ground and traveling from place to place. I cannot compare my two hours in Danville with the many visits the man I encountered may or may not have made to his grandfather's grave. We were like two ships passing in the night, even if we were moored in the same place. Maybe we saw things differently, maybe we did not. But when I imagine all the photographs I have taken, I see one great sepulture illuminated from above and time slows down.

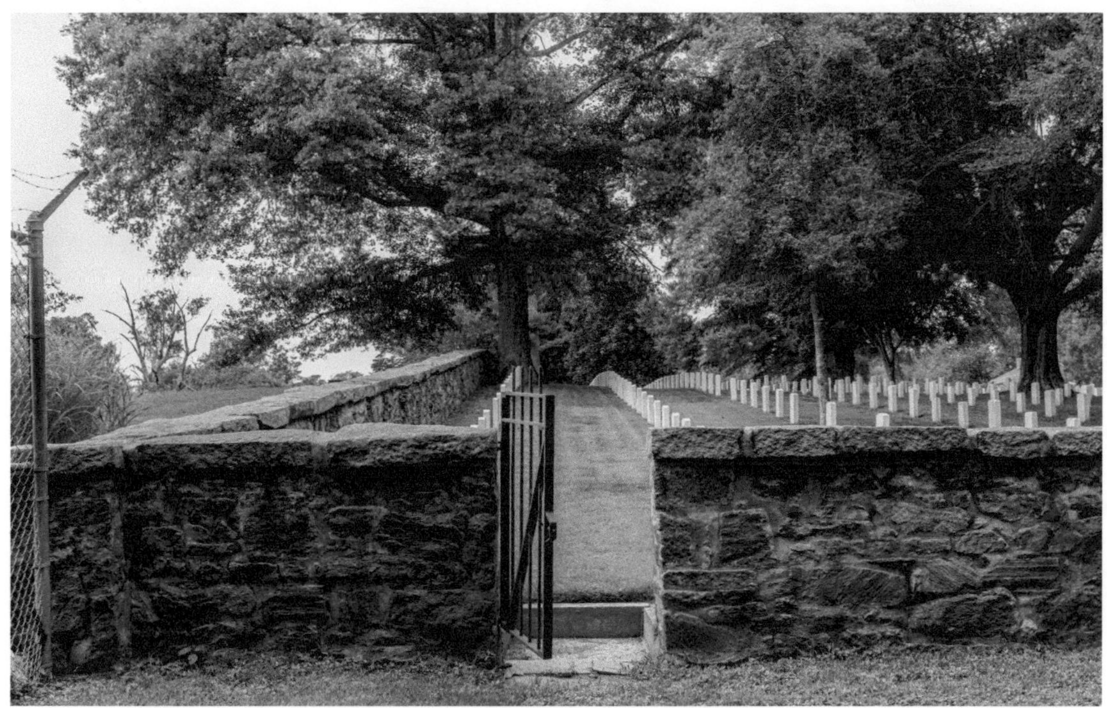

Danville National Cemetery (established in 1867), Danville, Virginia, 2019.

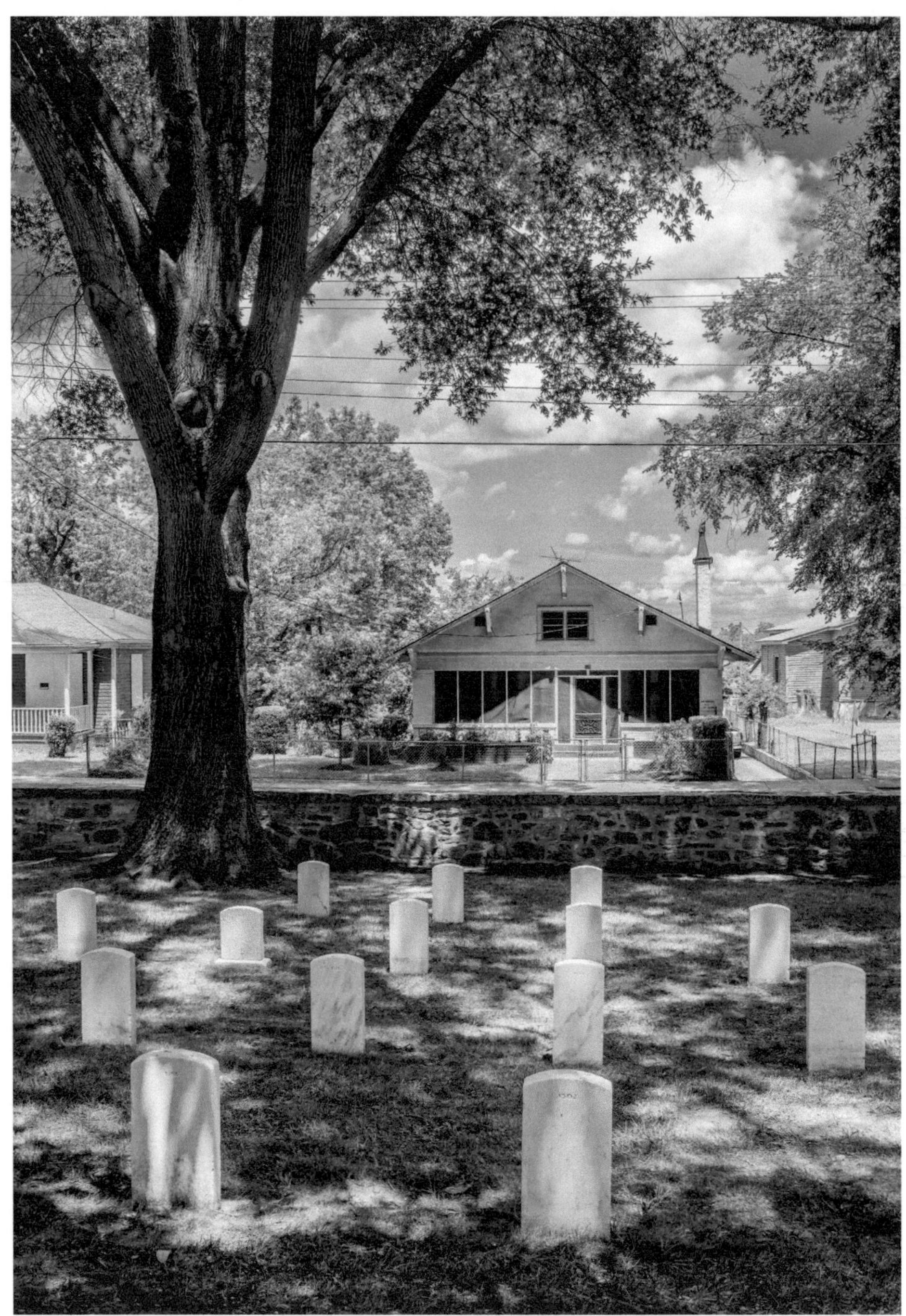

Danville National Cemetery, 2019.

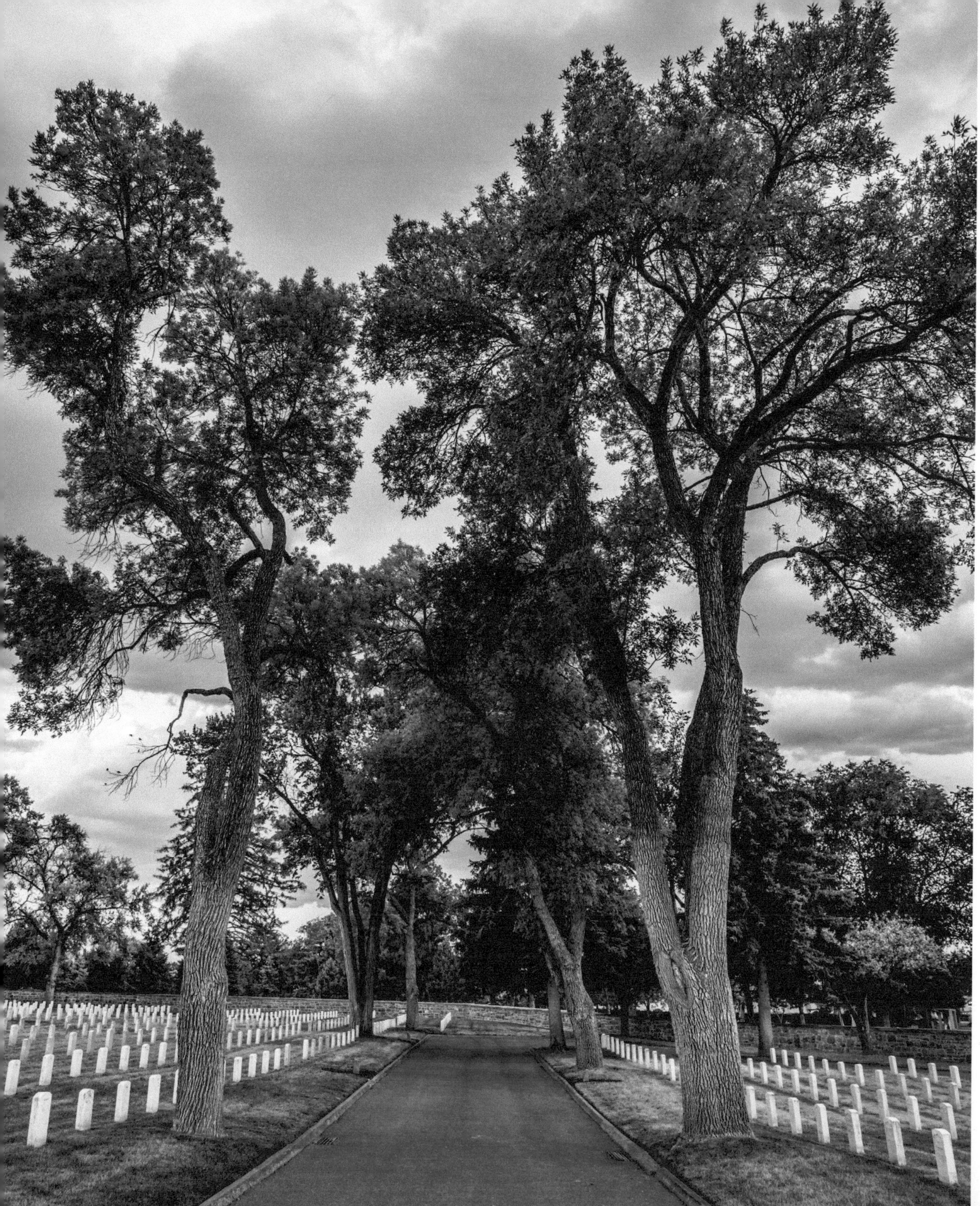

Santa Fe National Cemetery (established in 1875), Santa Fe, New Mexico, 2017.

4

X Marks the Spot

At Santa Fe National Cemetery, the remains of fifty-nine thousand American citizens are interred on seventy-nine acres set into the historic city's foothills and bordered on the west by a highway that curves down toward the cemetery's entrance on Guadalupe Street, one of the major surface streets downtown. Two hundred sixty-six Union soldiers were buried on the cemetery's south side, in graves dug in the 1860s and now shaded by mature elm trees, while, on the north end, there is a columbarium, built in 2004, to house the ashes of recently deceased military personnel, including those who lost their lives in Iraq and Afghanistan. The middle section spans the twentieth century and encompasses the remains of men and women who served in World War I, World War II, and the Korean and Vietnam Wars. The plots are tightly organized, and the white headstones, facing east and west in the desert sun, bring the mountains and horizon into a welcome and visually pleasing natural alignment.

In the summer of 2017, I spent three days walking the cemetery and taking pictures. I was there almost by accident, because I was in town to take a week-long class at the Santa Fe Photography Workshops that I hoped would advance the cemetery project I began in France. By the time I got to New Mexico, I had been to France three times, once over a three-day weekend in February when I got caught in a mini snow squall and found myself huddling with a group of British schoolkids at the top of the Thiepval Memorial to the Missing of the Somme. I had visited all the American World War I cemeteries in France and Belgium, compiling what I thought was a solid portfolio of photographs. In fact, I applied to the workshops to take a class with a photo editor, thinking that I would get advice on how to prepare my images for publication. But the class did not fill, and I ended up in a workshop on fine arts photography. The move was fortuitous, not only because I spent the week taking pictures and immersed in daily "crit sessions" but also because everyone in the workshop had to have a project and mine focused on the national cemetery.

The truth is that when I arrived in Santa Fe I was barely aware of the cemetery's existence. Two months after my winter trip to France, I visited the cemeteries at Andersonville and Shiloh to learn more about how the United States honors the military dead. I was moving forward on two fronts—one photographic, the other research oriented. I most of all wanted to make pictures of the distinctly American spaces in Europe, but I also wanted to understand their purpose and how they came to be, an approach that led me to the archives and a review of the historical literature. I knew about the national cemetery system but was focused on the American Battle Monuments Commission (ABMC), the government organization responsible for overseeing American military cemeteries abroad.

The growth of the national cemetery system certainly shaped the commission's work, which began after World War I, but scholars have tended to treat the two commemorative efforts separately. This is true even of the government's recordkeeping. While the documents pertaining to the national cemetery system sit in the National Archives in Washington, DC, the ABMC papers are stored at the National Archives research center in College Park, Maryland. Before I got to DC and read about Edward Whitman's travels through Tennessee, I combed through boxes in College Park.

Santa Fe changed all that. Or I should I say that exploring the Santa Fe National Cemetery while engaging the ins and out of fine arts photography broadened my sense of how I might understand these landscapes, giving me another view of what my project could be.

The landscape and light in the Southwest can have a bracing effect on photographers, which may explain why the workshops are based in Santa Fe. But it was not just the New Mexican atmosphere or the revelatory appearance of another military cemetery (with many more to come) that reoriented my perspective. The instructor of my workshop, photographer Michael Eastman, was a stickler for composition and attending to the edges of the frame, details that can distract or focus the image. Photos are like puzzles, he told us, and though some convey more tension than others, successful images cohere around a particular visual logic, rules artists have followed for centuries. To get us thinking and seeing in these terms, he asked us to spend a day in Santa Fe making abstract images of local scenery—random markings on brick walls, trash or traffic directions spread across pavement, and so on.

I found the exercise clarifying, for while cemeteries—and military cemeteries in particular—are formal spaces, I did not simply want to reproduce the symmetry on the ground. I wanted to see beyond the blueprint, impose some visual order and make the image my own. Yet the landscape itself was not my own. It belonged to the dead. Or, rather, the nation had claimed it for the dead. And these spaces, their sacred-ideological purpose so emotionally palpable, likewise made their claim on me, adding to the challenge of trying to fit a large group of headstones into the frame without cutting a stone in half or eliding a name. I encountered that dilemma in France and in Georgia and Tennessee. The marble or granite markers are not just objects in space. Death is not an abstraction. Each grave, each individual in those graves, deserves respect on his or her own terms. Each represents something bigger than itself.

We talked in the workshop one day about the line of vision one should take in photographing a building, a window, or object. What is the difference between viewing the scene head on and seeing it from the side? The angled view has the advantage of revealing spaces that might otherwise be blocked from sight, potentially bringing more information into the picture. On the other hand, the frontal view tightens the frame and provides a stable base of reference from which the eye can follow any radiating perspectives. Shooting from the front might flatten the image, but the effect creates a new visual environment, something unique to a photograph or work of art.

We were discussing the aesthetics of sight, but the exchange also had a philosophical dimension. In an interview he gave toward the end of his life, photographer Walker Evans spoke as he sometimes did about the beauty he found in everyday scenes and objects, commenting that "the thing itself is such a secret and so unapproachable."[1] Evans did not advocate for one camera angle or another—though his pictures of store fronts and signs show a preference for the frontal view—but insisted on the sanctity of the observed world and the photographer's commitment to trying to illuminate its inherent mystery.

Some photographers are wary about naming the thing since seeing is meant to reveal what words cannot convey. Still, for me the questions about how to approach the scene felt particularly important. I was happy to let the secret linger and hope that the picture I made captured something of the thing's essence. That was an article of faith that I surrendered to the process of showing up, pointing the camera, and clicking the shutter. But it mattered how I identified and framed my subject. Was I photographing a monument, a landscape, names on stones, loss and grief, a constellation of political statements, memory or a piece of history, an afterimage of the dead that now rose up through the ground by some technological sleight of hand, or my own mortality? Whatever I saw or wanted to represent, that thing needed to be at the center of the picture.

The national cemetery is three and a half miles from the workshops, on the other side of town, and because I was without a car, I walked there most days, following the Old Santa Fe Trail down to the plaza, past the Palace of the Governors and the New Mexico History Museum, and continuing on to Guadalupe Street. The federal site shares a wall with Rosario Cemetery, a nineteenth-century burial ground belonging to the Catholic Church with grass and graveled surfaces, family mausoleums, and a chapel that serves as the destination for the annual Novena de La Conquistadora, a festival procession that brings worshippers into Rosario for nine days of prayer centered around a three-foot high wooden statue of the Blessed Virgin Mary that is the oldest such figure in the United States. The Catholic Church occupied the area before the federal government did, and in 1870, the diocese donated the parcel of land that established the national cemetery.[2]

The city of Santa Fe has a shifting, sedimentary quality that makes any attempt to call the town "historical" seem shortsighted and trivial. The legacy of conquest and resistance that shaped the borderland culture in the region casts a long view on the history that gave rise to the national cemetery system, complicating my typically American—and perhaps provincial—conception of civil war. Touring the downtown by foot brings these layers closer to the surface, giving the history a more intimate feel that can be hard to distinguish from the town's commercial facade—an artful blend critical to any well-conceived tourist destination. The strands loosen though as I cross Paseo De Peralta and look at Wells Fargo Bank, Panda Express, and the businesses that sprawl along Guadalupe Street. Here, as in other municipal districts zoned for cemeteries, the history of the dead is removed from recent development.

Walking opens up sight lines, revealing spaces between buildings and objects and creating a rhythm of earth, body, and movement that evokes our own life trajectory. During the early 1900s, poet Edward Thomas trekked the paths and country roads of southern England to ward off depression. For Thomas, walking was a solitary activity that enabled him to surface and assuage his feelings of alienation and restlessness. By following trails "worn by hoof and naked feet and the trailing staves of long-dead generations," he stepped into the deeply grooved patterns of mortality, confirming in some visceral way his humanity.[3]

At home in Vermont, I walk the dirt road and hiking trail that run past my house almost every day. When we moved here thirty-odd years ago, I jogged or went to the gym to exercise. But now I find myself compelled as perhaps Thomas was to measure life with each step and find in the natural landscape a way to reflect on the losses that accumulate over time.

Now as I look out the window at the pre-Thanksgiving snow that is accumulating around my shed, I am at a remove from the preoccupations that pace my walks through the woods. More so than writing, walking feels like dreaming, fluid and expansive, and is essential to the picture taking I want to pursue. Although photography is a stationary act, pausing in place to capture a moment and scene, it is also—or can be—an embodied form of representation—legs, arms, and camera in flow with consciousness and an ever-changing landscape. If I used a large-format camera or a tripod to photograph these memorial spaces I might take greater care in composing the frame, but I would cover less ground and sacrifice the sense of being in and among objects and part of the picture.

But I am getting ahead of myself. At Santa Fe, I had three days to photograph the cemetery, and I approached the site as I imagined a naturalist might, walking the grounds from end to end and crawling military style toward headstones for close-up shots of names and telescoped views of what lay beyond. I remember that when I was maybe ten years old I would spend summer days searching my backyard and neighborhood for rocks, a hard-scrabble adventure that held the promise of discovering something that matched a picture in one of the science books I got at the school bookfair. That feeling of anticipation drew me across town each day in the hopes of making one or two photographs that stood out from the others and possessed intangible qualities that I would recognize long after I left Santa Fe.

I took thirty to fifty pictures each time I visited, shooting with a 50 mm lens. The "nifty fifty" is a great all-around lens that is supposed to mimic the view of the human eye. It is also a prime or fixed-focus lens, which means that I had to move my feet and body if I wanted a different view of my subject rather than rotate the glass in and out to adjust the sight. I used this lens in France and was happy enough with the results, but in Santa Fe, the long rows of headstones and boundless horizons made me wish for a bigger view. I borrowed a 20 mm wide-angle lens from the shop at the workshops (Nikon was a corporate sponsor), and the frame stretched dramatically, but the image appeared distended, and I struggled to control the edges. I later ended up using a 35 mm lens that enlarged my view while also seeming to maintain a natural perspective.

Santa Fe was my first focused exposure to a fully articulated national cemetery. By that I mean the cemetery includes graves that extend from the Civil War to the present and that it is

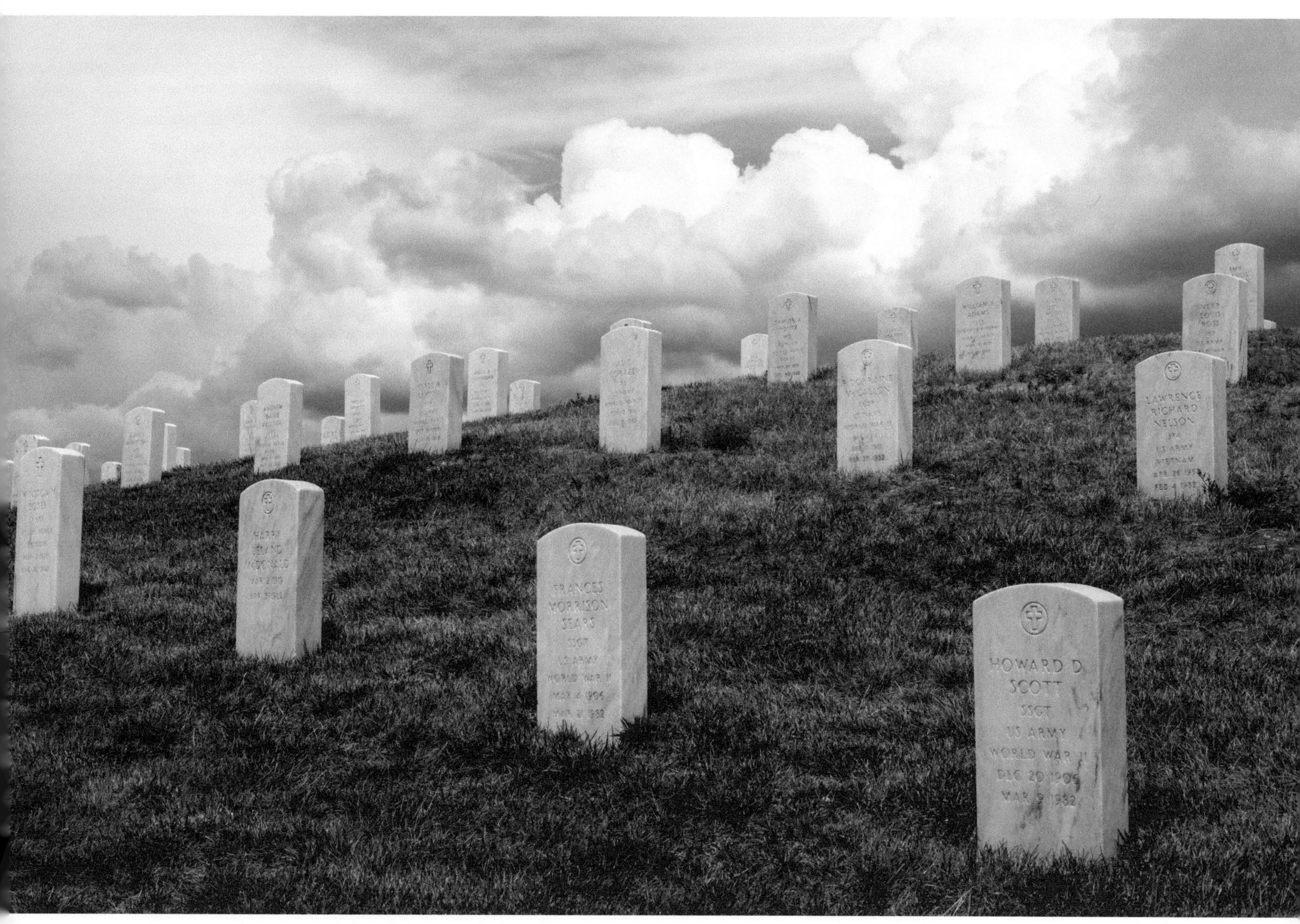

Santa Fe National Cemetery, 2017.

open for future interments. The walled section on the south side contains the Union dead and a few monuments built during the nineteenth century, while the columbarium and ground flush markers on the north end push up against interstate US 84 like a modern-day housing development. The superintendent's lodge, erected in 1895 and built in rough-hewn Pueblo style, sits at the middle of the cemetery, with a rostrum toward the front and several roads leading from one side of the site to the other. When seen on a map, the cemetery looks something like a plump sickle moon, and a wire-post fence follows a ridge on the east side, separating the gravesites from the private lands and homes, which are invisible from Guadalupe Street.

One morning, I followed the fence line north, hiking the rocky terrain up from the Civil War section, trying to get a picture looking down at the cemetery. As I scaled the hill, I watched a buckhorn deer bound over the fence and disappear into the sage brush, junipers, and pinyon pine. Although deer now overrun many suburbs and are tolerated at national cemeteries—at Eagle Point National Cemetery in Oregon, I saw a doe and two fawns nonchalantly circle the rubber figure of a wolf the landscaping crew had installed to slow down their grazing—the leap was a reminder of the wilderness that lies just beyond the dead.

As Thomas Laqueur notes, more than two thousand years ago, Diogenes the Cynic told his students in ancient Greece that, when he died, he wanted his corpse to be thrown over the city walls so it could be picked over by animals and returned to the natural order.[4] Although the philosopher's wishes may live on in certain green burial practices—the spreading of ashes on water and mountains or composting of remains—the idea of the cemetery was founded on the hope that X marks the spot where the dead will be remembered ages hence.

Of course, these distinctions are theoretical, the boundaries more blurred than human artifice can dictate. Although memory is meant to separate the dead from the forces of change, nature is always present, microbes eroding the wood panels on high-priced caskets and frost heaves exerting pressure on the concrete burial vault that insulates the coffin from the shifting soil around it. The body lies in state until it is claimed by the earth, though the process of decomposition can take many years. Indeed, the bones of the amputated limbs found at Manassas were intact 160 years later.

What exists on the surface is obviously more legible, with stones and words extending the identity of the dead into some uncharted future. But when we stand in front of a headstone, the future is already history since we are being asked to remember or imagine someone whose life is over. This irony is especially acute at older cemeteries that have fallen into disrepair and now appear stereotypically old. It is less pronounced at national cemeteries, not only because the government works to maintain these spaces but also because the cemeteries are designed to bring the past into the present.

Here at Santa Fe, looking down from the fence line at the headstones—spanning out like a regiment or phalanx—I did not see a nationalist imprint or feel any ideological nudge, emotional or cognitive, but instead beheld a uniform instillation of order on the land, perhaps stark and austere, yet beautiful in its rhythmic attempt to mark the brief passage of human presence on earth, not to cheat or ignore death or suggest some lives were more important than others, as individual memorials in private cemeteries can do, but open and emphatic about our shared mortality.

The collective got smaller when I headed down the hill but appeared no less symmetrical as I shifted the lens and reframed the scene—from seventy to forty and then ten headstones, each set square and upright, the vanishing point shifting as I moved this way or that. I was in the midsection of the cemetery, and this was not just an experiment in composition, though it certainly was that, as I tried to figure out how best to capture the essence that I continued to circle, first with my camera and now here in prose. The geometry of the cemetery yields a similar photographic aesthetic, which in theory means treating each section, each part, with equal weight or respect, this last concept—which is always on my mind—subject to interpretation when and if I step outside the sightlines I have drawn for myself.

Even closer, the headstones resolved into group shots and individual portraits, and I faced forward, first on my knees and then prone, to approach the grave of Reynaldo G. Valencia, a World War II Army veteran—a PFC—who died in 2004. His wife, Patsy, who died eleven years earlier, was buried next to him in Section 9 but with the stone and name pointed in the other direction. I have seen this practice of burying husband and wife in opposing graves in many cemeteries, often with the designation "His Wife" appearing as a prefix on "her" headstone. In this instance, Reynaldo is a "beloved father," and Patsy is a "beloved mother."

I took pictures of Reynaldo's and Patsy's headstones and, in the prints I made for my project, displayed them side by side, as a diptych. Before leaving Section 9, however, I turned back toward the hills and photographed the cluster of headstones from an angle, tilting up to catch the barge of clouds that filled the western sky. This image would also be part of my final presentation.

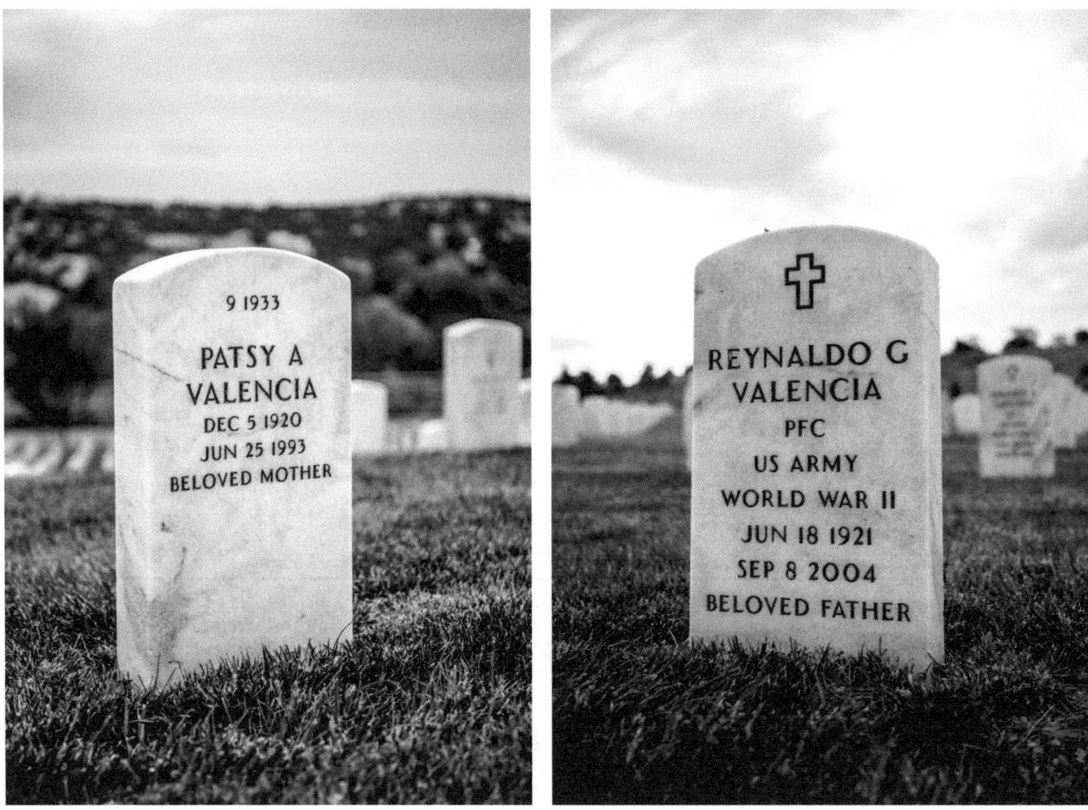

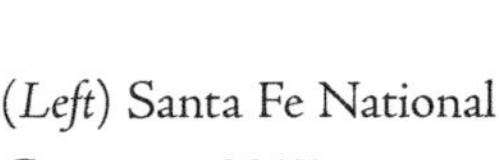

(*Left*) Santa Fe National Cemetery, 2017.

(*Right*) Santa Fe National Cemetery, 2017.

Through headstones and grave-locator database entries, what we learn about the dead at national cemeteries is limited to a few words and images. I did a Google search and consulted Ancestry.com and discovered that Reynaldo went by "Ray" and that Patsy's middle name was Aragon and that she died in Española, a small city thirty miles north of Santa Fe. I could learn more through additional research, but what about everyone else interred at Santa Fe?

On the south side of the cemetery—what I think of as the Civil War section, though that is incorrect since the Union dead are mixed in with other veterans—there is an individual memorial to Private Dennis O'Leary, who fought in the Spanish-American War but died at Fort Wingate (New Mexico) in 1901. Not only is the memorial large but it includes a nearly life-size statue of O'Leary, sitting and leaning against a stump on top of the grave marker's sandstone base.[5]

Uncomfortably out of place, the exception proves the rule. The dead appear in rows of headstones that surround O'Leary, while, at the north end, name plates on the columbarium span the perimeter, each marking the larger history of the landscape, a memorial to democracy that subordinates the individual to the whole but with the promise that what's been made of stone and metal will be remembered in perpetuity.

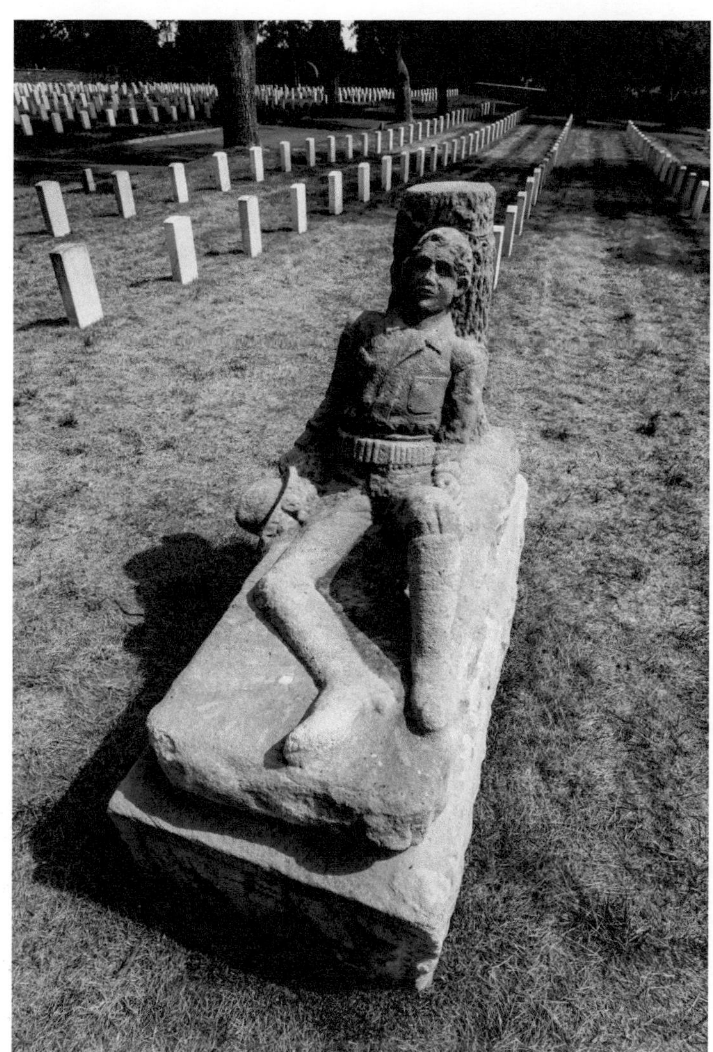

Santa Fe National Cemetery, 2017. The statue of the twenty-three-year-old soldier Dennis O'Leary was moved from Fort Wingate to Santa Fe National Cemetery in 1911 when the fort was disbanded and the graves at the post were disinterred and the remains relocated to Santa Fe.

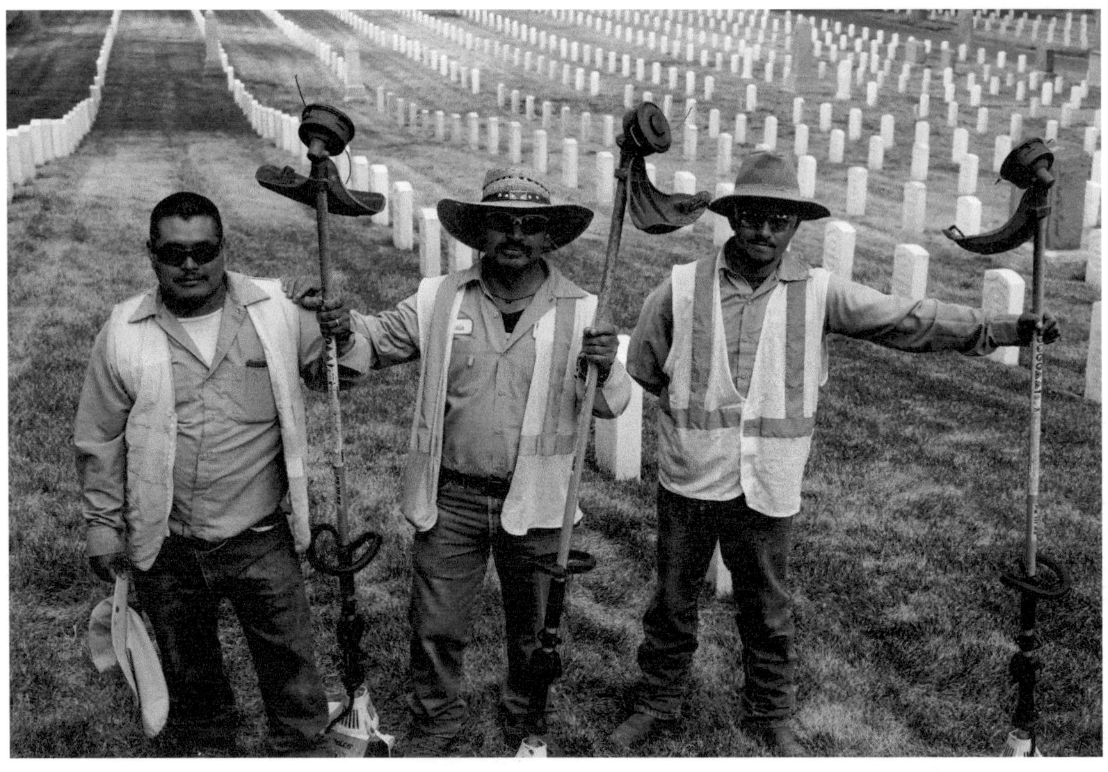

A landscaping crew takes good care of Santa Fe National Cemetery, 2017.

I got the idea and tried to photograph it, even if I worried that my pictures might ignore the people who are part of this place. One day, I found myself by the wall at the south section, where a landscaping crew was cutting grass. I said hello and asked if I could take their picture. They stopped and stood as a group, each man holding a weed whacker, like a soldier armed with his rifle, and I took my picture.

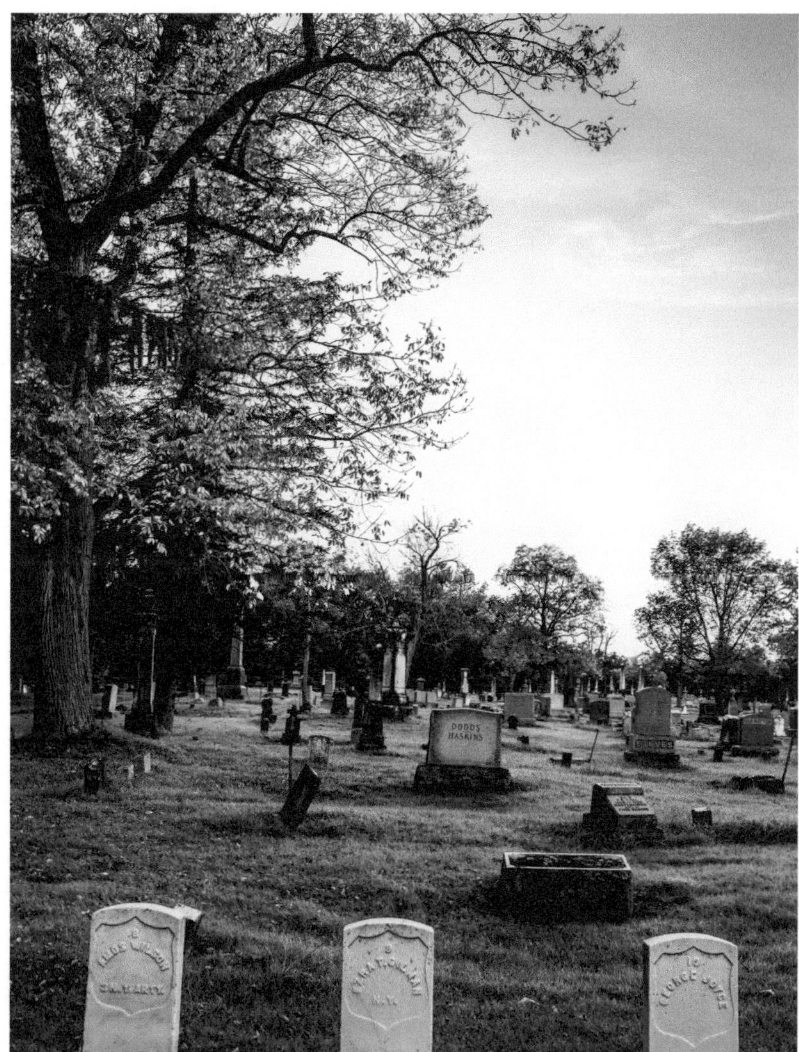

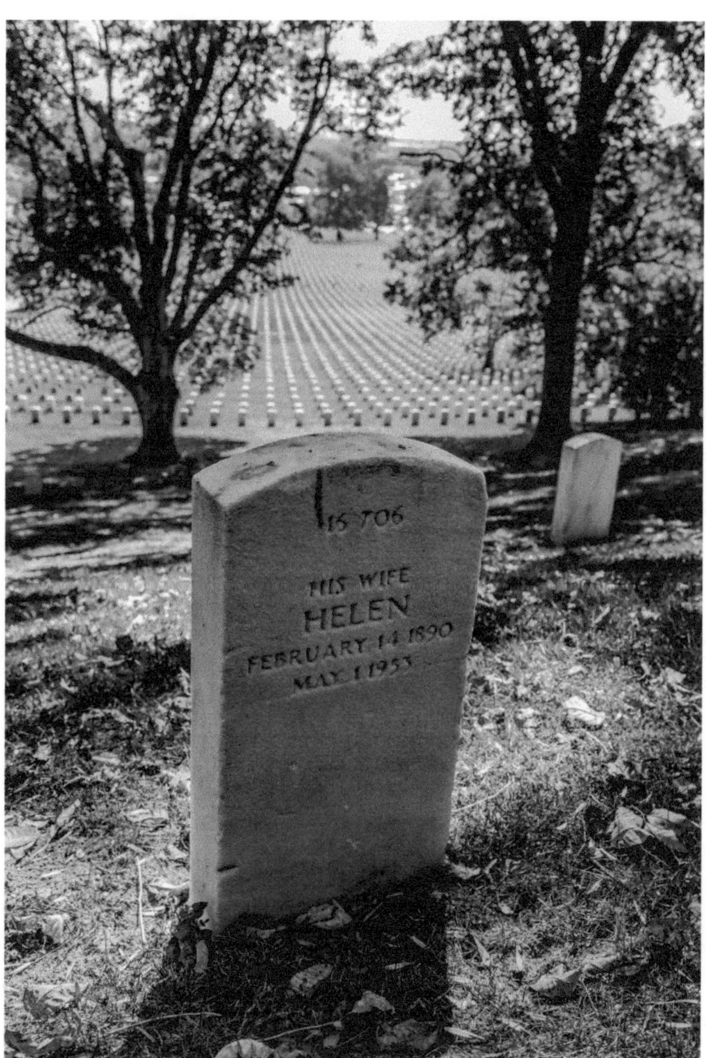

(*Left*) Soldiers' Lot in Albany Rural Cemetery (lot established in 1862), Albany, New York, 2017.

(*Right*) Cypress Hills National Cemetery (established in 1862), Brooklyn, New York, 2017.

5

Confederates Interrupt Us

After my week in Santa Fe, I purchased a Nikkor 35 mm lens (used), a spare battery, another memory card, and some lens caps. Buying these items did not make me a photographer, but at least I would be prepared for contingencies. If my equipment failed, I could always use my iPhone—the camera was sharp and the lens wide—but I wanted to hold the gear close, lean into a full-frame DSLR, and see the world differently. It was not just about taking pictures.

I was eager to extend my project, so I identified all the national cemeteries within reasonable driving distance and, late one Friday afternoon in September, headed to Albany Rural Cemetery, where in 1862 one of the first Soldiers' Lots was established. The bright sunlight was fading as I followed the narrow road through the up-and-down landscape, half expecting Ichabod Crane to emerge from the deepening shadows. Like many older private cemeteries, especially large ones, Albany can be hard to navigate. When I at last reached the 149 Union gravesites, it was close to 6:00 p.m., and I had less than an hour of light to shoot past the standing soldier monument to try and capture the stalwart rows of headstones with the crumbling private memorials as Gothic backdrop. Then it was on to downtown Albany, where I spent the night at the Hampton Inn and got up early the next morning to board an Amtrak train for New York Penn Station and crisscross my way through the labyrinth of corridors to take the subway to Cypress Hills National Cemetery in Brooklyn.

One of the original twelve national cemeteries, Cypress spans eighteen acres—as opposed to the 467 at Albany Rural Cemetery—and includes more than twenty-one thousand graves, but it feels bigger because of the horizon that unfolds at the hilltop of the cemetery, offering views of the flight towers at JFK, with Rockaway Beach and the Atlantic Ocean further beyond. As I stood on the platform of the stone-built rostrum, watching planes float in and out of the airspace and aimed my camera across the graffiti-scarred lectern at the sea of headstones that appeared lit from within by the bright morning sun, I considered how different the landscape was from the picturesque enclosures I had seen the day before.

Cypress Hills is closed to interments—and has been since 1954—and except for two teenage boys riding their bikes up and down the road leading to the rostrum, the cemetery was deserted. The superintendent's lodge, built in the 1880s, was also empty, and a notice on the front door indicated that the office space was available for rent to local community organizations.

Open and free. The words are so familiar to the American vocabulary that they hardly need to be explained. Still, my few visits to national cemeteries had already broadened—and complicated—my understanding of the terms. Spatially, the cemeteries were designed to draw people in—first by carriage, then by automobile, and always with the understanding that visitors are free to walk from one grave to another. That such liberty is permitted in a place where the remains of thousands of citizens have been so carefully laid to rest, like one row of beds after another, is testimony to the political-philosophical ideals these memorial landscapes are meant to ennoble.

I acted on this freedom when I took pictures. After several trips to cemeteries in the United States and abroad, I may have even taken it for granted, which was why I was brought up short when I was asked to put the camera down.

It was a bright Saturday morning, about a month after my trip to Brooklyn, when I drove to Woodlawn National Cemetery in Elmira, New York. Woodlawn is one of two national cemeteries in central New York, the other being in Bath, which is forty miles northeast of Elmira in the Finger Lakes region.

I arrived at Woodlawn around 4:00 p.m. and started to walk the grounds, lingering in the front-right corner, where the fence slants in to join an L-shaped columbarium that runs along the backside of several houses before it turns left to mark the cemetery's northern boundary. The columbarium functions as a wall, the dead guarding their brethren while providing privacy for adjacent homeowners. Whether veterans have objected to being memorialized in this way, I do not know, but at Woodlawn it is the only remaining option, since the ten-acre cemetery is otherwise full.

When I stood near the foot of the L, I had a clear view of the house next to the cemetery. It was a green-clapboard bungalow with a front porch and a driveway that ran close to the fence,

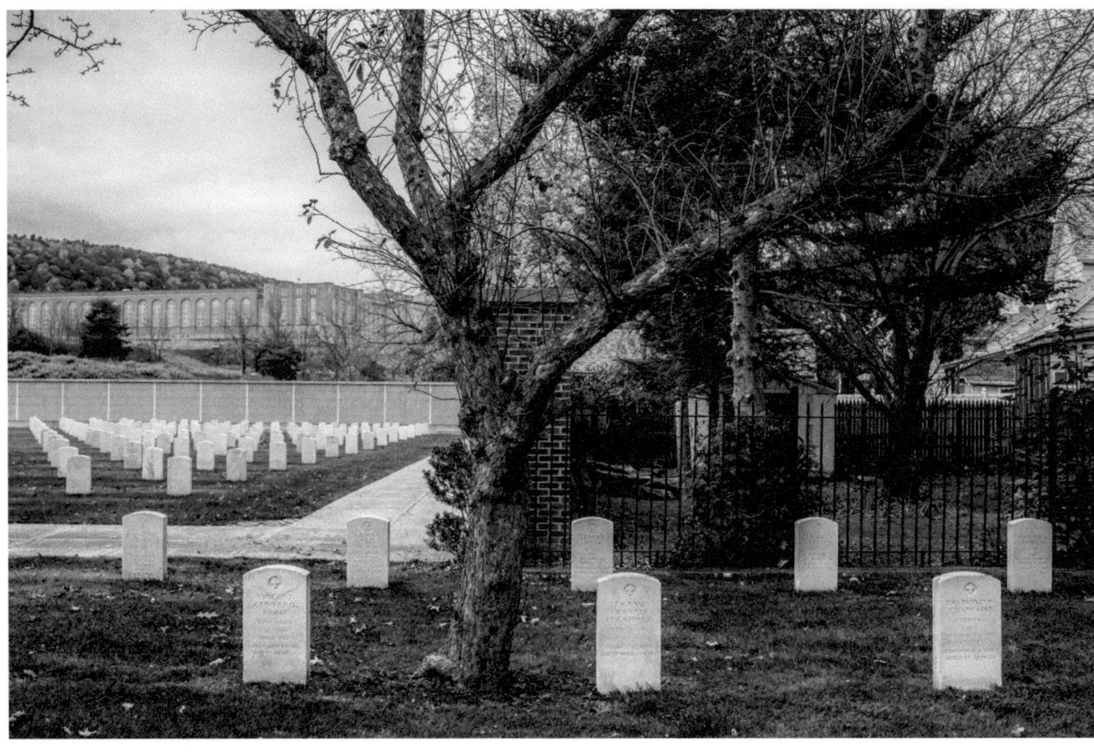

Woodlawn National Cemetery (established in 1874), Elmira, New York, 2017.

stopping at a gate that opened into the backyard. There was a dumpster in the driveway and a bunched-up carpet by the columbarium wall, signs of a renovation project. The black wrought iron fence was tied to the columbarium by a brick column with a flat capstone, while at the base of the column a small shrub screened the junction of rods and brick. I pointed my camera, and the headstones and the domestic odds and ends all became part of the same, oddly intimate scene.

I turned left and followed the columbarium toward the back of the cemetery. Above the wall, a half mile away, on a hill overlooking the cemetery, I could see the Elmira Correctional Facility. The complex opened in 1876, two years after Woodlawn National Cemetery was dedicated and sits on land that Union soldiers used as a training camp and later would become a prison for Confederate soldiers. The prison was known as Hellmira. Nearly three thousand men died there of malnutrition, smallpox, and other diseases. Their remains were buried at Woodlawn in a separate section on the west side.

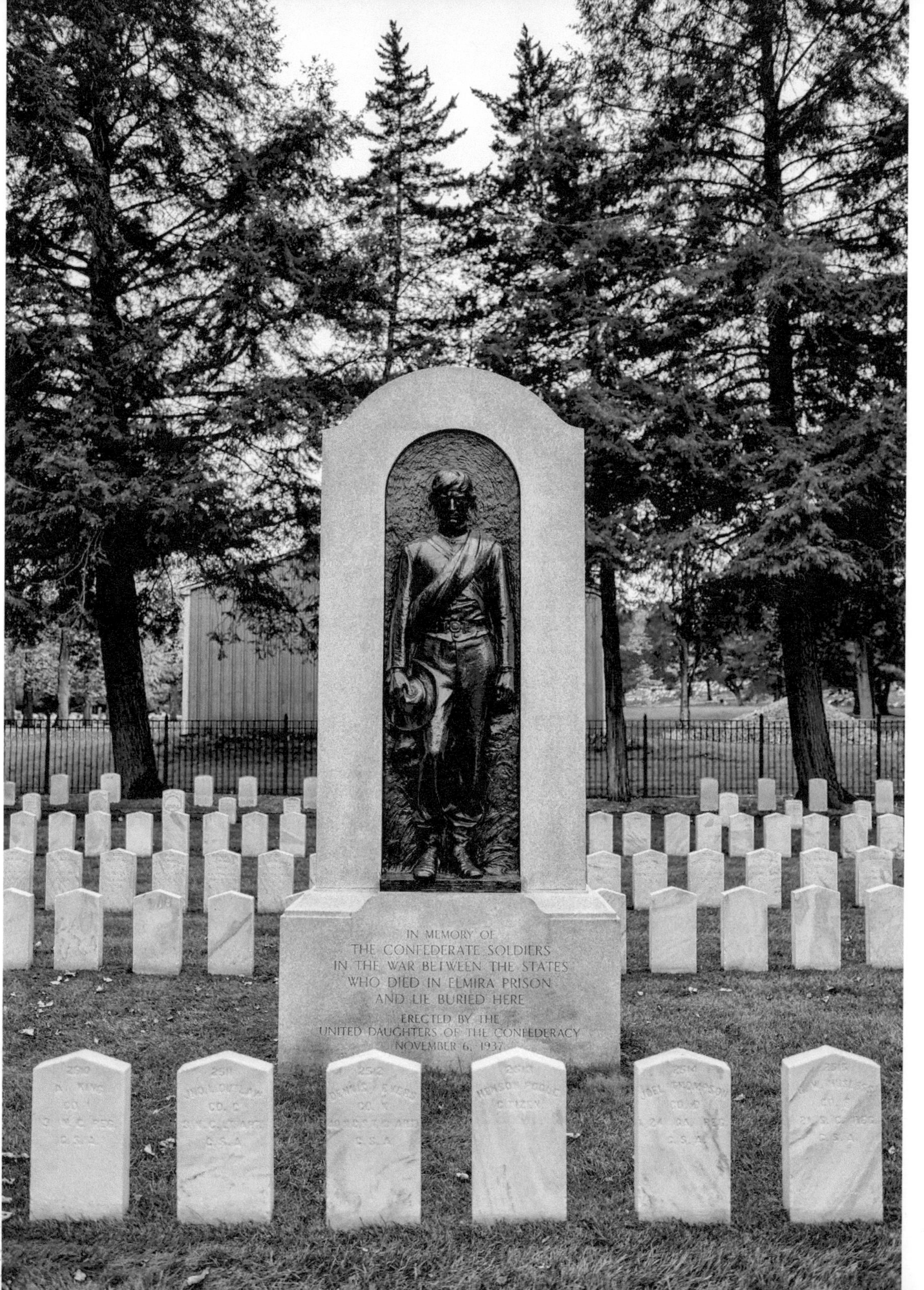

Woodlawn National Cemetery, 2017. The Confederate monument is in a separate section of the cemetery, surrounded by pointed headstones that mark the Southern dead.

I walked to those graves, moving through sections F, B, and C, across the central pathway, and past the superintendent's lodge and flagpole. Memorial space is regimented throughout the cemetery system, and where Confederates are concerned, it tends to be strictly regulated. Here, the pointed headstones of the South are flanked by several rows of federal graves, including the remains of World War II veterans. The graves are segregated, the newer headstones pulled back from the large middle section, the distance a reminder of the debate that must have accompanied the decision to honor US soldiers in the same cemetery where enemy combatants were buried.

I took several pictures and moved to the rear of the section, shooting toward an apartment building that faced the cemetery, where scores of Confederate headstones filled the better part of the frame. Behind me was a memorial to the Southern soldiers who fought in "The War Between the States" and died in the Elmira prison. The ten-foot granite pillar includes a bas-relief figure of a soldier—slender, young, and without a weapon—and the inscription on the monument says it was erected by the United Daughters of the Confederacy in 1937.

It was almost 5:30, and I circled the monument with my camera in front of me, concluding that it had been a good day and I had been lucky with the weather and the light, when I saw a man in uniform approaching me from the pathway. I paused, we said hello, and he then told me I was not allowed to take pictures here.

The patch on his shirt indicated he was a private security guard, not a police officer or cemetery employee, and I was tempted to say, as I did when I later encountered the volunteer at Saratoga, that this was a public space and I had every right to take pictures. Instead, I asked why, and he backtracked a little, explaining that the cemetery's director had said that all photographers must get permission beforehand. He gestured to the pillar, and then I understood. Across the nation, Confederate monuments were being removed and relocated and pictures of this one might appear on social media and attract protesters who wanted to deface or destroy it. There was no point arguing, so I said thanks and turned back to examining the headstones as he walked away.

As I drove to my motel, I could not help but think about the irony: the government outsourcing the protection of memorials whose very reason for being was to dissolve the Union. That irony only felt stranger as I continued to travel and encountered Confederate monuments and guards at Chicago, Alton (Illinois), Springfield (Missouri), Johnson's Island (Ohio), Finn's Point (New Jersey), and Point Lookout (Maryland).

I approached these places warily, but no one said anything to me about not taking pictures. The

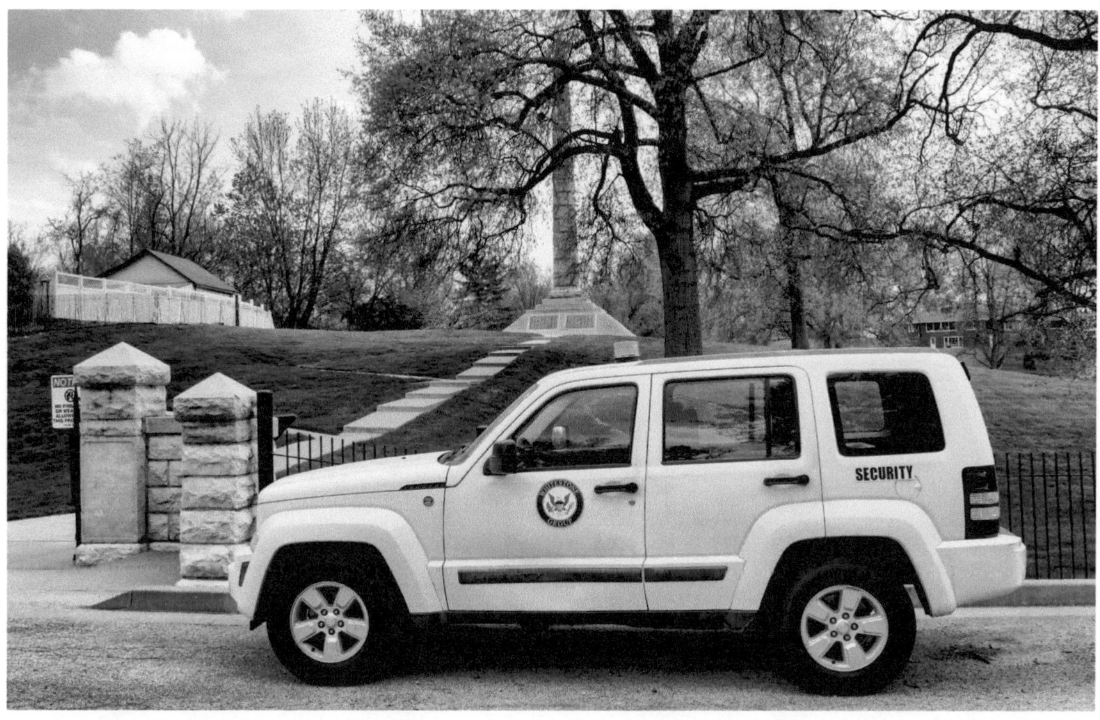

North Alton Confederate Cemetery (established in 1867), Alton, Illinois, 2018.

guards were mostly passive. I would see them on the perimeter, in their cars with their phones, or sometimes I just saw their patrol cars, with the company logo on the door panel—the Whitestone Group, the name encircling a screaming eagle, as if to say the Ohio-based security firm is a government agency and not an "Approved Federal Supplier."

There were two exceptions. At Finn's Point National Cemetery, located at the end of a gravel road in Salem, New Jersey, half a mile from the Delaware River, the guard followed me like a hawk. I visited on a soft day in June, and the cemetery was vacant except for a few bicyclists who had pedaled down from Fort Mott State Park, a landscaping crew, and the security guard who was standing by a trailer parked next to the superintendent's lodge. I moved deliberately across the freshly mowed lawn, composing pictures as I went but with the uneasy feeling of being watched.

Finn's Point is a two-acre cemetery established in 1875 and dominated on the north side by a large Confederate monument—a stone pillar or obelisk—built in 1910 to mark the 2,436 prisoners who died at nearby Fort Delaware. In the middle of the site is a smaller memorial, erected

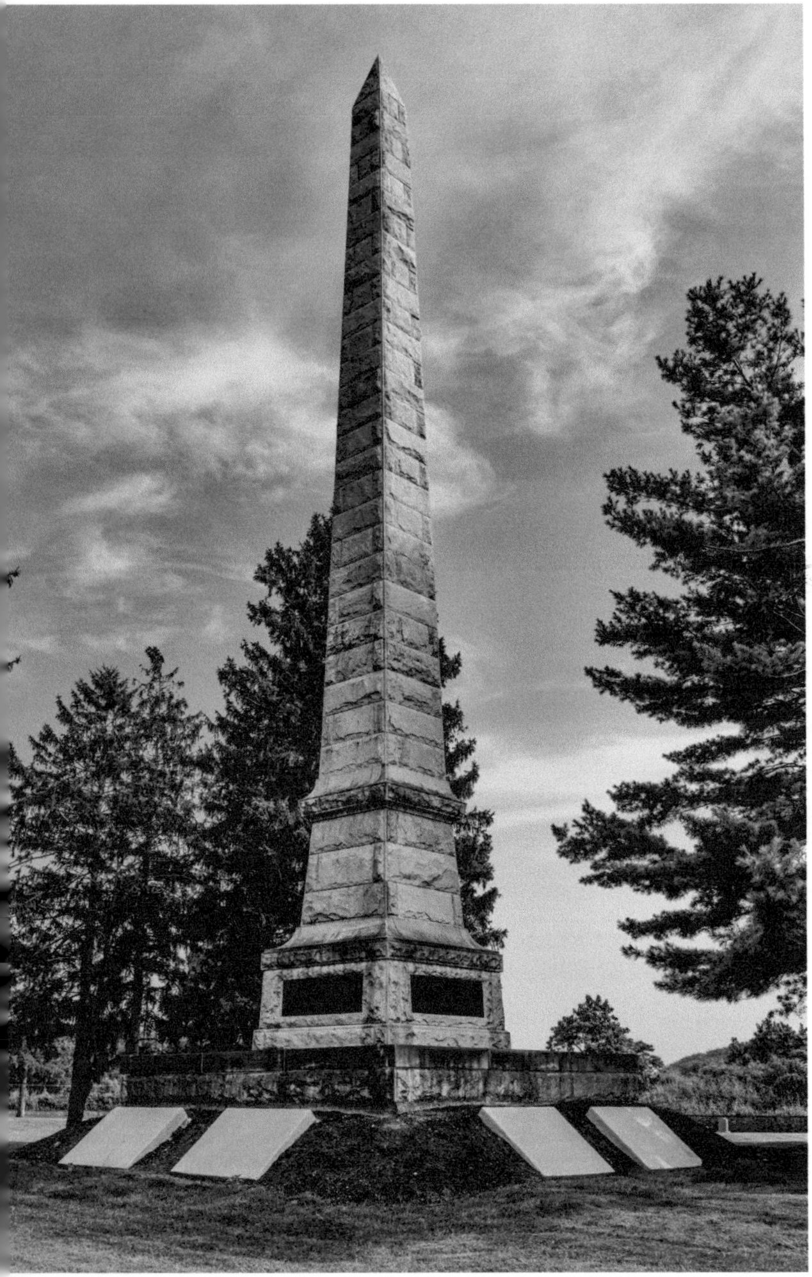

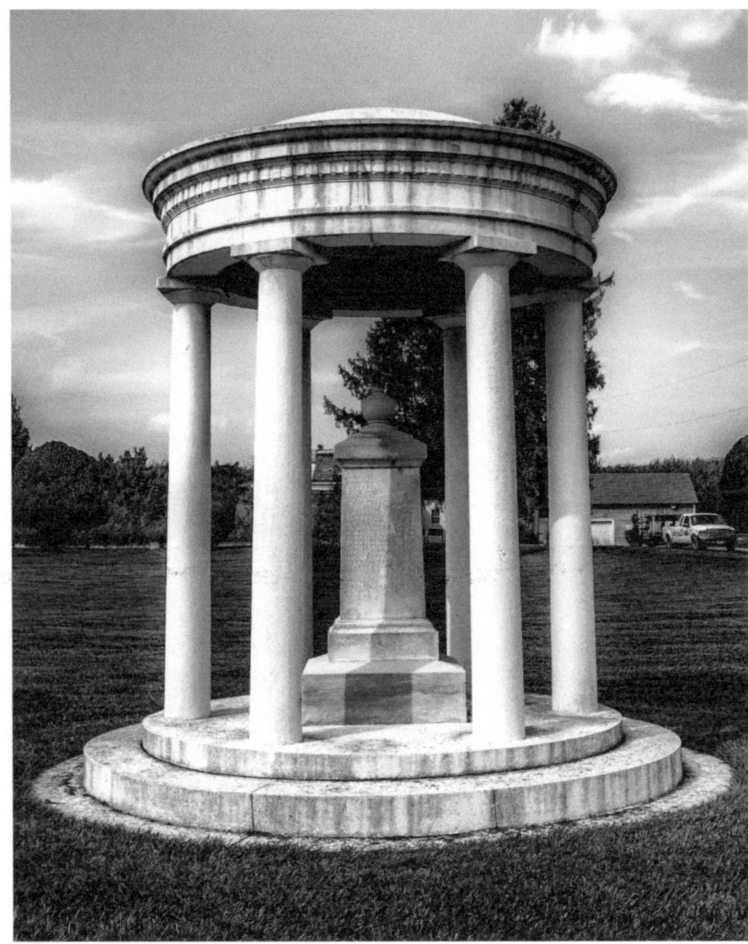

(*Left*) Confederate Monument at Finn's Point National Cemetery (established 1875), Salem, New Jersey, 2018.

(*Above*) Union Monument at Finn's Point National Cemetery, 2018.

in 1879, that honors the 135 Union soldiers who perished while guarding them. Beyond the cemetery wall toward the river are grass and wetlands. When I finished taking pictures, I walked out the gate and started to follow the wall around, hoping to get a shot of the cemetery from the outside looking in. But the guard yelled from the trailer and waved me off, so I settled for a photo of his patrol car.

By contrast, the guard at the Point Lookout Confederate Cemetery seemed almost happy to see me when I showed up on a Sunday afternoon after driving 120 miles from Richmond, not as the crow flies but up I-95, west on US 301, and then over the Potomac River by Dahlgren, Virginia, and into Maryland, where I turned south toward the tip of the western shore of Chesapeake Bay, a borderless region that feels neither southern nor northern. Point Lookout does not occupy what Edward Whitman would have recognized as a "conspicuous" spot near a "great thoroughfare." It is on the outskirts of Scotland, Maryland—population 250, as per the 2020 census—the former site of an army stockade, also called Point Lookout, which eventually became a prison for Confederates, 3,382 of whom died in captivity.

There are no Union dead at Point Lookout, which explains why it is not identified as a "national" cemetery. The same applies to the other Confederates-only cemeteries managed by the US government. Robert Penn Warren once remarked that Southerners fought the war because they believed "they had created the Union" and "the North was going to take it away from them."[1] But the South seceded, and the Confederate dead belonged to another country. The federal government marked the difference in the Southern memorials it constructed.

The Confederate headstones would be pointed, not rounded. After 1930, new headstones were also stamped with the Southern Cross of Honor. Where individual markers were not possible—for instance, at Finn's Point, Point Lookout, and the North Alton Confederate Cemetery in Alton, Illinois—the government constructed obelisks to memorialize the dead. While the marble for the headstones came from Georgia, the Van Amringe Granite Company of Boston built the pillars.[2]

The obelisks designate the remains of Confederate soldiers buried on site in single graves or group enclosures, usually trenches with one coffin stacked on top of another. The men died in Union prisons, and while they may originally have been buried nearby, their remains were reinterred after the war. Recordkeeping was poor, and where authorities marked individual graves—at the original or new burial site—they used wooden headboards that eventually disintegrated.[3]

The Confederate Mound in Oak Woods Cemetery on Chicago's South Side is marked by a

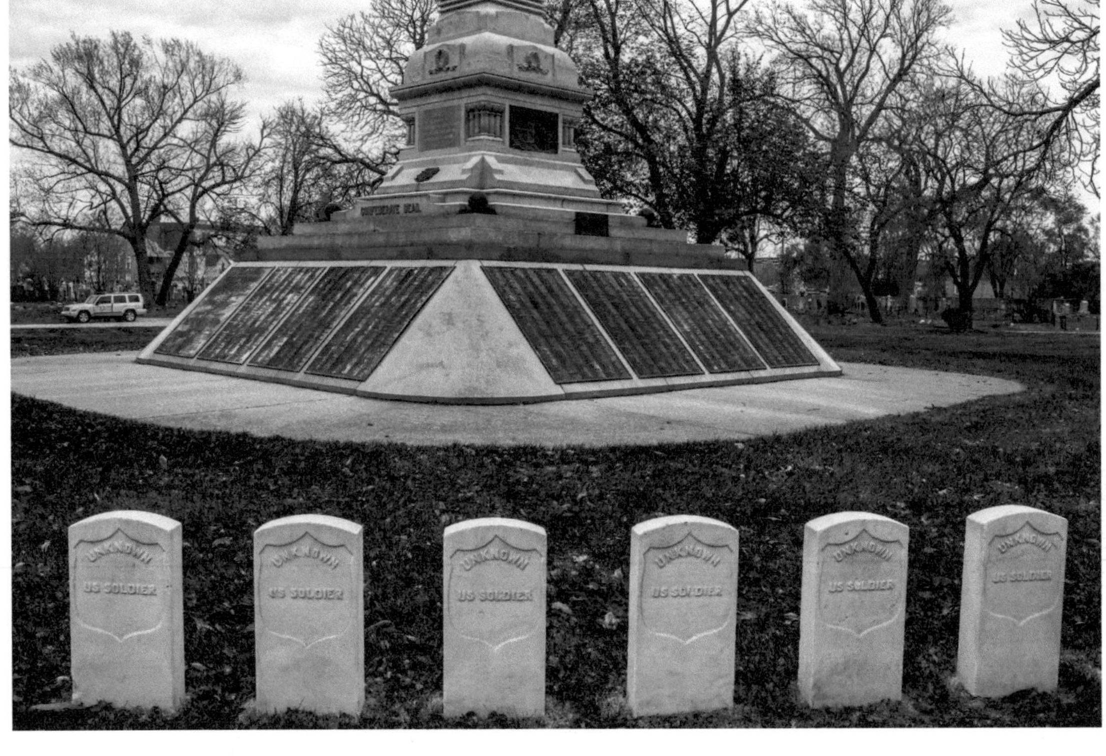

The Confederate Mound (remains transferred in 1866; monument dedicated in 1895) in Oak Woods Cemetery, Chicago, Illinois, 2017.

thirty-foot-high column with a standing soldier statue on top. Unlike the other group markers, the mound is truly a mass grave, the remains of more than four thousand men who died at Camp Douglas prison sharing the same space. It is similar to the Tomb of the Civil War Unknowns at Arlington, except here (and at Finn's Point, North Alton, and Point Lookout) the dead are known, and their names are listed on bronze tablets affixed to the base of the memorial, the identities tumbling over one another, sometimes hard to read given the dirt, tarnished metal, and shifting light, but still part of an effort to memorialize their deaths in singular terms.

Twenty feet from the mound, in a line extending across the corner of the concrete pad, are the graves of a dozen "Unknown U.S. Soldiers," men who worked as guards at Camp Douglas. I thought when I took pictures on a cold day in November that the sharp, straight row announces the landscape's primary purpose: This is a place for the dead. But a soldier looms over the spot and cannon balls anchor the column, so it is not surprising that some see the mound

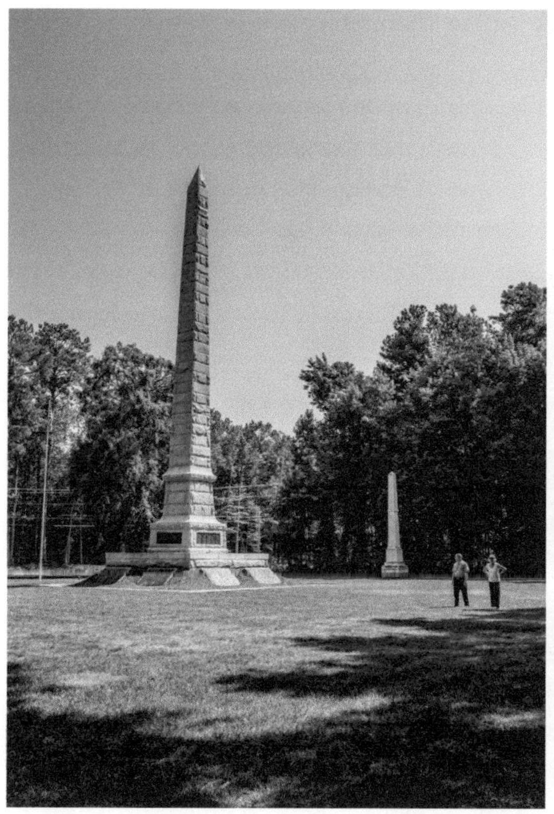

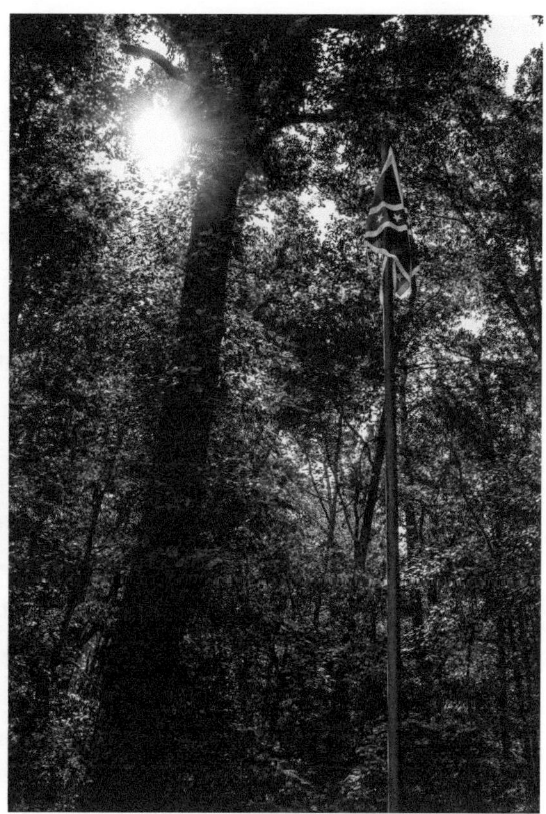

(*Far Left*) Point Lookout Confederate Cemetery (established in 1910), Scotland, Maryland, 2019.

Point Lookout Confederate Cemetery, 2019. The flagpole displaying the Confederate battle flag is located just behind the cemetery, on private property.

as a monument to white supremacy or that a security officer from the Whitestone Group was parked on the roadway to protect the memorial. As at Finn's Point the situation evoked the absurd: guards guarding guards who once guarded Confederates, who now share the earth with their captors. Beyond the mound many famous African Americans were buried at Oak Woods, including civil rights activist Ida B. Wells, Olympic medalist Jesse Owens, and Chicago mayor Harold Washington.

When I was at Point Lookout in Maryland, I asked the guard whether he had dealt with any protests or threats, and he said no, people were just curious about the memorial, that his job was pretty boring, and that the most exciting part involved breaking up fights at the convenience store down the road. He said he had fought in Iraq, more than fifteen years ago, was thinking about reenlisting, and that working security was a way to fill in the gaps until something better came up. He also reported that ghost hunters occasionally showed up at night looking for signs of dead Confederates. Yes, he said, there is a lot of history here. In fact, one guy who lived in the area tried to persuade the government to display a Confederate flag at the cemetery, and when he got tired of being told no, he purchased the land surrounding the site, installed a flagpole behind the fence, and established his own commemorative park next door.[4]

There was some logic behind that plan, I thought, as I wandered off to see the Confederate Memorial Park and then photographed the flag that shone defiantly in the trees above the cemetery, partially obscured by the thickened summer foliage. After rendering the sight I could not help but consider how other visitors might interpret seeing the Stars and Bars battle flag of those who fought against the Union and in favor of a slave-based economy.

After all, in 1898, President William McKinley, speaking to an audience in Atlanta, declared that "sectional lines no longer mar the map of the United States" and that it was time that "we should share with you in the care of the graves of the Confederate soldiers." Two years later, after relentless negotiating by Confederate veterans, the government opened a section for Confederate graves at Arlington National Cemetery. Newly designated plots followed at Camp Butler National Cemetery, Jefferson Barracks National Cemetery, and other national cemeteries, all mandated by the 1906 Commission for Marking Graves of Confederate Dead, with the stipulation—as the legislation put it—that they mark only the graves of men "who died in federal prisons and military hospitals in the North and who were buried near their places of confinement."[5] And, in 1914, the UDC arranged to have a monument built at Arlington, establishing a foothold in the federal landscape that was unimaginable during the 1870s and '80s.

So the dead carried the meaning of the war forward, their various legacies differentially carved in stone. The significance of those inscriptions was more than symbolic. Though McKinley spoke of reconciliation, his support of Confederate interests bolstered the legitimacy of the Jim Crow South and helped undermine some of the gains that African Americans made during Reconstruction. At the same time, the plan for marking Confederate graves placed the Lost Cause under federal jurisdiction. As historian John R. Neff has pointed out, the president's proposal that "we" share with "you" assumed that union would be achieved "through the subjugation of Confederate soldiers to the national purpose," a vision of future power borne of the North's "Cause Victorious."[6]

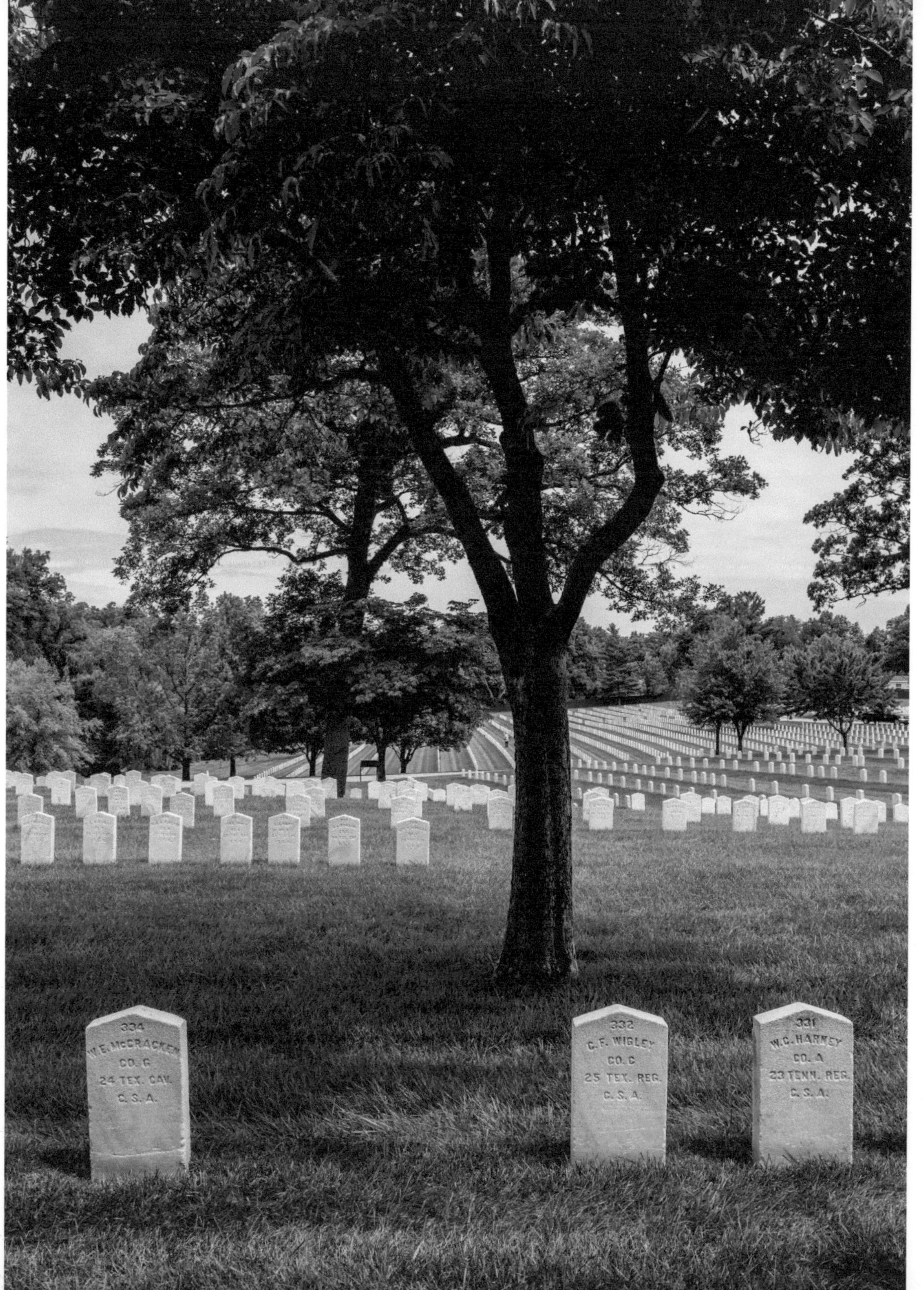

Camp Butler National Cemetery (established in 1862), Springfield, Illinois, 2018.

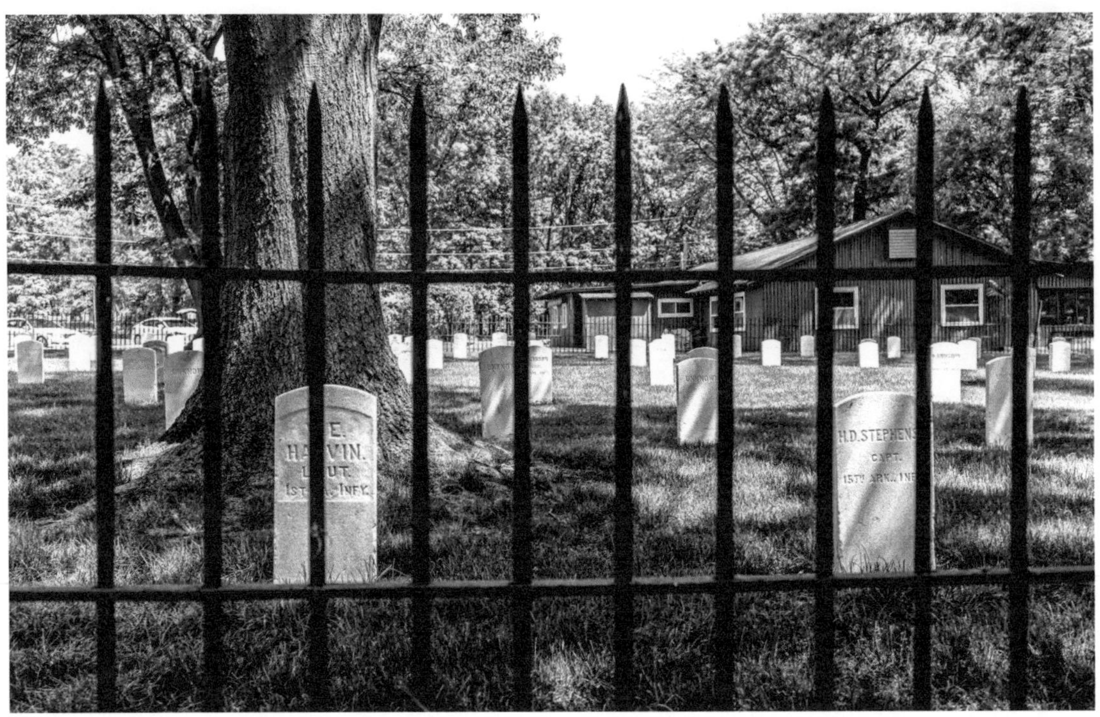

Confederate Stockade Cemetery (established in 1862), Johnson's Island, Marblehead, Ohio, 2018. Johnson's Island on Sandusky Bay in Lake Erie was a Union prison for officers of the Confederate Army. The headstones here are not pointed, as Confederate markers usually are.

That history is with us still—me and you—as we stand on well-manicured grass surrounded by rounded and pointed headstones. From a distance, we may see a unified whole, while closer in, we can find dissent. But always the future is literally rooted in the past.

Of course, that future may look different when we see it in on southern ground, as I did when I visited Soldiers' Rest in Vicksburg, Mississippi, one morning in March 2018. This was my first trip to a Confederate cemetery, one private burial ground within another, in this case, Cedar Hill Cemetery (formerly City of Vicksburg Cemetery). The street address for Soldiers' Rest is 366 Lover's Lane, and I followed the directions on my GPS through the city's hilly neighborhoods, which might have been shelled from the Yazoo and Mississippi Rivers when Ulysses S. Grant's Union forces lay siege to the city in the spring of 1863. It was early spring, and the luxuriant growing season had already claimed the land, the unkempt beauty and honeysuckle scents vying for attention.

It had rained overnight, and when I pulled into the cemetery, I looked over a field of grass and stone, everything glistening in the morning light, the grave plots of Cedar Hill dotting the horizon. I parked next to a large Confederate monument built in 1893. Behind me the land rose to a shaggy escarpment hanging over the cemetery. Before me were gray headstones for five thousand Confederate dead, grouped by state, the green pathways littered with Stars and Bars and Southern Crosses. Beside the monument was a stone rostrum in disrepair. Memory all around me.

I had the place to myself and was eager to take pictures, my excitement piqued by the sense of having stepped into forbidden territory. I moved quickly down toward the headstones but slipped on the water-soaked ground, clutching the camera as I fell, scared I would break it. My lens and clothes were wet and muddy, so I returned to the car, wiped down the equipment and changed my shorts and shirt before heading back.

The Gettysburg Address was nowhere to be seen, and there were no headstones for US Colored Troops nor any mention of Fort Pillow. To say the place was haunted by Confederates is not quite right because real people show up to honor the dead on Decoration Day, the southern version of Memorial Day. They come to Soldiers' Rest, Hollywood and Oakwood in Richmond, and Cave Hill in Louisville, some planting small Confederate flags just as people lay wreaths on graves in national cemeteries during the holidays.[7]

It goes without saying that these people are white, some certainly members of heritage organizations like the UDC. The fact I am also white enables my freedom to think I can just come here and take pictures. By stepping into these landscapes, I wonder if I am complicit. But complicit in what?

Two months before my visit to Elmira, in August 2017, alt-right nationalists clashed with protesters in Charlottesville, Virginia, who were demanding the removal of a statue of Robert E. Lee from a city park. A young woman was killed when a man with a history of white supremacist beliefs drove his car into a crowd of demonstrators. Two years before that, Dylann Roof murdered nine African Americans at a church in Charleston, South Carolina. Hoping to spark a race war, Roof drew inspiration from Confederate symbols.

The Department of Veterans Affairs began hiring private security guards soon after the Charlottesville conflict, and spent almost $3 million the next year to protect Confederate memorials at national cemeteries, according to records the AP obtained through the Freedom of Information Act.[8] Those measures were not enough to prevent someone from lopping off the head of

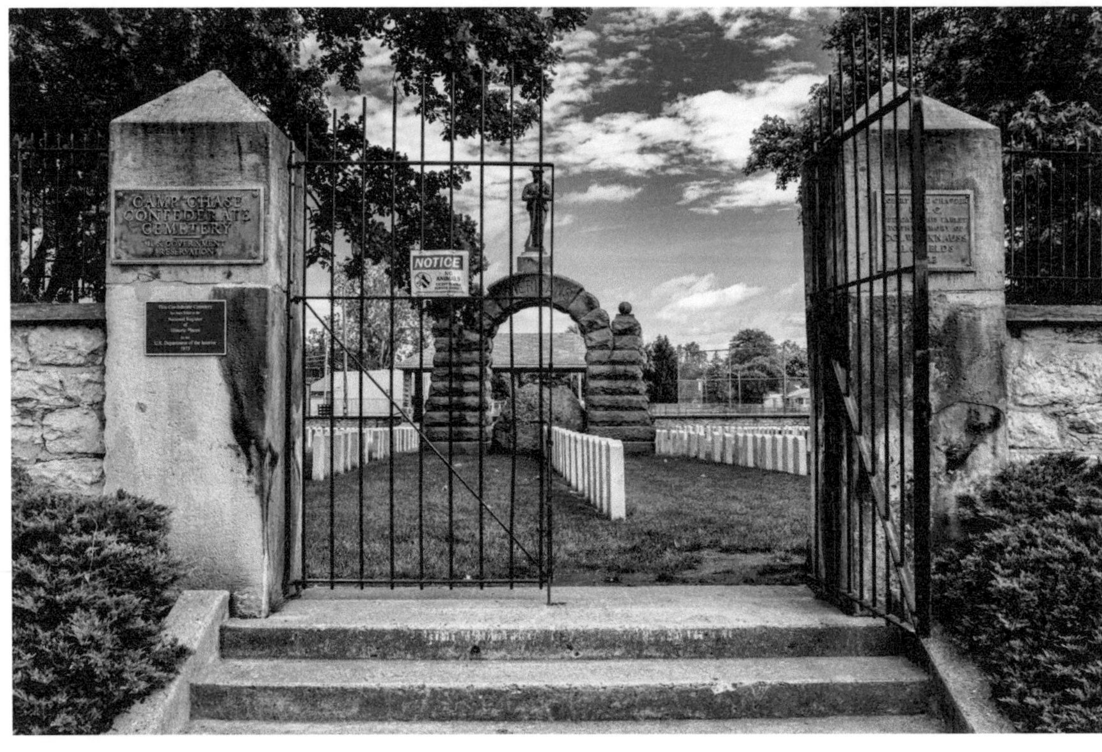

Camp Chase Confederate Cemetery (established in 1879), Columbus, Ohio, 2019.

the Confederate soldier standing on an arch at the Camp Chase Confederate Cemetery in Columbus, Ohio, the remains of the 2,260 prisoners spread out in the graves below him. When I visited the cemetery in the summer of 2019, the monument had been repaired.

Meanwhile, a few days after the decapitation in Columbus, a resident of Springfield, Missouri—625 miles to the southwest—contacted the information hotline at the *Springfield News-Ledger* to ask why a security guard stopped her at the gates of the Springfield National Cemetery, which includes 566 Confederate graves and a monument to General Sterling Price, the Missouri governor who fought for the South.[9] She had been walking through the cemetery for years. Why was it no longer open and free?

After Charlottesville, Democratic members of the House of Representatives drafted legislation prohibiting the display of the Confederate flag on federal property and the use of Confederate symbols in nationally funded programs. Responding to a request from legislators,

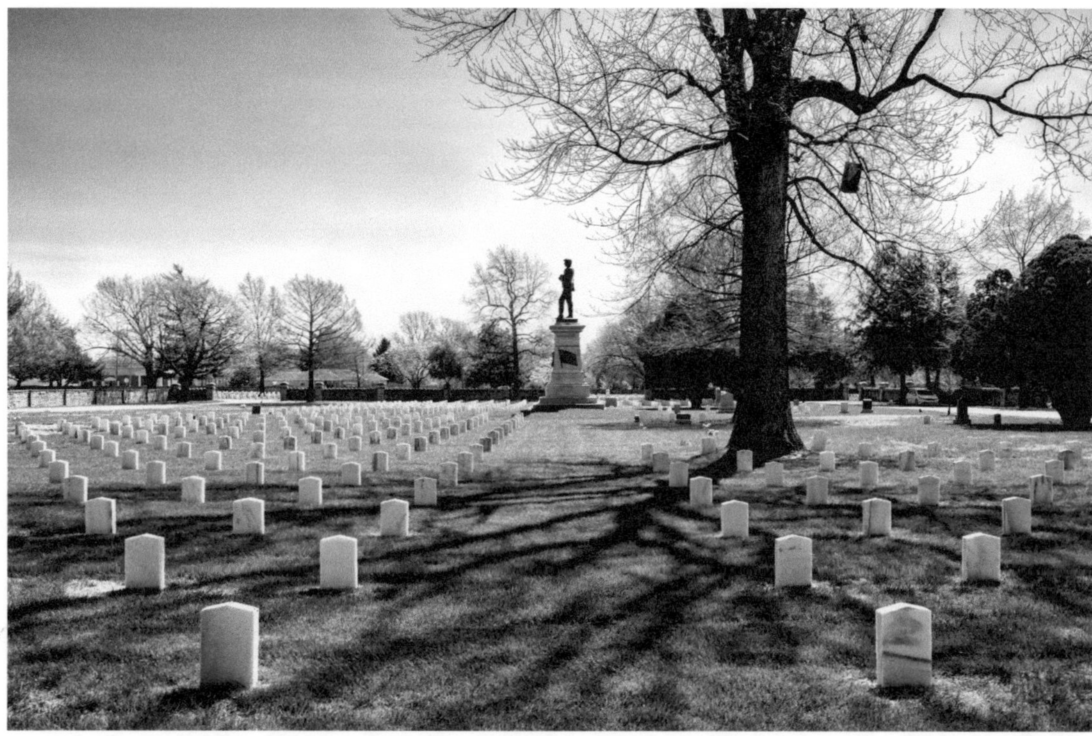

The Confederate section at Springfield National Cemetery (established in 1867), Springfield, Missouri, 2018.

the Congressional Research Service issued a report describing the challenges of enacting such a law. The researchers underscored the legacy of racism associated with Confederate icons but also noted that many Americans valued their historical significance. They mentioned that Confederate-themed symbols are in use at several National Park Service sites, that national cemeteries with Confederate graves periodically display the Confederate flag to memorialize the dead, and that personnel in some branches of the military are free to wear Confederate flag tattoos so long as the emblems do not disrupt unit morale. They also explained why it would be difficult to limit federal funding to state and local entities that permit the display of Confederate symbols on state flags, office buildings, and license plates.[10]

It is hard to say whether this report or the aptly titled "Federal Stewardship of Confederate Dead"—a 2016 study by the National Cemetery Administration—spells the bureaucratic end of history or just reveals the country's messy past. History is never monolithic, and we risk our

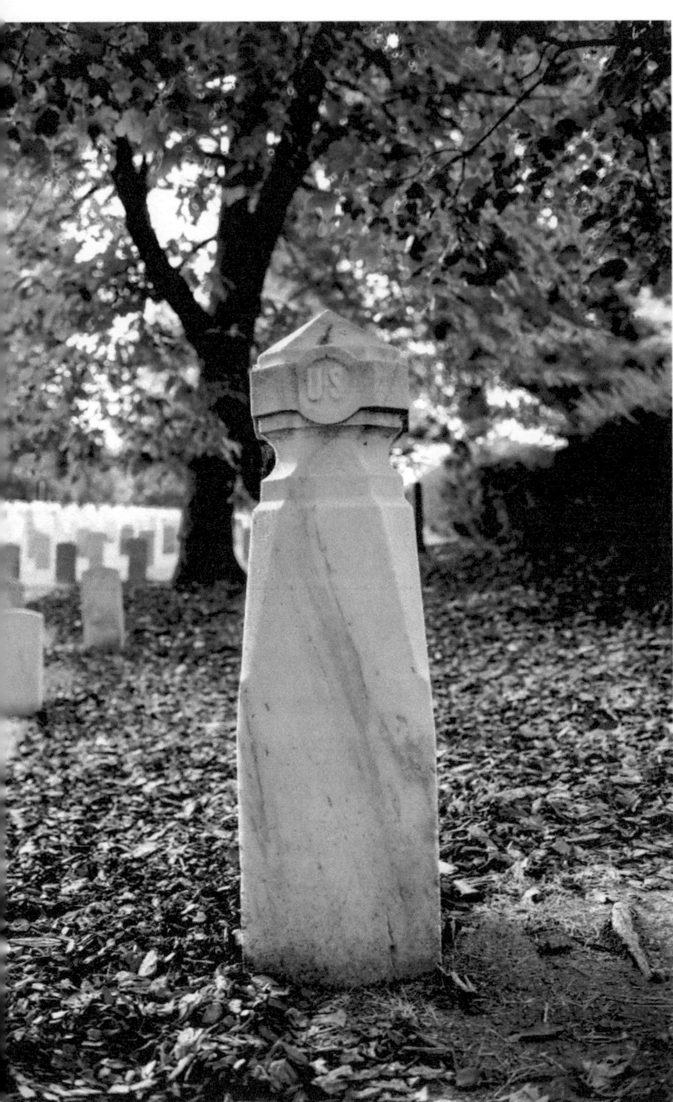

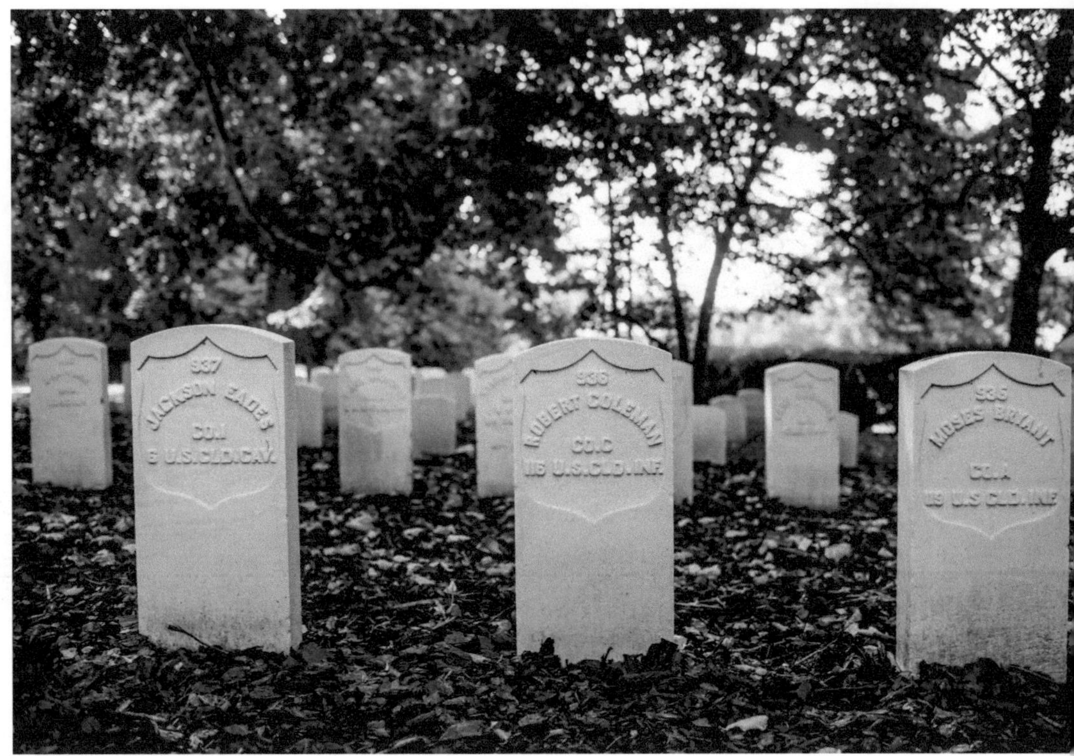

(*Left*) A boundary marker at Lexington National Cemetery (established in 1863), Lexington, Kentucky, 2019.

(*Above*) Lexington National Cemetery, 2019.

ability to understand its legacy when we alter the record. But "we" is a fraught term, and the politics of remembrance vary depending on who and what is on the ground.

Lexington Cemetery, in Lexington, Kentucky, offers an example of what compromise or political finesse can look like on a memorial landscape. Established in 1848, Lexington is a large private cemetery that includes both a Confederate section and a lot for 1,388 Union graves that, in 1863, was designated a national cemetery. The split between Northern and Southern graves reflects Kentucky's divided loyalties during the Civil War. Although the state remained in the Union, roughly 40 percent of its men who fought in the war sided with the Confederacy.[11]

Not quite an acre in size, Lexington National Cemetery sits on the eastern edge of Lexington Cemetery, nestled between a hedgerow and an internal roadway. The lot faces inward and includes several arced rows of headstones, flanked by ten marble boundary posts with the letters "US" stamped at the top. I visited the lot twice in two days, drawn by its elegant design and the classic beauty of the marble posts. I also took pictures at the south end of the lot, where two dozen African American soldiers—Union men—were buried together.

The second day, I walked north past the boundary markers and into the Confederate section, fifty yards away. There are family plots, individual graves, and a memorial to "Our Dead"—a stone tree constructed like a crucifix. There is also a monument to General John H. Morgan, a Lexington native who fought for the Confederacy at Shiloh and was killed in a Union raid at Greeneville, Tennessee, in 1864 at the age of thirty-nine. No standing soldier statue, the monument presents Morgan on a horse, and the horse on a pedestal, the general gazing intently at the road before him.

I learned later that the century-old memorial had been in the cemetery for only a year, that the statue, along with a monument of John C. Breckinridge (vice president under James Buchanan and later secretary of war for the Confederacy), had been relocated from downtown Lexington. The mayor and city council had been thinking about the character of civic space for some time—about addressing the sins of the past—but decided to move the figures shortly after the Charlottesville tragedy.[12]

History, it seems, belongs with the dead. But this phrasing is too glib, too dismissive of the complex politics that placed John H. Morgan in the Confederate section at Lexington Cemetery. The general will never cross the road to engage the Union soldiers just beyond him. The setting is frozen in time, deconstructed, and carefully segregated. I could not possibly fit all this in a single

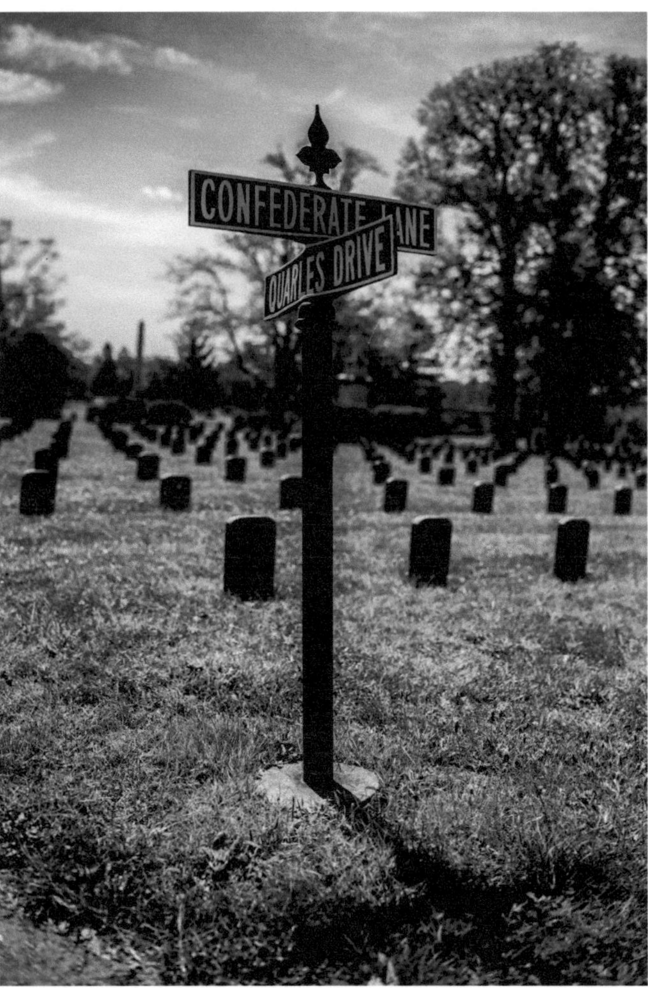

Stonewall Confederate Cemetery, Winchester, Virginia (established in 1866), 2019.

image. My lens was not wide enough, trees crowded the way, and I was unable to find common ground. Still, the fact I could try, that compromise was in sight, distinguished Lexington from Stonewall Confederate Cemetery in Winchester, Virginia; Soldiers' Rest in Vicksburg, Mississippi; or McGavock Confederate Cemetery in Franklin, Tennessee. These are unreconstructed landscapes, dedicated to memorializing the sacrifice that Southern men made in the name of the Confederacy. And there is no room for negotiation.

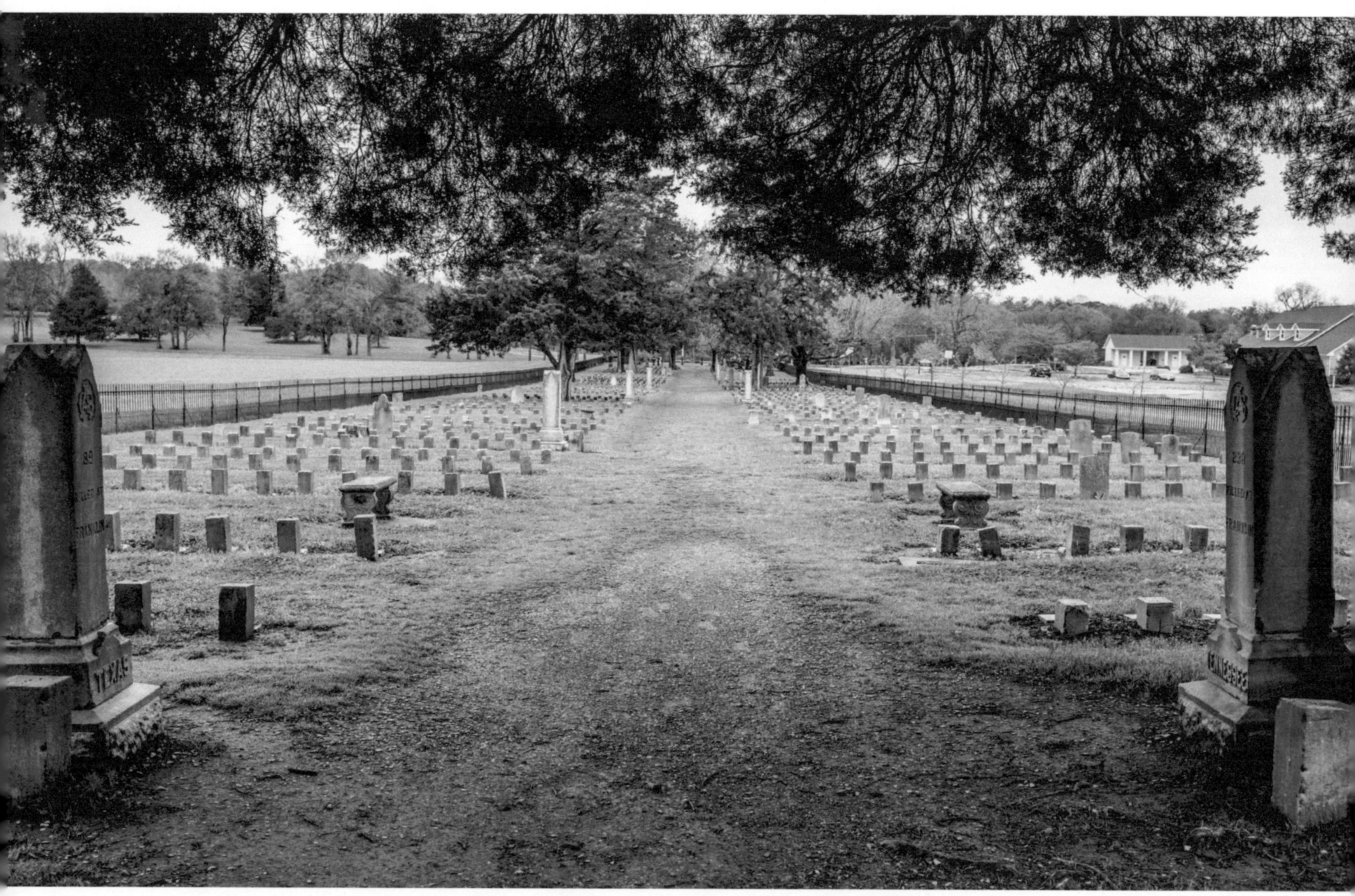

McGavock Confederate Cemetery (established in 1866), Franklin, Tennessee, 2018. Nearly 1,500 Confederate soldiers died at the Battle of Franklin (November 30, 1864) and were buried here by soldiers and enslaved men.

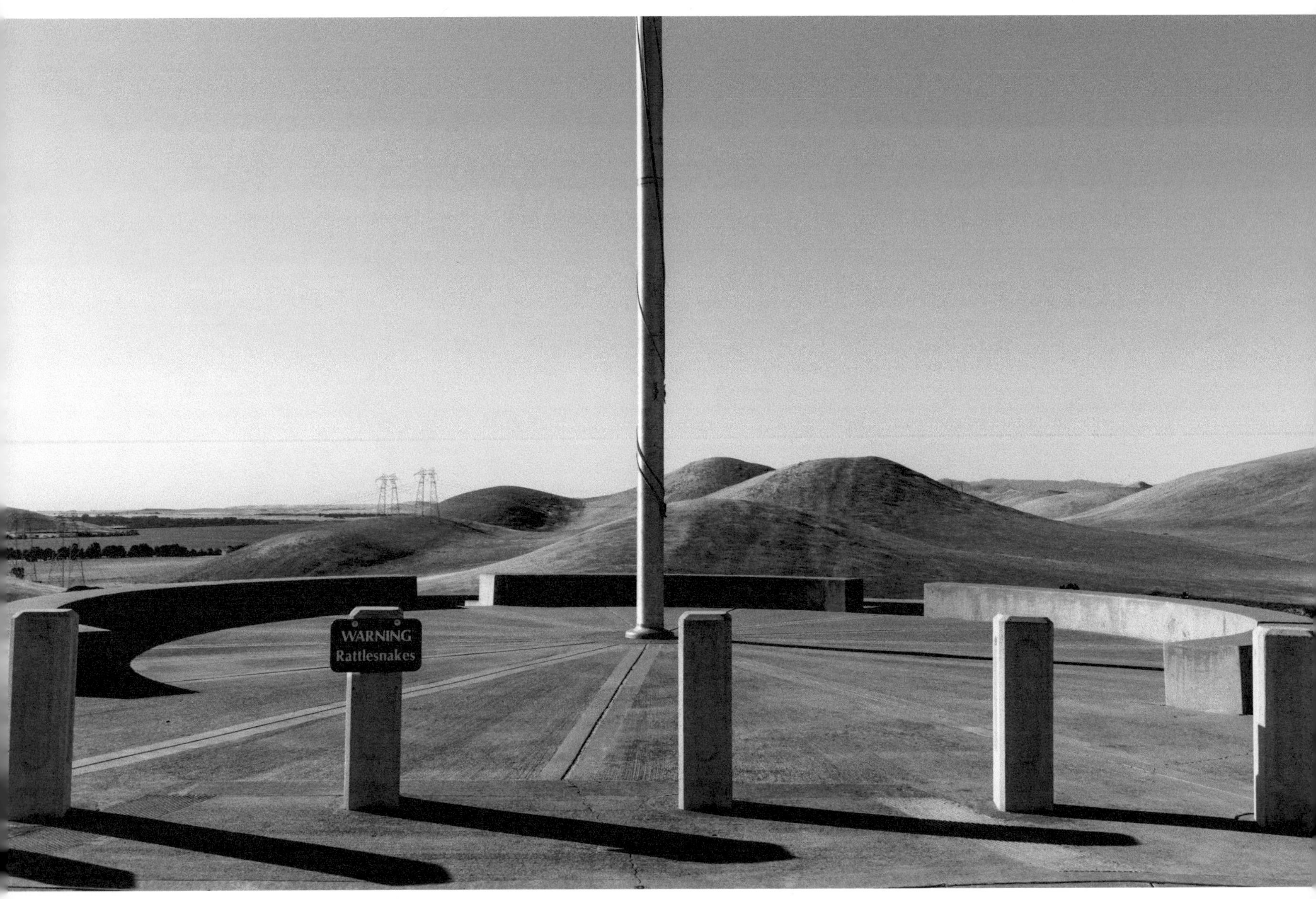

San Joaquin Valley National Cemetery (established in 1989), Santa Nella, California, 2018.

6

True Ground

If the arrangement at Lexington National Cemetery was meant to calm the volatile debate over the place of Confederate monuments, it seems to have worked. The disagreeable parts of history receded into the 170-acre cemetery, carefully positioned on a landscape already split along Mason-Dixon Lines, the spaces in between left to speak for themselves. The assumption here is that cemeteries are places for quiet reflection, the silence broken only by the need for burial services.

I know I share this assumption, and that no matter how I explain the situation at Lexington, I just want to be free to walk and take pictures. At home, clicking through the thousands of photographs stored on my computer, I return to this territory. In Lightroom, the software program for editing pictures and managing "workflow," I reframe scenes, sharpen fields of gray, and discover details I have not seen before. I pass through folders organized by place and time, revisiting images of Keokuk or Barrancas as I describe in prose what it was like being there, an experience and space that I now think of as my own.

There is a tension between the landscape as seen or composed from behind the camera, and the landscape as it was made or used. In the still space of a cemetery it is easy to pretend that it has always been thus, that the memorial functions are, in effect, immemorial, and that silence has also been the rule.

But history often pulls us back, and I did not have to go far to find evidence of a time when these places functioned more like public squares, places for serious debate and dissent. The signs were in front of me as I drove through the gates, the Gettysburg Address reminding me that

Lincoln spoke in a cemetery. Further on, I often found platforms or rostrums, where citizens gathered on Memorial Day to celebrate the idea of the Republic.

In describing these visits, I do not mean to suggest that I encountered the cemeteries as fully formed landscapes whose features fit into a pattern that I started to catalogue as soon as I arrived. I got to this point eventually, but it took me a while—and some research—to see these places historically, to see the rostrum and superintendent's lodge as standard features in a system that evolved over time.

The newer cemeteries also have venues for ceremonial gatherings and special events. So at the San Joaquin Valley National Cemetery in Santa Nella, California, there is a one-hundred-yard reflecting pool, which in 2016 served as the site for a spectacular Memorial Day celebration featuring speeches from veterans and politicians, as well as a fly-in by a Vietnam-era helicopter.[1] And nearly all functioning cemeteries have dedicated committal shelters located on the side of the road or tucked into cul-de-sacs, providing space for family and friends to congregate for funeral services. Where permanent shelters are not available, tents or pop-up shelters serve the same purpose.

On the other hand, rostrums—often underused and neglected—look like artifacts of a bygone era. Like the bandstands and gazebos found on small-town greens, they evoke the tradition of face-to-face democracy, of bringing people together. Now when I approach one with my camera, stand back and see it within the landscape or ascend the stairs and shoot out from the platform, as I did at Cypress Hills, I can almost imagine the crowd below, almost hear the words floating out from the podium.

In Latin, the word *rostrum* means "animal snout or bird's beak." At the Forum in ancient Rome, the rostrum was the platform used for public speeches. The speaker's platform was called a rostrum because it was decorated with the prows of ships—often shaped like birds' beaks—that the Roman navy stripped from conquered vessels and then brought home as trophies of war.[2] This definition is relevant in another way since an early verb form of rostrum (*rodere*) means to gnaw or scrape, which is what birds do with their beaks and military ships did with their prows when plowing into other vessels.

It is a stretch to get from scraping to speaking but worth the effort given the implications for how we think about civic speech. While the Forum, like the agora in ancient Greece, is loosely tied to current notions of free speech, the words that Roman emperors shared with their assembled constituency were not free. The language of state came from the spoils of war, and jingoistic celebrations of power, to stretch the metaphor, were aimed at stirring audiences, literally peeling them from their seats.

The connection I want to make here between rostrums and war, speech and landscape, comes into sharper focus when we consider the evolving role of commemoration at national cemeteries. In her history of Arlington National Cemetery, Micki McElya argues that the landscape serves as a model for "militarized nationalism and collective mourning."[3] Yet the idea that the military or the Department of Veterans Affairs should mobilize grief on behalf of a combat-ready United States developed over time. When Lincoln spoke, he could hardly ignore the role of the military; the dead made sure of that. Still, the questions that preoccupied him and many of the speakers that followed him into the national cemeteries were more elemental: What kind of nation should the United States become?

The impetus for building rostrums was the growing popularity of Memorial Day, first known as Decoration Day because people honored the Civil War dead by placing flowers on their graves. The custom of decorating graves began after the war, at federal and private cemeteries in the North and South. In 1868, General John A. Logan, who led the veterans of the Grand Army of the Republic, declared that May 30 should be the official day for honoring the Union dead. Although southerners established their own dates for Decoration Day (which varied from place to place), Logan's decree brought the occasion onto the national calendar, at least for northerners. It also established an official locus for the holiday: the national cemeteries.

But the cemeteries were not designed to accommodate large civic gatherings, so when men like Logan began giving Memorial Day speeches, the superintendents had to set up temporary rostrums. Faced with the surge in activity, the Quartermaster's Department (with Montgomery Meigs still in charge) decided to build permanent platforms. There was no construction budget for rostrums so they had to be creative with expense and design, while also responding to the needs of particular locations and the (political) requests to build at one cemetery instead of another.

Between 1873 and 1905, the department built forty-nine rostrums. Although the demand for speaking platforms declined in the 1910s and '20s, the quartermasters constructed more than forty rostrums during the 1930s and '40s with money from the Works Project Administration, the relief agency funded by the New Deal. The last rostrum was built in 1956, at Willamette National Cemetery, just south of Portland, Oregon.[4]

Not surprisingly, one of the first permanent rostrums was erected at Arlington in the spring of 1873. Designed by Meigs, the rectangular structure—really, an amphitheater—includes a built-in lectern with the words "E Pluribus Unum" inscribed on the front and a trellis that covers the entry paths on either side of the seating area. The Tomb of the Civil War Unknowns is one hundred feet away.

While most rostrums built in the nineteenth century were octagons—eight-sided concrete platforms, with nothing more than stairs, a railing, and sometimes a roof—the department also constructed rectangular rostrums at bigger cemeteries like Jefferson Barracks in St. Louis (1879) and Marietta, outside of Atlanta (1882). Like the one at Arlington, these rostrums are located in prominent spots, sometimes on axis with roads or flag stands and monuments, giving them a formal heft that the smaller rostrums lack. In the 1930s and '40s, when the Veterans Administration had the money to replace aging rostrums or construct new ones, they often built rectangular platforms in the neoclassical mode. So the brick octagonal rostrum at Cypress Hills, built in 1886 for $596, gave way to a bigger structure that cost almost $25,000.[5]

I could see as I walked through some cemeteries that the rostrums were an afterthought, an addition to the preexisting footprint and often a close fit. The rostrum at Lebanon National Cemetery in Lebanon, Kentucky, is an octagon that sits under a large oak tree, next to a row of headstones. When I shot toward the stairs one day in August, the headstones lined up on a tight diagonal, shadows dappling their faces and the concrete pad of the rostrum. Behind the rostrum is the tree trunk. Next to the tree is a service building. When people gathered to hear a Memorial Day speech—and the rostrum at Lebanon went up in 1932—they must have filled in around the graves.

The rostrum at San Antonio National Cemetery is likewise shaded by tree branches and flanked by headstones. When it was built in 1889, the octagonal structure, similar to the one at Lebanon, included a roof that was later removed. The rostrum is also steps from the informational markers explaining the cemetery's origins, an official acknowledgment that the cemetery—established in 1867—is now considered a historic site. The signs struck me as intrusive and a little ironic, since the placement of the signs, so close to the platform, makes it difficult to see how people once assembled here. When I photographed the rostrum, I managed to capture the entire scene. When I looked to the west, I saw downtown San Antonio outlined against the Texas sky.

The first Memorial Day, or Decoration Day, took place on May 1, 1865, at a racetrack in

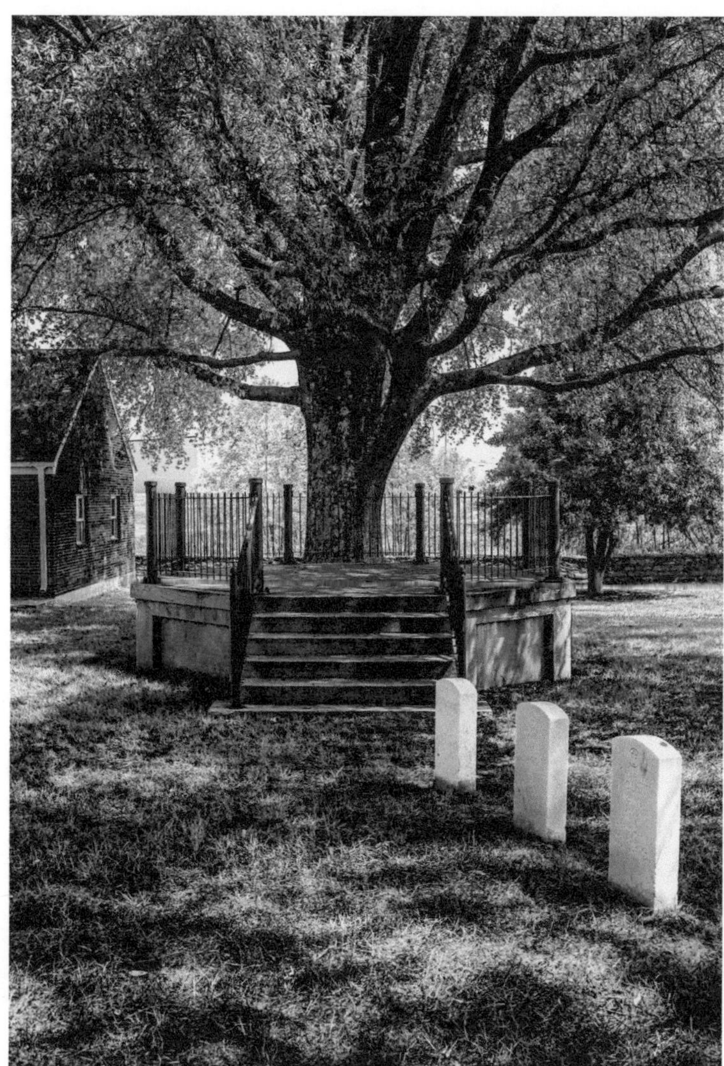

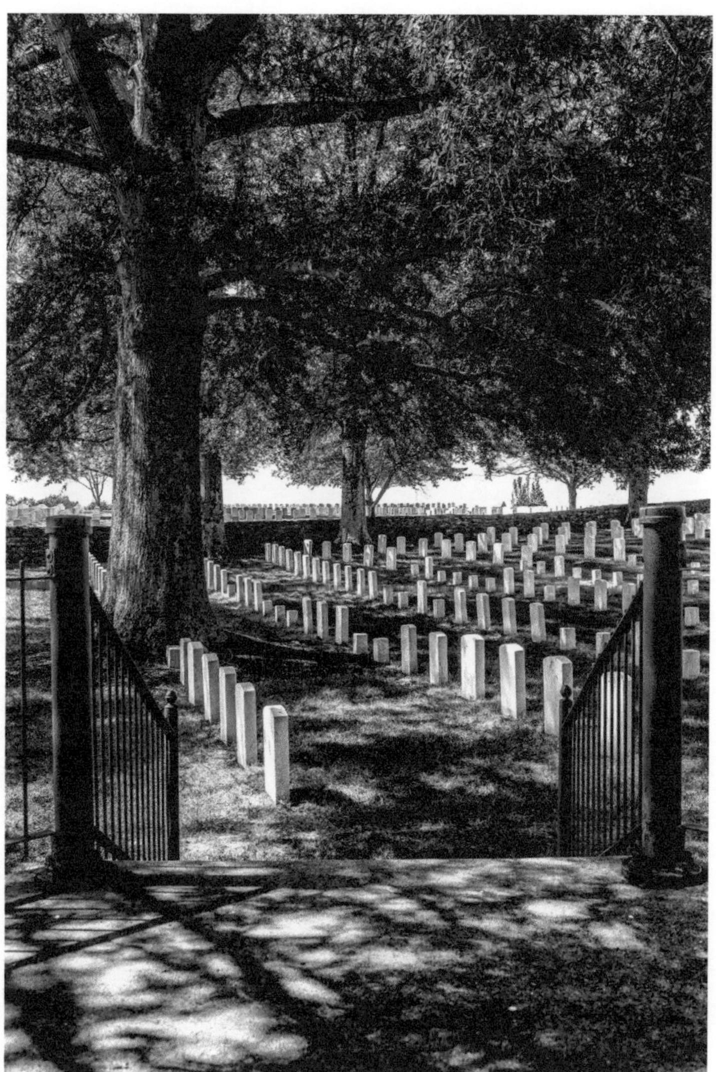

(*Left*) The rostrum at Lebanon National Cemetery (established in 1867), Lebanon, Kentucky, 2019.

(*Right*) Looking out from the rostrum at Lebanon National Cemetery, 2019.

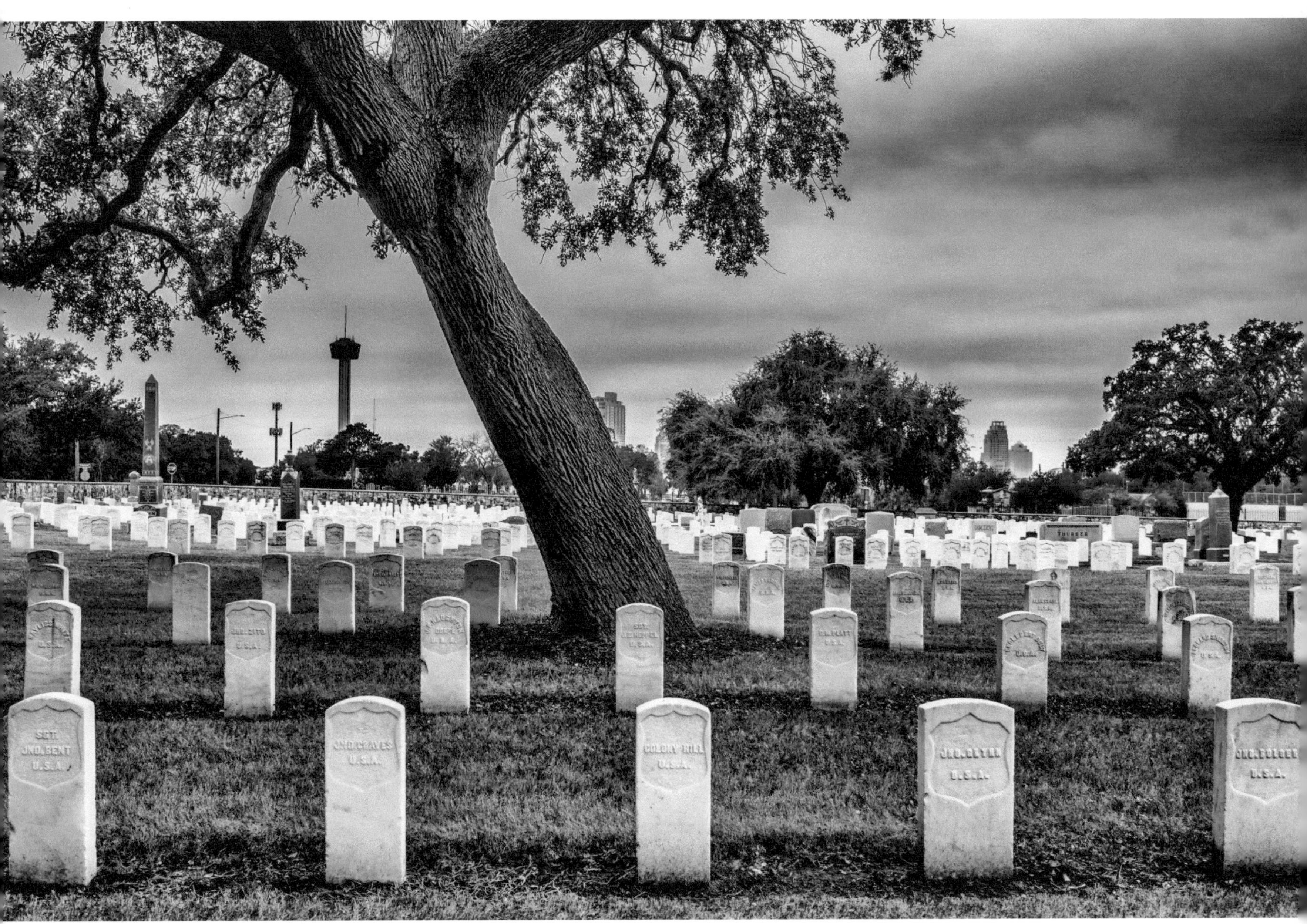

San Antonio National Cemetery (established in 1867), San Antonio, Texas, 2018.

Charleston, South Carolina, where the Confederates established a prison and then a graveyard. After the war, members of the city's Black churches improved the cemetery to honor Union soldiers who died in captivity—the "Martyrs of the Race Course." Ten thousand people, mostly African American, attended the dedication, which included musical performances, a prayer service, and speeches by Black civic leaders and Union officers. As "founded" by African Americans, Memorial Day was, in David Blight's words, a "ritual of remembrance and consecration."[6]

During the 1870s, similar events took place at national cemeteries elsewhere in the South as African Americans poured into Memorial Day events often organized by the Grand Army of the Republic. Like the energy that infused Charleston or the "sense of promise" that extended across Texas and much of the country after slavery was outlawed in that state—in Galveston on June 19, 1865 (Juneteenth)—the hope that animated these gatherings was aimed at a better future but also framed by years of darkness.[7] So it is hardly surprising that Black Americans came to cemeteries—where mortality meets a higher authority—looking for redemption.

Nashville's *Republican Banner* reported that, on May 30, 1871, hundreds of people took the train south from Louisville to attend the ceremonies at Nashville National Cemetery. The crowd, "composed almost entirely of negroes," walked down from the station "to a beautiful grove, on the eastern side of the Cemetery, to a stand decorated with flags and covered with a tarpaulin," where General William B. Stokes, a Unionist from Tennessee, saluted "our martyred President" for issuing the proclamation that "forever wiped from our national escutcheon the dark spot of slavery." Outside the cemetery gate, vendors sold food and drink, "giving the scene the appearance of a grand 4th of July celebration or jolly picnic."[8]

That same year, thousands of Black citizens also showed up at Richmond and Salisbury National Cemeteries to decorate the graves and celebrate the day. The atmosphere was jubilant, even raucous, and officials worried that the partisan Republican speeches had riled the crowds and undermined the cemeteries' solemn purpose. But Meigs was reluctant to curtail the gatherings, agreeing with colleagues that it was "best to put the grounds in order" and "not to attempt to limit free speech." The "observation of the day," he said, will "bring about a better feeling and in the end the graves will be reverenced on the true ground that they are occupied by men who died for their country."[9]

So, in the fluid and fraught postwar Republic, mourning became the generator of utopian possibilities, and the dead's silence (and sacrifice) enabled the living (Union men) to speak of the

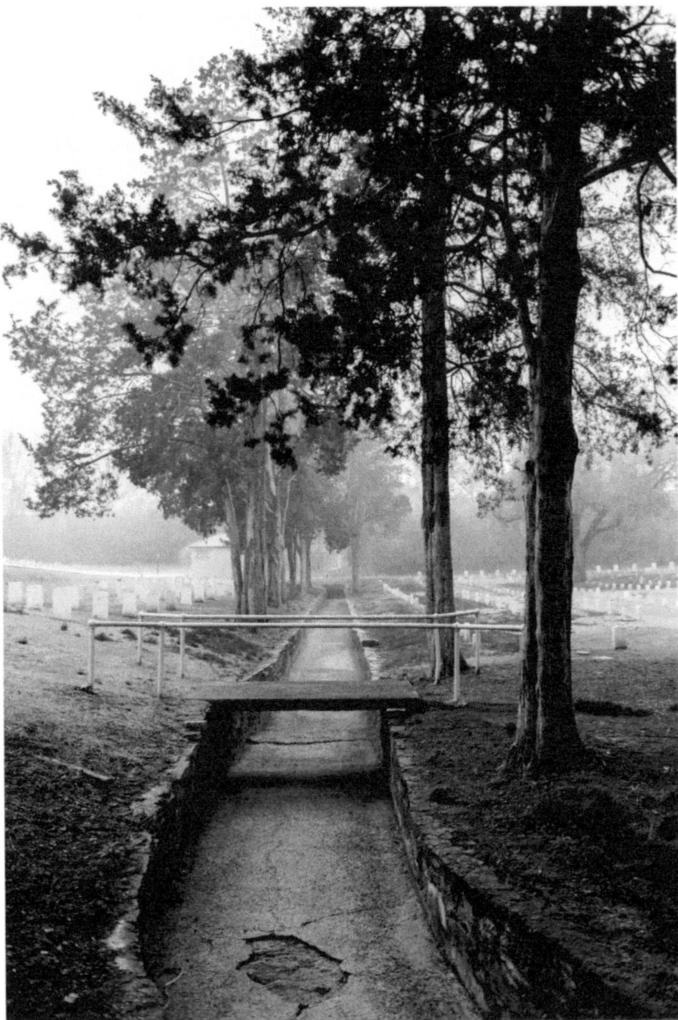

Nashville National Cemetery (established in 1867), Madison, Tennessee, 2018.

nation's future. The First Amendment was important to how men like Meigs understood the role of free speech, but even more important was the blood that leached out from the battlefield and into the cemeteries. The war's uncontestable reality was death, and now the purpose of all political rhetoric was to explain why so many men were gone and how the ground could be made true.

Cemeteries thus played a critical role in the battle for national identity, a battle because the

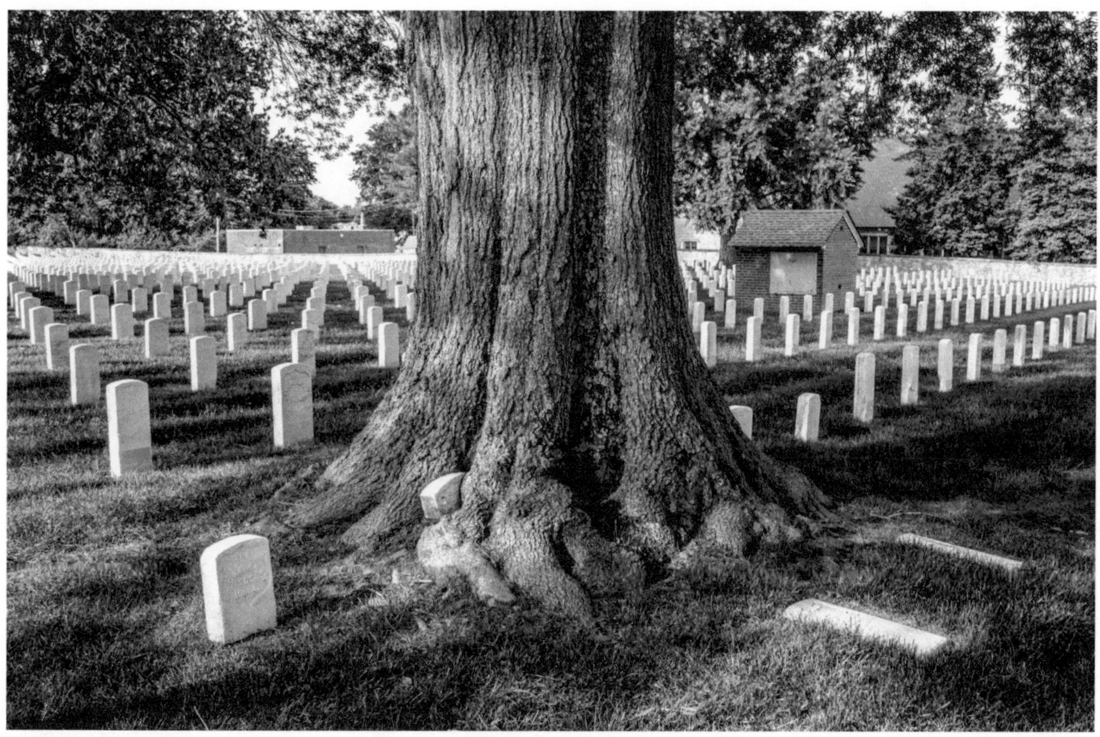

A large oak embraces a gravestone at Richmond National Cemetery (established in 1866), Richmond, Virginia, 2018.

future of the Republic was not yet clear and the official memory of the Civil War was unsettled. When I walk the grounds of the cemeteries, the signs of this battle are hard to see, but the antique rostrums, empty now, were once filled with the promise of change, especially for Black citizens. Historians are of mixed mind as to whether Memorial Day speakers during the late 1860s and '70s were more interested in addressing the future of the Union or the challenges of Emancipation.[10] Yet there is little doubt that the Republic was in transition and that the cemeteries were the backdrop for a national conversation, a space, I am tempted to say, for national dreaming.

Newspapers gave front-page coverage to these Memorial Day ceremonies. In 1875 the *Pittsburgh Daily Commercial* reported that at Cave Hill National Cemetery in Louisville, Secretary of Treasury Benjamin Bristow used his Memorial Day speech to affirm that "a great blight has been removed from the South by the abolition of slavery" and that the "immortal" principle that "all men are created equal" now "reaches forth to every man of whatever race or color." Meanwhile,

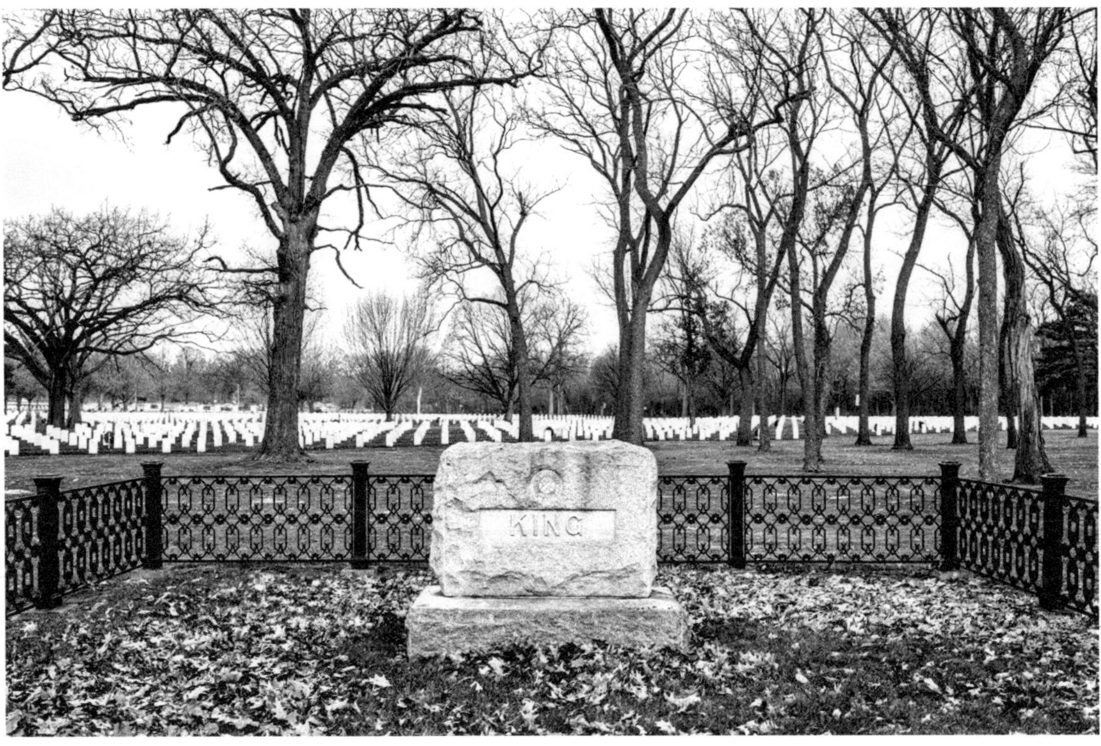

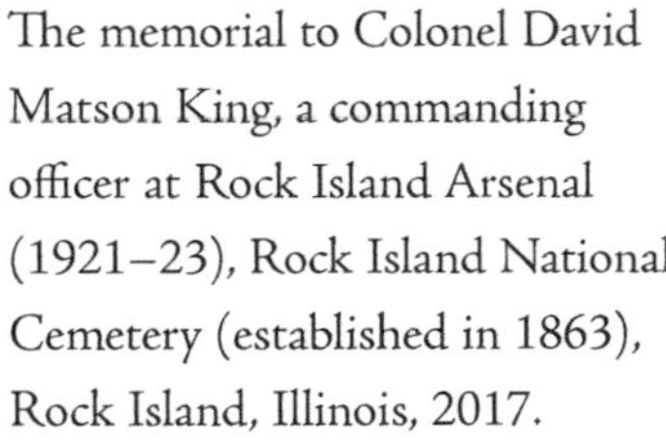
The memorial to Colonel David Matson King, a commanding officer at Rock Island Arsenal (1921–23), Rock Island National Cemetery (established in 1863), Rock Island, Illinois, 2017.

six thousand people gathered at the Rock Island National Cemetery in Illinois to hear Judge H. H. Benson of Davenport, Iowa, deliver a similar message, that Union soldiers fought for "love of freedom."[11]

Occasionally, Confederate veterans launched volleys from home territory. In 1869, at Battle Grove Cemetery in Cynthiana, Kentucky, William C. Breckinridge—who was a cousin of John C. Breckinridge and later served in the US House of Representatives—gave a Decoration Day speech blaming Northern aggression for the war, claiming that slavery had nothing to do with it, and arguing that the Union would never be restored unless the government also honored the Southern dead.[12] In Cynthiana, where the ground that Breckinridge defended appears undisturbed, the pointed headstones circling the Confederate monument are still in place, and the inscription on the monument says the names of the dead "shall never be forgot." Forty miles from Lexington, the history feels tenaciously local, and the sense of being lost in time is palpable.

The same could be said about some Union burial grounds, except that they were designed and maintained to reflect the nation as a whole.

Southerners often regarded the national cemeteries as territory seized by the victors over and against the loss of their sons and brothers. So in 1871, after the Memorial Day ceremonies at Fredericksburg National Cemetery (in Virginia), the local newspaper editor questioned why the community should decorate the graves of soldiers who destroyed much of the town during the war.[13]

By the late 1880s, the resentment seemed to subside as Union and Confederate veterans—white men—walked arm in arm at some Memorial Day celebrations, including the one held at Fredericksburg in 1884, which Black townspeople were barred from attending. During the early 1900s, the feeling of subjugation diminished further when the federal government began marking Confederate graves. This was not enough to satisfy southern heritage groups that wanted full control of the memorial process, while for African Americans, it was a startling reversal of the scenes at the first Decoration Day in Charleston. The promise of Reconstruction had vanished, and Jim Crow now ruled the South; literally, the ground had shifted.[14]

More than any public figure who ascended the rostrum on Memorial Day, Frederick Douglass recognized how difficult it would be for the nation to forge a shared memory around the war's most important outcome: emancipation.[15] Douglass resisted the idea that Northern and Southern soldiers should be honored equally for their courage, and in 1871, when he spoke at Arlington National Cemetery by the Tomb of the Civil War Unknowns, he urged listeners not to "forget the difference between the parties to that terrible, protracted, and bloody conflict" or that the war "made stumps of men" and "sent them on the journey of life armless, legless, maimed and mutilated" or that the "unknown heroes whose whitened bones" were in the tomb fought to preserve the Union and rid the country of "the hell-black system of human bondage."[16]

Douglass spoke of blood and soil, a rhetoric of violence and sacrifice sprung from the national cemeteries, words and images that Americans knew as the common language of the war. Implicitly, he reminded his audience—which included President Ulysses S. Grant—that the purpose of the war was to heal the nation, to piece together the dismembered body parts.

Like Meigs, Douglass was trying to forge new ground. Yet if the quartermaster general was mostly concerned with establishing the cemeteries as proper places for mourning, the once enslaved statesman was focused on bringing Africans Americans into civil society and creating a democratic culture that did not yet exist.

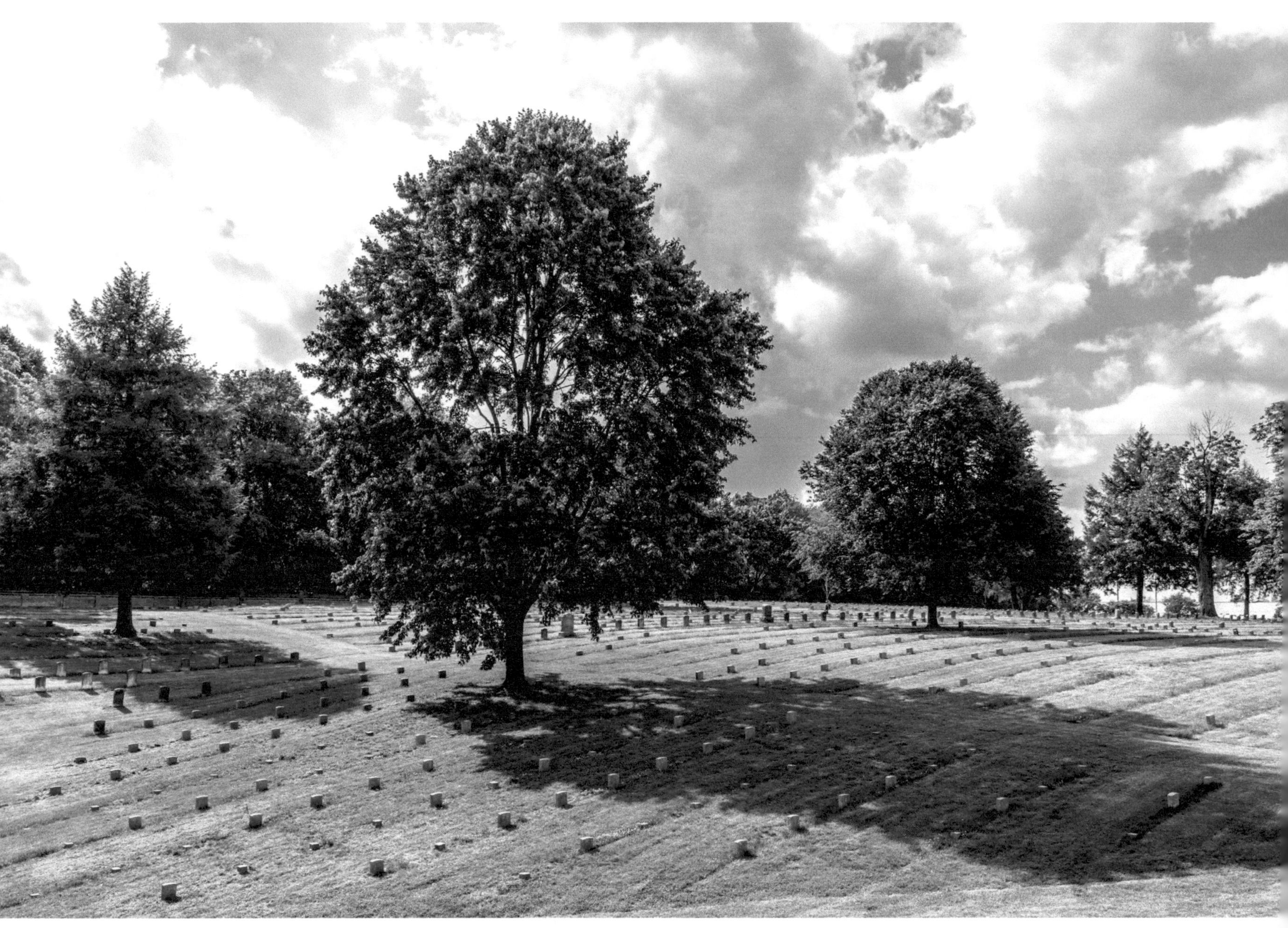

Fredericksburg National Cemetery (established in 1866), Fredericksburg, Virginia, 2018.

After his speech, Douglass headed down to the lower part of the cemetery—now Section 27—to honor the 1,500 Black Union soldiers buried there, all members of the US Colored Troops (USCT). The USCT graves were not included in the decoration ceremony he led, so he petitioned Secretary of War William Belknap to move them into the larger section of white Union soldiers buried by the tomb. Their remains stayed in place.[17]

More than 180,000 men served with the USCT, and when the war ended, the remains of thirty thousand Black combatants were exhumed from battlefield graves and reinterred in fifty-one national cemeteries and fifteen or so private burial grounds. Identified on headstones as "colored infantryman," "colored cavalrymen," or "USCT," they were buried in separate sections and segregated from the white soldiers.[18]

After the war, Black Americans continued to serve in separate units, the most famous being the Ninth and Tenth Cavalry, the "buffalo soldiers"—so named (legend has it) by Native Americans, who admired their bravery and associated them with the animals they hunted and revered—who fought in Plains wars during the 1870s, '80s, and '90s. The grim irony here, as historians have argued, is that Black men led by white officers helped to exterminate Native American tribes and advance the nation's imperial designs. The Ninth and Tenth Cavalry, along with the Twenty-Fourth and Twenty-Fifth Infantry—two other Black regiments that remained intact after the Civil War—were deactivated during the 1940s and 1950s.[19]

In 1947, a year before President Truman ordered the desegregation of the military, the War Department abolished the "caste system" in national cemeteries, announcing that "the policy of providing uniform burial facilities without distinction as to rank or race of deceased veterans will be effected progressively as new sections are laid out." This was an incremental approach to racial justice. Administrators did not exhume the remains of Black and white soldiers and shuffle the graves in order to achieve integration. In fact, they allowed existing sections to fill up under the old rules, as segregated—a practice that was not eradicated until the early 1960s—and then buried veterans without regard to race in the newer sections.[20] But the color line never really disappeared, at least not in the older cemeteries. For instance, at Alexandria National Cemetery in Pineville, Louisiana, where there are about two hundred USCT graves, the rows of headstones look like a single neighborhood. But when I moved closer and photographed the graves of two Colored Troopers and a Vietnam War veteran—whose race I later clarified through census records (he identified as white)—I could see the historical differences block by block.

The same pattern is visible at other national cemeteries that grew beyond their Civil War origins. So Beaufort National Cemetery, located on the coast of South Carolina and established in 1868 (a year after Alexandria), includes a combination of white and Black Union graves that are surrounded by newer plots. Beaufort is larger than Alexandria: forty-four acres as opposed to eight and more than twenty-five thousand interments in contrast to ten thousand. It also has more Civil War dead: 9,003 Union casualties, including the remains of 1,745 USCT, while at Alexandria there are 1,270 Union graves, of which 203 are UCST.[21]

I visited Beaufort in the summer of 2018 as part of a weekend trip that took me from Atlanta to the Atlantic Coast, and then up North Carolina, where I flew home from Charlotte. My route included stops at Marietta and Georgia National Cemeteries, then Beaufort, and finally Salisbury. When I arrived at Beaufort at dawn on Sunday, I looked out at row upon row of headstones, framed by the moss hanging down from the live oaks and streaked with dirt since it had rained hard the night before. The grass was patchy—perhaps because of the extensive tree covering—and the headstones appeared stuck in mud, while the soft, scattered light gave the scene a spectral quality.

One of the first pictures I took focused on a group of USCT headstones in Section 30, flanked, as at Alexandria, by more recent markers, with the cemetery wall in the distance almost hiding the sign for a marine equipment shop. The image, I thought, captured both the historical details and the eerie atmosphere. Still, as I walked away, I considered the picturesque qualities that inspired my shot and understood why the Beaufort Chamber of Commerce listed the cemetery on its website as one of the top attractions in the area. This was in contrast to the grittier, diminished grandeur of Alexandria at Pineville, which is nothing like a seaside, resort town.

I worked my way toward the back of the cemetery, the sections radiating out from the center like slices in a pie, a layout that is easier to see on a map and felt less formal than the circles of headstones that weave in and out of the hills at Marietta, which I visited the day before. The superintendent's lodge sits by the front gate, but there is no rostrum—the octagonal podium built in 1890 was demolished in 1966—and, as I passed through a break in the red brick wall, I saw how the cemetery was expanded in 2004 to add more plots, columbaria, a committal shelter, restrooms, a grave locator, and a service road that occupies the space in between. It was still early, and the sprinkler system suddenly turned on, drenching the new sections but not the old.

Like other Civil War–era cemeteries that have been recently updated, Beaufort tells the history

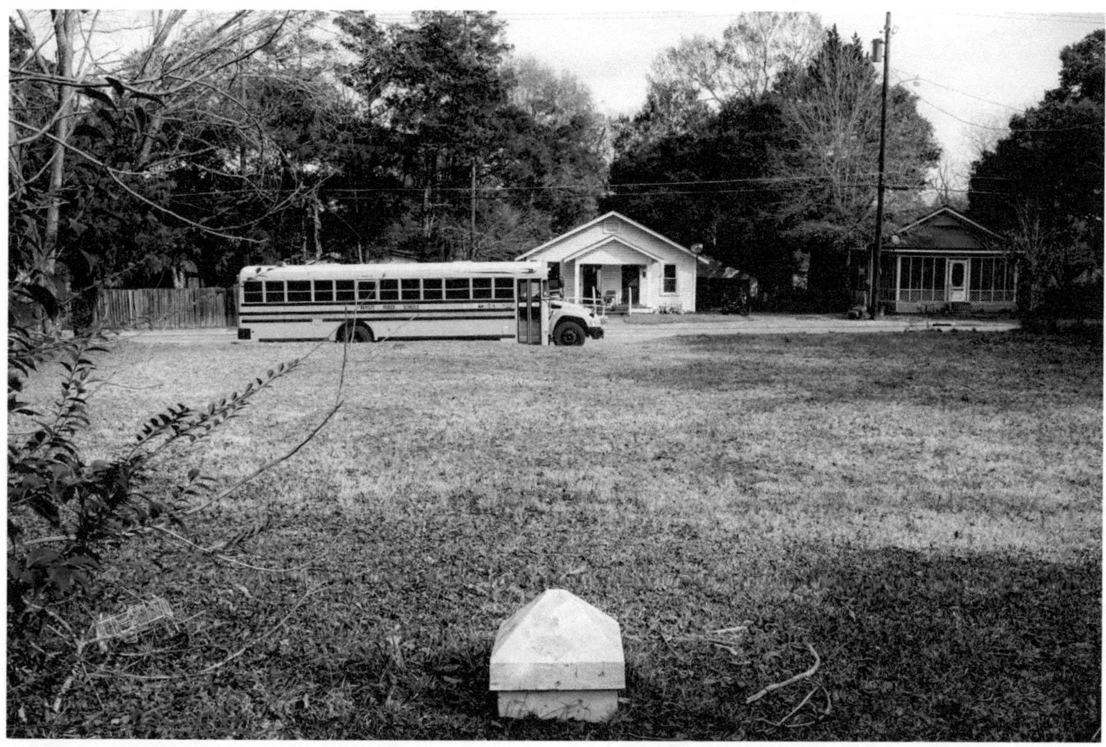

A view of the neighborhood that surrounds Alexandria National Cemetery (established in 1867), Pineville, Louisiana, 2018.

of the modern United States in a streamlined, inclusive fashion. Pieces of the past are accessible on the ground; visitors can pause at specific headstones and markers to focus on individual lives and stories. But as a whole, the landscape pulls these details into a larger narrative. Memory is brought to scale, and differences are assimilated.

In my journey across the cemetery system, I saw a similar story. The landscape reflects in memory the contradictions of American history. Draw back and behold a nation's progress, its ideals uplifted in stone marking the necessary sacrifice. Find a perspective closer in, a middling view, and locate its conflicts, the Confederate dead in one section and the USCT dead in another. I cannot resolve these differences and do not want to. They are irremediable. I took pictures of the markers and the spaces in between, and I was torn between my desire to see and understand these places and my desire to erase all monuments to the Lost Cause. The Confederate dead, I think, can stay.

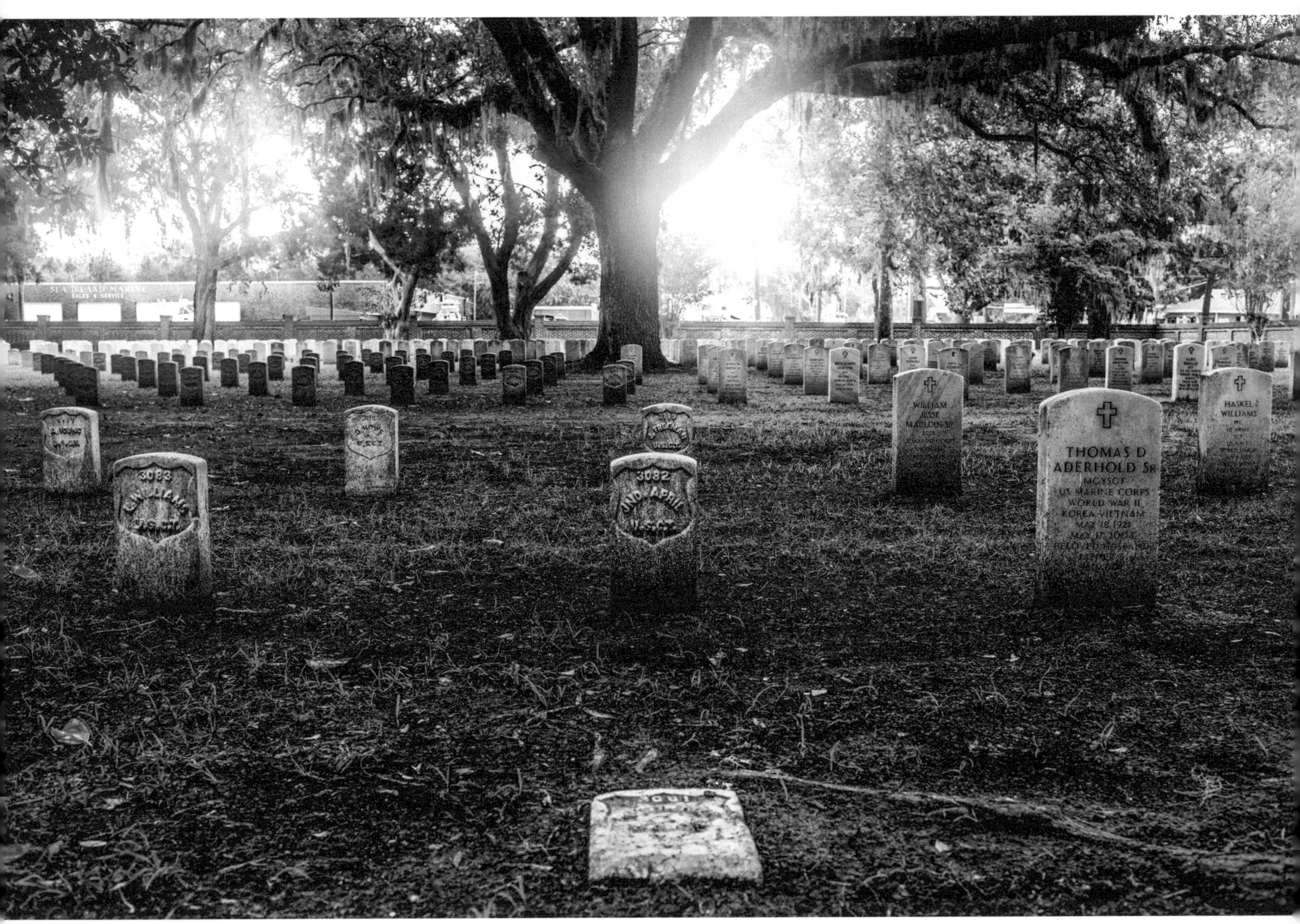

Beaufort National Cemetery (established in 1863), Beaufort, South Carolina, 2018.

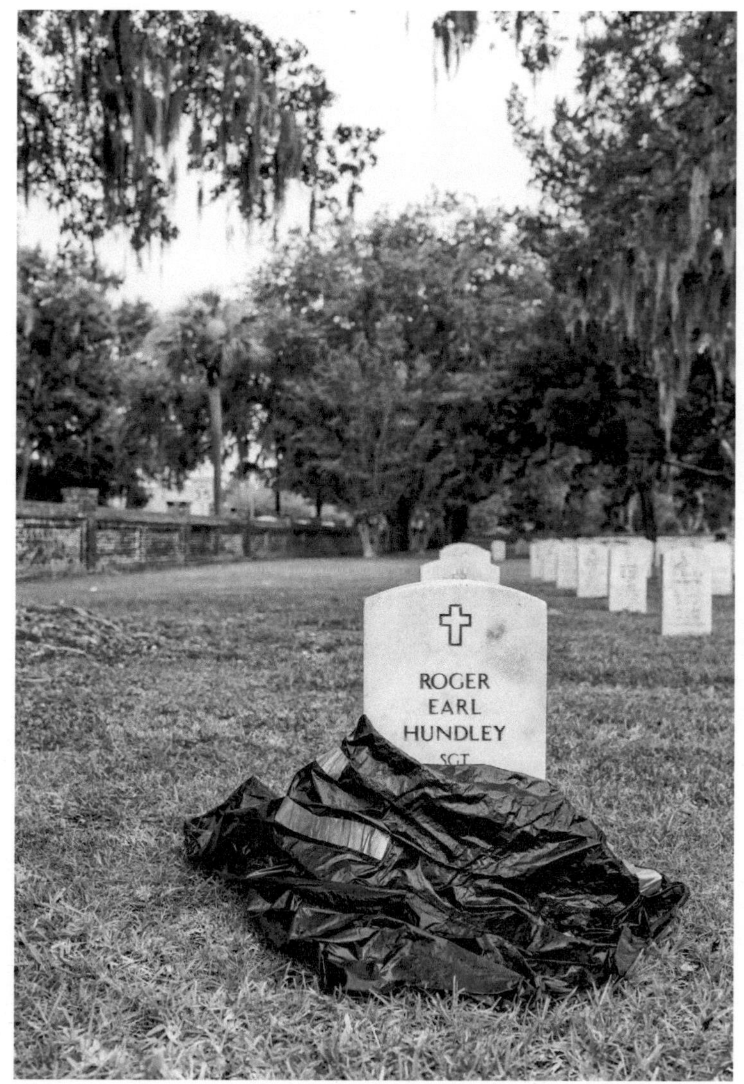

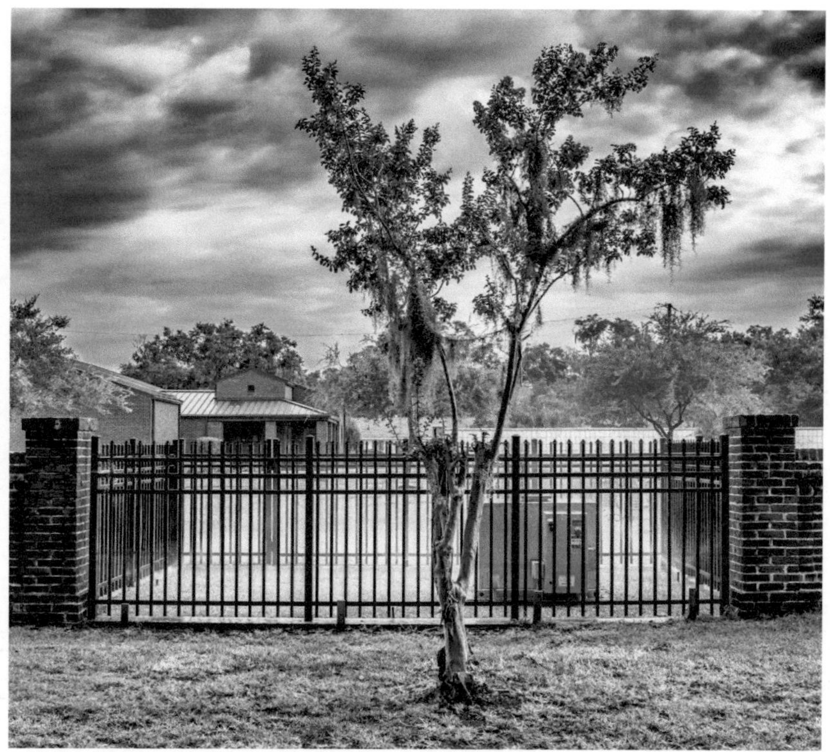

(*Left*) A wind-blown trash bag alights on a headstone at Beaufort National Cemetery, 2018.

(*Above*) Utilities quartered at Beaufort National Cemetery, 2018.

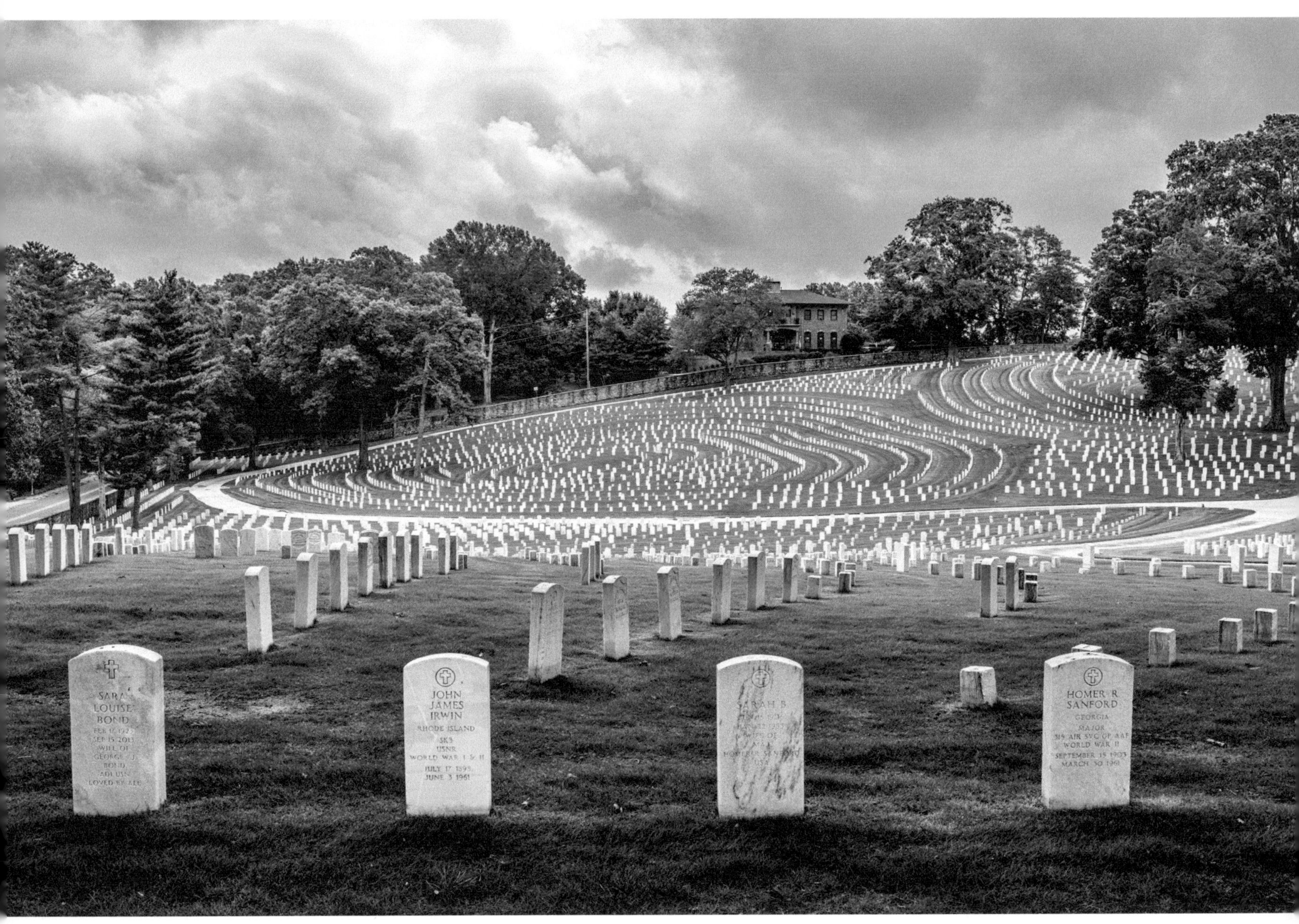

Marietta National Cemetery (established in 1866), Marietta, Georgia, 2018.

The national cemeteries are now more inclusive, more democratic than they were when Douglass spoke at Arlington. As built landscapes, they reflect the iterative course of progress, one generation at a time, the earth moved, the rhetoric (words and stone) revised and redesigned, to meet the evolving interpretation of American ideals. Maybe this explanation is too facile, too forgiving of the failures along the way. Or maybe it is possible to hold two conflicting views in balance. When I looked at the plots of "colored" infantrymen at Lexington or the signs at Memphis marking the Fort Pillow massacre, I was reminded of what journalist Nikole Hannah-Jones has said about the arc of racial justice: that Black Americans, even while enduring centuries of violent oppression, have fought harder for the idea of the nation than any other group of Americans.[22]

That trauma is at the heart of the National Memorial for Peace and Justice in Montgomery, Alabama, which I visited on a Sunday morning in December 2019, after stopping at Alabama National Cemetery and before driving to Fort Mitchell National Cemetery. On the route I mapped from Atlanta, Montgomery sat between the two cemeteries, and I mention the date because it places my visit in context. By the time I got to Montgomery, I had been to 130 or more cemeteries and seen millions of graves. But I did not feel like I could proceed without seeing how the memorial honors the thousands of Black Americans whose lynchings were a brutal rejection of the democratic vision the national cemeteries are meant to symbolize.

So I went to Montgomery. Montgomery, where Rosa Parks helped to spark the Civil Rights Movement. Montgomery, the state capital and also the first capital of the Confederacy. Montgomery, a thriving port on the Alabama River during the early nineteenth century and a busy slave market. The Equal Justice Initiative has worked to highlight the region's history of racism, both at its Legacy Museum and in public markers. The lodestar of its effort is the National Memorial, which opened in 2018 to give names and places to the known 4,400 victims murdered between 1877 and 1957, men and women lynched "at the hands of persons unknown," without public records or memorials to mark their deaths, which placed their life histories in kind of epistemological, spiritual limbo.[23] The installations change that: rectangular, steel boxes that hang from rafters like coffins with the names of victims, listed by county and state, an arrangement that is then duplicated, with the boxes lying flat like coffins, elsewhere in the park.

While this presentation of names, dates, and places has drawn comparisons to the Vietnam Veterans Memorial in Washington, DC, another antecedent is surely the national cemetery system, specifically the Civil War cemeteries, where the sacrifices made in the name of democracy appear in similar geometric forms. But the National Memorial also offers a rebuke to the Republic and seeks to find a new way forward—on true ground. That ground is actually quite old, as I learned when I crossed the street from the memorial to the Equal Justice Initiative Center and saw the Community Remembrance Project: a wall display of glass jars containing soil from the places where people were lynched, not quite remains and not exactly the trace elements of sacrifice that Douglass described.

Grief is blind to race and background, and at national cemeteries sorrow is in principle leavened by a sense of pride that death came in the service to country. At the National Memorial, as Black a space as any I have seen, the landscape has different intentions. Blackness is entwined here with what theologian James H. Cone calls "the lynching tree," a memory of violence and loss that has been passed down from one generation of African Americans to the next, always with the hope of redemption. That memory is marked here for all to see, so we can know their names, say their names, and bear witness to the truth.[24]

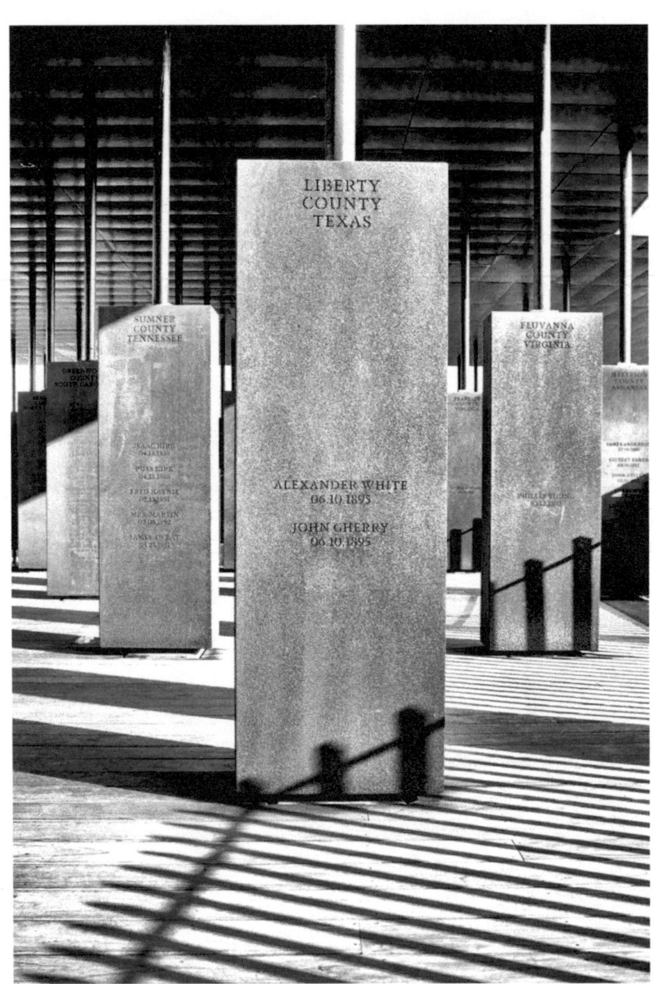

The National Memorial for Peace and Justice, Montgomery, Alabama (opened in 2018), 2019.

I moved on, persuaded as I walked and saw that the national cemeteries are compelling testimonies to the power of American ideals in all their imperfection. I say this despite and also because of their status as official channels of memory, standing now and then at the ragged edge of crumbling walls and on deserted speaking platforms, trying to get a better picture of my country's unfinished business.

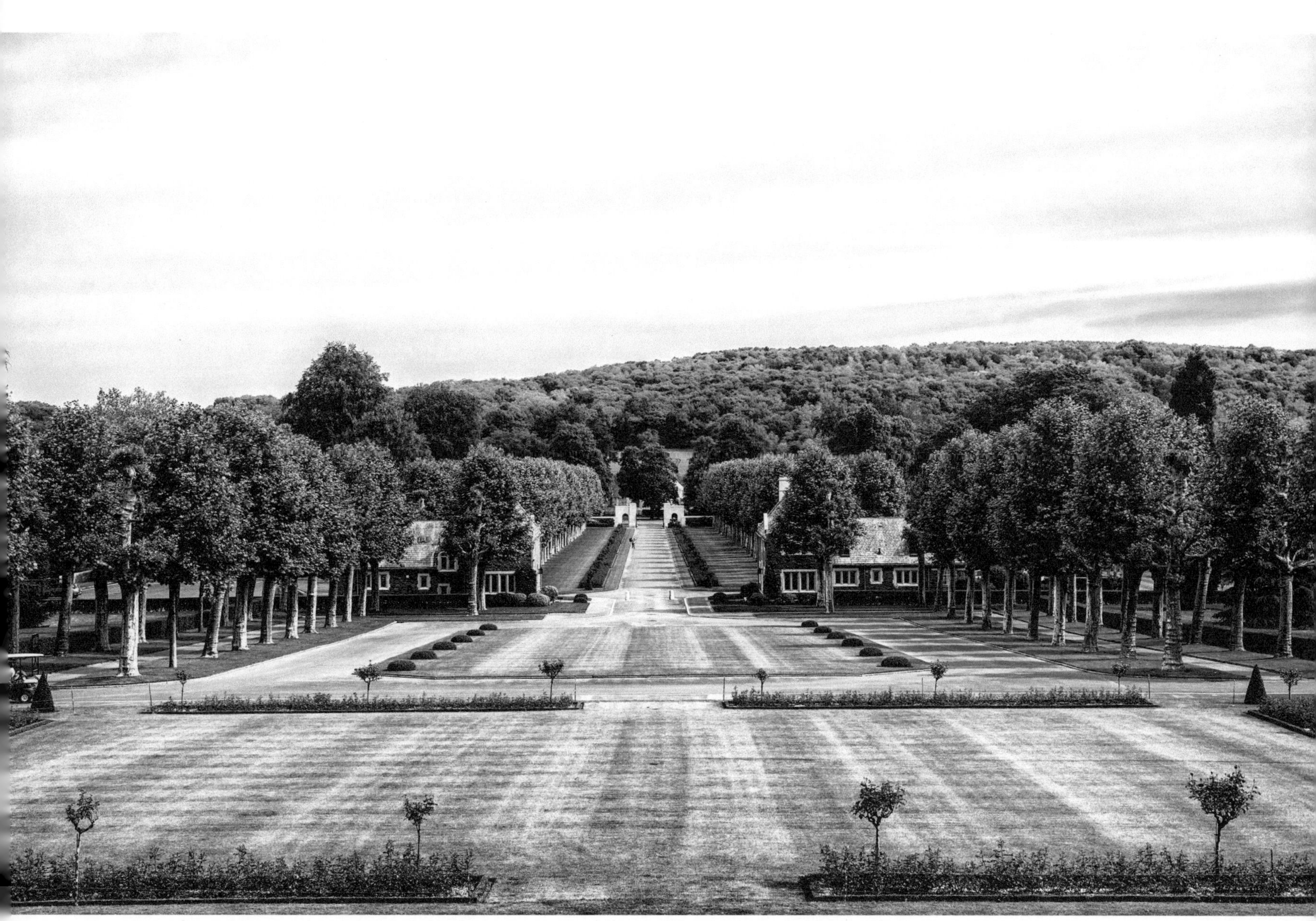

Aisne-Marne American Cemetery and Memorial (established in 1918; dedicated in 1937), near Belleau, France, 2016.

7

Abroad

I did not realize I was going to Europe to be Americanized when, in February 2017, I flew from Montreal to Paris, rented a car, headed northeast to Waregem (Belgium), backtracked to Lille (France), and then returned to Paris and went home. Over the course of three days, I visited Flanders Field American Cemetery, Somme American Cemetery, and Suresnes American Cemetery, three of eight sites that the United States established after World War I to inter solders who died while serving with the American Expeditionary Forces. In 2015, I saw the Meuse-Argonne American Cemetery; the following summer I visited Aisne-Marne American Cemetery, Oise-Aisne American Cemetery, and St. Mihiel American Cemetery, as well as several monuments in the area.

My itinerary evolved as I revised it on Google Maps, guided by previous visits and research I had done on the American Battle Monuments Commission, the government agency responsible for American military cemeteries abroad. The project I imagined after that first visit to Meuse-Argonne had morphed into a hybrid study of American memorial landscapes. To explain why I was going to France for the weekend to take pictures of places I could otherwise explore in the archives, I told people that I had to be on the ground to do the work. That was true, though I did not plan to visit the Brookwood American Cemetery (in England) or the Lafayette Escadrille American Memorial Cemetery (in France). I already knew these places were outliers in the commission's effort to mark the ground where American soldiers fell.

I also wanted to visit the two major British memorials in the area—Menin Gate in Ypres, Belgium, and the Thiepval Memorial to the Missing of the Somme in France—as well as some British cemeteries. Across the villages and farmlands that comprised the Western front, the Great

War is still remarkably present, and I wanted to see—and feel—how the British and European allies memorialized the dead. "By 1934, in the *département* of Somme alone," Geoff Dyer reports in his 1994 travelogue, *The Missing of the Somme*, "150,000 British and Commonwealth dead had been buried in 242 cemeteries. In total 918 were built on the Western Front with 580,000 named and 180,000 unidentified graves."[1] These numbers are hard to picture, and they say nothing of the French memorials, cemeteries, and roadside shrines, never mind German graveyards.

The point of any tally of the Great War's death toll is to dwarf the imagination because that is what the war did. Almost 3 million German and Austrians died, 1.7 million Russians, 1.35 million Frenchmen, more than 900,000 men from the British Empire, 650,000 Italians, and 116,000 Americans. And these numbers do not include civilian casualties. In the words of historian Jay Winter, the war "democratized death," killing masses of ordinary men, not just professional soldiers, whose bodies disappeared into the war-torn earth. Without remains or locations to hold funeral rites, the war also challenged how people mourned the dead. On November 11, 1919—Britain's first Remembrance Day—when thousands of citizens gathered around the Cenotaph in London's Whitehall district for two minutes of silence, nobody spoke, and the memorial that architect Edwin Lutyens designed for the occasion, the Cenotaph (or empty tomb), was free of rhetoric. Apart from the inscription on the side of the plinth—"The Glorious Dead"—there was nothing left to fill the vacuum.[2]

Except names. When Lutyens later designed the Thiepval Memorial, an enormous monument of interlocking towers, he made space on the walls for the names of more than seventy-two thousand British and South African soldiers who never returned from the Battles of the Somme (1915–18). Lists of names cover other memorials the Imperial War Graves Commission built after the war, with names also designating the headstones in Commonwealth cemeteries. Names helped fill the void and provided a focus for mourning; the walls and headstones gave people something to touch.

Before reviewing the scholarship on the Great War and memory, I knew little about Lutyens. I knew that Thiepval had influenced Maya Lin's design of the Vietnam Veterans Memorial on the National Mall in Washington, DC. But I was unfamiliar with Lutyens's role as the national architect of grief and how his efforts, like those of Montgomery Meigs, created the blueprint for memorializing the military dead. Like Meigs, though not to the same extent, he understood the obliterating effects of modern warfare. When he visited the Western front in 1917, he was

The War Stone at Thiepval Memorial to the Missing of the Somme (unveiled in 1932), Thiepval, France, 2017.

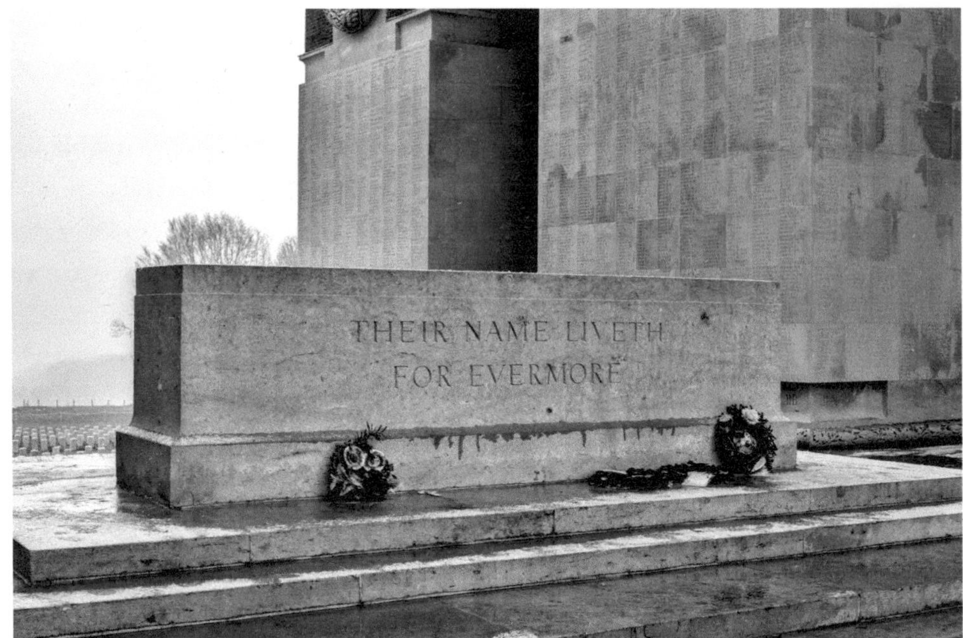

Vietnam Veterans Memorial (dedicated in 1993) and Washington Monument (dedicated in 1885), Washington, DC, 2016.

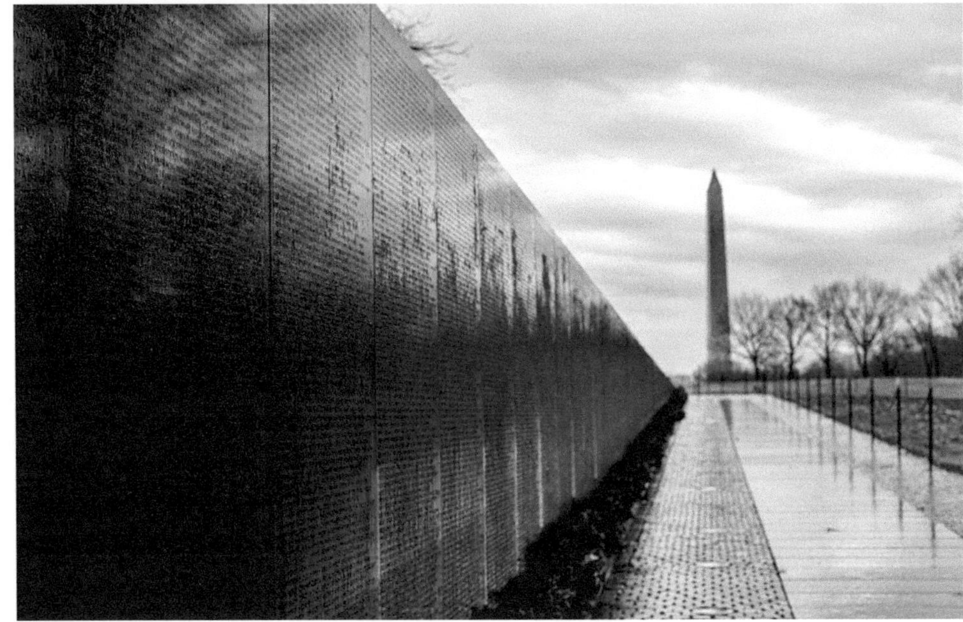

transfixed by the "ribbon of isolated graves like a milky way across miles of country where men were tucked in where they fell." Amid so much death, any conventional effort to memorialize the war's impact would seem weak and temporary. The "only monument," he wrote his wife, "can be one where the endeavor is sincere to make such monument permanent—a solid ball of Bronze!"[3]

Like the Cenotaph, the bronze ball is a stripped-down, classical form, a fundamental signifier of human presence. Lutyens was skeptical of ornamentation, and he resisted the use of traditional religious symbols in Commonwealth cemeteries. When the decision was made to include a rugged Christian cross in the cemeteries, the architects agreed that it would stand on axis with another one of Lutyens's innovations, the War Stone, a large, heavy altar, with an inscription on the side from Ecclesiastes (suggested by Rudyard Kipling, who lost a son in the war) that reads "Their Name Liveth For Evermore."[4] This was the next iteration of the bronze ball—the Cenotaph, flipped on its side.

Learning about Lutyens was a revelation. For as long as I had known anything about World War I, I identified the postwar era with a turning away from civilized values or disillusionment translated to iconoclastic creativity, as in T. S. Eliot's ironically constructive line from *The Waste Land* (1922): "I can connect nothing with nothing." But historians of British and European memorial culture have argued that the war did not prompt a significant break from the past, that even as modernists upended conventional modes of representation, most people relied on established (religious) symbols and narratives to express their emotional distress, especially when it came to honoring the dead. "Traditional modes of seeing the war," Winter explains, "while at times less challenging intellectually or philosophically, provided a way of remembering which enabled the bereaved to live with their losses, and perhaps to leave them behind."[5]

Seen here, Lutyens is a mediating force, a link between older expressive forms and the minimalist design that emerged in the modernist era. His memorial architecture was a fitting complement to silence and the failure of language, and I see how it resonates with the Vietnam Veterans Memorial, another kind of cenotaph that eschews conventional rhetoric.

But if Lin reached back to Lutyens for inspiration, the architects who designed the American World War I cemeteries and monuments in France worked within the classical tradition, creating Old World landscapes that look like extensions of the National Mall in Washington. DC. In his book about Thiepval, British architectural critic Gavin Stamp says (with a touch of chauvinism) that the American memorials establish "a ratio between the volume of masonry and the number of casualties far in excess of those of other nations," making them "monumental but rather pedantic."[6] Or maybe imperialistic.

I did not have to return to France in the winter of 2017 to know that the American Battle Monuments Commission erected the memorials as a show of American strength on the world stage. Yet reading about the memorials and seeing them are different things, and I was optimistic that my two-front approach, of photography and archival research, was leading me toward a revised understanding of these landscapes. For example, I knew that the commission went to great lengths to document the operations of the American Expeditionary Forces and then map some of that history—literally to inscribe it—on the cemeteries and monuments it built in France. The British and French did not mark the dead in this way, nor had Meigs and his colleagues.

I want to underscore the fluidity of this view because as I now try to summarize, punctuate, and draw connections, I am writing from a perspective that did not coalesce until I visited dozens of national cemeteries. In hindsight, I am able to view the American memorials in France in a broader context. I see that the commission wanted to enhance the commemorative practices the War Department used after the Civil War, and I see that Britain, which had greater reason to establish memorials in France and Belgium, avoided expressions of nationalism and martial power. The differences are striking.

It would be naive to think anyone could drive around northeastern France for a few days or wander into the Douaumont Ossuary in Verdun and arrive at a comprehensive understanding of how these national memorial practices differ from one another. That said, it is surprising there is not more encouragement for this sort of comparison. This may be because, as Stamp's comments suggest, the Great War remains a cataclysmic event that brooked no comparison, especially with the United States. Similarly, Dyer says that the British effort to inter and honor the dead was "without precedent," though he might have rephrased this point had he reflected on Edward Whitman's report on the Department of the Cumberland.[7] This sense of separateness is likewise reflected in the scholarly community, where there is little overlap between those who study the Civil War and memory and those who work on the Great War and memory.

Nonetheless, the British war memorials, strewn now with poppies every November 11, and the national cemeteries, newly clad in American flags on Memorial Day, illuminate a shared culture of remembrance, of necronominalism, to borrow Thomas Laqueur's apt phrase, that positioned the government as the arbiter of personal memory and identity. The lists of names on memorial walls accomplish what the grave locator at the national cemeteries does for American family members and friends, which is to identify a projection point—a place of rest, really—for the swirl of emotions that people bring to these places.

Speaking of his own internal navigations, Dyer explains that he began his pilgrimage to learn more about his grandfather, a man who "could have been anyone's grandfather" and who fought in the Great War—and survived—but whose individual qualities were overshadowed by his membership in the "1914 generation."[8] He speculates that Britain's decision to honor the dead in serial fashion, one name after another, all in the name of sacrifice, actually had the effect of erasing their memory. But he found that touring the Somme helped him see his grandfather more clearly.

One consequence of modern warfare is that familial and national genealogies are now more likely to converge and shape people's understanding of the past. I remember once when I was visiting my eighty-year-old grandmother in West Hartford, Connecticut, that I glanced at a document sitting on her desk in the den. It was a genealogy, and, I figured, fair game for further examination since it was my history too. I leaned in and read that when her "Granpappy" went off to fight in the Civil War he took his "manservant" with him. My grandmother grew up in Texas and Louisiana and "her people" came from Georgia and Mississippi, but she never mentioned this piece of history. When I walked back into the kitchen and said something like "I never knew someone in our family owned slaves," she responded, "Well, lots of people did back then." Irritated with my snooping, she let me know our conversation was over.

My grandmother left the South at the age of nineteen when she married my grandfather—a recently widowed flour salesman from Minneapolis—and never returned. She rarely talked about her childhood, and I did not see that genealogy again (which her sister had drafted) until after she died at the age of ninety-five. When I looked at the document more carefully, I discovered that two of my Confederate relatives were imprisoned at Johnson's Island in Ohio and on the Dry Tortugas off the Florida Keys. They apparently survived the war, but I do not know where their graves are or whether they were buried beneath a Southern Cross.

If this was a different project, I might claim these details in a story about my grandmother's secret past or a history of competing family legacies, since my grandfather, the flour salesman, grew up in western Pennsylvania and came from a family of French-German descent and may have had relatives who fought for the North. He also served in the army for a few months during World War I but did not go overseas. Or I might have engaged these antecedents through an

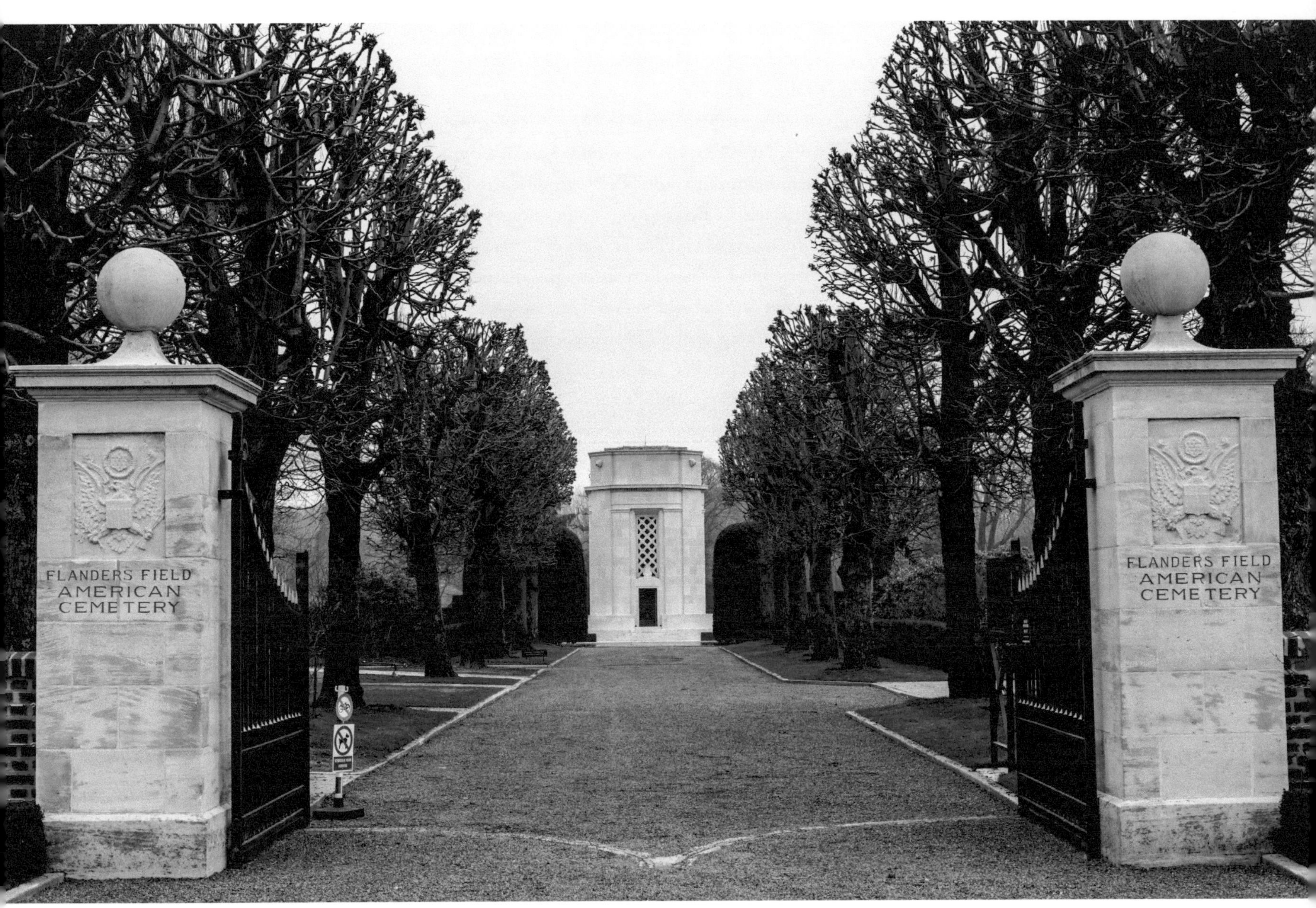

The entrance to Flanders Field American Cemetery (established in 1918; dedicated in 1937) leads to the chapel, Waregem, Belgium, 2017.

analysis of how the modern state, beginning in the 1860s, developed an infrastructure for tracking the personal histories of its citizenry, through census data, birth, death and marriage certificates, military records, or more recently, DNA profiles.

Instead, I was driving on the A1 toward Flanders Field American Cemetery, where I spent two hours taking pictures and then headed east to Ypres to see Menin Gate, before rounding out the day at a hotel I booked in Lille. I did not sleep much on the flight from Montreal, so I pulled into a roadside oasis outside of Kortrijk to get a coffee and pastry. It was late in the morning, and the cafeteria was empty, the commuting crowd having long since left. I had crossed into Belgium without knowing it and was fifteen minutes from the cemetery.

The cemetery is not actually in or near a field but takes its name from the lowland plains that extend through northeastern France and Belgium, where much of the Great War was fought and poppies bloom in the spring, symbolizing the regenerative cycle of death, life, and memory, which the Canadian John McCrae illuminated in his 1915 poem, "In Flanders Field." West and East Flanders are also provinces of Belgium—Waregem is in West Flanders—the place-names framing the cemetery, a walled enclave of 368 graves and six acres situated between two residential streets that come to a point about seventy yards in front of the entrance, forming a wedge-shaped, cobblestone apron that serves as a parking lot.

When I arrived, I took a picture of the front gate, shooting down the road that leads into the cemetery, the gravel way—like an *allée*—lined with cropped trees and terminating at a marble white chapel, with the words "Greet Them Ever With Grateful Hearts" engraved in the pediment, punctuated from above by carvings of lion heads on either side. I walked toward the chapel with the superintendent's lodge on my left and saw four paths extending out from the building to the corners of the cemetery and the wall that encloses the grounds, mirroring the privacy hedges that stand in front of the homes in the neighborhood. Inside the chapel, there is a small altar with flags on either side, representing the United States and its allies. On the rear external wall is an inscription explaining that the chapel was built in memory of the American soldiers who died in Belgium and whose graves "are the permanent and visible symbol of the heroic devotion with which they gave their lives to the common cause of humanity." Below is a bas-relief figure of woman in a robe writing on a tablet, an echo of ancient Greece.

The graves, identified by marble crosses and the occasional Star of David, underscore the ecclesiastical character of the place. I use that word, rather than "religious" or "Christian," because

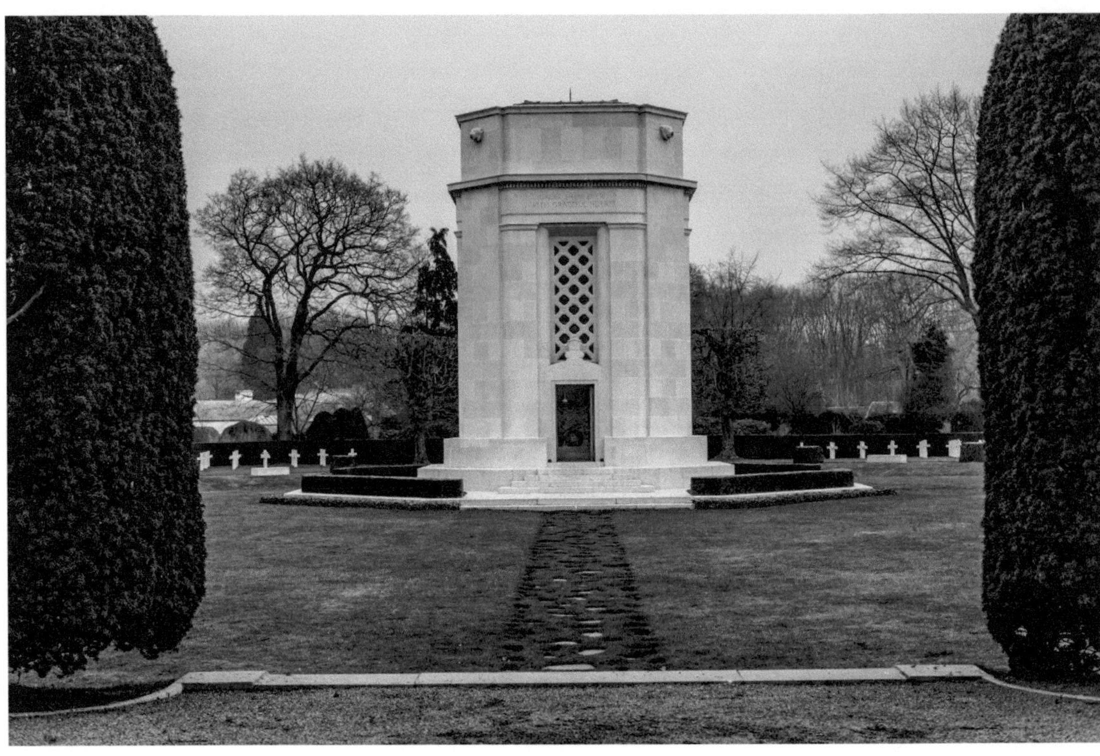

The chapel at Flanders Field American Cemetery, 2017.

of the deliberate effort to elevate the dead to a higher, more fully articulated order of remembrance, nationalism now blessed by God and undergirded by the Western humanistic tradition. Even the headstones marking the Unknown are more elaborate—marble crosses with the words "Here Rests in Honored Glory An American Soldier Known But To God."

Here, I want to stress how this landscape differs from both the British memorials and the dozens of national cemeteries I have visited, particularly the Civil War graveyards, some of which appear homespun by comparison. I also want to suggest (because "identify" or "define" would be too strong a term) how these differences match up with my response to these landscapes, that is, with consciousness, that hard-to-define, ever-streaming blend of thought and feeling. This last objective may be more easily named than achieved, or perhaps best approached through photography, but it should be part of the conversation.

Toward the back of the cemetery, where the headstones give way to stands of trees and rhododendrons and manicured lawn, I felt like I was standing in a private park or garden. Though it was February and the growing season was over, a small landscaping crew had arrived to rake and mow, and they brought a hydraulic lift to trim the trees. Meanwhile, the superintendent's lodge, completed in 1924, looked like it had just been renovated; a sleek new addition with lots of metal and glass extends from the rear. Flanders Field is really not an example of historical preservation, but the dead rest here in perpetuity without fear of disinterment, and the superintendent does not have to worry about finding room for additional graves, as many of his counterparts in the United States do.

Founded in 1923 by an act of the US Congress, the American Battle Monuments Commission set the aesthetic standards for all the cemeteries and monuments that the United States created on foreign soil following World War I. Flanders Field is one of twenty-six cemeteries that the commission built and now oversees, each laid out in the classical mode with religious grave makers and chapels. An independent agency that reports to the president, the commission was first led by General John J. Pershing, the former commander of the American Expeditionary Forces, and was staffed almost entirely by army officers. The military staff managed the construction of the memorials, working closely with the architects, who were selected by a governing board with input from the US Fine Arts Commission, which oversees the design of federal buildings in Washington, DC.

This high-minded alliance was relatively short-lived. After establishing cemeteries in Europe, Africa, and Asia for soldiers who perished during World Wars I and II, the government backed away from the tradition of interring the military dead abroad. The remains of military personnel who died fighting in distant wars would henceforth be repatriated. American families had this option during both wars, but after World War II, it became standard operating procedure. The change reoriented the government's approach to commemoration and settled the rituals for remembrance on domestic turf, thereby enhancing the role of the national cemetery system. The American Battle Monuments Commission became a legacy organization, responsible for managing existing "shrines" and sustaining the memory of American military service throughout much of the world.[9]

It is hard to know whether Americans these days regard the memorial sites in Europe as shrines or if they are even aware of their existence. President Donald Trump decided it was not worth his time to visit the Aisne-Marne American Cemetery in the fall of 2018, and he reportedly referred to the marines who died at Belleau Wood as "losers" and "suckers."[10] For their part, marines still consider Belleau Woods to be sacred ground, and some periodically return to camp out in the forested battlefield behind Aisne-Marne. And when I visited the Normandy American Cemetery and Memorial, the guide who led us on a tour of D-Day sites brought us through the gates and said, "Welcome home."

A century ago, the idea that Americans would travel in search of hallowed ground had wide currency. Indeed, the World War I sites were meant to attract Gold Star mothers, veterans, and tourists. In 1929, the American Battle Monuments Commission published a guidebook, which a young Dwight D. Eisenhower helped write, with photographs and maps, describing battlefields and villages, monuments and cemeteries, which were finally dedicated in 1937. An early plan for honoring the American Expeditionary Forces proposed that the United States build a memorial highway in northeastern France, like the loop road that was created at Gettysburg in the 1890s.[11]

In fact, that strategy is similar to what the British pursued at Menin Gate. When I got to Ypres in the midafternoon, I saw the gate is a monumental arch that extends over a street and serves as an entry into a closely packed commercial district, the tips of Gothic-style buildings leading toward the vanishing point, with St. Martin's Cathedral in the distance, much as the chapel at Flanders Field focused my view through the entrance gate. But while Flanders Field is a self-contained enclosure or cloister—and a destination—Menin Gate is part of the walking city.

There are two doorways on either side of the arch and a lion stretched across the top, above the salutation "To the Armies of the British Empire Who Stood Here From 1914 to 1918 and To Those of Their Dead Who Have No Known Grave." I walked through the door on the right, gazing up at the walls that stretch up from the sidewalk, thousands of names arranged in columns by nation, unit, and rank. Pedestrians passed under the gate on the other side without looking at the walls, and I took pictures as I crossed the street, heading toward a portal in the middle of the underpass.

I walked up the stairs, still surrounded by names and then wreaths and crosses made of poppies, all tokens of remembrance left by relatives or friends. The stairs lead to a promenade offering views of the river and neighborhood, as well some historical displays and a scale model of the gate, which was designed by Reginald Blomfield and dedicated in 1927. I had almost a bird's-eye view, but everything I wanted to see was behind me. Every night at 8:00 p.m., a British honor guard with bugles stands on the street I just crossed and performs the Last Post Ceremony in

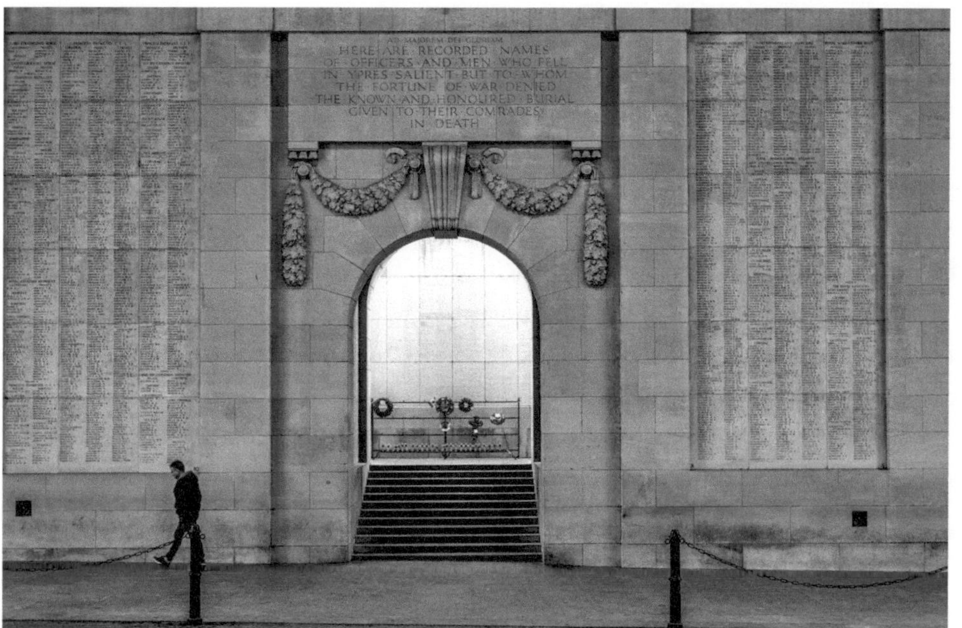

The Menin Gate Memorial to the Missing (unveiled in 1927), Ypres, Belgium, 2017.

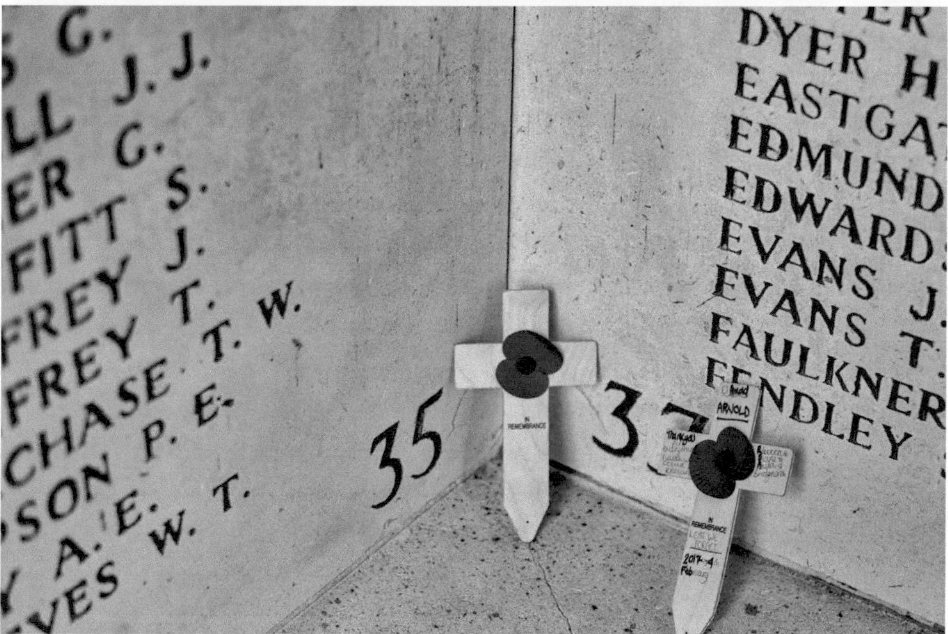

The Menin Gate Memorial to the Missing, 2017.

memory of the Commonwealth soldiers who died defending Ypres. But I could not wait for that since I had to drive to Lille.

At Menin Gate, the Great War brought the process of mourning into public view, the disembodied names of the dead now part of a shared, historical landscape. The estrangement of bodies from names—the missing—heightened the war's trauma, but the reincorporation of names on the streets of Ypres must have brought some comfort to the grieving. I realize, too, as I think back to Whitman's 1866 report, that he imagined the national cemeteries would also be part of a visible public landscape. While that did not happen as perhaps he hoped it would, the War Department tried again in the 1920s, this time connecting victory, death, and memory on ceded territory, European land now marked by American history. A radical proposition, really.

Lille is a forty-five-minute drive from Ypres and about an hour north of the Somme, and by the time I reached my hotel, the temperature had dropped, causing me to wonder as I walked through the town square whether my light winter jacket would be warm enough. The next morning, soon after I checked out, it began to snow, fine and wet, bringing mist up from the warmer ground and wrapping the horizon in a milky haze.

The area I was traveling through, like most of the places I visited in northeastern France, was rural: flat farmland, some rolling hills, rivers, the occasional factory, villages throughout, and cities like Lille, Reims, and Verdun the only echo of the metropole, Paris, that seems to represent the entire nation. Marine Le Pen, the right-wing politician, calls this region "forgotten France," and its current economic woes, she and other populists have argued, are the result of globalization and immigration, policies favored by European elites.[12] It is strange to think that a century ago this region was the center of the Western world, and stranger still to see that the effects of the war—trenches, cemeteries, and other memorial sites—remain a prominent part of the landscape.

When I arrived at Thiepval, the snow had picked up, and I aimed my lens through the flurries trying to get a full picture of the memorial, which is bounded on one side by two sections of British and French graves, with a path down the middle—like a nave—leading to the Cross of Sacrifice that faces the War Stone on the memorial. I photographed from the other side, without the intervening headstones, but I could not avoid the group of twenty-five British school kids, who were there on a field trip. I caught them on the platform of the memorial gathered around their teacher, and also in the cemetery, standing in the middle path, looking back at Lutyens's monument, snow coming down.

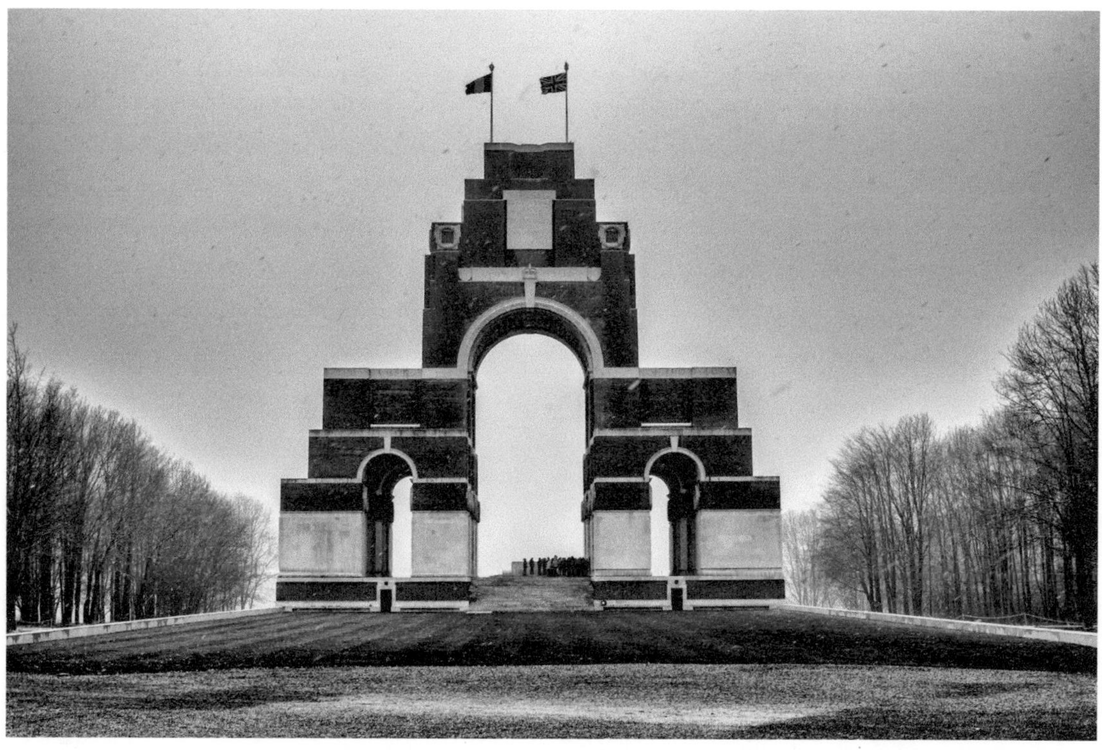

The Thiepval Memorial to the Missing of the Somme, 2017.

In a 1991 *New York Times* article, Vincent Scully, a Yale art historian, described Thiepval as an "enormous monster" with "demonic eyes" that towers over visitors with the death-making power of war. This was in an article that begins with the idea that Yale undergraduate Maya Lin shaped Lutyens's monument to "her own, gentle sorrowful vision" in the just-constructed Vietnam memorial. While there is no escaping the looming quality of Thiepval, I think Scully wrongly reads the Great War into the memorial when, in fact, Lutyens created a super-sized monument to loss and emptiness, unrestrained except by the headstones and cross below, and open to the surrounding countryside, a vertical expression of the limitless naming at Menin Gate.[13]

Before getting to Thiepval, I stopped at Warlencourt British Cemetery, one of many Commonwealth cemeteries designed by Lutyens. More than three thousand men were buried at Warlencourt, and the cemetery includes Lutyens's signature War Stone and a cross, so it is a formal

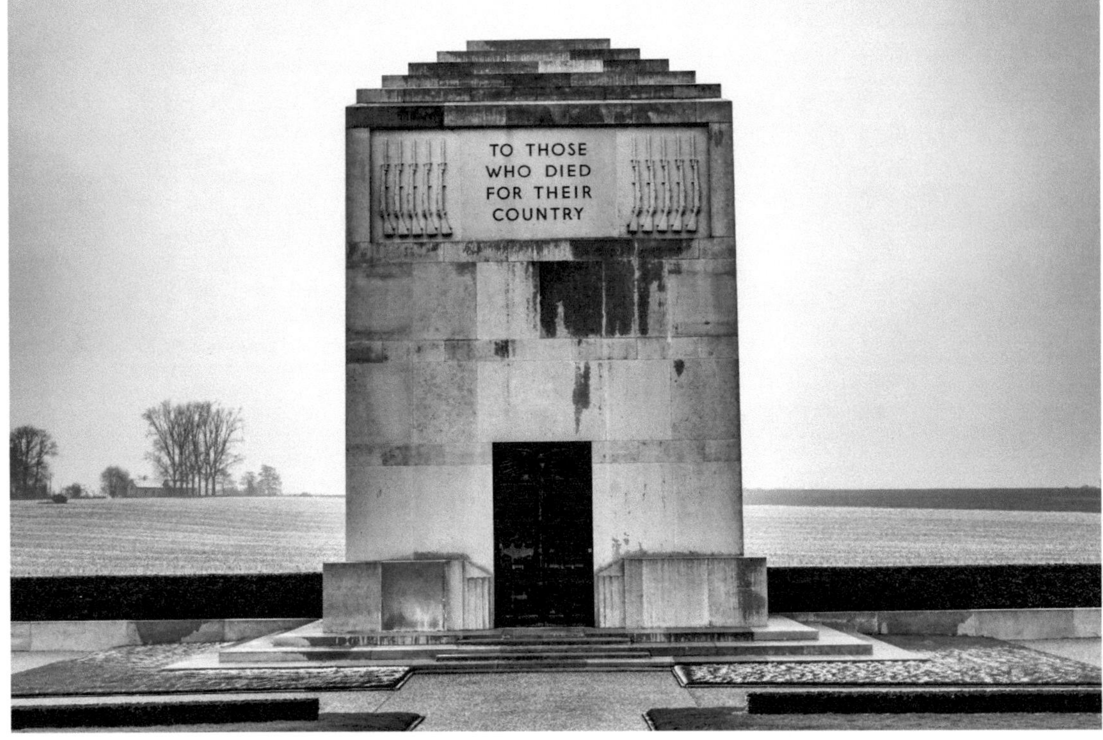

The chapel at Somme American Cemetery (established in 1918; dedicated in 1937), Bony, France, 2017.

landscape. Still, the grounds are separated from the adjacent farm fields by just a small hedge, which gives it a gently pastoral character.

Thirty miles to the east is the Somme American Cemetery and Memorial. Here, the Americans marked the cemetery's location by pushing the chapel to the perimeter and carving a large cross in the middle of its face, the name of the location at the bottom ("Somme American Cemetery"), and the French words "Morts Pour La Patrie" at the top, framed by three bombshells on either side. The military theme is echoed on the flip side of the chapel with the same message, now in English—"To Those Who Died for Their Country"—set in a panel framed by rifles. The chapel, probably twice as large as the one at Flanders Field, sits at the end of a paved path that leads to an American flag stand anchored by iron helmets, replicas of what "doughboys" wore into battle.

At St. Mihiel American Cemetery the imagery is similarly bellicose. The statue of the screaming eagle that stands in the middle above the words "Time Shall Not Dim the Glory Of Their

Deeds" does not just argue for national dominance. It also dominates the landscape. I wanted to photograph these objects from an angle to throw them off axis and question their command of the dead, though the symmetry of the space was hard to shake. At Somme, I approached the flag stand and chapel from several directions and hoped that the dusting of snow and milky white atmosphere suggested another reality.

When I visited St. Mihiel, the superintendent (who was walking the grounds) pointed to another statue, a figure of a young man, and explained that it was an exception, that monuments to actual people were not allowed in the cemeteries. But, in this case, a grief-stricken mother exerted political pressure, and the American Battle Monuments Commission permitted an unnamed statue of her son, Lieutenant Walker Blaine Beale, who died in the Battle of Saint-Mihiel.[14] Looking around the cemetery, I also saw birdfeeders in some of the trees, a welcome nod to nature's order.

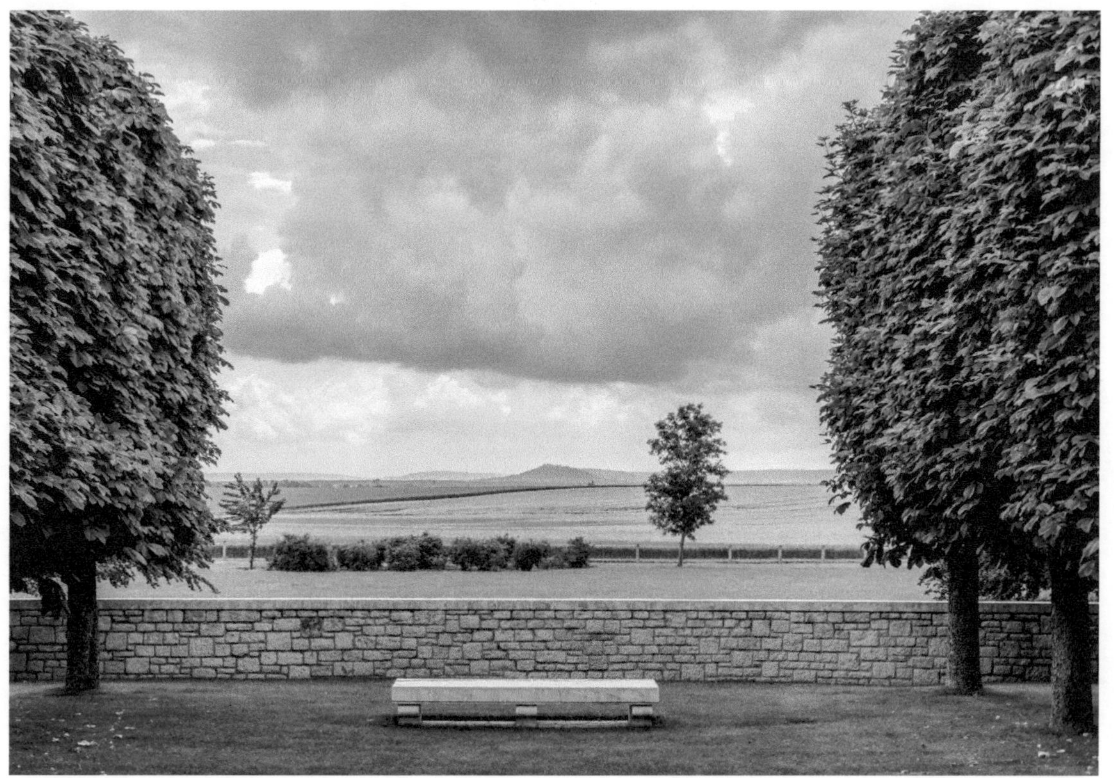

St. Mihiel American Cemetery (established in 1918; dedicated in 1937), Thiaucourt, France, 2016.

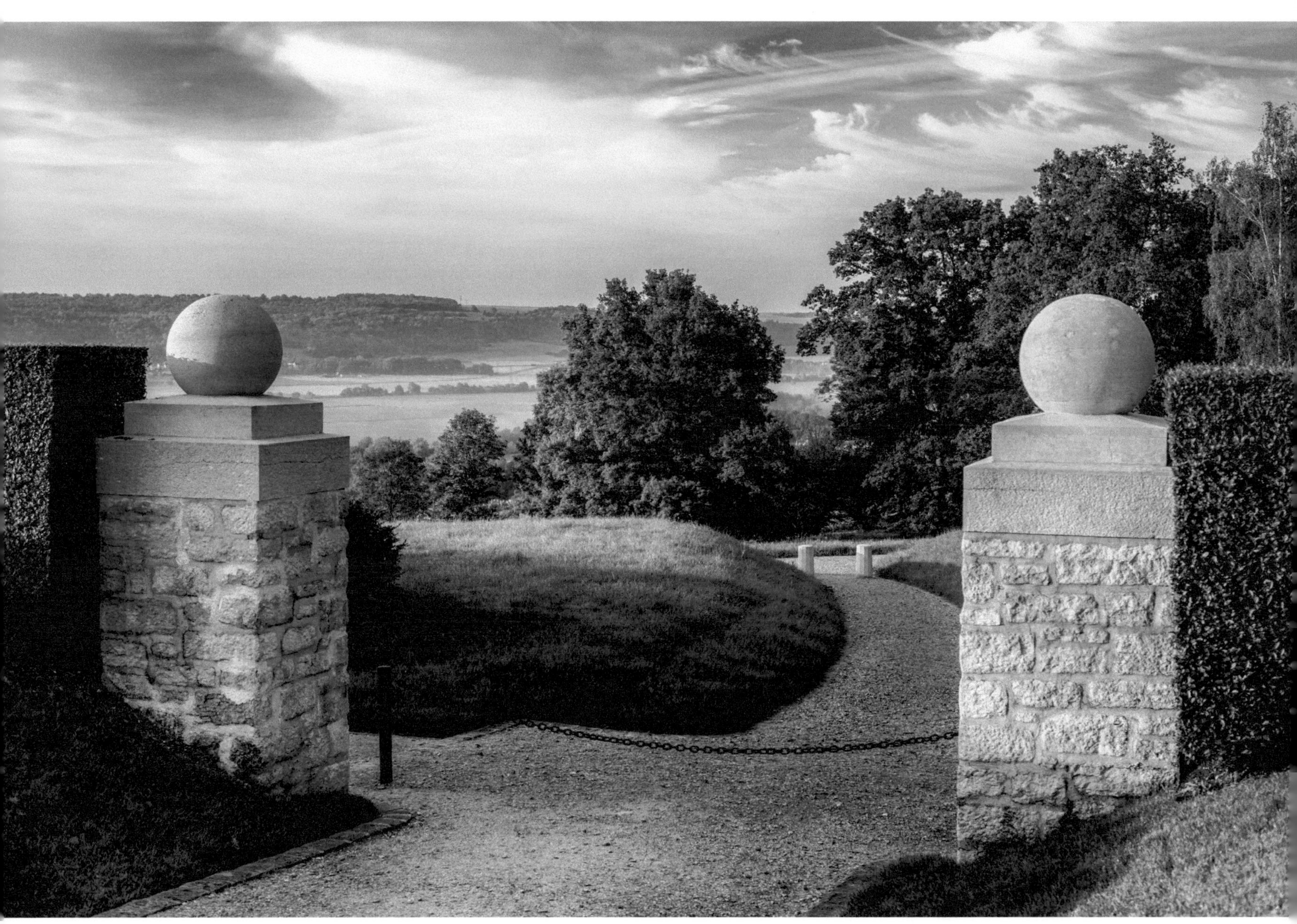

A walkway at Château-Thierry American Monument (dedicated in 1937), Aisne, France, 2016.

The geopolitical purpose of these memorials was to lift up the memory of the American military: its strength and glory. In 1931, General Pershing highlighted that goal in reviewing the proposal for the statue that was to be placed on top of the Montfaucon American Monument, which honors the army's role in the Meuse-Argonne campaign. He rejected the first design because, as he argued in a letter to architect John Russell Pope, the female figure (a Greek goddess) appeared to be grief-stricken and therefore signified weakness.[15] The sculptor revised his drawings, and the statue is now supposed to signify liberty.

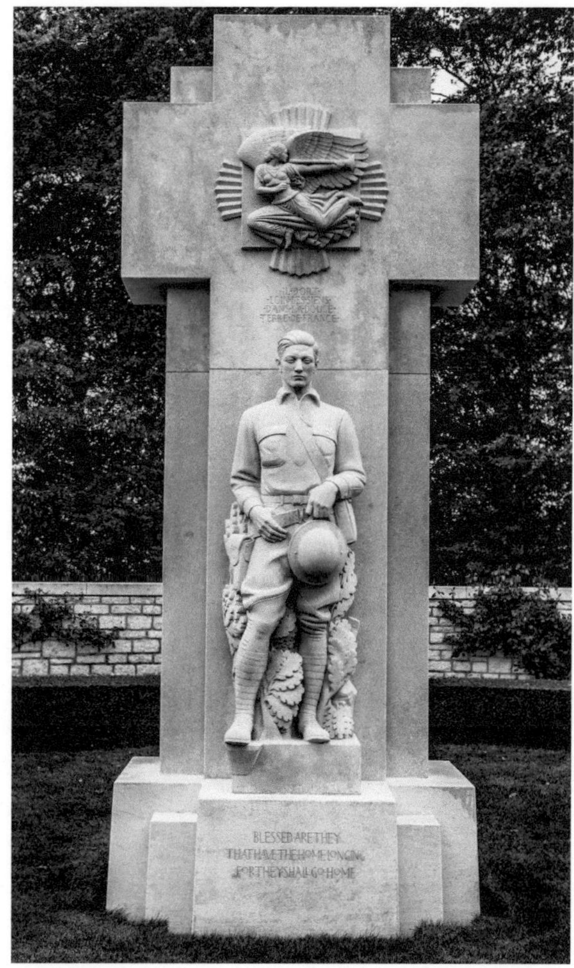

St. Mihiel American Cemetery, 2016. The unnamed memorial to Walker Blaine Beale includes two inscriptions. The first, at the top, is in French: "Il Dort Loin Des Siens Dans La Douce Terre De France" or "He Sleeps Far From His Family In The Gentle Land Of France." The second, at the bottom, is in English: "Blessed Are They That Have The Home Longing For They Shall Go Home."

The display of American military success was not simply figurative. At the Bellicourt American Monument, just around the corner from the Somme cemetery, I parked my car in front of the formal threshold, with steps leading to a stone block featuring a tableau of classical figures. But on the back side of the monument, facing the countryside, an elaborate display of maps and prose illuminates the attack that the Twenty-Seventh and Thirtieth Divisions made in September 1918 to break the Hindenburg Line. I say "illuminates" because the carved map is flecked with red and yellow to highlight routes and locations. At the foot of the monument is a large round orientation table, a compass or azimuth, maybe six feet wide. I gazed out at the snow-glazed farm fields and then down at the table and saw that I was looking west, toward Hargicourt, four miles away. I turned around and glanced at the map behind me and saw that Hargicourt was one of several villages important to the American Expeditionary Forces' 1918 fall campaign. I was then oriented.[16]

Back home, I can see that the photographs I took at Bellicourt stand out not only because of the vast whiteness that engulfed much of what I saw that day but also because they resemble pictures I took of similar drawings at American monuments and cemeteries in France:

- Covering a wall at the Chateau-Thierry American Monument: a map, like the one at Bellicourt, depicting the ground captured by the American divisions in the Aisne-Marne Salient.
- On the ledge of the balcony to the observation deck at Montfaucon: arrows pointing toward the American Cemetery (the Meuse-Argonne American Cemetery), 7 kilometers [4.35 miles] away.
- At the Meuse-Argonne American cemetery: a similar array, inscribed on a stairway, pointing to Grand Carre Farm, 5 kilometers [3.11 miles] away, Bantheville, 2 kilometers [1.24 miles] away, and other locations.
- In the rotunda of the Montsec American Monument: a large relief map key of the St. Mihiel Salient, with directions to the St. Mihiel American Cemetery, 17 kilometers [10.56 miles] away.

The displays put me in place to understand the region's historical geography, more specifically, how the American Expeditionary Forces helped beat back the Germans in 1918 and win the war. They were versions of the commission's 1927 publication, *A Guide to the American Battle Fields in Europe*, now set to stone and memorialized. Before making these trips and embarking on this project, I did not know what a "salient" is: "a spur-like area of land, especially one held by a line of offense or defense, as in trench-warfare."[17]

At the National Archives, I learned that these displays were part of the commission's decade-long effort to clarify the army's movements during the war. The document trail was extensive: forty feet of boxes containing maps and letters asking division commanders to confirm their actions during specific battles and at particular times and places. This was military history conducted by military men, using tools honed during the war—cartography and photography—resulting in a multivolume *Summary of Operations*, published in 1944, and sixty-nine folios of terrain photographs taken after the war showing the territory the Americans fought to control. The stone-hewn infographics were just the tip of an iceberg.

When the American Battle Monuments Commission hired Paul P. Cret, John Russell Pope, Egerton Swartwout, and others to design these memorials, it sought to enshrine this history in the timeless vernacular of classical architecture: Elysian Fields platted and built out in the French countryside. I took dozens of pictures of this otherworldly landscape during my first trip to the Meuse-Argonne American Cemetery, and dozens more during my return visits, often just trying to capture the visual order imposed upon the land. It was not until I got into the archives that I realized the drive for order came from the war itself and the military, as if the chaos of battle might be redeemed by the historical record.

One veteran spoke to this tension when the commission asked him to clarify the movements of his battalion on the night of October 6, 1918. "I have examined the map and marked the lines that I know from personal experience to be correct," he wrote in response to the materials the commission sent him in the fall of 1928. "I had no maps to refer to that I made during the campaign, but some of the territory is stamped indelibly on my mind. I would know Hill 263 if I would meet it in Hell."[18]

The architects also took direction from the military record. In 1929, Cret, the commission's consulting architect and probably the nation's foremost neoclassical designer, wrote Major Xenophon H. Price, the commission's administrative head, to say that the map they were engraving on the Bellicourt monument did not square with all the documents they had been given. The design team had to choose where to draw the battle lines, and he hoped Price would be comfortable with their decision, noting that, "as you know, the exact line of battle is never very accurately determined."[19]

If I linger here over time-stamped documents, the "real" stuff of history, it is not to correct the foggy vision of memory but rather to underscore the military's determination to authenticate the historical record and set that record in stone. I photographed these maps-as-monuments at Bellicourt and also at Chateau Thierry—a much larger memorial likewise designed by Cret—and I took pictures of the graven arrows, showing the way from monument to battlefield to cemetery, expressly linking victory and death and blurring the line between memorial architecture and military design.

The British landscapes are also in the classical mode, and the principal difference between them and the American versions is that the British memorialized the dead and the Americans memorialized the dead and celebrated the success of their military. The British memorials signaled the end of an empire, while the American landscapes announced the beginning of a new one. And unlike the first national cemeteries, the landscapes abroad present a united front—no divisions between Union and Confederate soldiers, no references to state affiliations, no separate sections for white and Black soldiers, and no need for the Gettysburg Address.[20] Just one nation under God.

It was Sunday morning, and my flight back to Montreal left in a few hours. I stood in the middle of the Suresnes American Cemetery, on the long path leading up to the chapel, a central portico flanked by colonnades and extensions on other side. Behind me was the gate—wrought iron with gold filigree—and below the gate is Boulevard Washington, whose two-way traffic and central median reinforce the cemetery's formality.

The cemetery is small, just over seven acres, and embraces 1,541 graves, including the remains of men who died in World War II, but the chapel is so large it looks like a small college library.

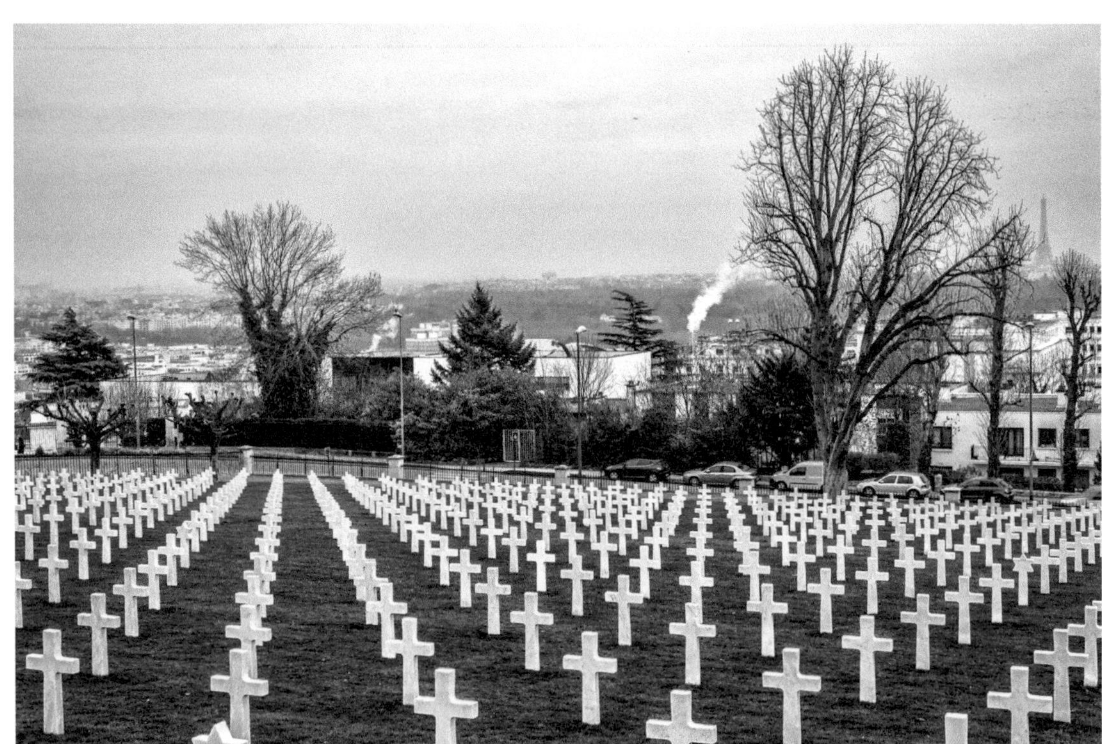

Suresnes American Cemetery (established in 1917; dedicated in 1937), Suresnes, France, 2017.

The grounds were quiet and empty of other people, though I could occasionally hear the hum of a car passing along the boulevard below.

Suresnes is a suburb of Paris, and the cemetery sits on a hill, overlooking the city, two miles away. It is an imperial view, and I took pictures, but I could not quite see the skyline because of the fog. To complicate matters, the settings on my camera were off kilter, the autofocus did not work, and I fumbled trying to adjust the view, blaming my ineptitude on the weather the day before. But, fortunately, one image emerged that captured the mood, the place, the lives lost and remembered, and the surrounding neighborhoods and the many lives therein.

Normandy American Cemetery (dedicated in 1956), one day after the seventy-first anniversary of D-Day, Colleville-sur-Mer, France, June 7, 2015.

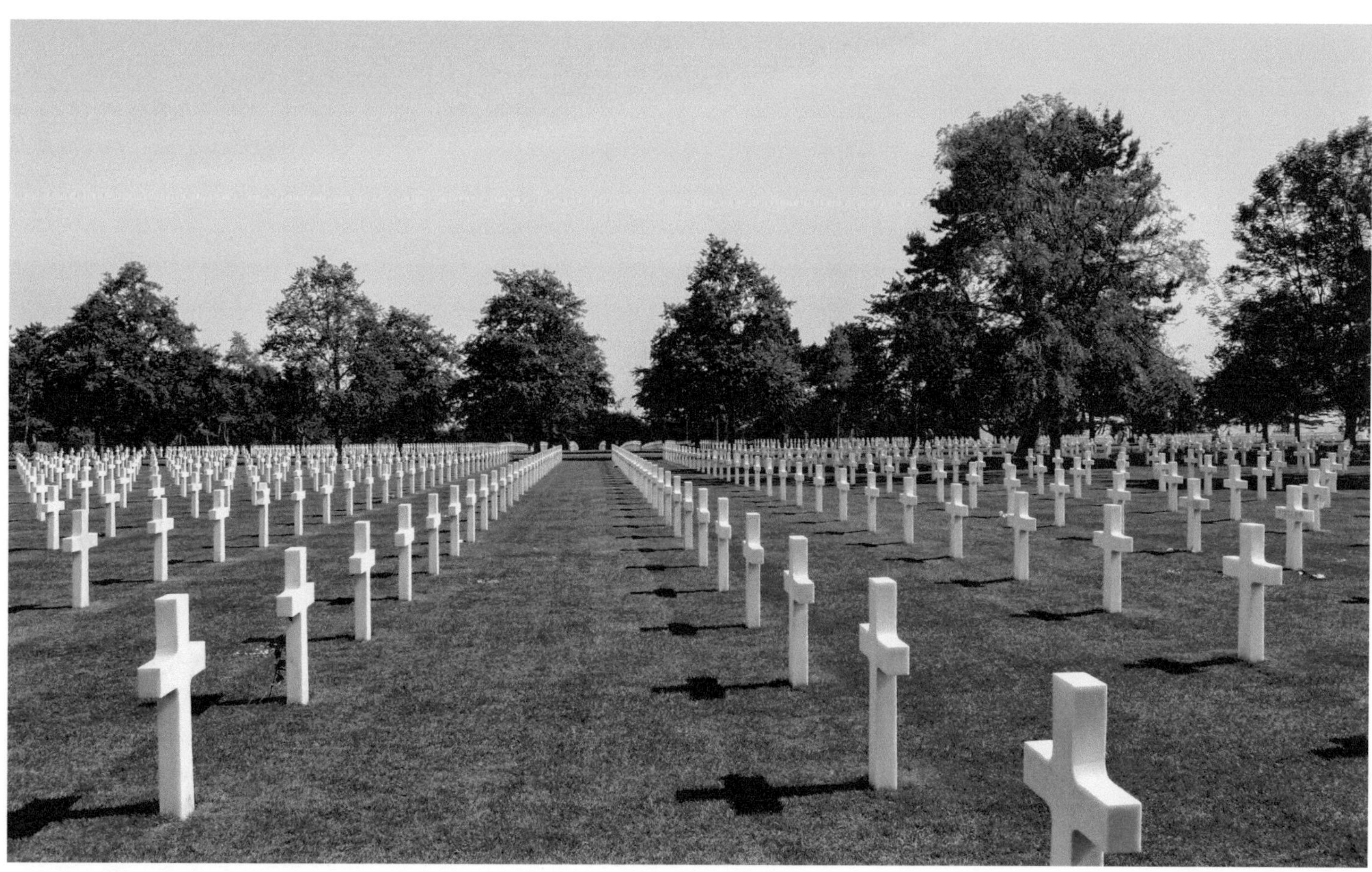

8

Good Wars

In the final scene of *Saving Private Ryan*, Steven Spielberg's 1998 film depicting D-Day and the Allied invasion of France during World War II, an elderly James Francis Ryan stands by Captain John H. Miller's grave at the Normandy American Cemetery and Memorial. Ryan asks whether he has been worthy of the sacrifice that Miller and others made so that his younger self—the Private Ryan of the movie's title—could survive. That sacrifice is bound up in feelings of patriotism, valor, brotherhood, and family, and these emotions are never more acute than when Spielberg examines them through the lens of memory. Although the early and extended sequence on Omaha Beach provides a gut-wrenching portrayal of combat, the film's real heart-tugging power resides in its retrospective vision, beginning with the very first scene when the Ryan family arrives at the cemetery and we see the good American man—the true private Ryan—that the movie's rescue plot is meant to save.

The graveside scenes that frame *Saving Private Ryan* underscore the film's main purpose: to recognize World War II as a "good war" and commemorate the ordinary Americans who defended their nation's way of life. The measured presentation of marbled headstones with the graveled pathways and finely manicured vegetation and ocean in the backdrop is critical to that message. The landscape appears majestic but restrained enough in its grandeur to make it an appropriate venue for solemn grieving and reflection. In fact, the scenes are so evocative that I wonder whether just seeing the movie is sufficient for understanding the cemetery's memorial power, whether it makes any difference to my view of the landscape that I have visited so many other cemeteries in France and the United States.

Of course, it matters to the film's consideration of what is a good war or good man that

Normandy American Cemetery is just up the hill from Omaha Beach, the epicenter of D-Day, which figured as the turning point in the war's European theater. Journalist Tom Brokaw highlights this proximity in his best-selling book *The Greatest Generation* (1998)—which appeared the same year as *Saving Private Ryan*—when he describes his experience of being at the cemetery on June 6, 1994, to cover the fiftieth anniversary of D-Day for NBC's *Today* show. Brokaw says the occasion "was a somber and celebratory moment, as veterans of that daring and dangerous invasion, unparalleled in the long history of warfare, gathered to pay tribute to those whose sacrifices were marked by the simple headstones and to share with the world their own remarkable stories of survival." Not surprisingly, the television show mostly focused on the heroics of the war until historian Stephen Ambrose—who was present at the broadcast and had recently written *Band of Brothers* (1992)—broke in to remind viewers of the horrific violence of D-Day, how men were torn apart by artillery and had their limbs "'blown off.'" Brokaw says that he welcomed the interruption because it shifted the focus to the men who survived and went on to lead productive lives, exemplifying the values they defended in battle.[1]

These memorial salutes follow in the tradition of the Gettysburg Address and President Woodrow Wilson's reflections at the Gettysburg reunion in 1913—stories of sacrifice that serve to reconsecrate the American mission on blood-soaked soil. But setting aside the rhetoric, the main point I want to make here is that these metanarratives must wait their turn. As Brokaw and Ambrose remind us, this vision of national unity is based on the experiences of individual men, and before the Republic can be invoked, the dead must be honored. For the military, this order is sacrosanct, as is clear from the Concurrent Return program, which was established during the Korean War. During World Wars I and II, the military buried their dead in temporary graveyards and subsequently reinterred them in permanent cemeteries abroad or shipped the remains back to the United States. With the advent of Concurrent Return, all soldiers killed in action were repatriated as soon as possible, following a carefully scripted process for returning the dead to their families. That protocol is still in effect. A designated member of the family is informed of the soldier's death, and a military officer transfers the remains in person.[2] So a government policy became a ritual that put personal history—the needs of Private Ryan—ahead of any public knowledge or discussion of how and why the death took place. The order is a delicate one, and too much emphasis on the violence of war—an expansion of Ambrose's perspective—can disrupt the bond to nation. For instance, as the Vietnam

War unwound, many Americans watched the body count rise on television, which galvanized the antiwar movement.

The idea that World War II was a good war assumes that such a concept is even possible. "Just war" theory begins with the proposition that taking human life is inherently wrong and that for a war to be just it must be fought for the right reasons—to defend innocent people or protect moral values—and that it must be waged in an ethical manner, which is to say, as Thomas Aquinas postulated more than seven hundred years ago, that a just war must promote good and avoid evil. On these grounds, the Allies' war against Nazi Germany and Imperial Japan was undeniably just and their victory a courageous defense of the civilized world. Critiques of this claim—and there are some—come from at least two points of view. One says that the United States and Britain gave up the moral high ground when they firebombed Dresden and Hamburg and dropped atomic bombs on Hiroshima and Nagasaki, unnecessarily killing thousands of civilians. Another, shared by conscientious objectors and skeptical realists alike, contends that war is by definition an immoral struggle to destroy human life, and further, in the case of World War II, that poor decision-making, absurd bureaucracies, and ideological posturing—themes dramatized by novelists such as Joseph Heller and Kurt Vonnegut—contributed to more deaths, making it difficult to maintain that the war was "Justified," "Necessary," or good. In the words of historian Paul Fussell (who was a World War II veteran), war is always "stupid and sadistic."[3]

Some of this criticism has come from rank-and-file soldiers, whose battlefield accounts underscore the faith they placed in the men they fought with but skewer the higher logic for war. There is an understandable irony here: that for many Americans the ideals used to justify World War II were less important than the ground-level sacrifices made to defend them. "War is brutish, inglorious, and a terrible waste," E. B. Sledge concludes in his memoir of fighting in the Pacific. "The only redeeming factors were my comrades' incredible bravery and their devotion to each other. Marine Corps training taught us to kill efficiently and to try to survive. But it also taught us loyalty to each other—and love. That esprit de corps sustained us."[4]

At the national cemeteries, you can find this devotion lodged between names etched on stones marking the shared graves from World War II, for instance, at Zachary Taylor National Cemetery in Louisville, where a good-sized marble slab, probably four times larger than a typical in-ground marker, displays the names and ranks of eleven men from the US Army Air Corps who lost their lives in July and September 1944. Their names are divided into two groups, one on top of the other, to separate the five men who died on July 7 from the five who perished two months later on September 13. When I spoke to the assistant director at Zachary Taylor, he told me that this form of burial was unusual and that few cemeteries have them, though I also discovered group interments at Fort McPherson National Cemetery in Nebraska. Here, too, the stones are oversized and include the names of air corpsmen—in one case, also split into two groups—as well as one marking the remains of eight US Army soldiers—a M SGT (master sergeant), a TEC5 (technician fifth grade), two S SGT's (staff sergeants), a 2d LT (second lieutenant), a 1st LT, and a TEC4—who died on June 18, 1945. The only other mark on these stones is the number embossed on the lower right-hand corner, identifying the grave's location in the cemetery's inventory.

The photographs I took of these stones show weathered streaking that blurs some of the letters, creating a kind of hologram effect. I wonder if someone, maybe the families, decided to bury

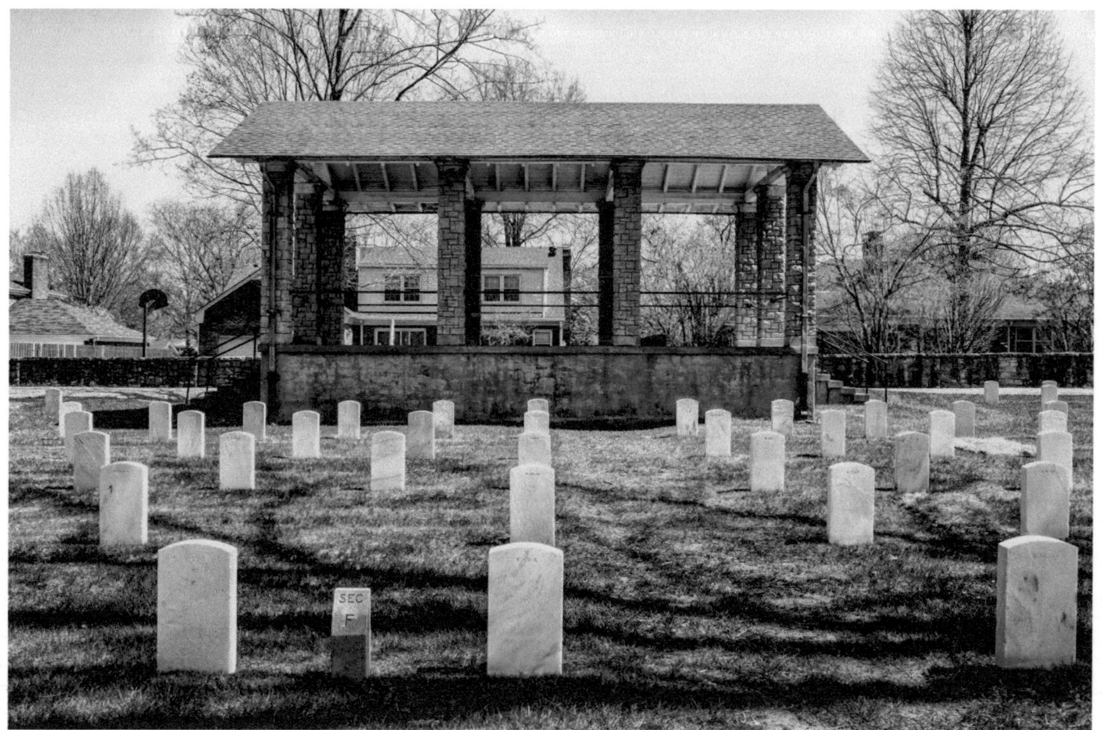

The rostrum at Zachary Taylor National Cemetery (established in 1928), Louisville, Kentucky, 2018.

the dead in their units, memorializing their shared fate and camaraderie. There is nothing to indicate how these men perished, though I assume the men in the air corps—the aerial unit of the army that after World War II was reconstituted as the US Air Force—went down together in their planes and their remains could not be separated from one another. The deaths of the eight soldiers are harder to imagine.

The largest of these group interments, and probably the most dramatic, is the USS *Arizona* Memorial in Pearl Harbor, which honors the 1,102 sailors who died on December 7, 1941, when the Japanese bombed their ship. Their remains are underwater with the sunken vessel, and the memorial is a long, white rectangular structure with a curved roof and view below to the ocean in the middle of the deck and a formal exhibition hall at the end, where the names of the dead appear on a marble wall. The memorial looks like a cenotaph turned on its side (though the tomb is not empty), and the names on the wall (of "gallant men") resemble the lists found at Thiepval and Menin Gate. The only way to see the memorial is to take a navy boat across the harbor. When I visited in the fall of 2020, COVID-19 restrictions were in place, and I was one of maybe thirty tourists, all in masks, who moved carefully through the sunlit spaces, each of us reflecting, I am sure, on the strange phenomenon of deflecting the virus in a place where so many died. As a site of remembrance, the memorial is unusual in that it marks a spot where men not only died but were entombed. It is also remarkable that the memorial has remained open to interments—for more than seventy-five years—and that survivors of the USS *Arizona* bombing may choose to be buried with their shipmates. Between 1982 and 2019 the remains of forty-four navy veterans were placed under the water, suggesting how resilient the bonds of brotherhood can be.[5]

Clean swept and resplendent on azure water, the USS *Arizona* Memorial is now almost far enough removed from the terrible events of December 7 to be called beautiful. Taking pictures of the space no doubt encourages that perspective, though the aesthetics of memorialization also serve to bring the horrors of the war and the sorrows of loss into a larger framework. This is what nationalistic memorials are meant to do: enlist reverence on behalf of the state. In this case, I depart from political scientist Benedict Anderson's contention that "no more arresting emblem of the modern culture of nationalism exist than cenotaphs and tombs of Unknown Soldiers." No doubt the dead are "saturated with ghostly *national* imaginings," as Anderson says, but here and in the national cemeteries, the ghosts emanate from specific names etched in stone.[6]

My goal in traveling to Honolulu was to photograph the National Memorial Cemetery of the

Pacific, located about ten miles from Pearl Harbor. Situated in the hollowed depression of a volcano (a caldera) that was formed more than 250,000 years ago, the cemetery—the Punchbowl, as it is often called—occupies long-treasured ground and at the perimeter offers spectacular views of the city and the coastline. Although it is part of the national cemetery system, the site includes a large monument, the Honolulu Memorial, which the American Battle Monuments Commission erected in 1964, eighteen years after the cemetery's founding. This makes the cemetery something of a hybrid landscape, as it brings the domestic elements of the American memorial landscape in touch with its international components. Symbolically, it complements the Normandy American Cemetery, providing the Pacific theater's explanation as to why the war was "good."

The Punchbowl received its name from English-speaking visitors who came to the island during the nineteenth century, though, to Hawaiians, the mountain was known as Puowaina or "hill of sacrifice," a reference to the sacralized deaths that took place there and throughout the Polynesian islands up through the early 1800s. During the 1890s, the city rejected a plan to turn the mountaintop into a cemetery, in part because of concerns that the dead would contaminate the water supply but also because the summit was a popular gathering place for Honoluluans. The Punchbowl retained its civic status until the bombing of Pearl Harbor, when the land was given over to military uses and the government renewed the proposal that the hilltop be converted into a cemetery—a military cemetery—a recommendation based on the high number of casualties in the Pacific and the lack of suitable burial space, as well as support from the Hawaiian veteran community, which had grown since the United States established a naval station on the island in 1899, a year after Hawaii was annexed. Construction of the National Memorial Cemetery of the Pacific began in 1948, and the first burials took place in January 1949 in a private ceremony that involved the interment of bodies stored in local mausoleums and held in temporary graves on Guam and other islands. Between January and August, in scenarios reminiscent of the reburial program following the Civil War, but now, with tractor trailers and bulldozers, the Office of the Quartermaster General supervised the burial of more than ten thousand caskets. The public dedication of the Punchbowl took place on September 2, 1949, V-J Day.[7]

This history complicates the Punchbowl's identity as "hallowed" ground, prompting questions from scholars about how its transformation into a national cemetery erased or sustained the landscape's traditional character and cemented the United States' imperial claims on Hawaii. The argument for erasure comes from the idea that a standardized military landscape was

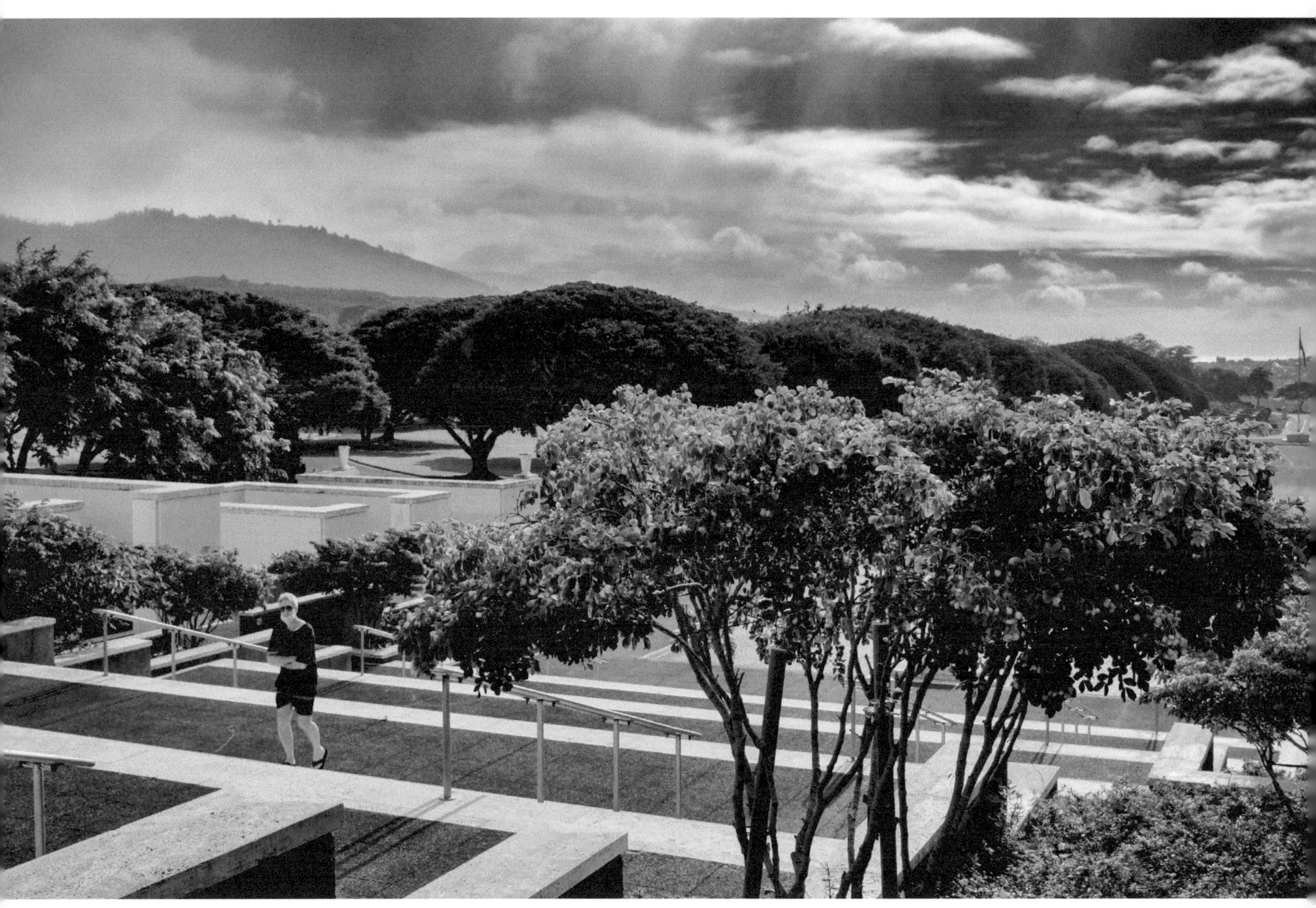

Walkway to the Honolulu Memorial at National Memorial Cemetery of the Pacific (established in 1948), Honolulu, Hawaii, 2020.

imposed on native ground, while the notion that the cemetery represents continuity draws on the interplay of colonial power and Indigenous order that has shaped Hawaii since the arrival of Captain James Cook and British settlers in the 1770s. In this second scenario, the national cemetery's reclamation of sacred ground signified yet another interpretation—or reassertion—of the authority and honor that comes from sacrifice.[8]

If I were making a documentary film about the Punchbowl and wanted to place these rituals in historical context, I would try to find footage not just of the cemetery's construction and dedication—newsreels showing the slow parade of caskets onto the grounds, preceded by clips of the bombing of Pearl Harbor—but also of how the mountaintop was used during the nineteenth century, supplementing with still photographs and paintings or drawings of the sacrificial executions that took place in earlier times. To expand the scope, I would cut to similar images of World War I cemeteries in France and Civil War graveyards at Shiloh, Beaufort, and other places in the South, all to make the point that these sites of honor and loss are joined by their allegiance to nation and to emphasize that they were put in place by the victors, not without humility or thought of the war's terrible costs but certainly with the understanding that they are all meant to sanctify the American creed.

As it stands, I was grateful to have made it to Honolulu from Vermont and was glad to roam the grounds with my camera. During my morning visit to the Punchbowl, as I walked the road that winds up to the cemetery from the administrative offices and the neighborhood below, the houses nestled into the hill sides just above the Abraham Lincoln Elementary School, I wondered where the representation of nationalism began. Did it start after I passed through the gates and gazed out over the city, with a reservoir and pump station on my right and mulched flower beds and trees to the left, one tree marked by a stone block telling me the tree was adopted by the Veterans of Foreign Wars, Department of Hawaii, on the "50th Anniversary of this Cemetery, September 2, 1999"? It was good that I was on foot instead of in a car so I could easily stop to take pictures, though I had to remind myself that it was difficult to photograph the smells and sounds of a tropical breeze.

At the top of the hill, the road bends right and leads directly into the cemetery, the view framed by two pillars on either side of the road, one taller than the other, both clad in the same white stucco that covers the pump station, the edges of the posts with indented channels and topped with silver caps, a decorative flourish in the Art Deco mode. The bigger left-hand pillar

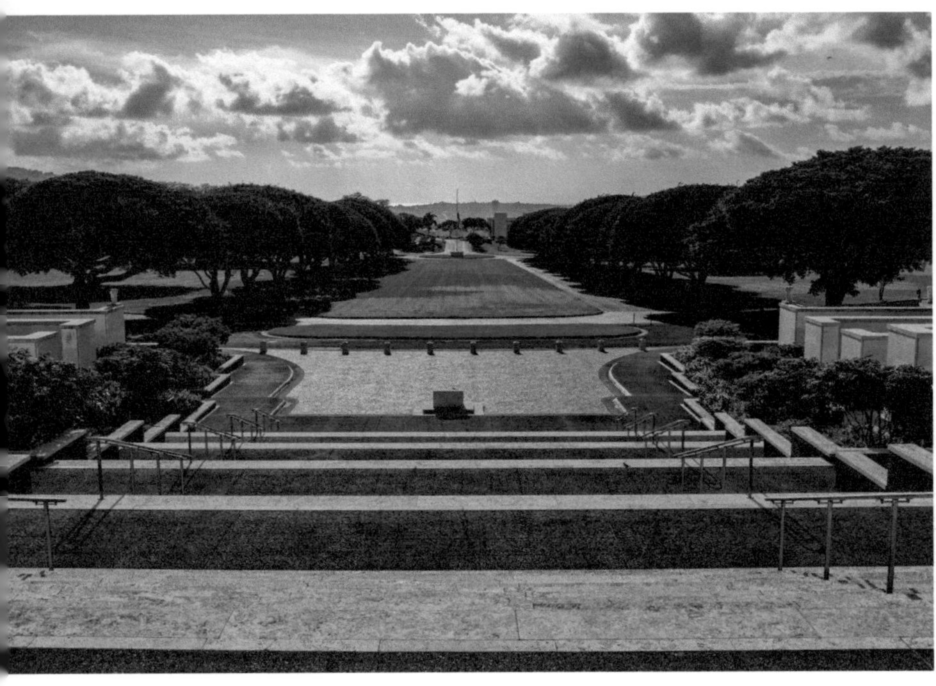

(*Above*) Looking toward the entrance of the National Memorial Cemetery of the Pacific from the Honolulu Memorial, 2020.

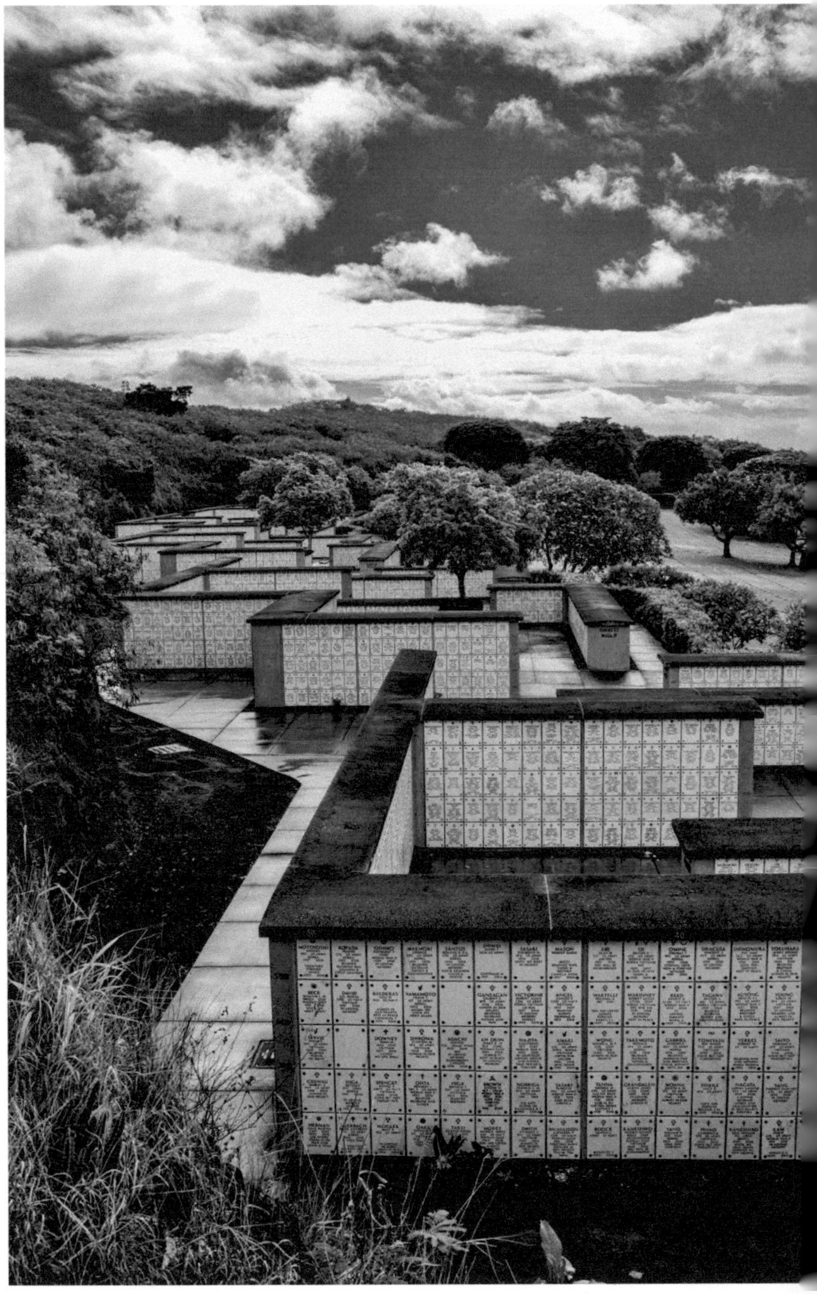

(*Right*) National Memorial Cemetery of the Pacific, 2020.

reads "National Memorial Cemetery of the Pacific," and above and below the lettering, there are two plaques, one with the ubiquitous excerpt from "The Bivouac of the Dead" and the other a sign from the Department of the Interior noting that the cemetery is on the National Register of Historic Places. The right-hand post identifies the grounds as "Puowaina" and "Punchbowl Crater," though the traditional names sit below medallions, one of which displays the spread-wing American eagle. Beyond the gates is a traffic circle with the flag, and behind the flagpole is a lawn stretching up to the steps of the Honolulu Memorial, flanked by roads and banyan trees along the boulevard and additional flagpoles on either side of the memorial.

I am caught up now in describing a space that I could just as easily photograph (which I did) because the experience of balancing the left- and right-hand views along a central axis is critical to the overall meaning of the Punchbowl. Maybe it goes without being said, but the landscape's formal qualities, not to mention its layered history, are inseparable from the sensual dimensions so that when I strolled across the football field–sized lawn and looked down at an in-ground stone marker (there are no standing headstones here) and then up at the Honolulu Memorial or out at the gangling roots and shading branches of the banyan trees, I saw and felt in circular motion, sweeping the individual history evoked on the marker into the larger history represented by the memorial. Some of the stones along the sides of the lawn appeared wedged in place, the plaques were not quite orthogonal to the curb, and the design looked flawed. I took pictures from several perspectives in the bright sun to try to catch this effect, with the memorial looming over my shoulder.

While over time the Pacific dead were joined by World War II veterans and men and women who fought in the Korean and Vietnam Wars as well as their spouses and sometimes dependents, the Punchbowl retains its identity as a cemetery dedicated to the good war or maybe good wars since the United States is now the world's preeminent power. And the memorial record keeps pace. So the Honolulu Memorial was built by the American Battle Monuments Commission in 1964 to "honor the sacrifices and achievements of American Armed Forces in the Pacific during World War II and in the Korean War." In 1980, the installation was expanded to honor "the Missing of the Vietnam War." In 2012, the commission installed another set of battle maps to document the Vietnam War. The panels appear at the rear of the memorial, next to similar displays of World War II and the Korean War and the nonsectarian chapel, and behind the thirty-foot bas-relief carving of a goddess-like figure of Columbia—meant to signify the prow of a navy carrier—which looks out from the front of the memorial.

In a 1965 *New York Times* review, art critic John Canaday observed that this "bosomy Liberty girl" was just one of several "puerile disasters" the commission had erected, also noting that the neoclassical memorials in Europe were "blocky, antiseptic wastes of marble." Explaining his disgust, he wrote: "These memorials do not say 'Remember.' They do not even say 'Forget.' They simply give no sign of awareness that anything at all ever happened. The agony of the men who died need not be commemorated for itself, since the accepted function of war memorials is to distill an expression of an ideal from the bestiality employed in defending it. But the living men who create war memorials, men who were lucky enough not to get drowned, shot, burned alive or disemboweled, have no right to fold their hands over their paunches, so comfortably intact, and say, 'It was all pretty glorious, and when you come down to it, downright pretty.' That is what these memorials say."[9]

This is a remarkable censure and worth quoting at length because of the way it echoes other criticism of how the war was remembered. Canaday, who served with the marines in the Pacific, insists that aesthetics must reflect the soldier's experience, but he does not explain how that should happen or whether an ideal can be pulled from the wreckage to represent the cause or acknowledge that nations should even construct memorials in the first place. And was World War II a good war? Like Fussell and Sledge, he cannot quite say.

Reflecting on my visit to the Punchbowl, I realize that in condemning the sculpture, Canaday overlooked the Courts of the Missing that flank the steps leading up the top of the memorial, a significant omission since the lists on the court walls represent a more restrained approach to remembering the dead. They contain the names of almost 30,000 men lost in action: 18,096 in World War II; 8,195 in Korea; and 2,489 in Vietnam, the last list, like the battle maps, added in 1980. From afar the enclosures do resemble marble blocks, but up close, they feel intimate, and the names appear one after the other, each matched with rank and home state and listed on separate panels, fourteen names per panel, three panels from top to bottom, spanning the length of the rectangular blocks and wrapping around the ends.

I circled the courts, shooting over the hedges that line the outside edge, trying to find the right angle, and wondering whether if I had a wider angle lens, a 22 or 24 mm rather than my 35 mm, I could show the walls and sculpture together, in effect making the connection that Canaday abhorred. The search for perspective also begs the question of how the serial naming of the dead serves the memorial process in general. The question has been with me since my trip

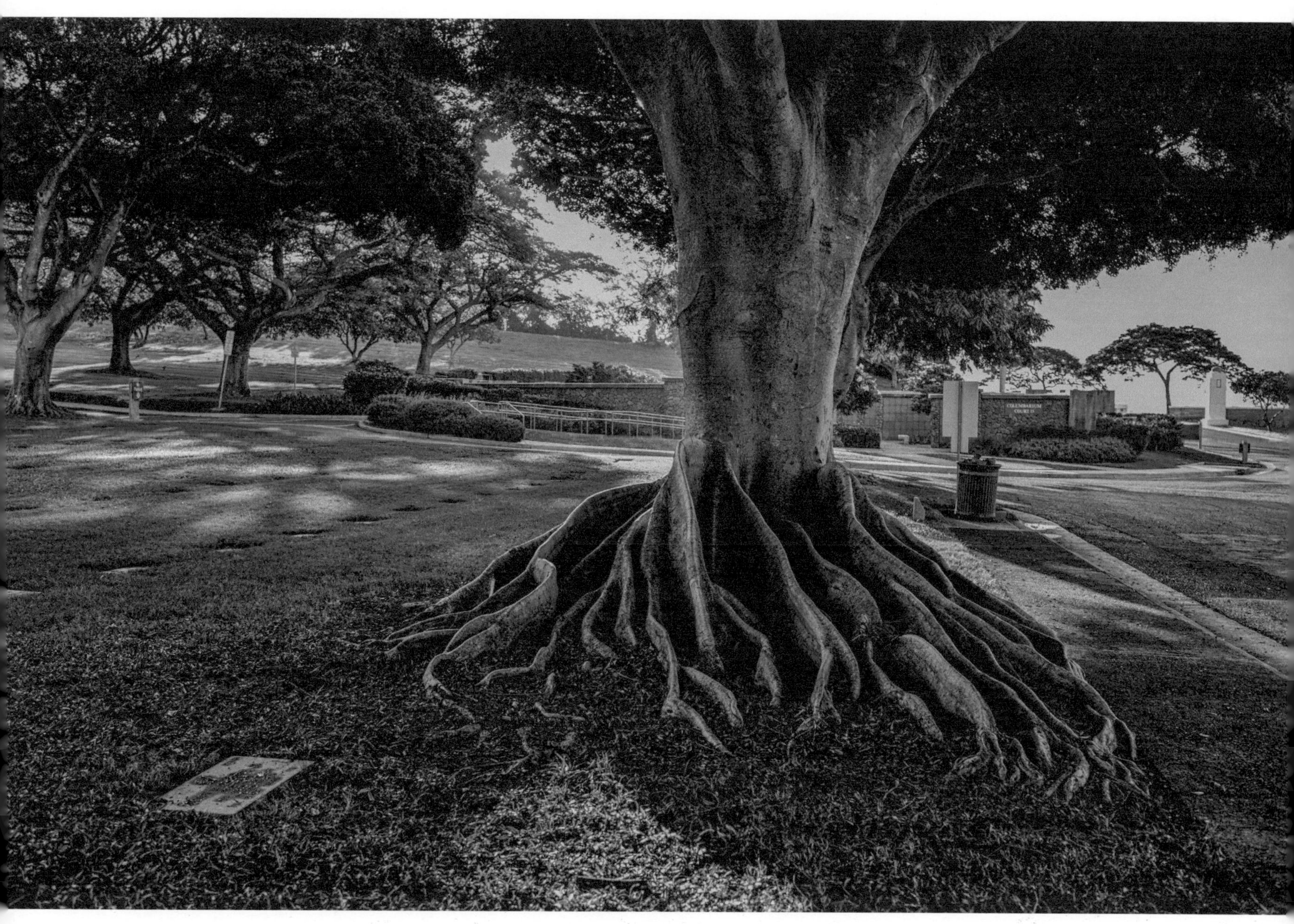

Banyan trees permeate National Memorial Cemetery of the Pacific, 2020.

to the Somme and Ypres, intensifying as I continued my travels and sending me back to the example of the Vietnam Veterans Memorial and its understated, emotionally resonant display of names—the missing and the dead—on a long, V-slanted black wall.

My answer begins with the observation that the Vietnam Veterans Memorial is not free of nationalistic rhetoric. Rather, the wall sits between the Lincoln Memorial and Washington Monument, where it is in dialogue with those sites, both symbolic of the Republic's highest ideals. The connection is loose and, given Maya Lin's graceful design, visitors can join the conversation, or not. At the Punchbowl, standing in one of the courtyards, the situation was similar. I could see and touch the names on the wall, conscious of the sculpture, maps, and iconography above me, heavy-handed perhaps, but—and this is the important point—the names have a tactile presence all to their own.

The thought stayed with me as I turned away from the Honolulu Memorial and made my way across the Punchbowl just as I had at other national cemeteries. The in-ground plaques stretched out before me, and the columbarium niches were stacked one on top of the other. At a remove from dramatic representations of nation and warfare but still framed by the mission set forth during the Civil War, they provide space for the kind of individual reflection you see at Thiepval and the Vietnam Veterans Memorial. Here, as at all the national cemeteries, the work of commemoration is both personalized and historical, idealized and pragmatic.

At the Punchbowl, these juxtapositions are dispersed across a compact, tropical landscape with Chinese banyan trees, monkey pod trees, and various native plantings that I could not begin to identify, a miracle-grown garland enwrapping the names of more than eighty-four thousand service men and women (and some dependents), including almost thirty thousand at the Court of the Missing and more than fifty-three thousand etched on flat stone markers and columbaria. There is also a Memorial Wall honoring different veteran groups that complements the trees on the gateway drive. Although the cemetery is closed to in-ground burials—with the exception of "casketed remains" that may be placed "in the same gravesite of previously interred family members"—the columbaria are open to interments.[10] From above, it is hard to see the scale of death because without the upright headstones, the cemetery appears to be an open field, like the names on the wall that are unreadable at a distance. When I walked to the northern rim of cemetery, where the paths look out over the inland neighborhoods of Honolulu and there is a sign that says, "Quiet Please," I gazed down through the foliage at a bank of columbaria arrayed in zig-zag fashion, like interlocking Legos, and took pictures of the enclave below.

The National Cemetery Administration estimates that more than five million people visit the Punchbowl each year. Like the cemeteries at Gettysburg and Normandy, its identity is closely tied to a single war. Yet I do not want to miss the Punchbowl's connection to the overall growth of the national cemetery system, an expansion that was part of World War II's rippling impact. Between 1930 and 1950, the federal government built eleven new cemeteries and added several "post" cemeteries—for instance, what is now called Fort Logan National Cemetery—to the national cemetery system. All of the new cemeteries are located in metropolitan areas, and most of them are much larger than the cemeteries established during the nineteenth century. Some, like Long Island National Cemetery (established in 1936), encompass more than 175 acres and have room for future growth.[11]

Building new cemeteries represented a shift in thinking for the army, the military branch that was responsible then for the cemetery system. With the exception of the cemeteries that the American Battle Monuments Commissions established in Europe, the government did not create any new cemeteries immediately after World War I. Instead, the quartermasters made room in existing cemeteries for the military dead. But in 1929, the War Department surveyed its existing cemeteries and discovered that although there was enough space to inter World War I veterans who might die as late as the 1990s, most of the cemeteries were at a distance from the nation's biggest cities and therefore not accessible to many veterans or their families. The United States was now a predominantly urban population, and the construction of Baltimore National Cemetery (1941), Golden Gate National Cemetery (1942), and other cemeteries near big cities reflected that reality.[12]

The participation by the United States in World War II confirmed the need for more national cemeteries. This need was based not just on the number of casualties (405,399 Americans died in World War II compared to 116, 516 in World War I and 620,000 in the Civil War) but also on the projected number of veterans who would subsequently be eligible for burial in a national cemetery. For instance, while five million veterans came out of World War I, twelve million served in World War II.[13] This increase meant that as the greatest generation began to die, the national cemeteries would increasingly be dominated by the men (and some women) who fought in World War II. It also underscored the system's primary identity as a burial ground for veterans. So, in

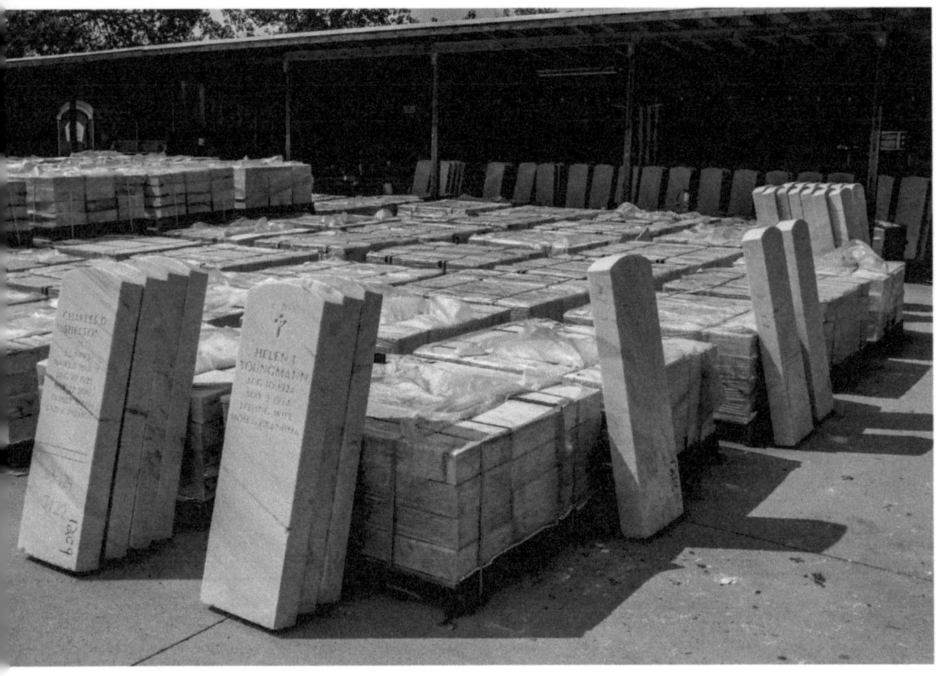

(*Above*) Preparing headstones at Fort Logan National Cemetery, 2018.

(*Right*) Fort Logan National Cemetery (established in 1950), Denver, Colorado, 2018.

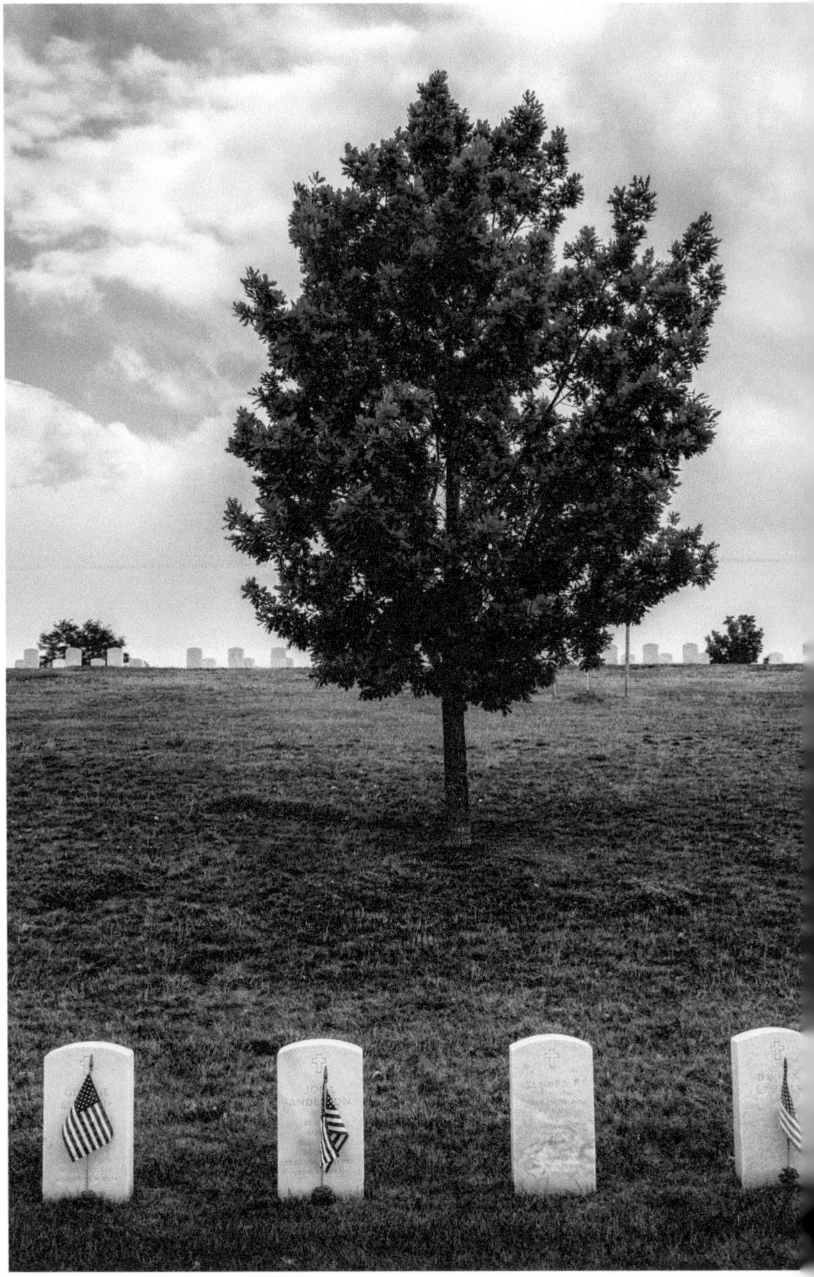

1973, the Department of Veterans Affairs assumed oversight of nearly all national cemeteries, a bureaucratic shift that signaled their importance as a civilian asset. Finally, the large number of Americans who fought in World War II points to the evolving character of the military. While the responsibility for defending the nation is now carried out by professionally trained military personnel, World War II was a "good war" in part because it was fought by citizen soldiers, the Private Ryans and Captain Millers of the world. This understanding of the "good"—the idea that all Americans should be prepared to die for their country—helps explain why the cemeteries are called national cemeteries, not military cemeteries.

To be sure, I cannot actually prove that World War II had a decisive impact on the image or "brand" of the national cemeteries. I can count the number of headstones marking the remains of men and women who served in World War II and try to estimate the proportional cost of accommodating the greatly expanded veteran population. Ultimately, the case hangs on cultural factors and attitudes about nation, war, and sacrifice. As historian (and retired army officer) Andrew J. Bacevich points out, World War II was the last time the United States relied on citizen soldiers to wage a successful war. The Korean War, a much smaller conflict, went forward in a similar fashion, but the Vietnam War "demolished" the idea that military service is an obligation of citizenship. Thereafter, the government would rely on professional volunteer soldiers, while promoting the "myth" that American armed forces were still liberating captive nations and making the world safe for democracy when in fact they were more often involved in "imperial policing."[14]

One implication of this thesis is that the landscapes I visited are founded on an outmoded understanding of nation and duty, and that by photographing them, I am eulogizing the disappearance of an older America. On the other hand, this nostalgic view of cultural declension is somewhat shortsighted. As historical landscapes go, the national cemeteries are expansive, resilient, and capable of containing multiple perspectives. This is particularly true of Arlington National Cemetery, the nation's flagship burial ground. There is a reason why schoolchildren take field trips to Arlington. More than any other commemorative site in Washington, it presents a sequential narrative of American history, offering numerous vantage points for patriotic reverence, the dead doing their part for the Republic long after their demise. Arlington is also big and complicated, and though it never wavers on the question of the nation's greatness, it resists easy interpretation.

I visited Arlington as a boy, and when I returned as an adult, first for a funeral and then to take photographs for this project, I was struck by how little the place had changed. The cemetery appeared ready to educate visitors about the nation's illustrious past through colorful maps, the Welcome Center and bookstore (with a security checkpoint), interpretive bus tours, and prominent destinations within the cemetery, such as the Custis-Lee Mansion and memorial to Pierre Charles L'Enfant that looks out at the city the military engineer helped design, as well as the gravesites of the many famous people whose names on the headstones complement their place in the history textbooks. At 639 acres, the cemetery is difficult to see, never mind assimilate, in a single or two-day visit.[15] Yet when I describe my project to people who do not know much about national cemeteries and say, "Think of Arlington, plus 150 more cemeteries," they appear to understand what I mean, as if Arlington were code for some unarticulated connection to nation. Sometimes I mention that the other national cemeteries are every bit as hallowed as Arlington and Gettysburg, even if they are relatively unknown and isolated. I have become like an evangelist for the dead.

The first time I returned to Washington with my camera, I took the Metro to the Arlington stop, the entry lights glowing in the still-dark morning as I walked up the steps from the platform and waited for the cemetery to open. The gates are maybe one hundred yards from the station, and the direct access can obscure the cemetery's place in Washington's larger symbolic landscape, which became clear to me when I later walked back across the Potomac River on the Arlington Memorial Bridge, which is a straight shot to the Lincoln Memorial and the National Mall. Although the distressed infrastructure of many national cemeteries may count as vernacular architecture, Arlington skews toward the monumental, an orientation best appreciated on foot or by driving across the bridge toward its enormous stone gates.

Much of Washington is dominated by block-shaped buildings and big public spaces, and the scale can take some getting used to. As a graduate student in the 1980s, I had a summer fellowship at the Smithsonian Museum of American History and received an ID card that gave me access to various government facilities and a kind of insider's status. Decades later, as I stood by the chain link fence and a No Trespassing sign, near Arlington's entrance, and took pictures of joggers rounding the bend in the river, I thought about the tension between inside and outside and how being affiliated with federal institutions seems to bring you closer to the nation's business. Given their proximity to the nation's business, the dead at Arlington seem like the ultimate insiders, and when we pass through the cemetery gates, we are meant to share the ground—and the history—with them. When I click through the pictures that I took during the several visits I made between 2016 and 2021, I can see that I focused on specific aspects of this history while also trying to photograph the landscape as a whole and understand it from within.

During my first trip, I walked up the hill almost a quarter of a mile to the Tomb of the Unknown Soldier and moved around in the light rain to photograph the tomb as well as the large gathering space behind it—the Memorial Amphitheater, which was dedicated in 1920 to supplement the older and smaller amphitheater where Frederick Douglass spoke in 1871. On my second visit, a year later, I returned to the tomb because it is closely tied to the memorial landscapes I was studying in France—the losses of World War I symbolized on domestic soil—and because the image of the military guard pacing the marble terrace was an iconic childhood memory. By the time I visited Arlington as a ten-year-old, President John F. Kennedy's grave attracted an estimated four million visitors a year, and I remember that my parents also took me to see it.[16] If I pull these childhood frames into focus, I can track the evolution of national identity across the two World Wars, the Eternal Flame serving as a memorial to the martyred president and navy veteran of the Good War. Walking south on Eisenhower Drive from the Welcome Center toward Patton Drive, which circumscribes one end of the cemetery, I can also speculate that Arlington's place in the firmament of memorial landscapes would look different were it not for United States' rise to world power after World War II.

With so many grave plots spread across a large historical expanse, it is clear that Arlington is an iterative landscape. But it is not what some might call a palimpsest because the past layers (excepting the dead) have all been brought to the surface and named, the nation's genealogy organized into memorials, ceremonial gates, and avenues. This is the case at all national cemeteries, but it is especially true at Arlington, where the guided paths lead you from one historical moment to another. So I stop to take a photograph at Ord and Weitzel Avenue and Lincoln Drive, where the street signs meet at a right angle to honor two Union generals (Edward Ord and Godfrey Weitzel), just down the road from Section 27 and the gravesites of the US Colored Troops, who are buried next to so-called contrabands, formerly enslaved people (often designated "citizen" on their headstones), who were permitted to build homes and live on the north side of the property after it was claimed by the government—in Freedman's Village—but were expelled in 1900 so their land could be added to the cemetery.[17] The iconic weight of Arlington

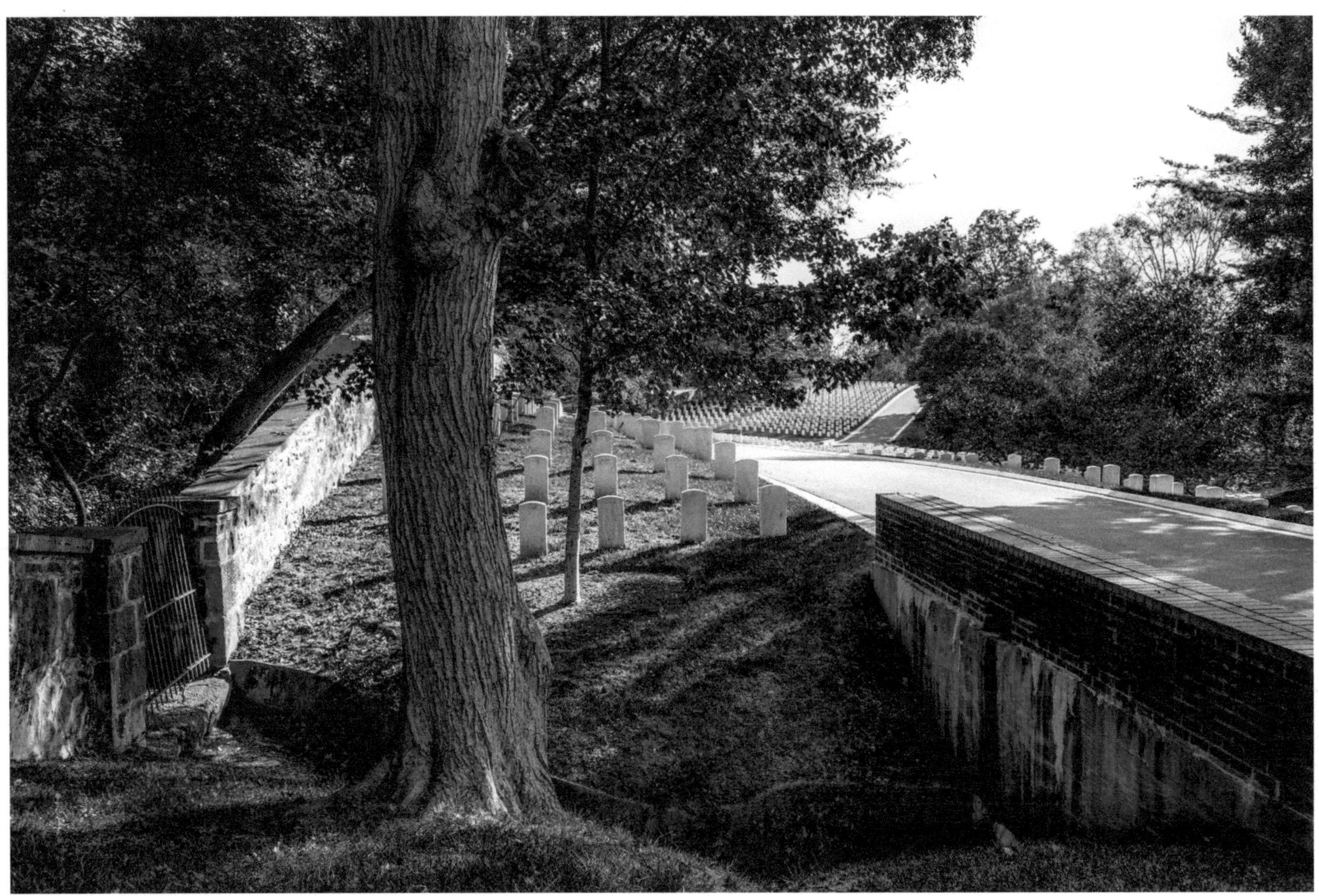

Section 27, Ord and Weitzel Drive, Arlington National Cemetery, 2020.

is evident in the stone benches that dot the grounds with the acronym US affixed to the gray surface in thick block letters and the curved saddle seat more appealing to look at (or photograph) than sit on, a bit like those antique chairs that occupy the corners of some living rooms as reminders of a more decorative past.

During my visit to Arlington in December 2017, I went off trail in the northwest section to see what I could see along the perimeter of the cemetery, still among the headstones but away from the frequently traveled paths. It is not like you can wander into unmarked territory at Arlington since the cemetery is bordered by Fort Myers and the number of buildings and amount of infrastructure, as well as the gravesites, give the landscape a thickly settled feeling. Still, when I walked through Section 1 into Sections 80–84 (rarely do the section numbers align with the topography), I found myself at the top of a hill looking down at a construction fence and beyond that a complex of newly built columbaria, roads, and walkways, spread out on a park-like plain where there also seemed to be space for in-ground interments. This new section was not quite finished, and with the fort's barracks rising up above the columbaria, I resisted the urge to step over the fence and take pictures. I found out later that this was the Millennium Project, the first effort in forty years to expand Arlington, begun in 2007 and recently supplemented by yet another expansion project to be completed at the southern end of the cemetery, next to the Air Force Memorial. Because of demands on space, the government has also narrowed the eligibility for burials, making Arlington "the most stringent of all U.S. national cemeteries." And, over the

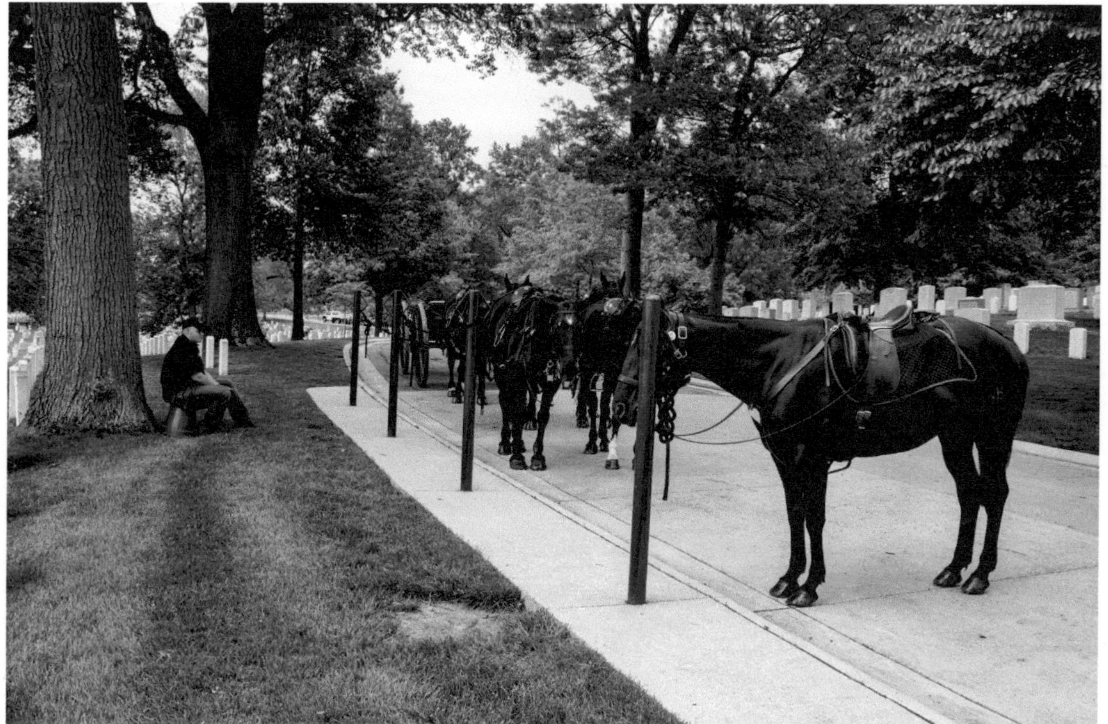

Arlington National Cemetery, 2021. As part of a long-standing military tradition, horse-drawn caissons carry the remains of eligible service members to their gravesites at Arlington. These off-duty horses pause to rest on Grant Drive.

objections of veterans, the military may establish additional restrictions by limiting in-ground burials to "combat heroes, battle casualties and a small pool of notable dignitaries."[18]

Legend has it that Arlington's future was guaranteed when, in 1864, General Quartermaster Montgomery C. Meigs demanded that Union dead be buried in the flower beds next to the Custis-Lee mansion, an interment plan that eventually included the Tomb of the Civil War Unknowns (located steps from the house). Up to this point, perhaps out of deference to the family, the soldiers had been digging graves on the outskirts of the property. The accommodation enraged Meigs, who was determined that the temporary cemetery become permanent and that the Lees never set foot on the property again.[19] Whether this story is true in all respects is not as important as the fact of its existence and the ongoing effort to establish a moral point of origin for the cemetery when, in the face of civil war, that center could be hard to see and when, as the deaths mounted, there was no edge, no end to expansion.

One hundred sixty years later, the ground that Meigs occupied remains vital territory for engaging the meaning of the Republic. While the national cemeteries were established as burial grounds for the Union dead, over time they transcended their function as military cemeteries to became evolving "sites of memory," places where the rituals of grief give way to wide-ranging reflections about the relation between self and nation, where the promise of freedom and democracy is explicitly invoked. In this respect, the dynamics of feeling, thought, and imagination that the national cemeteries enable are just as important as what and whom these landscapes honor.[20]

I write in the optative mood, recognizing that my description of this would-be dreamscape may seem wrongheaded. After all, signs of memorial dissonance are all around us. Monuments to once hallowed political leaders are coming down across the United States and Europe. In 2020, the Andrew W. Mellon Foundation launched its Monuments Project, "an unprecedented multi-year commitment" focused on "transforming the nation's commemorative landscape to ensure that our collective histories are more completely and accurately represented." With a budget of $500 million dollars, the foundation will award grants to support "publicly oriented initiatives"—usually the creation of new installations—that "express, elevate, and preserve the stories of those who have often been denied historical recognition." Erika Doss likewise suggests a crisis of representation in *Memorial Mania: Public Feeling in America* (2010), when she underscores Americans' "obsession with issues of memory and history" and their "urgent desire to express and claim those issues in visibly public contexts." Here, the single-minded commitment to memorials dedicated

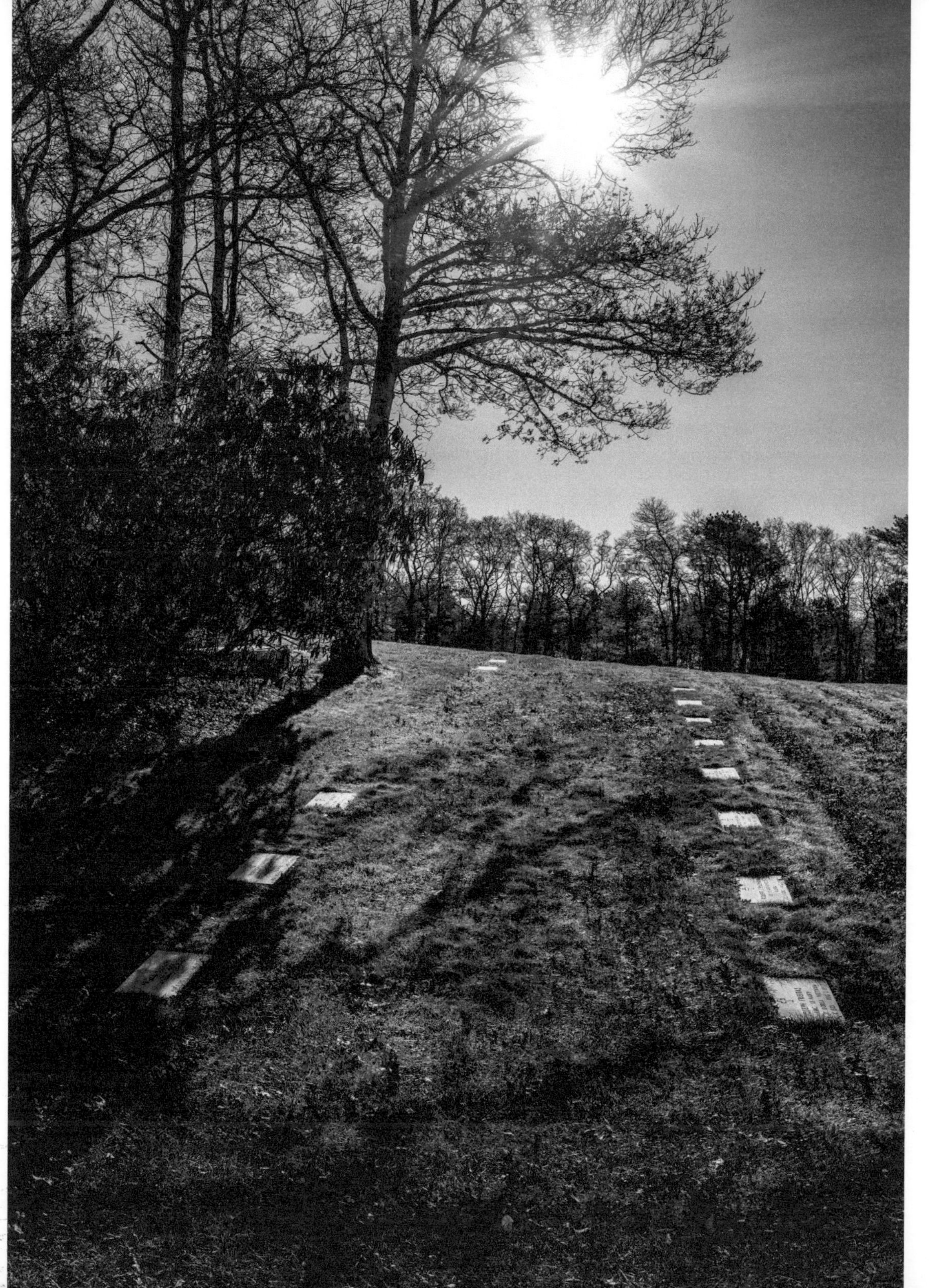

Massachusetts National Cemetery (established in 1976), Bourne, Massachusetts, 2018.

to particular causes is tied to a corresponding belief that no one commemorative site can speak for the whole. Other scholars of American memory have made similar observations.[21] In a nation increasingly divided by competing versions of history, conspiracy theories, and "alternative facts," your collective memory may not be mine.

In highlighting the distinctive mission of America's national cemeteries, I do not mean to claim that these landscapes celebrate or promise to restore a consensus-based view of US history. Rather, I want to suggest that the cemeteries, taken as a whole, reveal the realities and thus the imperfections of the American story in poignant, often unsettling terms while also providing an expansive, open-ended context for assessing American political imperatives. Moreover, and borrowing from John Bodnar and Pierre Nora's theoretical framing of the relation between history and memory, I would stress the cemeteries' potential for mediating the "ideological formulations" that define American nationhood.[22] In practice, this abstract proposition means that visitors have the space—both physical and figurative—to interpret the memorial record inscribed across 155 cemeteries and assess and judge accordingly. This is one way of bearing witness to America's ever-changing role in the world since the Civil War and acknowledging the nation's complicated relation to its shared democratic project. We may be tempted to dismiss the cemeteries' representative status by objecting to their military nature and deploring the "bad" wars that they honor, but in my view, having visited all but a few of America's national cemeteries, this would be a mistake. The place for protesting military decisions lies elsewhere, not among the dead. Here, in the national cemeteries, we are all on common ground.

9

Trees and Stone

THERE IS A WAY IN WHICH CEMETERIES APPEAR TO HAVE LITTLE TO DO WITH HIStory, at least the kind that gets written down in books and taught in schools. This distinction is less about the difference between history as a narrative of human accomplishment or the epigraphic remembrance of the past than the fact that cemeteries are part of the natural environment. Left alone or buried and burned, human corpses molder and return to the elements. Dust to dust. Headstones, a kind of writing on the earth, bring the dead into the historical record and distinguish graves from the scraped depressions and skeletal remains left by scavenging animals and insects. To be human is to mark the traces of our ancestors and the limits of mortality.

In the deserts and mountains of the American Southwest, a body can disappear in a matter of weeks. Take the experiment that anthropologist Jason De León carried out in the Sonoran Desert just south of Tucson, when he placed the carcasses of three dead pigs by a mesquite tree and under some rocks and installed a motion-sensor camera to record what happened to their bodies. De León's larger interest was estimating the number of migrants willing to risk their lives in order to cross the border into the United States. The pigs were a proxy for those who attempted the journey but died along the way and left no trace of their passage. The fate of the dead pigs helped explain why. Within two weeks, the flesh on their bodies was completely gone, picked clean by scavengers and withered by the sun and sand and wind, the skeletons well along in the process of decomposition. What survived were the tattered remains of the clothes that De León dressed the pigs in, the vestiges of civilization.[1]

To a certain extent, the memorial process is meant to resist the ravages of decomposition. Bodies placed in caskets are insulated by burial liners and concrete crypts, and cremains end up in metal urns to be buried or stored in columbaria. Activists, beginning perhaps with Jessica Mitford, whose book *The American Way of Death* (1963) exposed the funeral industry's price gouging, have pushed for more control of the mortuary process and developed new ways of disposing of dead bodies and reinstituted ancient practices that state and local regulations sometimes prohibit.[2] Many advocates want to manage what they see as a deeply personal ritual, while others are concerned about the environmental impact of standard undertaking.

I would not describe the national cemeteries as personal or private spaces. In mission, they are anything but. Still, perhaps because they were conceived during a civil war defined by geography and slavery and land—and fought in places like the Wilderness and Atlanta—and because the dead were initially lost to nature, the architects of the system were especially concerned with protecting the dead from the elements even as they remanded them to the earth in the most efficient ways possible.[3] In death as in life and regardless of the inconsistences surrounding the designation, the United States has remained nature's nation.

In 1997, the Los Angeles National Cemetery opened the Rose Garden Ossuary, becoming the first national cemetery to give veterans' families the option of dispersing cremains across an open space. Cemeteries built during the early 2000s, such as Fort Sill National Cemetery in Oklahoma and Great Lakes National Cemetery in Michigan, incorporated scattering gardens in their original designs. The ashes drift into the foliage and on to the ground to become part of the natural environment, the names of the deceased appearing on a nearby plaque. When I visited the Scattering Garden at Georgia National Cemetery—established in 2006, fifty miles north of Atlanta—I hesitated, not sure where to point the camera. Scattering challenges the idea that commemoration should take place around a fixed point, and my search for perspective reminds me of the free-floating "unknowns" and lists of names on the walls of Thiepval and Menin Gate and the Vietnam Veterans Memorial. But I realize that the added pain of not being able to identify or locate a soldier killed in war does not apply in Georgia since the bodies were presumably accounted for, and the families simply decided to commit the ashes to the earth—where they would end up anyway—and hold on to the names.

Cemeteries are built around this tension between the memory of human presence and the return to nature. In eighteenth-century Europe, the modern cemetery evolved as a cosmopolitan landscape—in Thomas Laqueur's words, a "luxuriantly protean space"—with gardens, sculpted pathways, and "a historicist jumble" of statues and mausoleums borrowed from the classical world to create a setting in which the memory of each individual body is assumed to be sacred. This was in contrast to the churchyard, where for centuries the dead took their place in the kingdom of God, and time was measured in Providential terms. The first cemeteries were private property, and the grave plots, purchased as real estate. They were also specially designed; indeed, the profession of landscape architecture emerged alongside the cemetery. Cemeteries such as Père Lachaise in Paris, Kensal Green in London, and Mount Auburn in Cambridge, Massachusetts, became famous for their artful integration of architecture and nature. Trees known for their spiritual properties, like the yew and the weeping willow, which had positions of stature in the churchyard, were included in cemeteries as vestiges of the earlier regime.[4]

In early nineteenth-century America, particularly in the Northeast and, most of all, in Cambridge, Massachusetts, where, as conceived by transcendentalists like Ralph Waldo Emerson (1803–82), the human soul was at one with all living things, nature came to play an almost

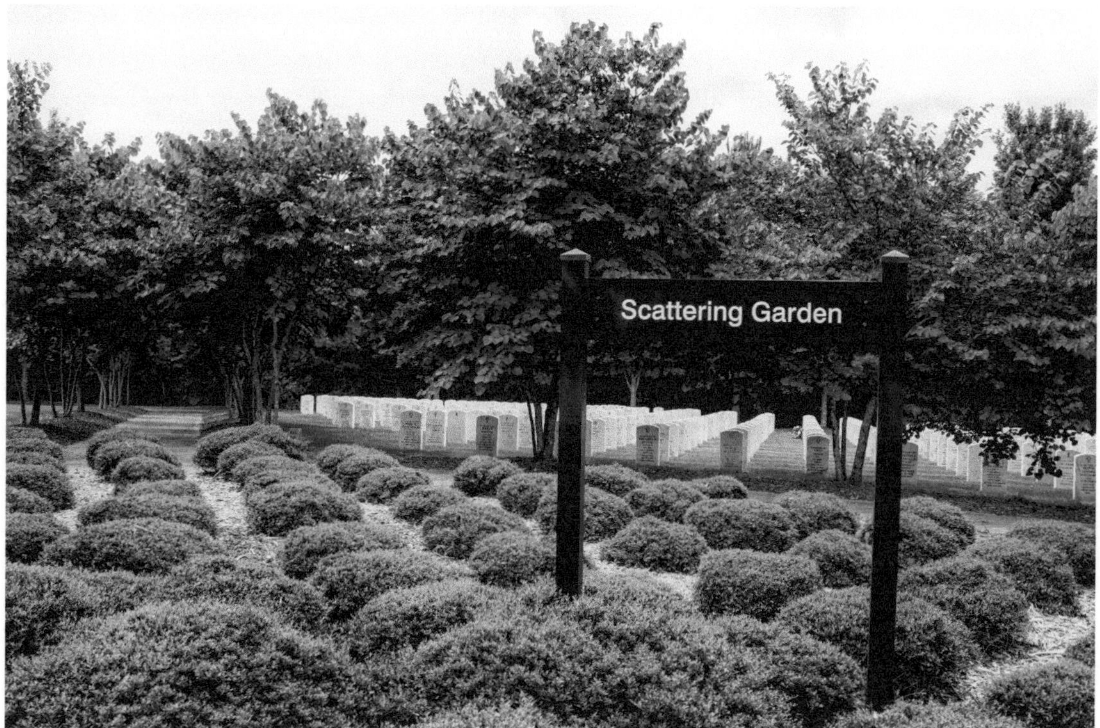

Georgia National Cemetery (established in 2001), Canton, Georgia, 2018.

metaphysical role in the disposition of the dead. Historian Aaron Sachs argues that the environmental ethos that developed at this time was based on the understanding that life and death are integrally related, a concept that unfolded in the design of Mount Auburn (founded in 1831), which encouraged visitors to assume an attitude of "repose" so they could peacefully share the pleasures of nature with the dead. The rural cemetery movement carried this vision to a larger cross-section of the population, giving upper- and middle-class Americans the chance to purchase grave plots in beautifully constructed tree-lined parks or arboretums. The sensory allure of these landscapes can also be a challenge to memory. For while cemeteries were built to help people remember the dead, nature is an ever-shifting panorama that can trump the landscape's "didactic" purposes and eclipse the fine print on headstones.[5]

With their regimented display of headstones, the national cemeteries departed from the meandering appeal of the rural cemeteries. But they did not leave nature behind. I remember that when I visited Cypress Hills in Brooklyn (founded in 1862), I spent an hour photographing the headstones beneath the branches of an enormous, graffiti-clad beech that dominates one side of the cemetery. The tree must have been at least a century old. I continued to find stands of what looked like old-growth trees in other Civil War–era cemeteries, and the first time I saw a tree swallowing a headstone—at Vicksburg National Cemetery—I wondered if Frederick Law Olmsted's instructions to Montgomery Meigs were ill-advised. While Olmsted encouraged him to plant native species and establish sacred groves, it appeared that nature had exceeded its order. At the National Memorial Cemetery of Arizona, outside Phoenix, I found palm trees and junipers spread throughout the grounds. In the middle of one section, next to a small enclosure marked "First Burials, March 14, 1979"—the lettering over the entryway mimicking the signs found at graveyards in old Western towns—I saw a huge saguaro cactus, probably thirty feet high, so big that a cable had been run from its trunk to the ground to keep the plant from collapsing onto the fence.[6] The saguaro also appeared to be damaged or diseased since long strips of canvas were wrapped around its midsection, like bandages on a wounded soldier.

I may have misjudged Olmsted's advice and not taken the word "sacred" seriously enough. Because it is clear that many of these trees are not merely ornamental. They are full participants in the landscape, like the "witness trees" that stood in place when men died on the battlefields of Antietam or Gettysburg and survive today as a living connection to those traumatic scenes. At Arlington National Cemetery, trees play a formal role in the commemoration process. Of the 8,000 trees

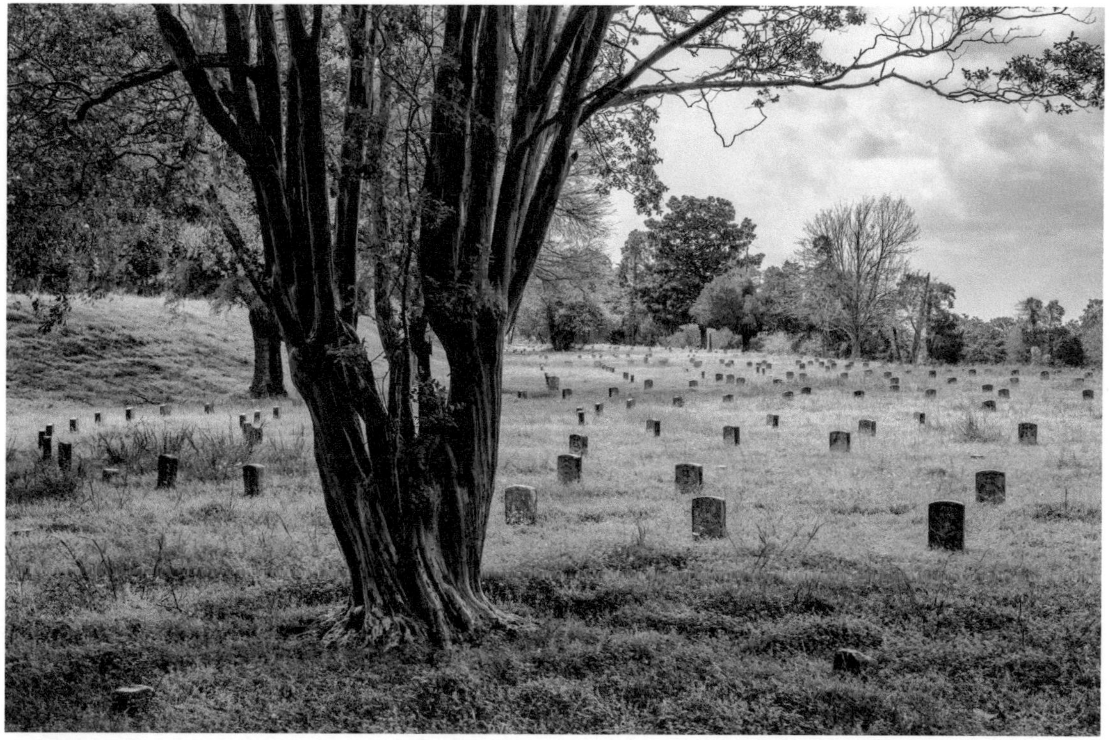

Vicksburg National Cemetery (established in 1866), Vicksburg, Mississippi, 2017. Only five thousand of the approximately seventeen thousand Union soldiers interred here are identified.

on Arlington's 652 acres, approximately 150 are memorial trees, planted to honor specific veteran groups. There is Tree #3 in Section 44, a Japanese flowering cherry, dedicated to the Veterans of the Battle of the Bulge; Tree #66 in Section 2, a pin oak, dedicated to the 454th Bombardment Group; and Tree #104 in Section 22, a Kousa dogwood, honoring the Ninth and Tenth US Cavalry Association (buffalo soldiers). But many of the older trees at Arlington are accidental witnesses and also receive care. If a spouse (usually a widow) is to be buried next to a veteran who died forty years earlier and a tree seems to be crowding the future grave, the Arlington foresters will excavate the site and trim the roots to make room for the entering casket and extend the life of the tree.[7]

This scenario reminds me of the bones that the National Park Service found near the Manassas battlefield and the effort to piece together the bodies. Undertakers do something similar when they "restore" corpses—cutting hair, shaving whiskers, and applying makeup—in advance of an open viewing so that the body resembles the person the grieving family remembers. In a

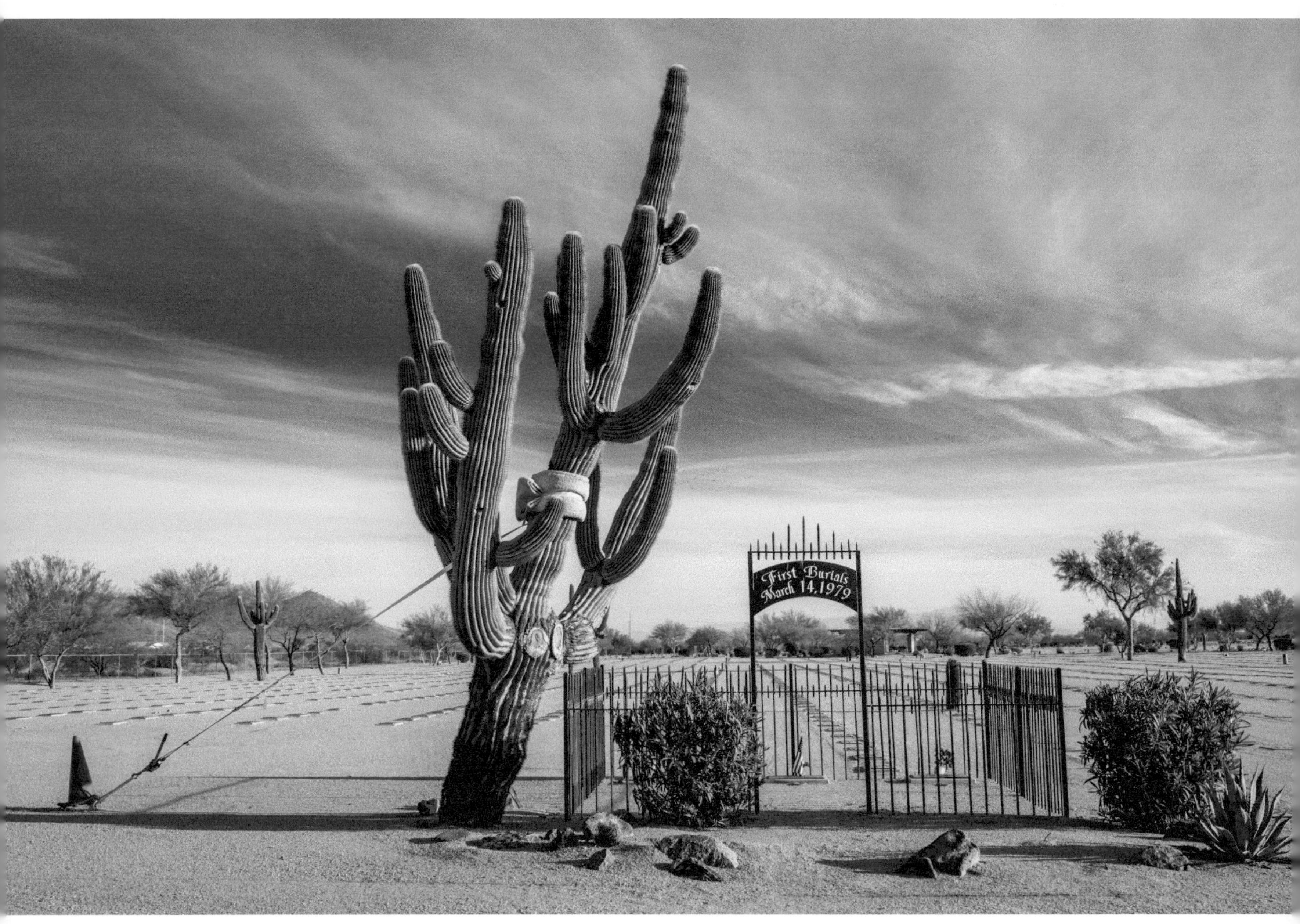

First burials at National Memorial Cemetery of Arizona (established in 1989), Phoenix, Arizona, 2018.

centuries-old practice known as pollarding, arborists cut back the tops of trees to prolong their life and enable a more juvenile appearance. I knew nothing about this tradition until I looked at the weirdly shorn trees along the alleés of American cemeteries in France and did some research. The historical explanation made sense, but I still could not understand why I was finding visual linkages where there was no logical reason for doing so. Then again, given the richly allusive necrogeography, maybe I was putting too fine a point on the matter.[8] In *The Overstory* (2018), novelist Richard Powers places trees at the center of a multigenerational saga in which the survival of humans depends on the sustainability of old-growth forests. And German forester Peter Wohlleben suggests a related genealogy in *The Hidden Life of Trees: What They Feel, How They Communicate: Discoveries from a Secret World* (2016), the subtitle making the not-so-subtle point that humans might learn something about how to cultivate their own future—and the planet's—if they were just more attentive.

During my travels, I encountered several remediation projects, with landscaping crews deployed to move soil or dig up headstones to address one problem or another. At Natchez National Cemetery in Mississippi, I took pictures of an eroding hilltop that was under construction, sweeping my lens across the purplish, stripped-out soil as if I were photographing an action sequence. The pictures did not turn out the way I hoped, as the composition looked as haphazard as the despoiled ground, but I tried again at Long Island National Cemetery, this time focusing on a section where headstones had been pulled from the earth to realign them. The scene was unsettling, though in my effort to impose order the photos did appear more carefully framed.

The day I visited Fort Leavenworth National Cemetery in Kansas (in May 2018), I was kneeling by some nineteenth-century grave plots getting ready to photograph a headstone discolored by green blotches, when I looked up to see a member of the staff, who introduced himself as the assistant director and told me that the distress marks were mildew and that the drainage system in this part of the cemetery needed to be repaired. He said he submitted a renovation proposal to his superiors, but they decided instead to replace the sod at a cost of a million dollars. He was unhappy with this outcome, but he did not need to explain their reasoning. The cemetery is on post, and Fort Leavenworth is a large, generously resourced US Army base. There are houses, commercial establishments, and, across from the cemetery, a golf course, where I saw carts, strollers, and joggers blocking my view of the fairways. Appearances matter. Why not just replace the grass and save the environmental engineering for later?

Two weeks after my visit to Fort Leavenworth, I was at Glendale National Cemetery in Virginia, a small cemetery, with the graves of Union soldiers laid out in circular fashion, when I struck up a conversation with an older Black man who was loading his pickup with landscaping equipment. I remarked how well maintained the grounds were, and he thanked me but said the grass was dry and brown and that he needed to figure out why so he could prepare the cemetery for Memorial Day. Then, pointing to the road, he said there is still a lot of gunpowder out there and that thousands of men died in the Seven Days' Battle, when Lee's army turned back George B. McClellan's forces as they approached Richmond in the summer of 1862. Only now—and he made one of those imperceptible shifts to the present tense—people are not willing to stand up for what they believe in and they do not want to fight. I nodded, and he replied, yes, it is a serious problem, that his wife teaches in a pre-K school program, that kids are being shot in classrooms and we need to "harden" the schools.

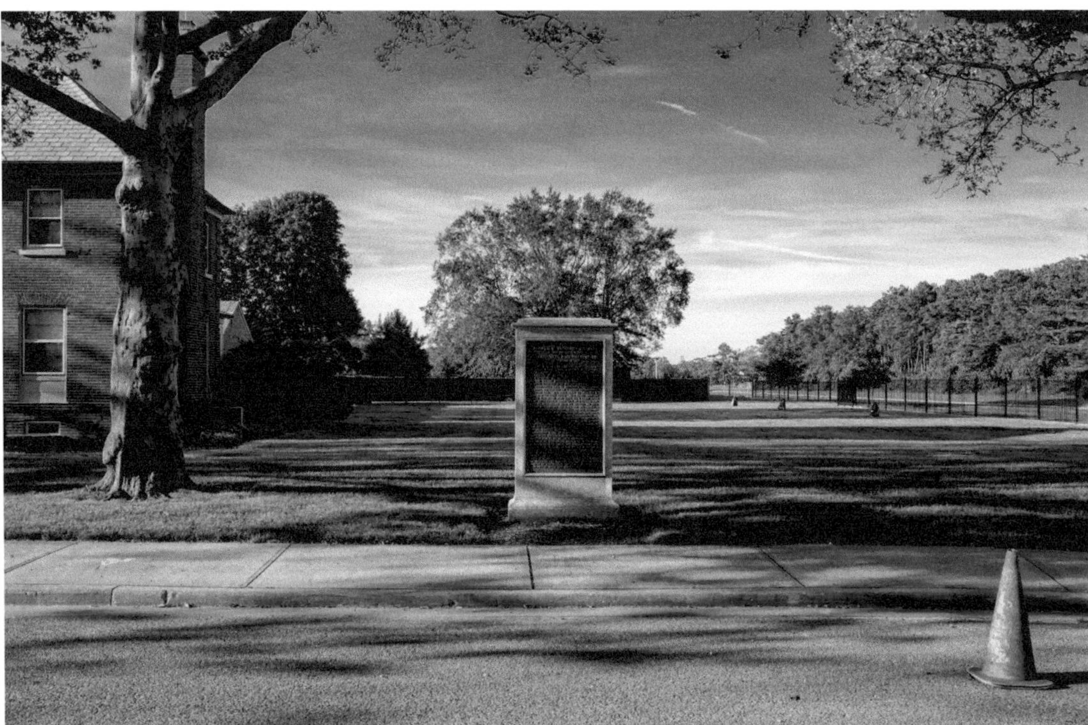

The Gettysburg Address displayed at Long Island National Cemetery (established in 1936), Farmingdale, New York, 2019.

There is no easy way to give the environment separate standing in these cases, nor is it possible to insulate history, or the marking of it, from natural forces. Also, we may come to these sites with our own conceptions of why they should be remembered, not necessarily because we disagree about the facts in or on the ground (though we might) but because we have different ideas about what these outcomes mean to the nation's history and culture. The architectural preservationists who work for the National Cemetery Administration and National Park Service contend with these tensions when they decide how history should be represented through the built environment. For instance, though the cemeteries built after the Civil War were designed in particular ways—some with headstones arrayed in circles, most with roadways for carriages—their aesthetic character changed as new graves were added and curb cuts were built for automobiles. At what point, if at all, did these alterations degrade the landscapes' expressive power, and how should the government safeguard their original memorial purpose?[9]

I am drawn to these historical skirmishes, and it occurs to me that what shows up in my lens as the juxtaposition of headstones and houses beyond the fence—the memorial and quotidian—is also a picture of time passing. In a tradition that goes back to ancient Egypt, we place flowers on graves to highlight the beauty and fragility of life. We know they will wilt and deteriorate; that is part of the ritual. The flowers return to nature, and the cycle of renewal continues.[10]

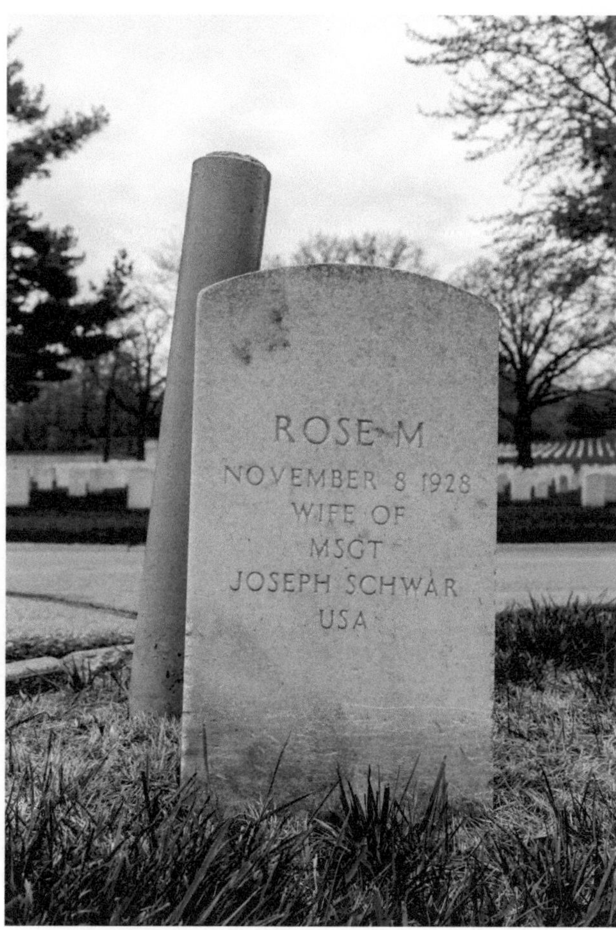

Fort Leavenworth National Cemetery (established in 1862), Fort Leavenworth, Kansas, 2018.

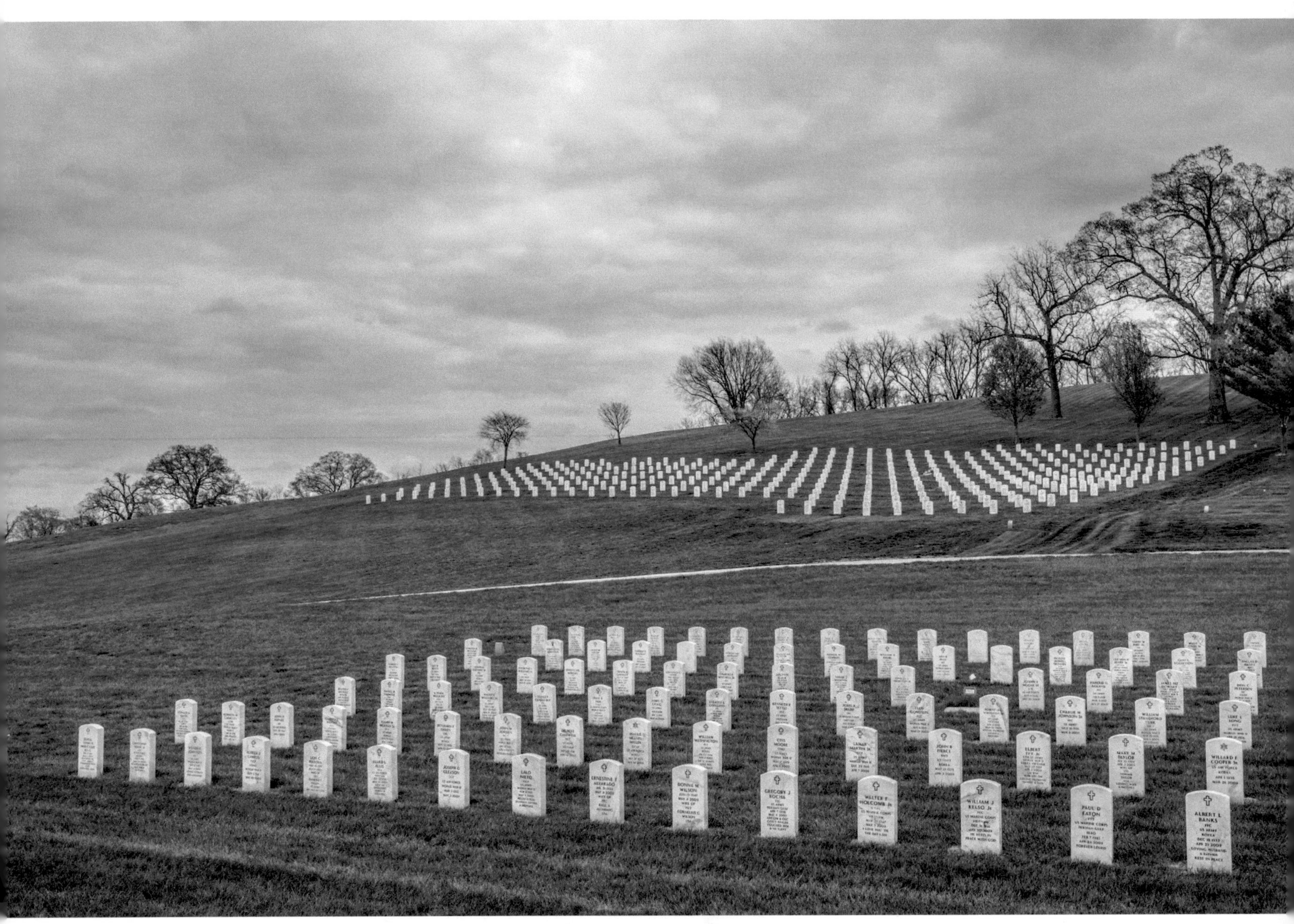

Leavenworth National Cemetery (established in 1886), Leavenworth, Kansas, 2018.

I may be straining poetic license here, but it seems to me that I am engaged in a kind of nature photography in this project, an effort to show how the dead and the nation are tangled up in the substrate, just as the tree roots and graves at Arlington are. Memory presents itself not only as graven images and words set in stone but as objects in the stream of natural history.

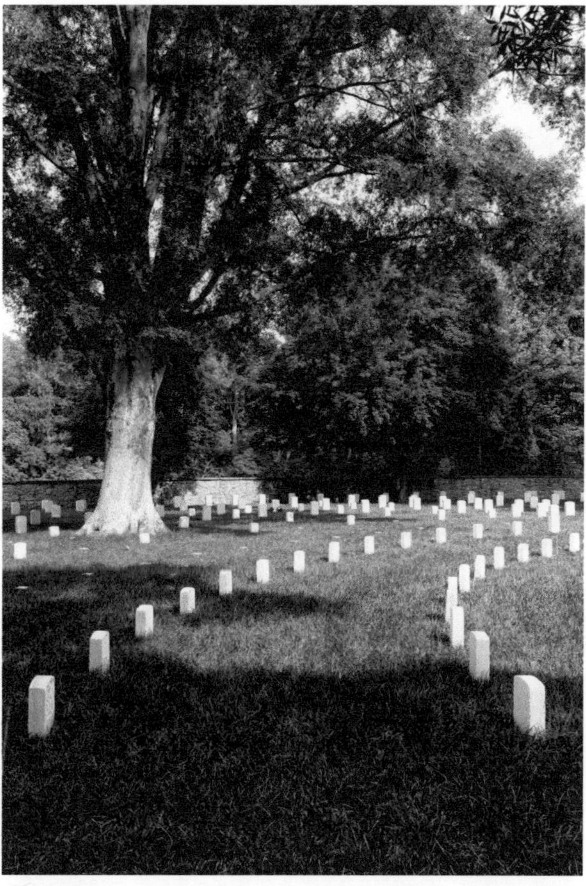

Glendale National Cemetery (established in 1866), Richmond, Virginia, 2018.

Sometimes, pursuing this line of vision flattens my subject matter, creating equivalencies where none were intended. To be specific: if I take a picture of an old water pump next to a row of headstones as I did at Camp Nelson National Cemetery in Nicholasville, Kentucky, am I showcasing a piece of infrastructure that is best left in the background or responding to what the memorial landscape is now showing me? The question is misleading as an either/or choice. At least I want to resist this framing because, in the late afternoon summer light with newly cut grass, the hammered metal appears to me in the fullness of nature, luminous in its distinct singularity. And it is not just the pump I have in sight. I get stuck on other things too, from the perches of stone that made the walls at Antietam National Cemetery to the concrete "floral containers" at Fort Snelling National Cemetery that were placed by the side of the road so people can throw away those plastic containers used to hold flowers. The national cemeteries have strict regulations about how long floral arrangements can remain on graves.

"To give an object poetic space is to give it more space than it has objectivity," Gaston Bachelard writes, "or, better still, it is following the expansion of its intimate space." In his 1958 book, the French philosopher explains how these dimensions take shape around the correspondence between psychological states and specific locations in the outside world, usually houses where corners, stairways, or attics hold archetypical yearnings and fears shaped by childhood experiences. Resisting the logic of positivist criticism, he lays out a place-based theory of the "poetic act" that "has no recent past." Instead, he is most interested in images of what he calls "felicitous" or "eulogized space." Bachelard says we are all daydreamers, drawn by primal memories of a receding past, an emotional geography we barely understand but that we revisit, reclaim, and re-create in the landscape before us.[11]

Bachelard's meditations suggest why I might want to photograph scenes and objects whose appeal I cannot fully articulate other than to point to their texture and solidity and the light and shade that constitute their seen reality. His reference to eulogized space also helps explain why a space ordinarily understood as a place of sorrow can evoke happiness and comfort. In other words, the dead are never just the dead and memorial landscapes may be surrogates for other structures of feeling. Scholars in memory studies have also stressed memory's elastic, multidimensional nature.[12] So when I stand by a grave at the edge of the cemetery and look through the fence at the back of a house, my field of vision expands in time, maybe to the sunroom at my grandparents' home in Birmingham, Michigan, where I sat and read as a child when I was not playing in the backyard gazing into that room, or to the interiors of other houses that I glimpsed from afar, perhaps from a car

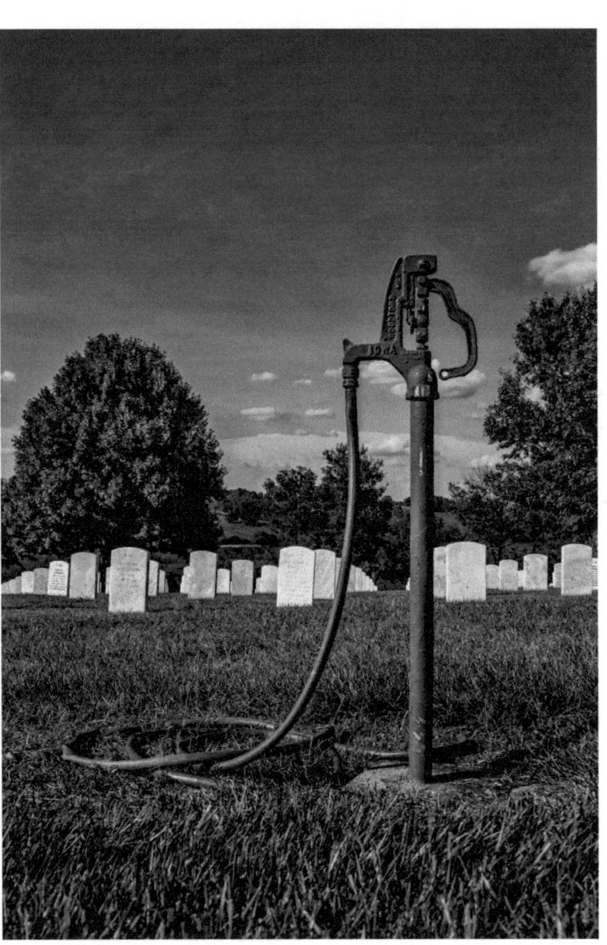

Camp Nelson National Cemetery (established 1866), Nicholasville, Kentucky, 2019.

when I rode through suburban neighborhoods at night, the warmly lit mysteries of other people's lives facing me across front lawns and sidewalks.

I can speculate based on Bachelard or any number of theorists that what we "see" through a camera is something other than what appears in the frame. But this is true for much photography. What stands out at a cemetery is the seemingly irreconcilable other—the dead—and at national cemeteries the memory of that person is inevitably connected to the military. If the service member died in combat, you would think that the poetic space accorded the dead—to stick with Bachelard's terminology—would tend toward the dark and violent. Yet the rituals accorded the dead are meant to grant peace and closure to the survivors, making the cemetery a final place of rest. This sense of resolution comes even for families whose relative's remains were MIA in Vietnam or Korea and recovered years after the combatant's death through the efforts of the military's Defense POW/MIA Accounting Agency. Sometimes the remains are limited to a tooth or a single bone, yet that object has enough emotional resonance to fill the space with an expanse of memories and meanings. In her account of the "exceptional care" the government takes to recover the missing, anthropologist Sarah E. Wagner moves from the forensic identification of remains to the memorial celebrations that ensue when the dead finally return to families and friends. Much like the mission that Edward Whitman and others undertook after the Civil War, this is a journey home that begins in remote, hidden places—for instance, in helicopter wreckage buried on jungle hillsides—and concludes with gatherings in living rooms, churches, and VFW meeting halls.[13] These scenes also comprise a kind of nature photography, really, a narrative that builds toward a happy ending and the rituals that restore the dead to the earth so as to distinguish them from the elements.

Pausing to mourn and remember or take a picture highlights the contradictions inherent in cemeteries: the dead are at rest in perpetuity and life goes on. The national cemeteries accommodate these discrepancies and, despite the assumptions we might make about repose, they are built to enable automobile traffic and momentary stops. There are a few formal parking spots, some by the office building, others in front of columbaria complexes or designated areas, but the landscape is mostly reserved for the dead. If military cemeteries are "silent cities," they are not necessarily walkable. Many older cemeteries are no more than three or four acres in size and can easily be strolled, usually with the flagpole and superintendent's lodge in sight, but the newer cemeteries are difficult to cover by foot if your aim is to be comprehensive. Calverton National

Fort Snelling National Cemetery (established in 1936), Minneapolis, Minnesota, 2018.

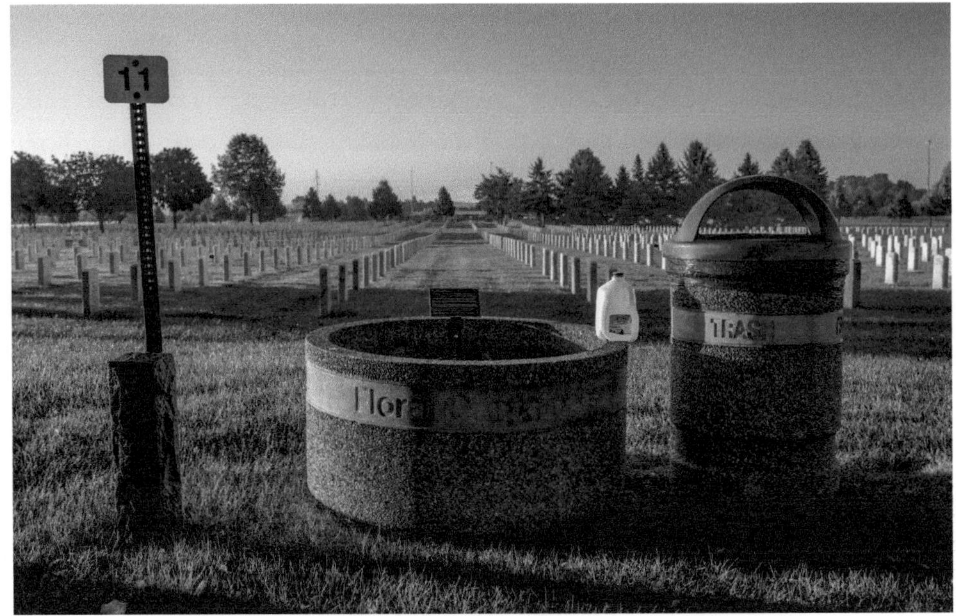

A view of the Minneapolis-Saint Paul International Airport from Fort Snelling National Cemetery, 2018.

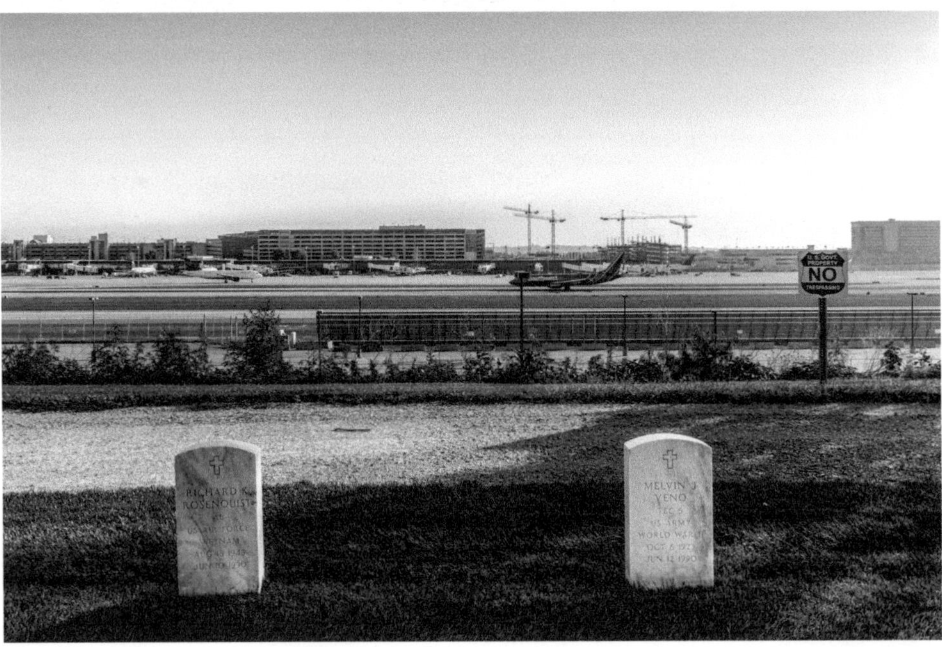

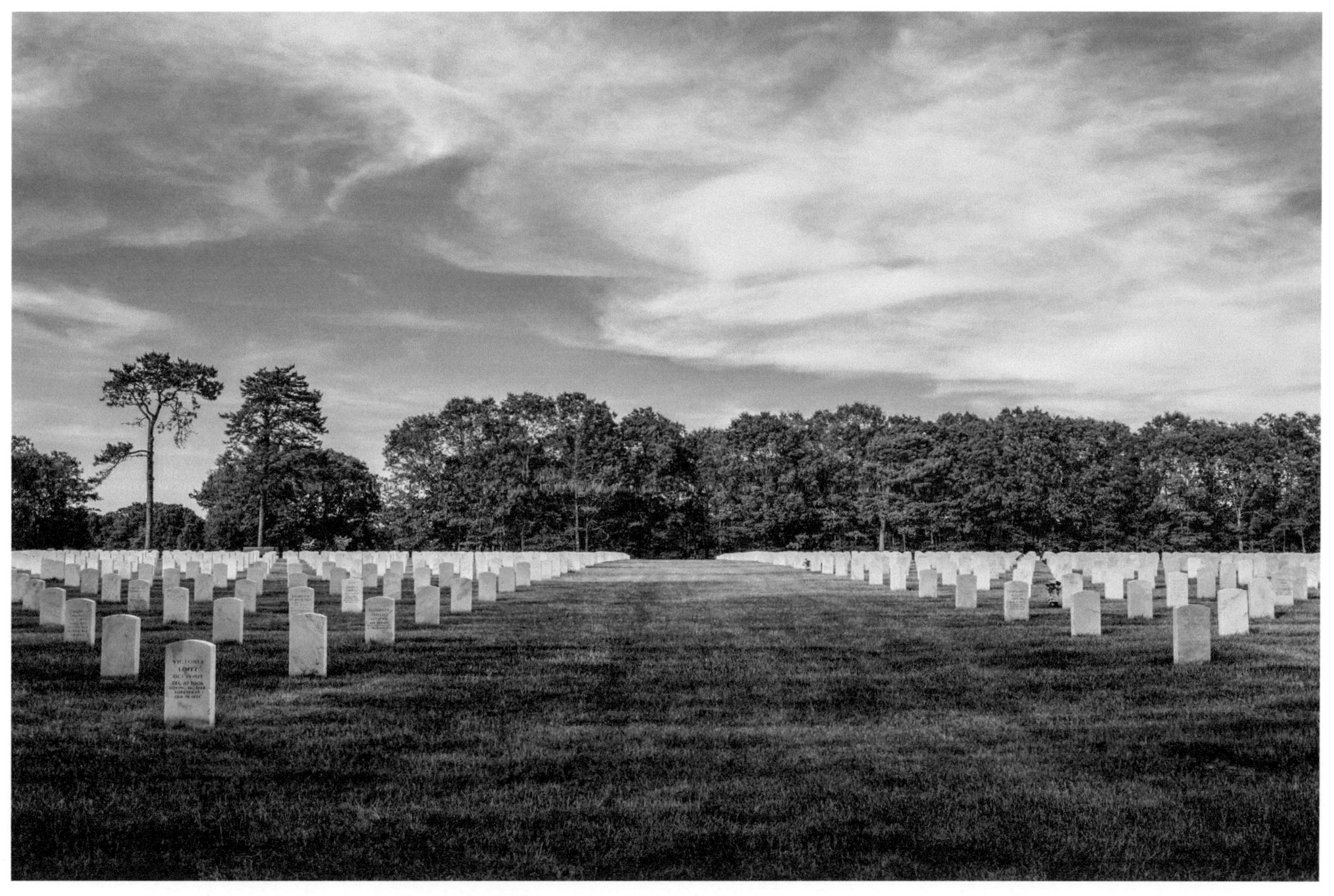

Calverton National Cemetery (established in 1977), Calverton, New York, 2019.

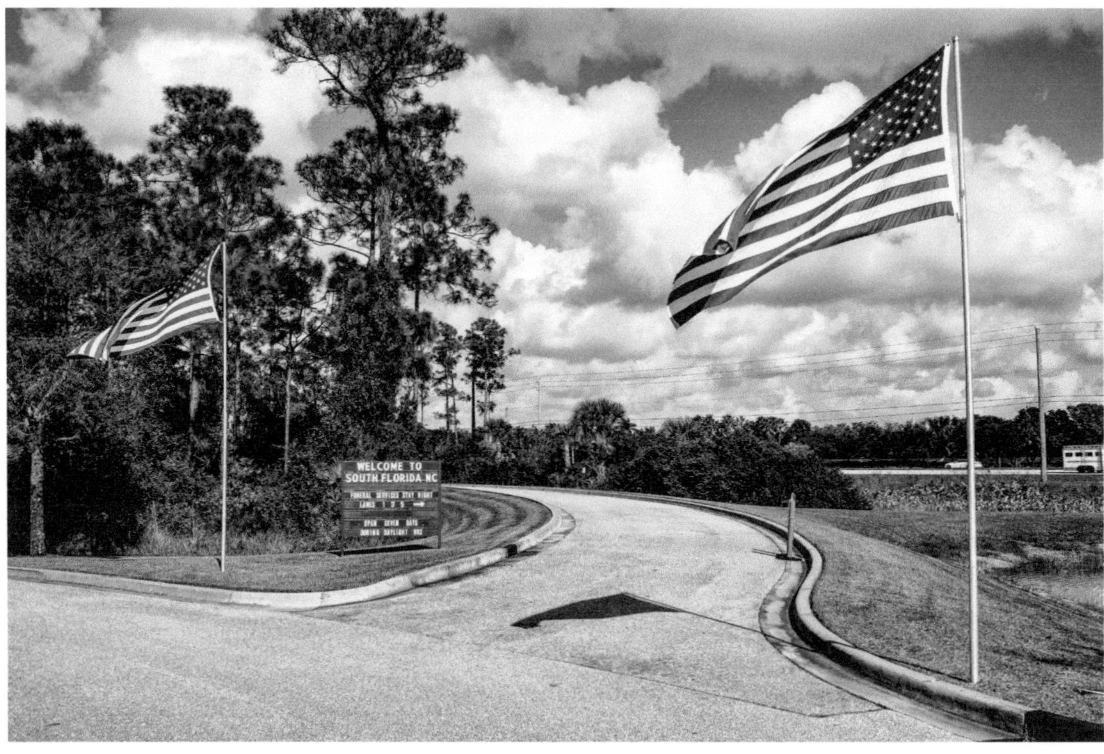

The entrance to South Florida National Cemetery (established in 2002), Lake Worth, Florida, 2019

Cemetery—at more than 1,000 acres and with 210,000 interments—stretches out into sections arranged like housing subdivisions, and you soon lose sight of the center if there really is one. The natural world opens up on all sides, but to see these places on the ground, you have to drive to a section, park by the curb, and then walk to a grave plot, columbarium, or scattering garden.

I got to Alabama National Cemetery in Montevallo on a January afternoon, and I was cutting through the woods between sections in the crisp winter light, when a woman called to me from the road, where she was standing next to her car and pointing to the headstones behind her. It was the day after the Wreaths Across America group had visited the cemetery to remove the holiday wreaths placed in December, and I guess, because I was taking pictures, she thought I had an official role at the cemetery. Anyway, she wanted to know why her father's and father-in-law's plots had not received wreaths. Last year, she said, they both got wreaths, and now a lot of graves had been left out and that did not look right—it just was not fair to the families. I said,

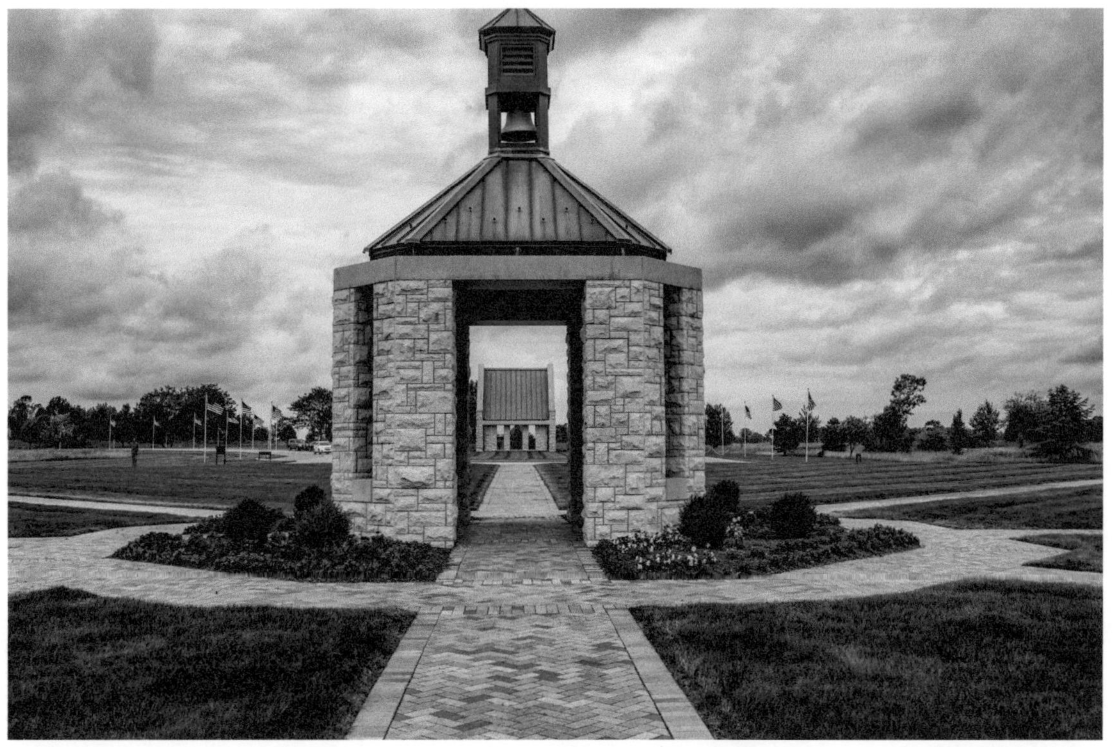

The Carillon Bell Tower at Ohio Western Reserve National Cemetery (established in 1995), Rittman, Ohio, 2019. The first carillon was installed at Arlington National Cemetery in 1949 as part of the AMVETS (American Veterans) Memorial Carillon Program that dates to 1948.

yes, that was too bad and maybe they ran out of wreaths. We wished each other Happy New Year and moved on, like neighbors passing each other on the block.

Spread across rural land and built in a style known as "corporate pastoralism," cemeteries like Alabama, Calverton, and Massachusetts may seem to lack character, but they allow a more privatized sense of intimacy. Commemoration is decentralized, the burial sections joined by curving streets and interlocking loop roads, with columbaria and memorial paths sited along the routes. During the 1980s, the National Cemetery Administration began to erect committal shelters to support the interment process.[14] Whether as open-air or glassy pavilions, the shelters bring mourners together for thirty-minute military ceremonies with honor guards and taps. Cars line up at the shelters for the ceremonies and then depart. Sometimes I saw that the cortege includes motorcycle riders. Given their age and dress—leather and jean jackets or vests—I guessed they were Vietnam War veterans. The roads are designed to funnel traffic, and at South Florida

National Cemetery in Lake Worth, Florida, there are dedicated lanes just beyond the front gate to guide funeral processions. The views at these places may be flat and uniform, as opposed to the weathered, picturesque scenes one often sees at Civil War cemeteries. But despite their streamlined design, the newer cemeteries are also part of history—or will be—and so I looked for the commemorative threads that tie them to their antecedents. I found them when I photographed the trees that line the memorial boulevard at Long Island, echoes of the neoclassical monuments in France, or the kiosk at Ohio Western Reserve National Cemetery that is on axis with the flagpole.

The national cemeteries have always been characterized by a blend of memorial stonework and utilitarian infrastructure. With the exception of some monuments and buildings, they lack the imprint of individual design. This is in keeping with their democratic ethos and distinguishes them from the military cemeteries in Europe, all neoclassical landscapes designed by renowned architects. It may also be what gives them a distinctly American identity. It is likewise fitting that during

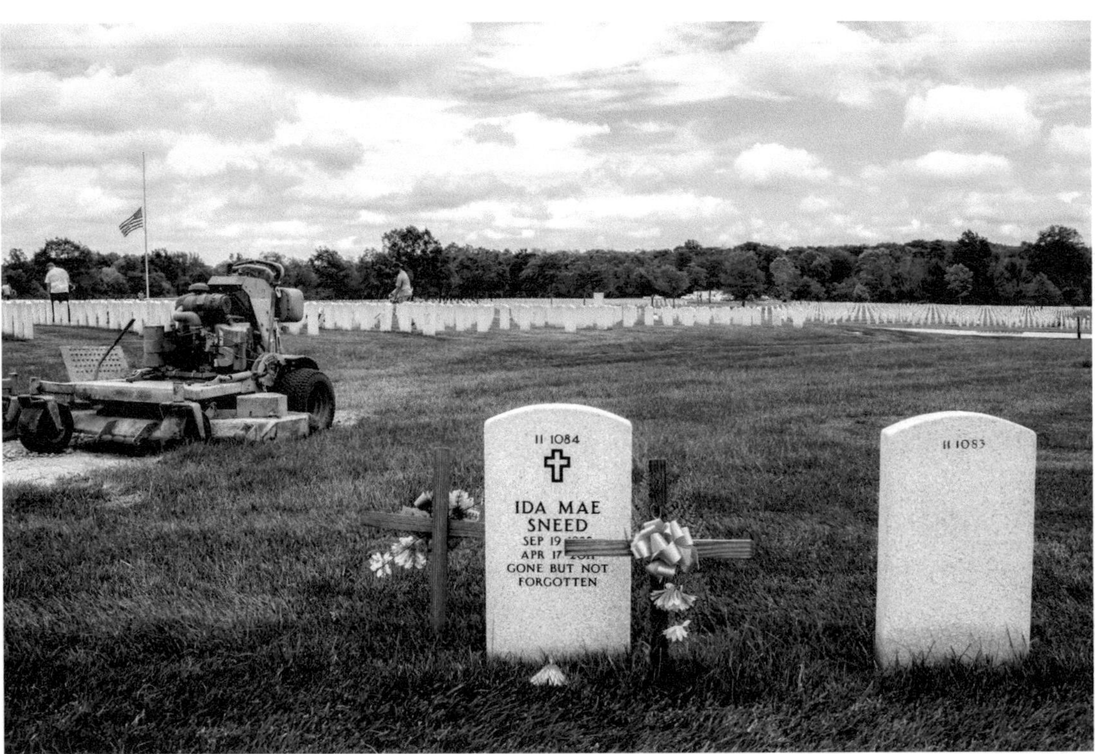

Ohio Western Reserve National Cemetery, 2019.

the last twenty years or so landscape architects have been responsible for designing the cemeteries. The qualifying prefix suggests that the architect's primary role in shaping these places is to give way to the earth, rather than press his or her design upon it, because those marks belong to the dead.

Compared to more traditional monuments—for instance, the equestrian statues and standing soldiers built in the nineteenth century—contemporary memorial design appears almost self-effacing. In reflecting on modern modes of remembrance, historian Jay Winter has proposed that the mass violence and death wrought by the Great War "pulled" commemorative forms toward the "horizontal axis." Forgoing the vertical shapes that once signified heroism or sacrifice, artists and architects now design war memorials that "bring us down to earth with a thud" and encourage contemplation, sorrow, and even regret among onlookers.[15] Yet this thesis does not quite capture the emotional dynamics of the low-slung American model, which, as it developed in the national cemetery system, sought to bring the individual mourner in line with the soaring needs of the nation.

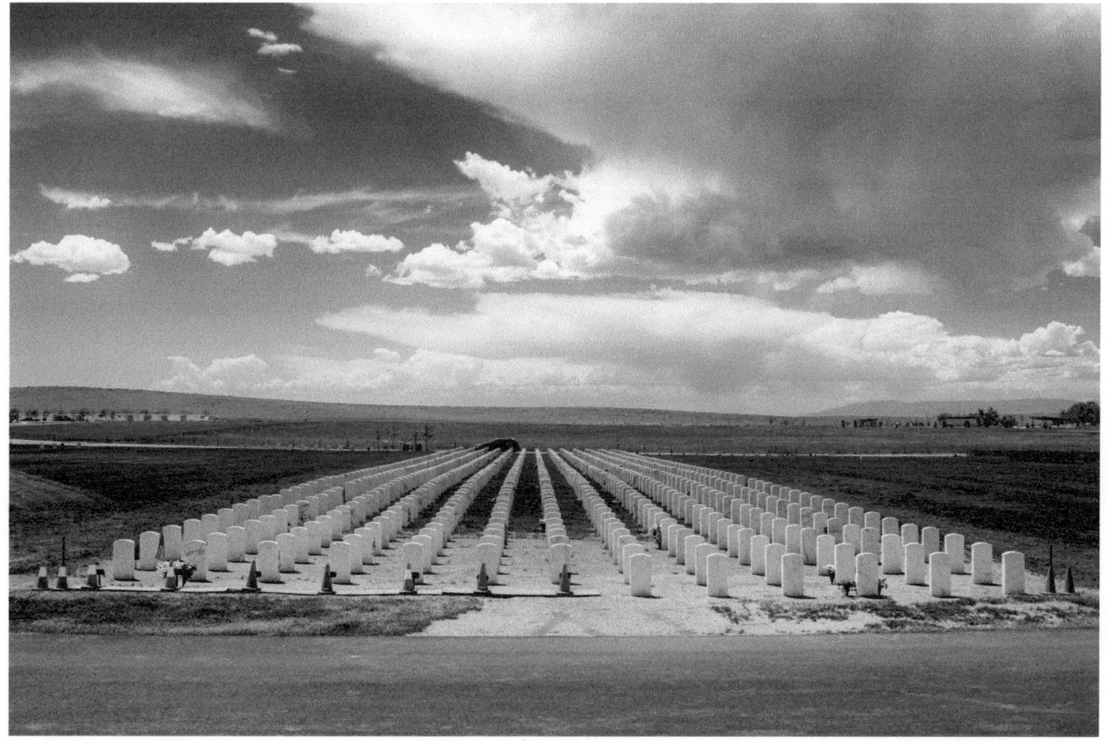

Pikes Peak National Cemetery (established in 2018), Colorado Springs, Colorado, 2020.

As if to explain how this happens on the ground, the LA Group, a landscape architecture firm based in Saratoga, New York, emphasizes four aspects of their work on national cemeteries (the Gerald B. Solomon Saratoga National Cemetery and Pikes Peak National Cemetery, among others). The architects describe their engagement with these spaces as a "journey through design" that begins with the entrance area (gate and roadway), proceeds to the administrative offices and public information center (including grave locator and bathrooms), continues on to interment spaces (grave plots and columbaria), and concludes with the ceremonial areas (committal shelter and flag stand). The design process combines functional and symbolic elements, which together "create a subconscious 'language' of the land" meant to speak primarily to the visitor, for it is "*the visitor's experience*" (their italics, not mine) that is of "utmost importance."[16] At Pikes Peak, a tight grid allows for the efficient placement of grave sites, while the big western sky and a seemingly endless horizon evoke transcendence.

The LA Group's description says that my visits have been anticipated and, moreover, that our collective orientation toward the dead—conscious or not—has been part of the cemeteries' design since their inception and that what appears to be up-to-date and out of sync with older parts of the cemetery is meant to extend the memorial process across time and space. In less poetic language, the National Cemetery Administration's design guide (2024) notes the importance of this inner pilgrimage with the reminder that the committal shelter is "not intended to be a focal point or a vital visual element of the total cemetery experience"—that symbolic role is reserved for the American flag, the "single most significant feature" on the landscape—but rather is meant to "preserve the privacy of committal services" in a "sheltered area visually isolated from the administrative, maintenance, and burial operations."[17]

I am not a veteran, nor have I lost family or friends who fought in war, so it is not for me to characterize the sense of loss that bring other people to the cemeteries, only to respect the gap in feeling and perspective. Nonetheless, I am encouraged to believe that these landscapes are open to all and that I have a place by the flag, whether it is surrounded by cannonballs and identified by metal signs from the Civil War era or machine tooled in silver rubbed steel and flanked by curved walls with a screaming eagle statue guarding the pathway into the amphitheater as it is at Patriot Plaza (built in 2014) at Sarasota National Cemetery. The difference between old and new is just a matter of time, and consciousness fills the gap.

At Togus National Cemetery in Chelsea, Maine, there are two burial sections located on the grounds of a medical complex run by the Department of Veterans Affairs. The facility began as one of several Soldiers Homes established after the Civil War to care for sick and infirm Union veterans. The original building, a resort hotel built during the 1850s, opened in 1866 as the National Asylum for Disabled Volunteer Soldiers. Togus was the first of its kind, the founding piece of what is now a vast health care system for veterans, and the government built several other Soldiers Homes during the 1860s and '70s, most of them attached to national cemeteries.[18]

I saw my first example of this multiuse landscape at Bath National Cemetery in New York, which I visited the day after seeing Woodlawn in Elmira. The grounds are extensive, and the cemetery stretches out into the hills almost as a necessary adjunct to the hospital beside it. When I toured Dayton National Cemetery almost two years later, I followed the interior road toward the southern perimeter and looked out over the flat stone markers in Section 18c at the Dayton VA Medical Center that was maybe 150 yards away and with no wall or fence in between.

Togus is split into two parts. Togus West is a cool, tree-shaded grove, surrounded by woods and studded with rock outcroppings, as you might expect in this part of New England, with several sections linked by paths across the craggy land and headstones designating the Union dead and some irregularly shaped memorials from the nineteenth century. Togus East (established in 1936), a half mile away, is laid out in a more contemporary fashion with headstones arrayed on a large field cut into four sections by crossing roads. A flag stand in the middle of one section appeared tied by invisible string to a row of saplings in the adjoining section and then tethered to a pole displaying the Gettysburg Address plaque—the idea of the monumental but not the thing itself. At the north end of the cemetery there is a Celtic cross (a gift made in the 1930s), behind which is a corridor of mature pine trees. Togus East is bordered by wetlands and looks like a place in Maine, though it is more open than its western counterpart so that a century from now arborists will not have to try and separate the trees from the dead. Both sections at Togus are closed to new interments.

The fact I can travel from east to west to visit national cemeteries, or that millions of veterans and their spouses are interred in these landscapes and that other Americans are free to visit their graves to remember them, illuminates the difference between this nation's citizens and the migrants—real or imagined—whose deaths marked the beginning of this chapter. The migrants began their journeys to the United States with the hope that they or maybe their children would

Bath National Cemetery (established in 1879), Bath, New York, 2017.

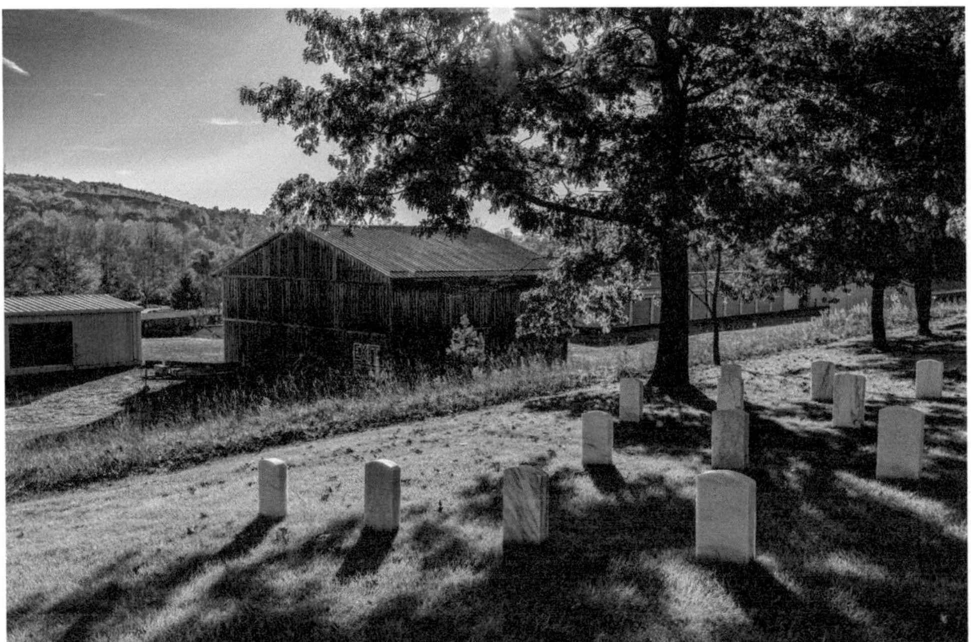

Dayton National Cemetery (established in 1867), Dayton, Ohio, 2019. Both Bath and Dayton National Cemeteries border a medical facility managed by the Department of Veterans Affairs.

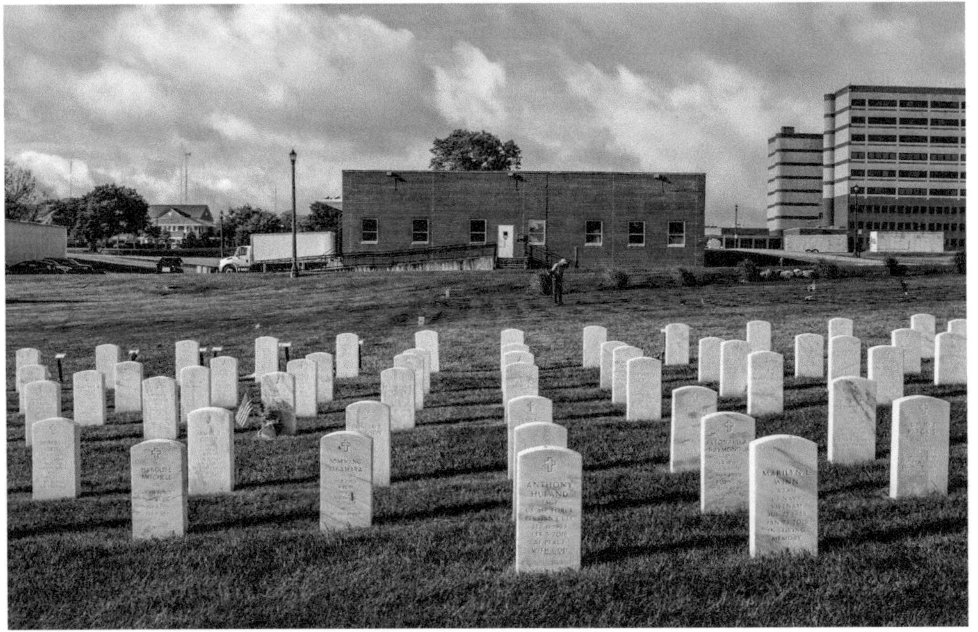

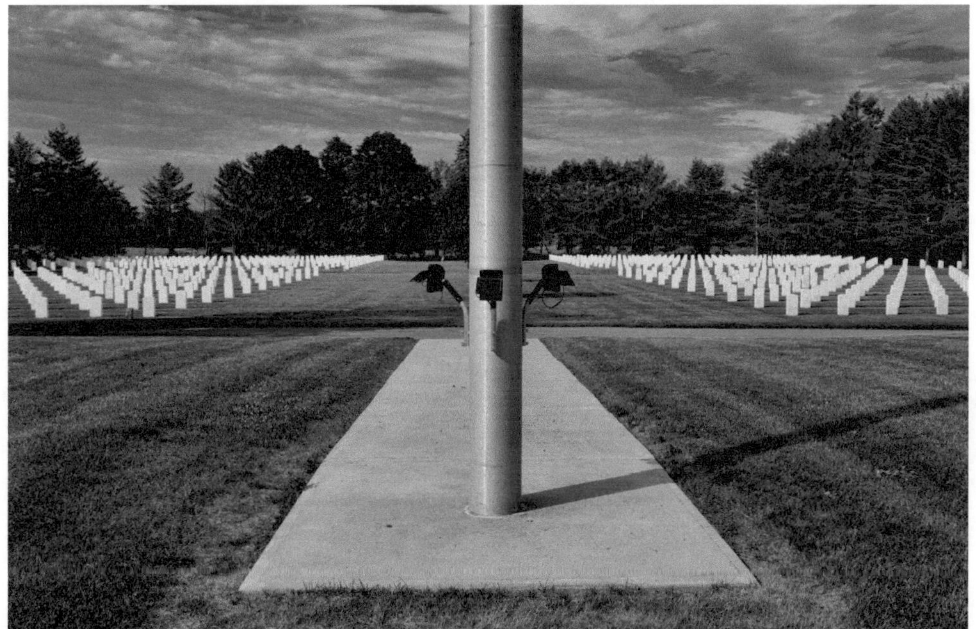

Togus East, Togus National Cemetery (established in 1936), Chelsea, Maine, 2018.

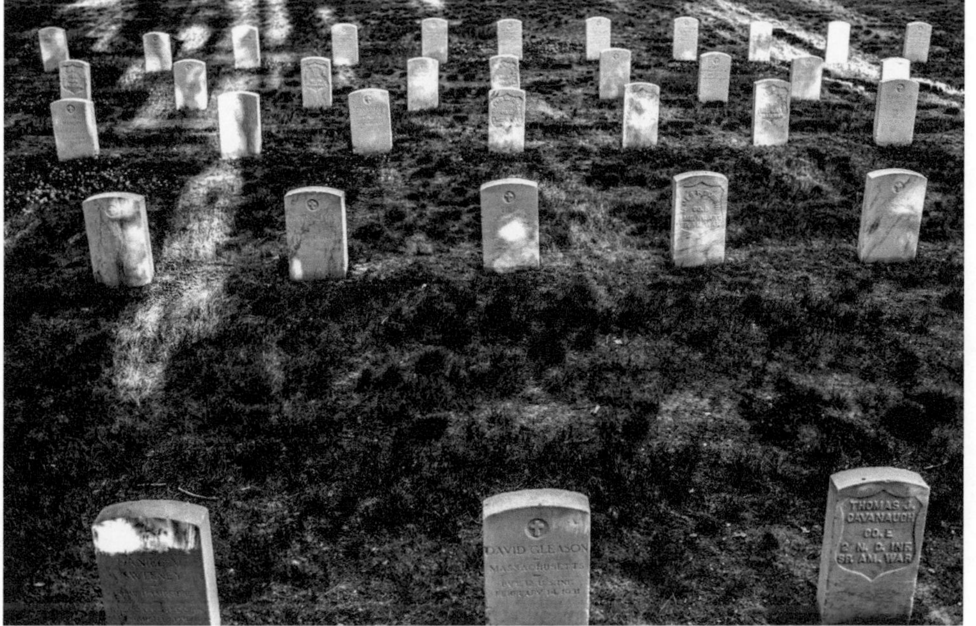

Togus West, Togus National Cemetery (established in 1866), 2018.

be eligible to take their place in these memorial landscapes but instead died in the desert, their remains now part of unmarked nature.

It may seem strange to speak of national cemeteries and freedom in the same breath, but it matters to me—more than I would have imagined ten years ago—that I can travel from one memorial landscape to another without encumbrance. And I want to believe that my journey to the cemeteries is about something larger than myself, that, in my slow walk through the sections, I find in each headstone, each columbarium niche, a sign of the self I might attain, a self that perhaps I have already attained even if I do not know it. At the same time, I know that my assumption of physical freedom is part of a history that has limited the mobility of other citizens, especially Black Americans.[19] And I realize that the encounter I hope to have with my imagined self is in many ways a privileged meeting.

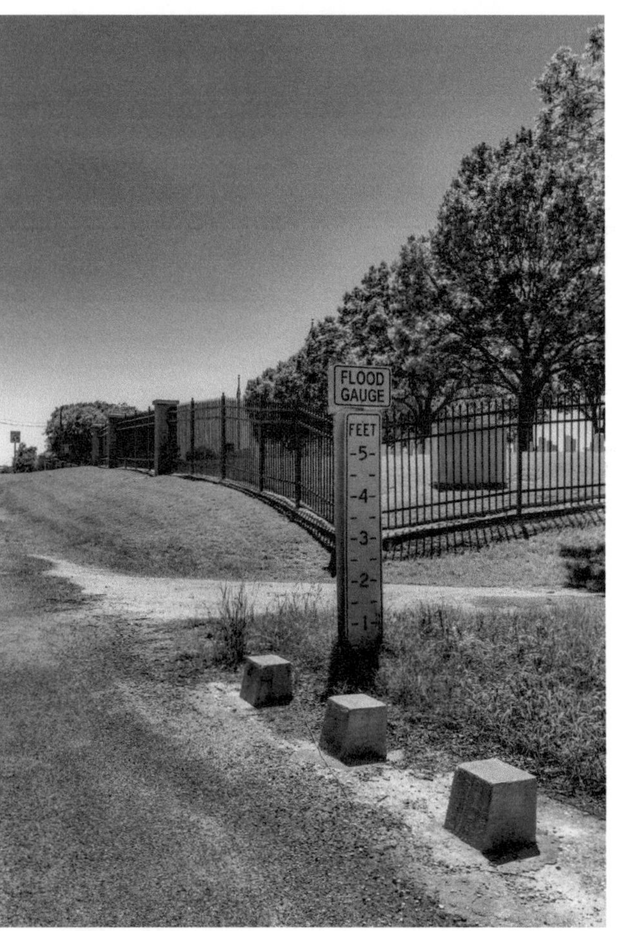

Kerrville National Cemetery (established in 1943), Kerrville, Texas, 2021.

Still, if you visit as many of the cemeteries as I have and see the dead spread out on hills and in valleys, near oceans and lakes, and within groves of trees surrounded by city streets, the United States can begin to look like nature's nation. This description only slightly exaggerates the visual, indeed visceral, impact of the cemeteries. What is more, as Katherine Verdery explains in her study of "dead-body politics" in East Europe, interring the remains of political figures in sacred locations or near significant natural landmarks can enhance the causes these leaders represent, even after death.[20] Generally speaking, this observation holds true at sites like Shiloh and Antietam, Arlington and Alexandria, where the proximity to battlefields and the nation's capital lends a measure of gravity and prestige to the cemetery. Yet at Black Hills National Cemetery, which sits on land once occupied by the Lakota, the symbolic link between nature and nation may be harder to sustain; the region's history of dispossession is too close at hand.

Meanwhile, nature takes hold in small, powerful ways. There is nothing illusory about the interment of remains on federal land. Corpses decompose, mingle with the soil, and nourish trees and grass. Above ground, stonework deteriorates and infrastructure wears out. Thus, the differences between natural and built environments seem to blur, while the cemetery evolves in an apparently organic manner. And this highly symbolic landscape starts to resemble the rest of the country.

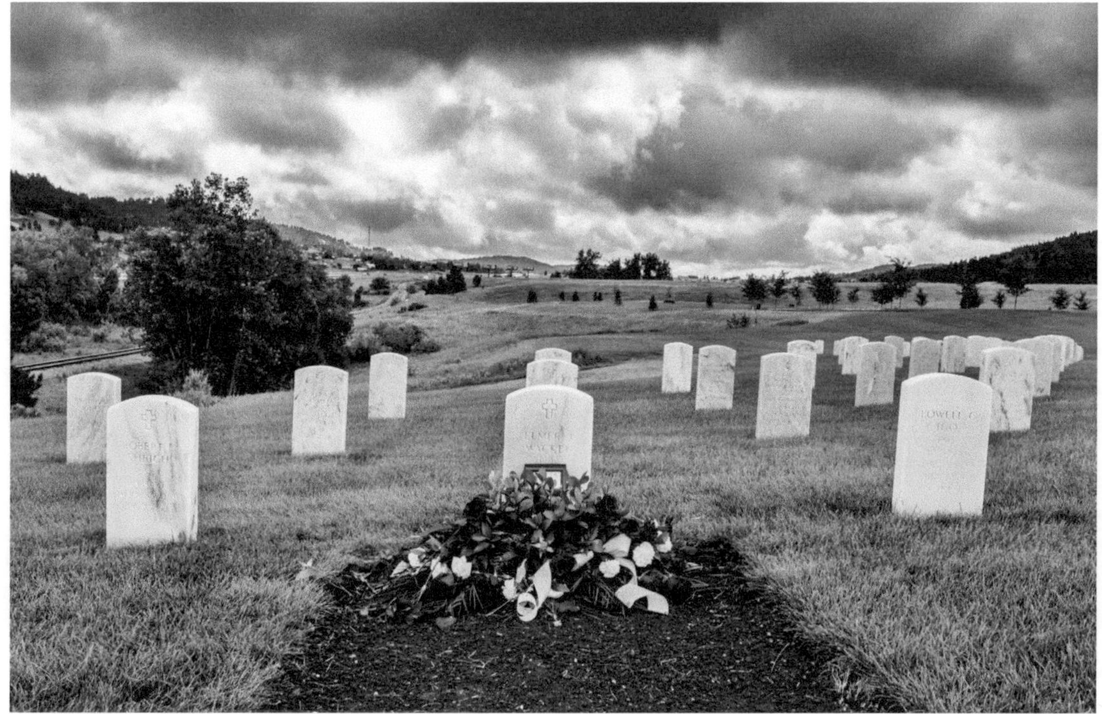

Black Hills National Cemetery (established in 1948), Sturgis, South Dakota, 2018.

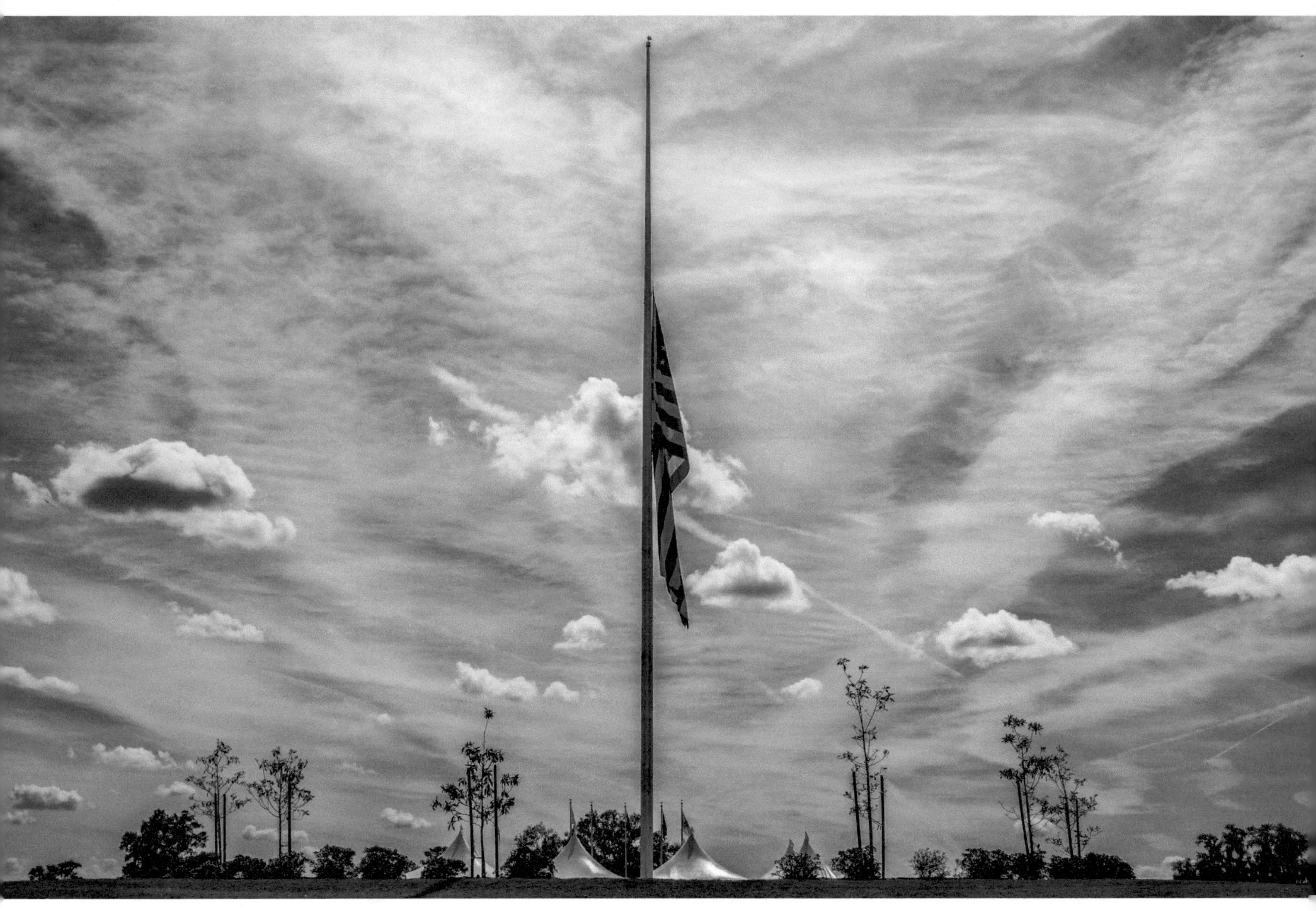

The flag stand at Tallahassee National Cemetery (established in 2015), Tallahassee, Florida, 2019.
According to protocol, the American flag is lowered to half-staff before, during, and after an interment.

10

COVID Times

So much changed in early 2020 when COVID-19 turned the world upside down, and communities of all shapes and sizes tried to halt the virus's spread through quarantines and lockdowns. I was teaching that spring until one day students were told to leave campus for an extended March break—destined to complete their classes online, though at that point nobody really knew how the semester would end. Many of my students were seniors, and they struggled to absorb the emerging truth that their final days of college would be spent at home and on Zoom. Theirs was an understandable quarrel with reality that was but a small part of a larger war being waged over the dangers of the pandemic and the associated curtailment of activities and (some said) freedom.

When the semester ended, I was concerned with my own liberty since I had a year's sabbatical ahead of me to finish this project and I planned to visit a dozen or so cemeteries, return to the National Archives for a few days of research, and settle down in front of the keyboard to write. The archives were closed, as were all government facilities in DC, but the cemeteries were still open to visitors and available for funeral services on a limited capacity. So when the virus relented a bit in June, I drove with a friend to New Orleans.

We followed I-95 south to Baltimore, angled southeast to Chattanooga, and made it to Louisiana in three days. After two days in New Orleans, I took a plane to El Paso, rented a car, and drove west to New Mexico, north to Colorado, and finally east into Nebraska, flying home from Omaha, visiting six cemeteries along the way.

In September, I flew to Alaska—Sitka and Anchorage—for four days. Then in November, I went to Honolulu for a long weekend, giving me two days at the National Memorial Cemetery of the Pacific. I traveled fast to go slow, photographing cemeteries during a time of sickness and death, telling myself and others that even though I was not an "essential worker," these trips could not wait. There were a handful of sites that were critical to my project—the Punchbowl was one—and then there were others in hard-to-reach places that I had not yet visited. Was it important for me to see all the national cemeteries? From a research perspective, the answer was no, a representative sampling would do. The same logic obtained on the aesthetic side. I did not need to photograph all 155 national cemeteries to capture the visual character of these landscapes. Quality was more important than quantity. And that master list of cemeteries was never going to be final. The government would continue to establish new cemeteries, like Tallahassee, and add to existing ones, like Fort Sheridan in Illinois, a Civil War graveyard that the US Army managed for more than a century before it was reclassified as a national cemetery in 2018.[1]

But my thinking about these places was not all based in logic. I wanted to reengage a familiar landscape and finish the journey I began three years earlier. Aiming a camera and tripping the shutter has own its logic and appeal, as does being on the road, and if I could extend that experience, I would. I calibrated my trips like an engineer conducting a time-motion study so there would be no wasted gestures, but the sense of being free never disappeared from the itinerary.

Maybe that is the point—that I have never felt less encumbered than when I am walking among the dead, trying to make order and art on a landscape as old as humankind. "Make" might not be the right word because taking pictures in these spaces feels like an act of discovery, not creation, but it does line up with Martin Heidegger's description of "being-toward-death." The German philosopher suggests that when we confront the reality of death and envision the end toward which all possibilities lead, we conceive of ourselves as free, self-creating individuals, potentially the authors of our own lives.[2]

Without getting into the details of phenomenology—which I do not fully understand anyway—it is enough to say that I felt the force of Heidegger's proposition as I sought not just to finish this project but to reorient my professional work and pay more attention to the world in front of me through the lens of a camera. While I cannot map the evolution of my interests with great precision, I know that as a sixty-four-year-old man I see and feel the world differently from how I did in my forties or even fifties. Aging is a subtle phenomenon, and for me the occasional, but distinct, awareness of mortality—a strange, intangible sense that the horizon is narrowing—fueled my desire to finish the plan I conceived after my first trip to France. The particulars of how I got to this point really did not matter. The Heideggerian project was now mine, and I was resolved to complete my travels, with the proper signposts along the way. Besides, I joked to anyone who would listen, how could I not take photographs of national cemeteries during this pandemic?

In fact, the pandemic had little effect on my ability to take pictures. If anything, the closing of some cemetery offices and the social distancing requirements gave me more room to move. Also, when I drove through the gates, it was hard not to feel that I had crossed into some protective zone. I am not sure that the photographs that I took during these trips were much different from the pictures I made before the pandemic—certainly, some of the details changed—but the space felt different, the memorial landscape, ironically, now a haven, now free from the uncertainty and unrest beyond the gates.

The trip I took in June was aided by local circumstances. My friend Jamie was employed in New Orleans but had been working remotely in Vermont and needed to return to pick up some belongings and rent a different apartment. I was happy to come along, take a slower route to Texas, and see what life was like outside northern New England. But the decision was not just mine to make. COVID-19 had reset the conversation, and I left with the understanding that I would travel with caution and quarantine when I got back home.

When we turned on to the highway in upstate New York, we were surprised to see a steady stream of traffic. When we left our motel in Maryland the next morning and crossed into Tennessee, the roads seemed as crowded as they would have been a year earlier. When we got to Chattanooga, the pandemic almost receded from view. We ordered take-out BBQ for dinner and discovered at the crowded, open-air restaurant that only the servers were wearing masks. The staff at the motel wore masks and spoke from behind plexiglass. There was a sticker sealing the door of our room, and the TV remote was wrapped in plastic, but most guests were bare faced, as if they had considered and rejected the safety measures.

The third day on the road, we walked into a gas station in Meridian, Mississippi, to buy drinks, and nobody, not even the employees—and there were maybe ten people inside—was wearing a mask, despite a sign saying that anyone who entered the premises was required to do so. Back in the passenger's seat, iPhone in hand, I read a story in the Jackson newspaper about how Governor Tate Reeves had implored people not to shame their fellow citizens for wearing masks. In New Orleans, there appeared to be more compliance, with shoppers honoring the municipal orders

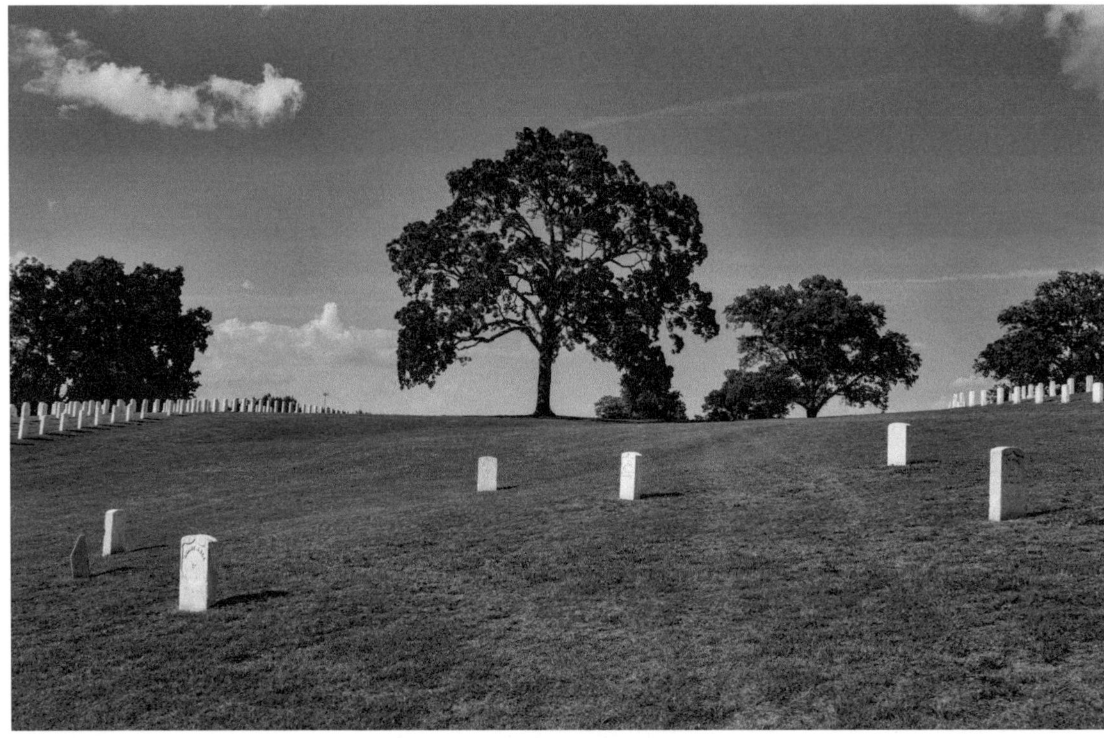

Chattanooga National Cemetery, Chattanooga, Tennessee, 2020.

posted on store fronts. So it went throughout the trip, the country splintered into conflicting belief systems. Or so it seemed. During a year marked by George Floyd's murder by Minneapolis policemen, street demonstrations driven by the Black Lives Matter movement, forest fires out West, and a volatile presidential election, it was difficult to read the room.

In Chattanooga, we stopped at the national cemetery and drove to the highest point, my second time in those beautiful, rolling hills with 360-degree views of the city and the mountains beyond, a piece of history marked by twelve thousand Union graves. As I walked with my camera down toward some rock outcroppings and large trees, a place where half a dozen headstones appeared randomly placed, apart from the uniform rows and circles of plots, I thought that if I took a picture there, I could reframe the space, map the still eye of the storm. In fact, I was doing what I do at nearly every national cemetery I have visited. The landscapes are generous and often spacious. You can settle by a grave or under the sheltering branches of an oak or drive a half mile out from the welcome center at the larger, usually newer, cemeteries and discover a section of burial plots tucked into a wooded hillside with deer nibbling on the foliage and never know you are on a federal property dedicated to military service.

Of course, it is the cemetery's hard-scaped polity that affords me this liberty: the dead arrayed in a final order of unity ready to defend and uphold the nation, regardless of the violence that claimed many of them or the differences that might lie within. I see, you see, we all see.

It is hard to demonstrate by empirical means what I want to claim here, and metaphors are only slightly more helpful since the freedom to move and see implies an expressive power that lies outside language. Why else take photographs? Why, indeed, if not to evoke the spirit of a place that, while marked by graven words, is occupied by the dead? The questions themselves are liberating. Still, it seemed increasingly clear to me, especially at a time when each citizen's move was under scrutiny, that the freedom I exercise when I photograph, or how I see, is the extension of ideals hallowed in the cemeteries. This privilege—the so-called imperial I, or eye—formed the contours of my project.

Also, given what I knew of the traumas that punctuated these landscapes, I could not help thinking that the cemeteries reflected favorably on the current political divisions. Besides our birth, the only truth we can be sure of is that we will die, so it should be of some comfort to know that the Republic has persisted despite, or because of, four million deaths stretched out over 150 years. Perhaps we understand this view of history—the dead honored in serial fashion in an (almost) unbroken sequence leading back to the 1860s, progress unspooling in reverse—to be a construction and believe that death only becomes beautiful by virtue of human design. Still, what is left beneath the memorial stonework and rhetoric is a natural history impervious to ideological critique and literally part of the nation's DNA. If you list the names on the headstones, including the unknowns, you begin to forge a collective genealogy, and the "I" becomes "we."

It may be that I came to these reflections over time and gathered them up in a moment of duress. Perhaps I was romantically searching for a composite American self to be revealed in original American landscapes, as in some old Western, the black-and-white tones highlighting the contrasts in culture, all the while clinging to an old-fashioned form of representation: one guy trying to picture a nation's history or some memory of it. But if I was naively optimistic about these goals, my project was no less valuable because of its sentimental nature.

It may also be true that the military is an imperfect if not unacceptable proxy for American culture. Militarism in general and professionalized killing in particular may be vital to national defense, but that does not necessarily make them representative of the culture. Nor, some might argue, does the honoring of servicemen and -women on hallowed or sacred grounds mean that we can all see ourselves on these landscapes, as if the cemeteries were a kind of national reflecting pool. On the other hand, one can plausibly argue that the current military in all its branches does exemplify the culture as a whole. Demographically speaking, it has never been more representative of the general population. A 2017 Pew Research Center study found that 57 percent of the active military are white, 16 percent are African American, 16 percent are Hispanic, and 16 percent are women, with this last number on the rise. In 2020 and 2022, the Council on Foreign Relations and the Department of Defense likewise underscored the growing number of minorities and women in the military. These trends are expected to carry into the veteran community in future decades and will no doubt be reflected in the cemeteries' increasingly diverse population.[3] The memorial landscape is truer now than it was during the 1870s.

Then again, these gains are offset by enduring problems. As critics have pointed out, the military's drive to build a more inclusive organization has been stalled by systemic racism. Senior leadership positions are dominated by white men, and the path forward for minority candidates remains narrow. Moreover, the tendency to focus on successful outcomes and downplay incidental problems—for example, not punishing service members for uttering racial slurs so long as the unit remains productive—has reinforced long-held patterns of discrimination.[4] Indeed, the involvement of former military in violent, alt-right political activity, including the failed Capitol insurrection on January 6, 2021, highlighted the legacy of white supremacy within the ranks. In this light, the military's commitment to redesignate bases named for Confederate generals amounts to a confession that it must do more to eradicate symbolic expressions of racism throughout the branches.[5]

The national cemeteries are not utopian spaces. Not all American conflicts have been so-called good wars, regardless of the concerted effort to remember them as such. And many of the combatants buried in the cemeteries did not choose to fight and die as they did. They are innocent. And the rest of us citizens? My sense is that we hold ourselves apart at our peril. If we do not share a genealogy, then at a minimum we enjoy the benefits of American power. Expunging the sins of the past is bad faith. There is a good argument to be made for eliminating or repositioning public monuments erected in the name of causes that are inconsistent with the ideals of the Republic, and here I would include some of the Confederate monuments that sit in national cemeteries. But the dead are different. They do not simply represent our tangled, human history: they embody it.

When I flew from New Orleans to El Paso, I had the impulse to think—call it muscle memory—that I was leaving some of this strife behind. I was headed West, lighting out for the territories and the open horizon. But that was a flight of mythic indulgence. History was still ahead of me, and throughout my drive into New Mexico and up toward Nebraska, I followed the tracks of empire across dramatically stark landscapes.

In El Paso, Fort Bliss was established to guard the southern border following the Mexican War and fend off attacks from Apaches and Comanches. Similarly, Fort Bayard (New Mexico) served to protect white settlers and travelers, many en route to California and Oregon, from Native American attacks. That military policy was part of a process of ethnic cleansing consistent with the racist philosophies that supported slavery.[6] When, in 1873, the government opened Fort McPherson National Cemetery (Nebraska), the grounds included the graves from the original fort cemetery as well as the remains of soldiers reinterred from twenty-three other cemeteries affiliated with frontier forts that the War Department had decommissioned. With the completion of the transcontinental railroad in 1869, those forts were no longer necessary since travelers could go west without extensive military protection.

Initially, the plan for converting fort cemeteries into national cemeteries was controversial. After all, the cemetery system was created to honor the Union dead. The Grand Army of the Republic particularly objected to the idea of granting the same privileges to soldiers who died fighting Indians or battling Mexico when there was no plan or budget for honoring Civil War veterans when they died. To address these concerns, Congress passed legislation during the early 1870s granting burial privileges in national cemeteries for all "honorably discharged" military personnel who served in the "late war." Decisions like this were important to expanding the nation's great sepulture beyond its original purpose and creating the memorial footprint that exists today. During the late nineteenth century, the War Department designated new cemeteries and enlarged and improved existing ones. And throughout the West, as at Fort McPherson, the quartermasters moved remains out of older frontier posts and into new spaces, such as San Francisco National Cemetery and the Santa Fe National Cemetery.[7]

Are many of these dead not the remnants of empire? I might not ask the question in that

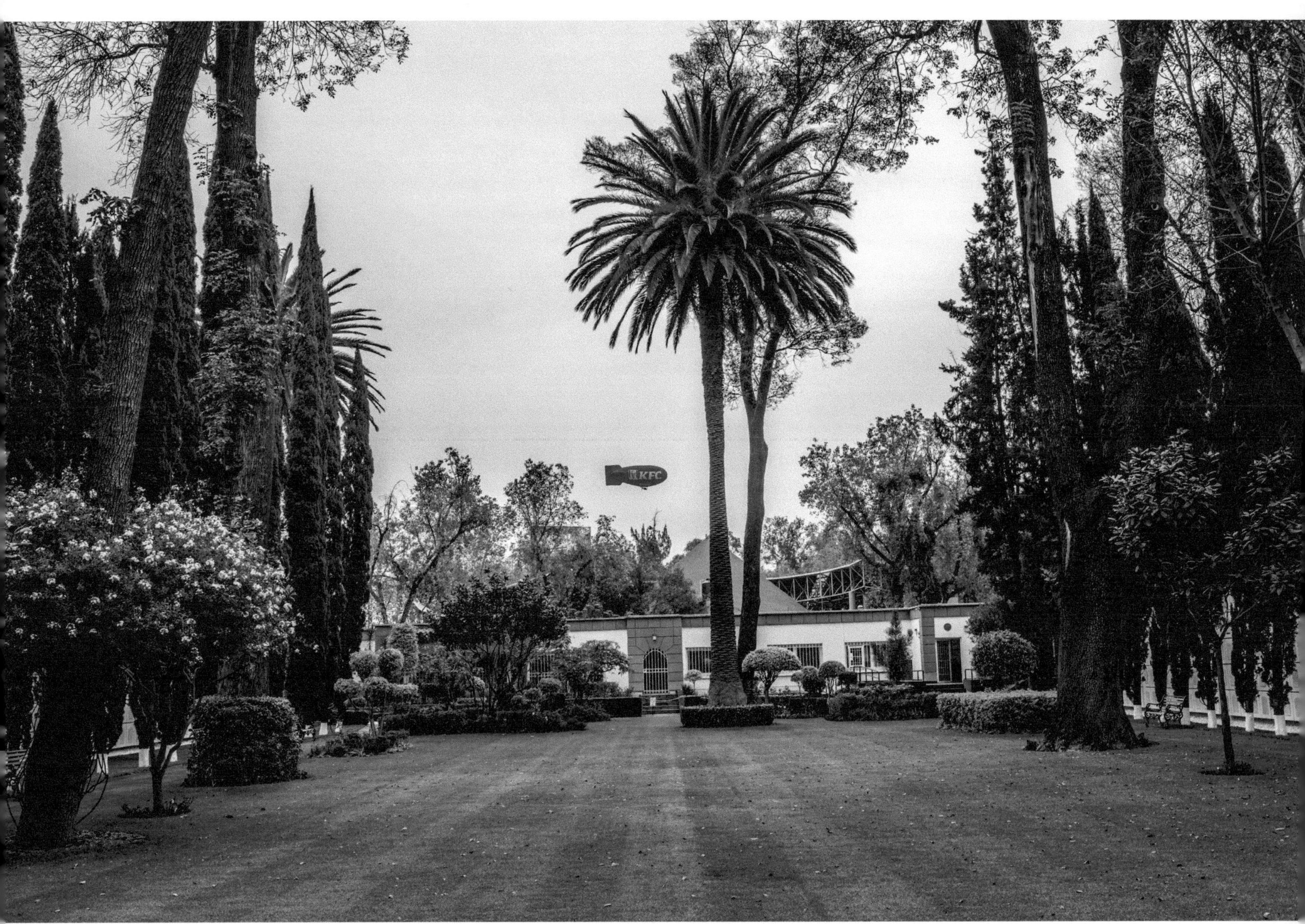

Mexico City National Cemetery (established in 1851), Mexico City, Mexico, 2020.

way if not for a trip I took to Mexico City—and the Mexico City National Cemetery—several weeks before the coronavirus hit.

The Mexico City National Cemetery holds the remains of 750 US soldiers who died in the 1847 invasion of Mexico City—part of the Mexican War—and is located a mile from the American Embassy in a walled enclave just off a highway in the middle of town. Managed by the American Battle Monuments Commission, the cemetery is the legacy of conquest. Even the commission concedes this awkward fact, noting in a 2007 press release that while in World War I and World War II "we were the liberators, we were going over to fight tyranny," the cemetery in Mexico City is "definitely" in "a different niche."[8] No wonder some Mexicans question why the dead—why "we"—are not back in our home country.

Behind the wall is a one-acre rectangular garden with a lawn in the middle, bordered by flagstone walks, wrought iron benches, and cypress trees and with a plinth at one end, honoring the memory of 750 Americans who are "known but to God," and a fountain and office building at the other. There is one large palm tree and tropical plants with pastel colors that looked exotic to me but are native to Mexico. The flowers in one of the beds near the entrance have been sculpted to spell "ABMC."

The dead are on the perimeter, their remains interred in two long columbaria or crypts affixed to the twelve-foot-high wall that stands behind the walkways, the name plates for the individual niches cast as small headstones, something I have not seen at other cemeteries. The columbaria date to the late 1970s when the cemetery was dug up and reduced in size to make room for the Circuito Interior Highway. Apparently, the commission tried to maintain the visual identity of the grave plots by lifting their faces to the wall.

Visitors are not permitted on the lawn, so I took pictures of the columbarium from the sidewalk, framing the name plates in serial fashion like a poster, sometimes aiming through the cypress trees. My best shot came at the end of the wall, where I photographed the headstone of Conti Luigi Joannini, next to a water faucet and plantings, the dark stone wall in the background and the gray surface of the columbarium set off by the white pebble ground covering. Conti Luigi died in 1882, and I found out later that she took her life. She was the wife of an Italian diplomat, who died two years before she did, and is one of 813 civilians buried alongside the soldiers from the Mexican War.[9]

The formality of the space was constraining, and when I looked up I saw a KFC (Kentucky

Fried Chicken) blimp slowing moving across the sky at the north end of the cemetery. When I reviewed my photographs at home, I noticed a huge picture of the Mexican pop singer Gloria Trevi peeking out over the eastern wall from a billboard next to the highway. One kind of imperialism has given way to one another, though that glib comparison does not really express what happened here during the nineteenth century.

Fort Bliss National Cemetery occupies similar territory. Dedicated in 1939, the cemetery, like the fort, is named for Lieutenant Colonel William Wallace Smith Bliss, a West Point–educated mathematician, who taught at the military academy, served in the Mexican War as General Zachary Taylor's adjutant, married Taylor's daughter, worked to remove the Cherokees from the Southeast in the 1830s, and ultimately died of yellow fever in New Orleans in 1853 at the age of thirty-seven. His remains were buried in a New Orleans cemetery beneath a twenty-foot plinth honoring his military service and in 1955 moved to El Paso so they could be reinterred in

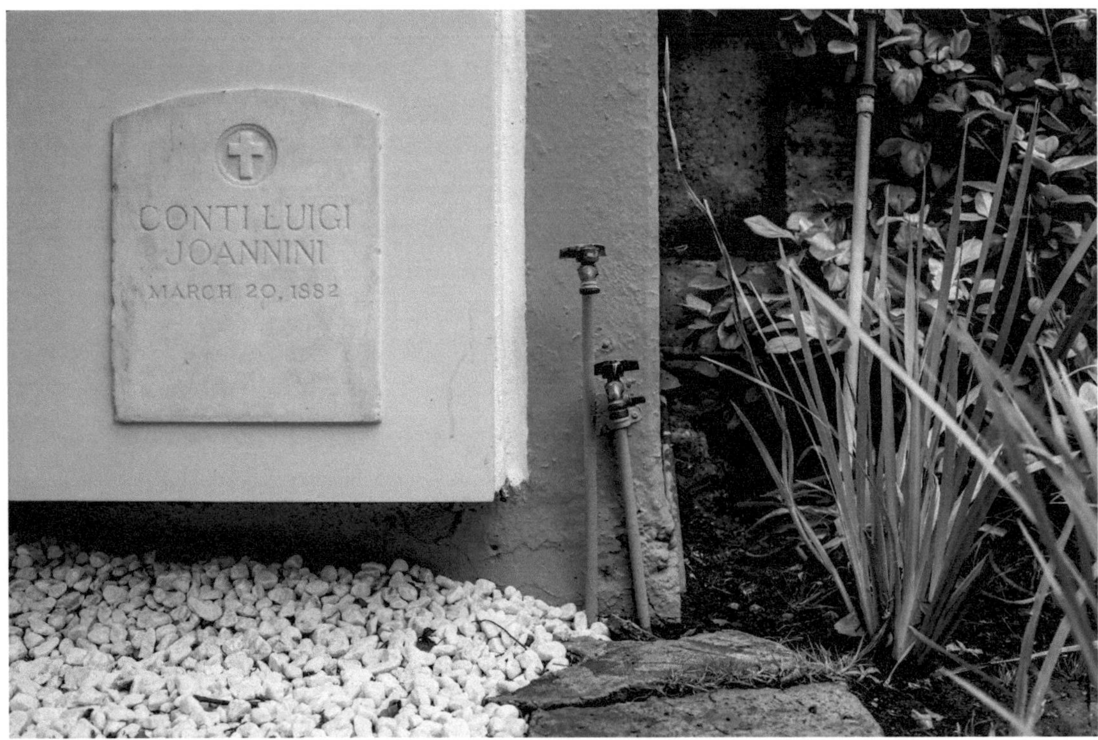

Mexico City National Cemetery, 2020.

the cemetery that bears his name (though the fort has been called Fort Bliss since 1854).[10] Bliss had a short but consequential life, and I was interested to find out that he was born in Whitehall, New York, which is just over the line from Vermont. According to the historical marker I see every time I drive through the town, Whitehall was also the birthplace of the US Navy.

Whitehall's unexpected appearance in this history underscores the American military's ever-stretching, always evolving presence on the nation's westward-oriented frontier. That layered development is evident at Fort Bliss National Cemetery, even if the original monument to Bliss currently stands on Parade Field—Fort Bliss is a large and active military base—two miles from the burial grounds, where his grave is designated by a headstone that stands by the entrance, apart from the other fifty thousand markers, between the flag stand and rostrum, like a sentinel. To the west, the cemetery is bordered by J. E. B Stuart Road, a reminder that the fort served as a Confederate garrison during the Civil War.

I got to El Paso at 3:30 p.m. and discovered when I left the gate that airport authorities were serious about enforcing safety protocols. As opposed to the Dallas-Love airport, where I changed planes, everyone was wearing a mask, and there were signs telling travelers to follow the rules and maintain social distance. When I picked up my rental car, the sales agent asked the customer behind me to stay out of the kiosk until we had finished. After leaving the airport, I drove to a Mexican restaurant the agent recommended and parked under a tree to eat my enchilada combination plate.

Just four miles from the airport, the cemetery sits below the Liberty Expressway, the better part of its eighty-three-acre expanse almost indistinguishable from the surrounding city. From above, as seen in Google satellite images, it looks like a desert oasis with trees planted in rows along the section edges and in clusters (with some palm trees) around the entrance. There is little grass, and what does exist extends from the front gates to the rostrum, the planted turf encompassing Bliss's grave but no others. In 2007, the National Cemetery Administration xeriscaped the grounds, which means they removed most of the grass and replaced it with rocky soil and native plantings to conserve the use of water and restore the environment to its original character. The project was successful—Bakersfield National Cemetery and the National Memorial Cemetery of Arizona received similar treatment—though veterans complain that the lack of grass is undignified.[11]

I realized as I walked the grounds in the heat after two flights and with two hours of driving ahead of me that I was not paying as close attention as I should to the historical details, for

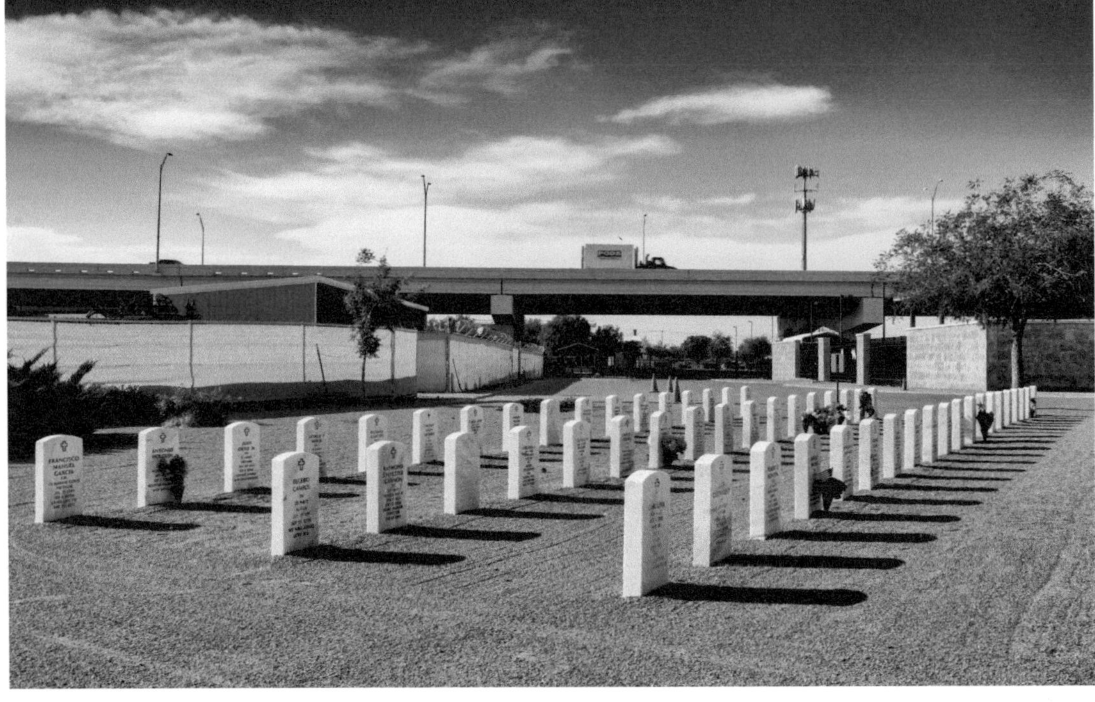

Liberty Expressway passes by Fort Bliss National Cemetery (established in 1936), El Paso, Texas, 2020.

instance, finding the graves of the fifty-five Chinese pilots killed in training exercises during the 1940s or the twenty or so German World War II prisoners who died in camps in Arizona and New Mexico.[12] This is always a challenge, balancing the particulars with the whole. The composite view of headstones, mountains, and highway is compelling, and I liked to think that if I just pointed and clicked, I would archive the drama in my memory card. But I knew that probably would not happen. I knew it was more likely that the harsh light would whitewash the images and that I was better off focusing on smaller scenes, what lay in the shadows. I saw a McDonald's cup that someone had thrown on the ground and a discarded plastic flower and concluded that the pandemic had prevented regular maintenance. No one else was around. If I stayed until sunset, I was sure the waning light would have opened up new views.

Instead, I headed west on I-10, the brown-gray moonscape turning pink and then purple, trucks passing me on the left, an electric billboard telling me as I crossed into New Mexico that there was a pandemic going on and I needed to mask up. I got to my motel in Deming around 8:00, not

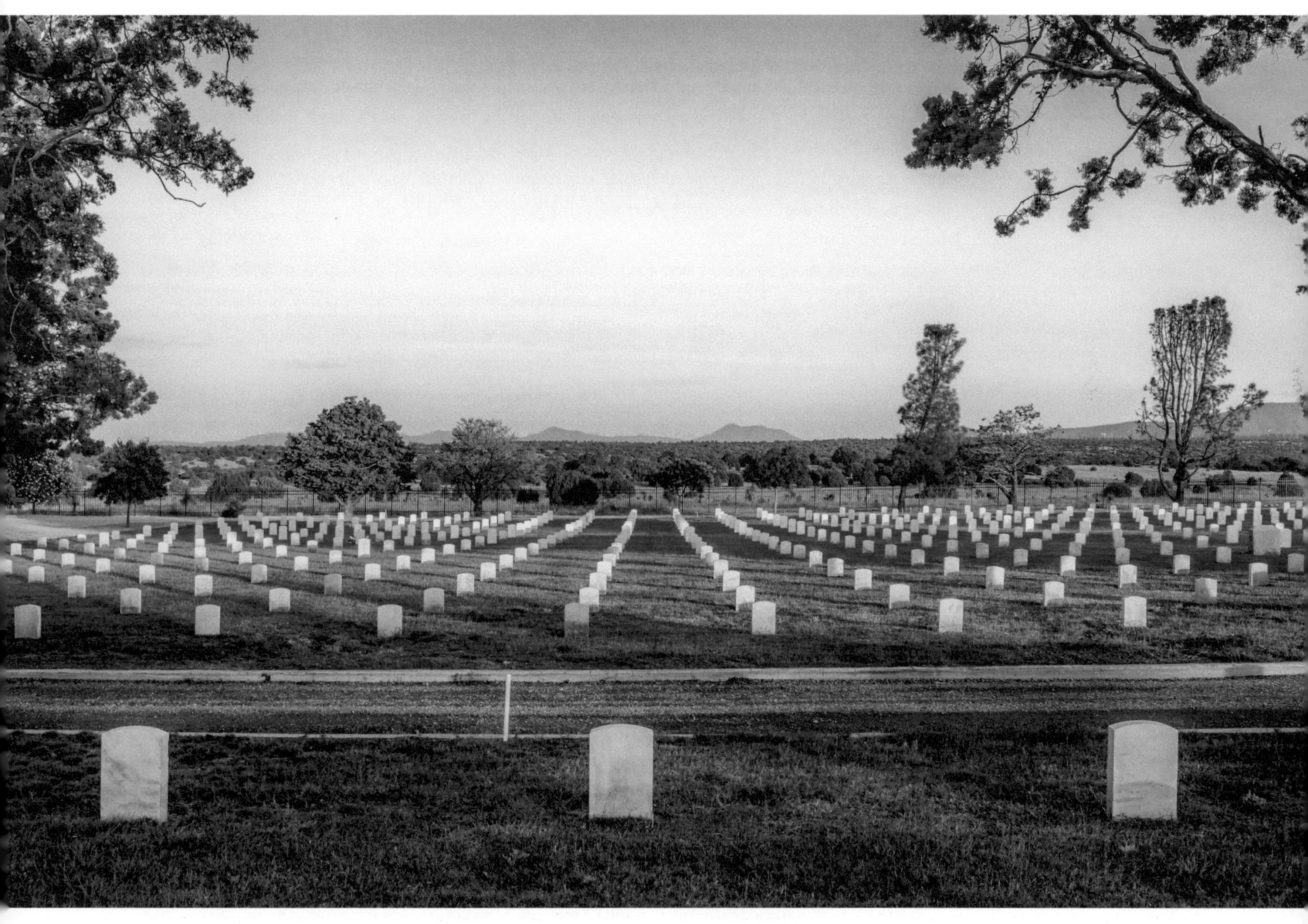

Fort Bayard National Cemetery (established in 1922), Fort Bayard, New Mexico, 2020.

bothering with dinner because I ate at 4:00, and I was asleep by 9:00 so I could wake up early to go to Fort Bayard National Cemetery before driving nine hours to La Junta—"the junction"—in southern Colorado, where I would visit Fort Lyon and Pikes Peak National Cemeteries.

The strong light was in my favor when I arrived at Fort Bayard since every figure on the ground, each headstone, outbuilding, bench, and tree appeared distinct from one another while at the same time the glow from the sunrise suffused the landscape with a soft binding agent. There at six thousand feet in the Arenas Valley the world had been re-created, and Eden restored—for a while.

The eighteen-acre cemetery was founded in 1866 and officially dedicated in 1922. You can track the history from the graves of soldiers from the Ninth and Tenth Cavalry and the Twenty-Fourth and Twenty-Fifth Infantry Regiments—buffalo soldiers—and an adobe shed that appears to date from the nineteenth century.[13] There were 3,732 grave plots, some of them very recent, and I saw from the piles of gravel and quadrants roughed out on the west side that they were expanding. I photographed the shed with my lens facing north, bringing into view the Pinos Altos Mountains to the north and open range in between. To the south are the abandoned buildings of old Fort Bayard, which was shut down after the Indian Wars and then reactivated during World War II. During the 1880s and '90s, the buildings served as a medical facility, run by the state of New Mexico, and more recently, in the 1970s, they came back online as a drug rehabilitation center. During World War II, the government maintained a camp for German POWs in Lordsburg, New Mexico, and some of the prisoners were transferred to Fort Bayard, where they worked in the cemetery and did other odd jobs. Some of the Germans who died at Lordsburg were buried at Fort Bliss.[14]

Out west, the land bends reluctantly to human design, and as I drove north from New Mexico into Colorado through little, hard-scrabble towns, I saw few masks, as if people already knew what to expect from nature and their neighbors and did not feel the need for additional protection. I saw more masks when I got to Nebraska, but in Omaha, where I spent my last night before flying home, the downtown scene resembled Chattanooga, and I ate my dinner on the sidewalk down the street from TD Ameritrade Park Omaha, where the College World Series is played but was not this year because the virus forced its cancellation.

In life there is always death, but I doubt Meigs and his colleagues imagined the national cemeteries would someday hold the remains of more than four million soldiers, sailors, airmen, and marines, plus their loved ones. And if they did foresee growth, I doubt they expected the proliferation of tens and dozens of cemeteries not in the "great thoroughfares" that Whitman envisioned but in small, out-of-the-way places that few people actually visit and that, as a result, are honored collectively on Memorial Day, Veterans Day, or during the winter holidays. Quite a few are in poor repair and underresourced, in stark contrast to the generous recognition of the dead at Arlington National Cemetery and other well-maintained sites.

But this is frontier territory, and I assume the landscape should look a little rough. When I approached Fort Lyon Cemetery, I passed the Kit Carson Chapel, a neatly preserved stone structure, named for the frontiersman I read about as a kid in *Kit Carson: Boy Trapper* (1945), one of many volumes in the postwar Childhood of Famous Americans Series.[15] But Carson's exploits—once considered heroic—are now shadowed by his reputation as a vicious killer of Native Americans, and the civilizing process that Frederick Jackson Turner eulogized in his 1893

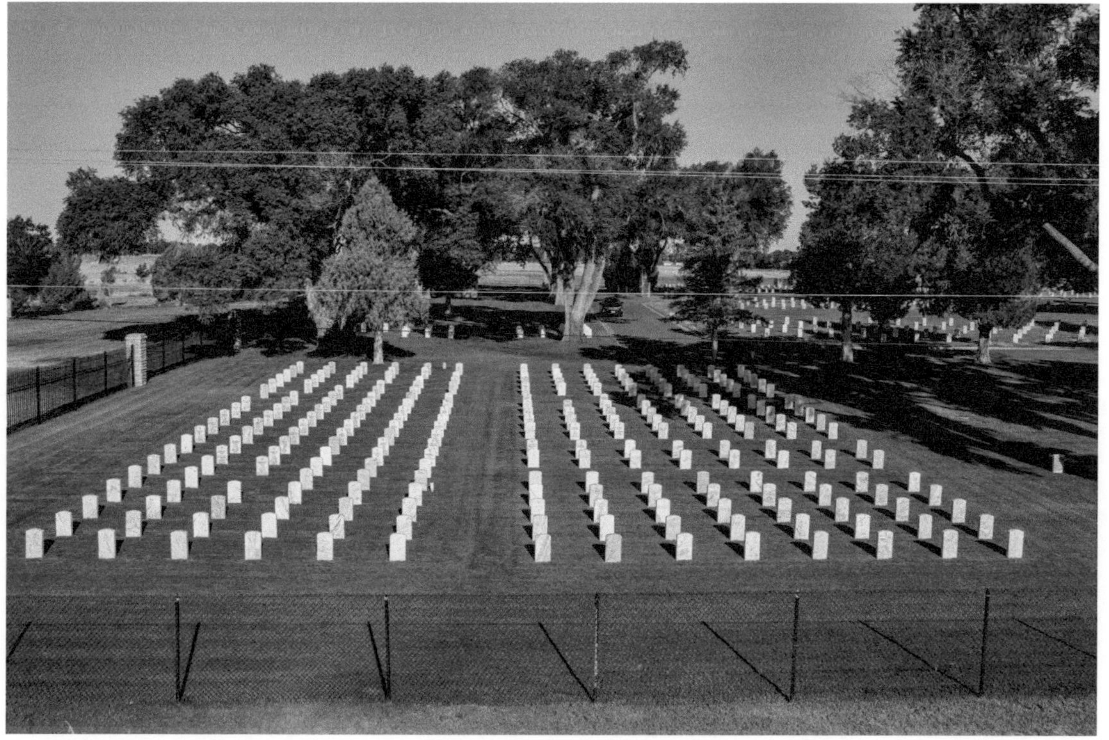

Fort Lyon National Cemetery (established in 1922), Fort Lyon, Colorado, 2020.

essay, "The Significance of the Frontier in American History," has given way to a darker portrait of western democracy.

Like Fort Bayard, Fort Lyon takes its name from a Civil War general who died in battle, and, like Fort Bayard, it functioned as a bulwark against tribes in the region, serving as a launching point for Colonel John Chivington, who led a slaughter of Arapahoe and Cheyenne encampments at Sand Creek, Colorado, in 1864. Fort Lyon lasted until 1897, and the surviving compound, as at Fort Bayard, was put to other purposes. It was used as a sanitarium, psychiatric ward, prison, and so on. Fort Lyon National Cemetery was established in 1887.

Yet this legacy had little bearing on my appreciation of the visual power of the cemetery—a fifty-two-acre site that felt smaller than it was, perhaps because of its clean, rectilinear design and the large trees that cast shadows over the lawn and dark stone walls and seemed to pull to the landscape into a more intimate arrangement. I showed up early in the morning and was alone except for a man with his dog, who left soon after I arrived. Although Fort Lyon is open for interments, I had the place to myself for two hours and worked the sides, photographing the trees and headstones, and then walked along an embankment paralleling the east side of the cemetery, which gave me an unusual chance to shoot down into the cemetery.

Here, it is useful to think of the frontier not just as a border, region, or stage of development but also a frame of mind. Art critic John Berger, in describing the fundamentals of perception, claimed that "the way we see is affected by what we know or what we believe." I cannot honestly deny that my assumption that I can go wherever I want when I want may be the product of a distinctly American (and imperial) belief in limitless expansion, a view of history that lacks a "sense of the tragic."[16] I may feel I am free, but I may be stuck in my own version of frontier thinking. Although I like to believe I had come here to register history's impact on the land, it would be shortsighted to claim that I am not part of this larger picture. I might have been complicit simply by traveling during a pandemic. And would the photographs I took of these spaces reflect my limited perspective? I do not know.

For then, though, I was on the road. So I drove northwest to the newly constructed Pikes Peak National Cemetery, then followed I-80 east to Fort McPherson National Cemetery in Maxwell, Nebraska, just beyond North Platte, and finally got to Omaha National Cemetery, which, like Pikes Peak, was new and a model of efficient design, with an array of burial options, including a metal capped ossuary for the general interment of cremains, which I photographed

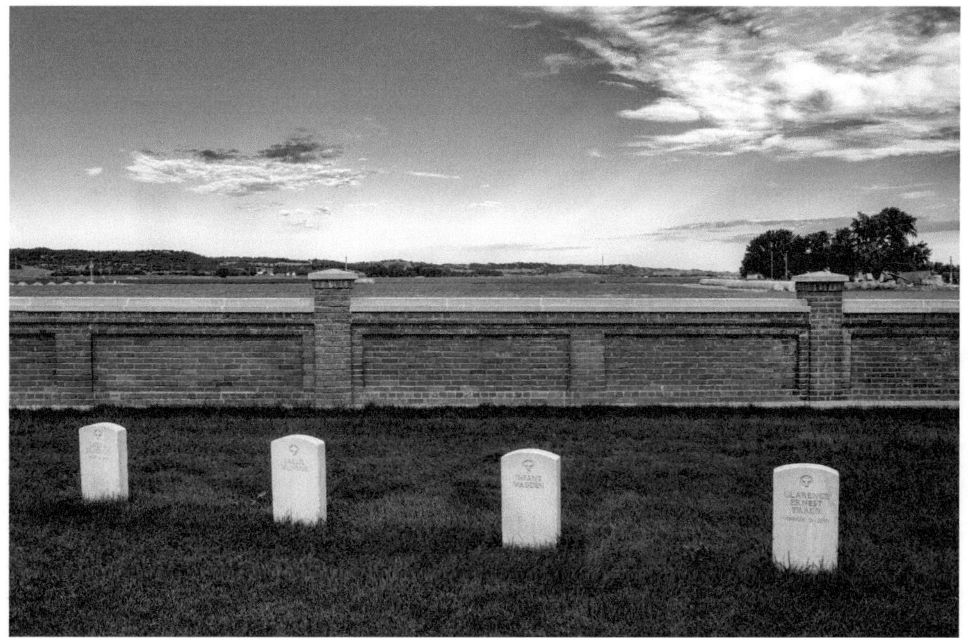

Fort McPherson National Cemetery (established in 1873), Maxwell, Nebraska, 2020.

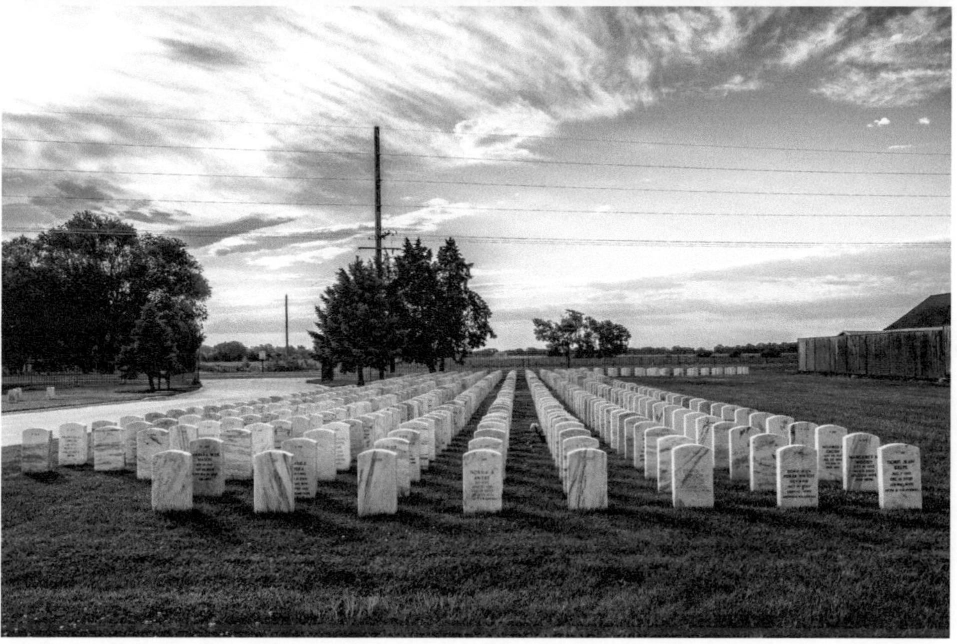

Fort McPherson National Cemetery, 2020.

with the Westmont town water tower in the background, beyond the fence line and flanked by cornfields.

The last stop on my frontier tour, Fort McPherson National Cemetery, was the most recent iteration of a burial ground once associated with Cantonment McKean—"cantonment" being a French word for military post—which, in 1866, was renamed for another Union general who died in battle: James B. McPherson. The twenty-acre, square-shaped cemetery was established in 1873 to accommodate the remains at Fort McPherson and the dead from other fort cemeteries. This transferal process continued into the twentieth century, when, in 1947, the remains of sixty-three buffalo soldiers were moved to the cemetery from Fort Robinson, also in Nebraska, the headstones a mark upon the region's unsettling racial history. Fort McPherson is open to interments—in 2013, a columbarium was added in the northwest corner—and, until Omaha National Cemetery's dedication in 2016, it was the only national cemetery in Nebraska.[17]

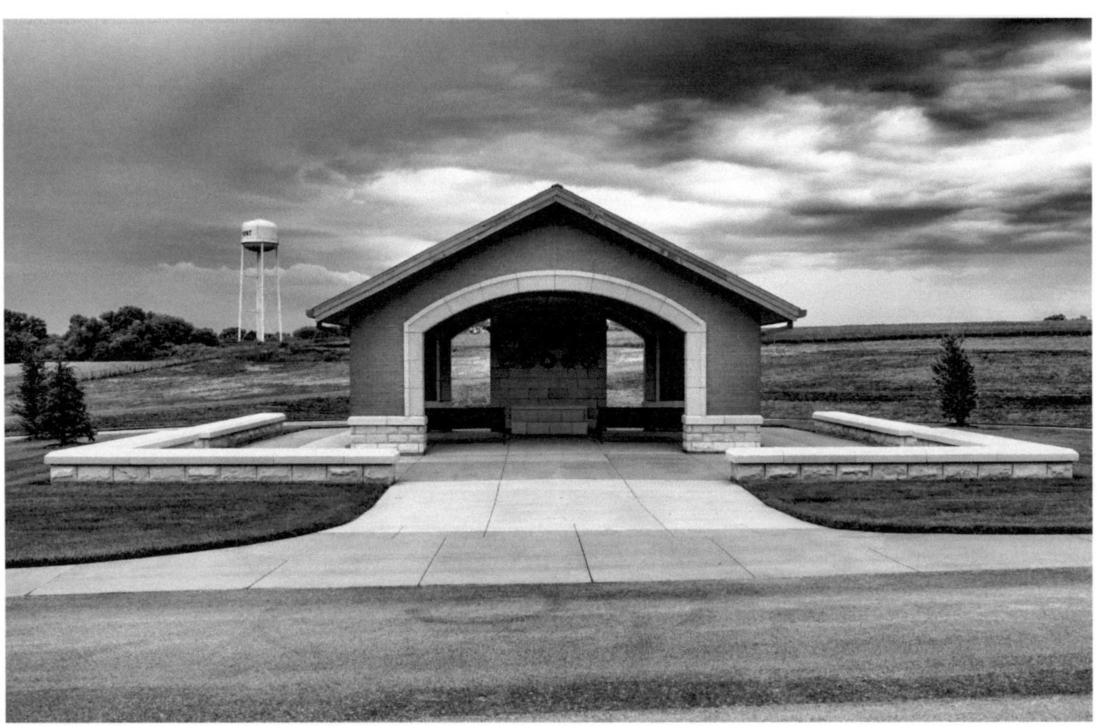

A committal shelter at Omaha National Cemetery (established in 2016), Omaha, Nebraska, 2020.

Although there is no ossuary at Fort McPherson, I found the flat markers designating the group graves of World War II casualties mixed among the headstones. The names of the eight US Army soldiers, killed in Europe or Asia or maybe even the United States—the stone etching does not say where—underscore the concrete, if paradoxically expansive, nature of memorial power. The dead were right below me and their names were on the grass, though the marker, which gathered weight from the mass burial, pointed beyond the cemetery's rural setting and the place's former identity as a fort.

The design and rhythm of the landscape—the formal entrance, flag stand, and superintendent's lodge—brought me back to a fuller view, reminding me that though I was standing in Maxwell, Nebraska (population 312), I was also someplace else. I took pictures at the front of the cemetery, focusing on the wrought iron fence, and when I examined them later, they were hard to distinguish from the photographs I took at the entrance to the St. Mihiel American Cemetery in France. In the distance, as I looked through the gates at both cemeteries, the furrowed plains seemed to stretch to oblivion. Inside was something else.

But the relation between inside and outside is not the same in Maxwell as it is in St. Mihiel. Over there, the fence separates borrowed American territory from the sovereign lands of France. At Fort McPherson, as at other national cemeteries, what lies within is loosely but obviously connected to the landscape outside the walls, whether it be farm fields, houses, a car dealership, or a vacant lot.

Throughout the early months of the pandemic, as the outbreak gave way to periods of relief and I looked for opportunities to travel and complete my project, the difference between inside and outside took on new meaning and borders emerged where none existed before. For instance, to go to Alaska and avoid a fourteen-day quarantine I had to prove that I had tested negative for COVID-19 within seventy-two hours of arriving in the state. The same was true when I flew to Honolulu.

Sitka is on an island in southern Alaska that is accessible only by sea or air, and when I landed on a Friday afternoon, we were met at the gate by a state health officer who reviewed our test results (downloaded to our phones and computers) and cleared us for passage as if we were going through customs. It was just a short ride into town, and my cab driver, an older woman who said she got to the island in the 1960s and never left, claimed that I did not need to wear masks except in some stores and restaurants, that in fact masks were nonsense, and that Sitka, after all, was made up of free-thinking individuals.

Sitka National Cemetery (established in 1924), Sitka, Alaska, 2020.

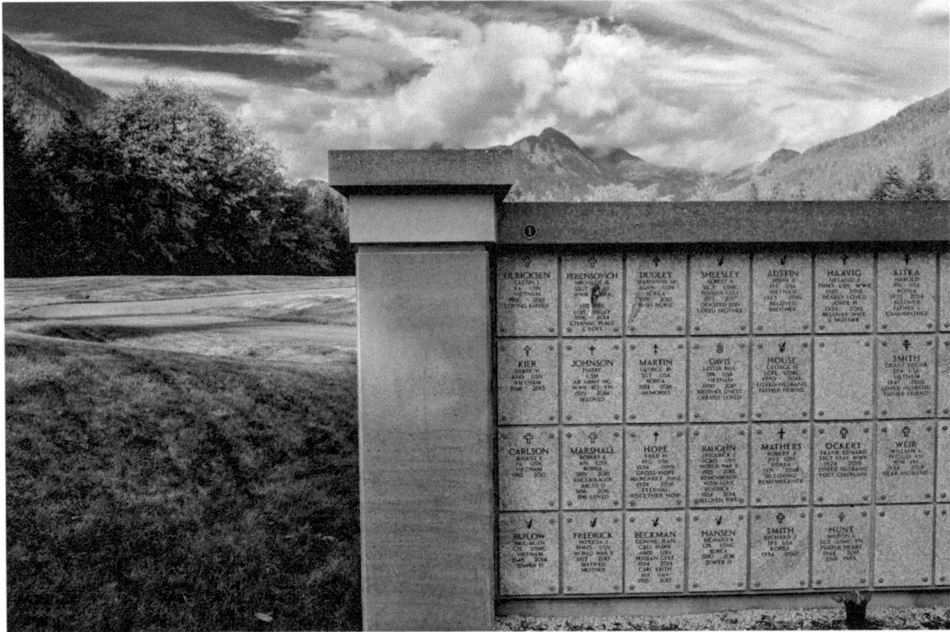

Sitka National Cemetery, 2020.

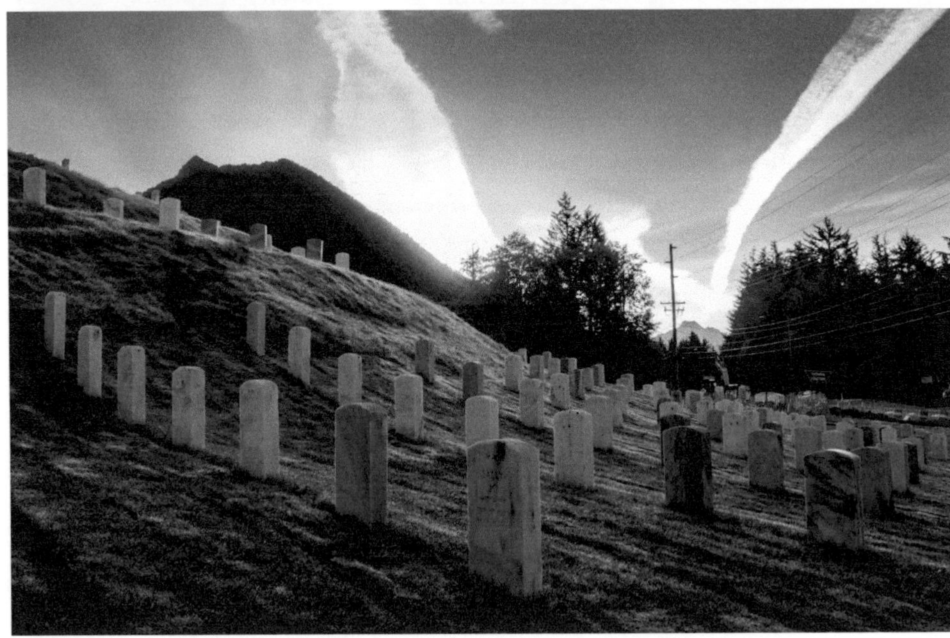

I did not argue with her, and nothing I saw over the next few days conflicted with my impression of Alaska's frontier character. The salmon were running during my visit, and the streams and inlets around the bay teemed with fish, and there were signs along the pathways warning of increased bear activity. I later saw similar postings at Fort Richardson National Cemetery in Anchorage, telling visitors not to wander outside the cemetery. More unusual were the blue X's taped on the benches and floors in the committal shelters, diagrams of where people were allowed to sit and stand during funeral services to reduce the possibility of contagion.

Sitka National Cemetery is located a half mile from downtown, on a four-and-a-half acre site with just over one thousand interments. The cemetery is small and carved into a hill, with several headstones that appear to sit precariously on the steep incline. Behind the hill is a columbarium with views of the mountains and also a huge white cross that stands on the edge of Sitka Memorial Park, the municipal cemetery, like a sign pointing to the outback. Although the national

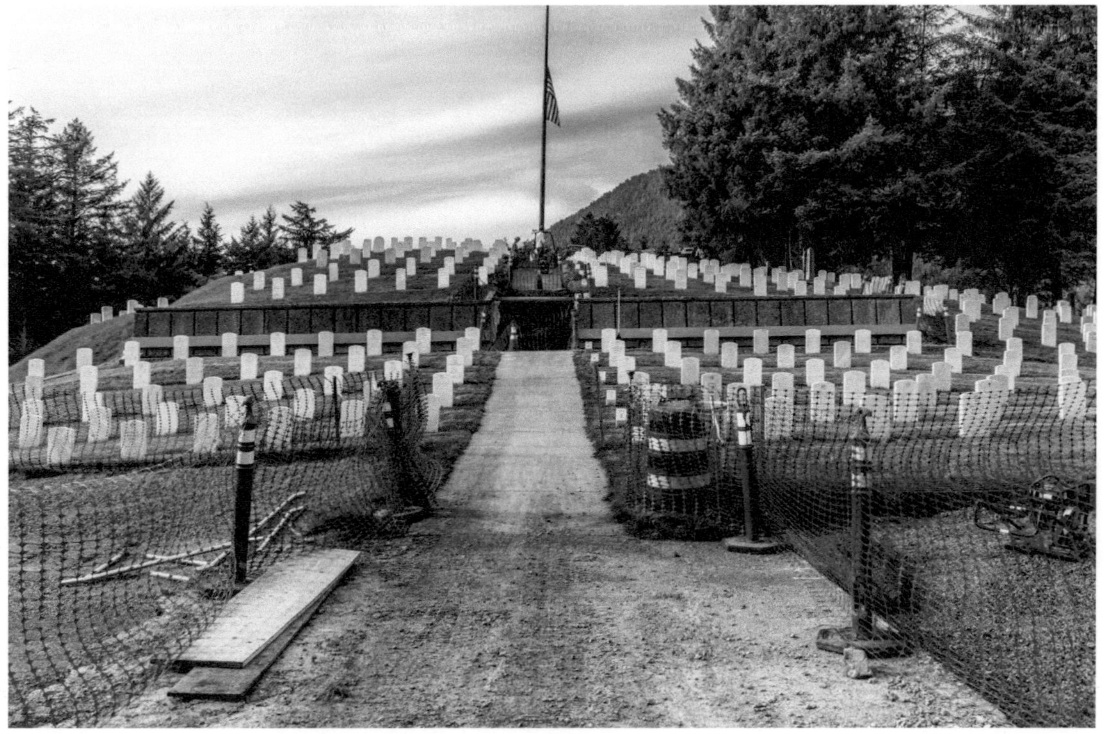

Sitka National Cemetery, 2020.

cemetery was laid out during the late 1860s, it was not brought into the system until 1924. The United States acquired Alaska from Russia in 1867, and the transfer ceremony took place in Sitka, where the Russians had struggled to colonize the Tlingit, the Native people who had been in the area for thousands of years. For a population of nine thousand, Sitka has an unusually high number of cemeteries—between fifteen and twenty—including a Russian Orthodox Cemetery, dating to 1805, with DIY grave markers and crosses spread across a deeply forested thicket north of downtown. Here the national cemetery's location seems particularly important, if only because its official designation—more than fifty years after the Civil War—aligned American commemorative practices with the Republic's imperial reach.[18]

I got to the cemetery around 3:00, winding my way past the marina and houses with electric cars parked in the driveways (more than you might see elsewhere because there is not much opportunity for long-distance driving in Sitka), and saw from the orange tape and machinery and hard hats moving across the brow of the hill that the site was under construction. But there was a way past the mesh and the excavated retaining walls, and I walked to the rear, my camera out, keeping my distance from the work crew, who were packing up for the day, some with masks pulled down (as mine was) and others with nothing at all.

After a few minutes I headed back to the top of the hill and paused by the flag stand, shooting down across the sloping rows of headstones and the street, when one of the workers, a big, white guy with a beard, stopped and asked what I was doing. It seemed my flat-footed response—I was just taking pictures—was the right answer to his conversation-starting question, and we talked.

I told him about my project, and he told me about their work: they were adding a section to the cemetery and remediating erosion problems. He said his grandfather, a World War II veteran, was buried here and so was his grandmother. He said he grew up in Sitka and that, except for a few years of college in Oregon, he had lived in Alaska his entire life. He told me his wife was from Long Island and attended graduate school at the University of Washington after going to college in New York City. I wanted to ask how they met, what their path back to his hometown looked like, but instead we talked about the quality of life in Sitka, the importance of getting away occasionally, and that he hunted and fished a lot. "Subsistence living" (his term, not mine) was not just a throwaway phrase but also (I found out later) a tradition protected by Alaska law.

We said goodbye, and he went back to cleaning the site, and I walked over to the columbarium to take more pictures. When I returned the following morning, I was alone. The sun was coming up, and I was the farthest west I had ever been. History is often local—it certainly is where the dead are concerned—and the cemetery has its share of distinctive residents. Still, the landscape was familiar, and I fell back on known rituals, roaming the grounds until my feet were wet with dew and I returned to town. I flew to Anchorage early the next day, and I ate reindeer sausage for breakfast before heading to Fort Richardson, where I registered to visit the cemetery because it is on post.

Looking back on my travels, I recognize that I did not need to visit Sitka, Baton Rouge, Philadelphia, or Maxwell to understand what the national cemeteries look like or how they developed. After all, the cemeteries are not that different from one another, and if you have seen a few, then maybe you have seen them all. But seeing is also believing, and over and against this commonsensical observation, I would say that viewing the country as a whole is no easy thing. And it is particularly difficult now, given the political and social conflicts that divide the Republic. When I began this project, I did not expect to discover a vision of unity embedded in the national cemeteries. But I did. And it was, and is, a sight to remember.

View from the Public Information Center at Alabama National Cemetery, Montevallo, Alabama, 2019.

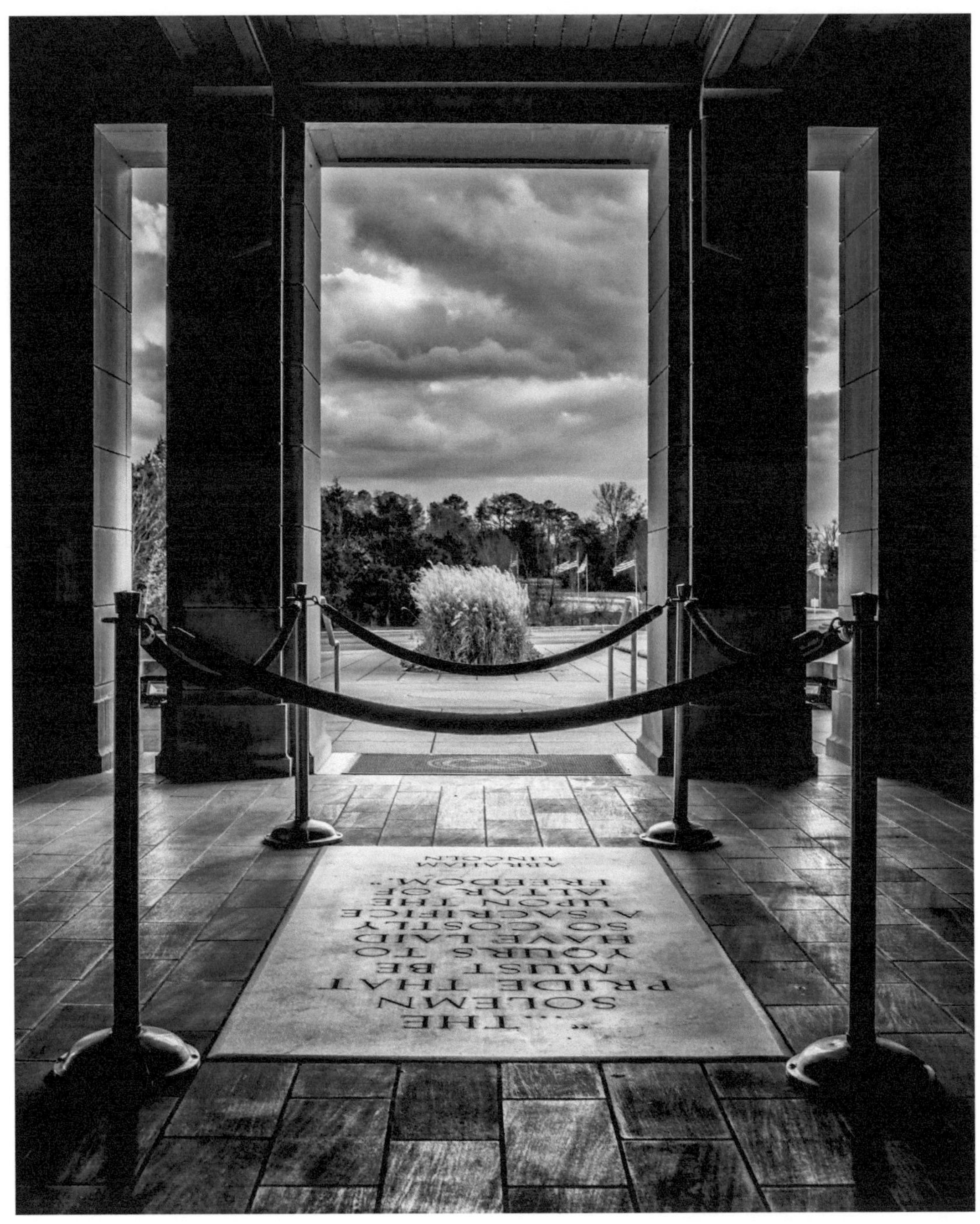

Coda

On May 31, 2021, the *New York Times* published an opinion piece titled "On Memorial Day, the Veterans Who Bury Their Own." The article was a profile of the men who work at Calverton National Cemetery, veterans who find purpose by maintaining the grounds, caring for the dead, and looking after each other—a sacred duty, the article said. I knew that the groundskeepers employed by the national cemeteries were veterans. I learned that during one of my first trips, when I visited the Bath National Cemetery in New York early on a Sunday morning and spoke to a guy watering the grass, who told me a little about the cemetery and how he came to work there. A couple years later, as I walked up a hill at the West Virginia National Cemetery, a man in his thirties, younger than the landscaper I talked to in New York, stopped in his utility vehicle and asked me if I had any questions or needed help in finding anything. I said no, I was just admiring the cemetery and told him I thought they did a great job maintaining the grounds. He replied, "Thank you, sir. We owe it to those who are here and those who were left behind."

I did not speak much on these trips. Most of the time there was no chance to talk. I was either the only person at the cemetery or alone among other visitors. When I did speak, usually with workers, the conversation addressed the details of remembrance, as shown in the landscape or infrastructure (those mildewed headstones at Fort Leavenworth). This is not surprising. What are cemeteries but places of memory and spaces we visit so we do not forget? The *Times* piece underscores this purpose when it quotes Randy Reeves, an undersecretary at the Department of Veterans Affairs and a veteran himself, who said in a Memorial Day speech at Calverton that we all potentially die two deaths: "We die the first time when breath leaves us. But we only truly die sometime in the future when no one speaks our name or tells our story."[1]

Hallowed. Shrine. Sacrifice. Honor. Consecrate. Reconsecrate. The commitment the United States made during the Civil War to remember the names of the Union dead brought a heavy force to bear on the act of remembering. The words used to describe the cemeteries—so evocative of holy purpose—are made by man, not God. Perhaps, to some, this construction seems false. By this measure, a death is honorable and the ground sacred only because the government made it so. Through the act of naming, the government also claims to speak for us all. These are national not military cemeteries, and it is this conjunction, eliding the various sins made in the name of American democracy, that can bring critics to the ramparts.

If I slow walk this argument, it is not necessarily because I disagree with the premise but because ideological analysis can lead to closure and rule out imaginative possibilities. I prefer the rhythm of show and tell and taking a broader view of the territory. As a memorial landscape, the cemetery is a figurative space, never more so than when it encourages a commitment to

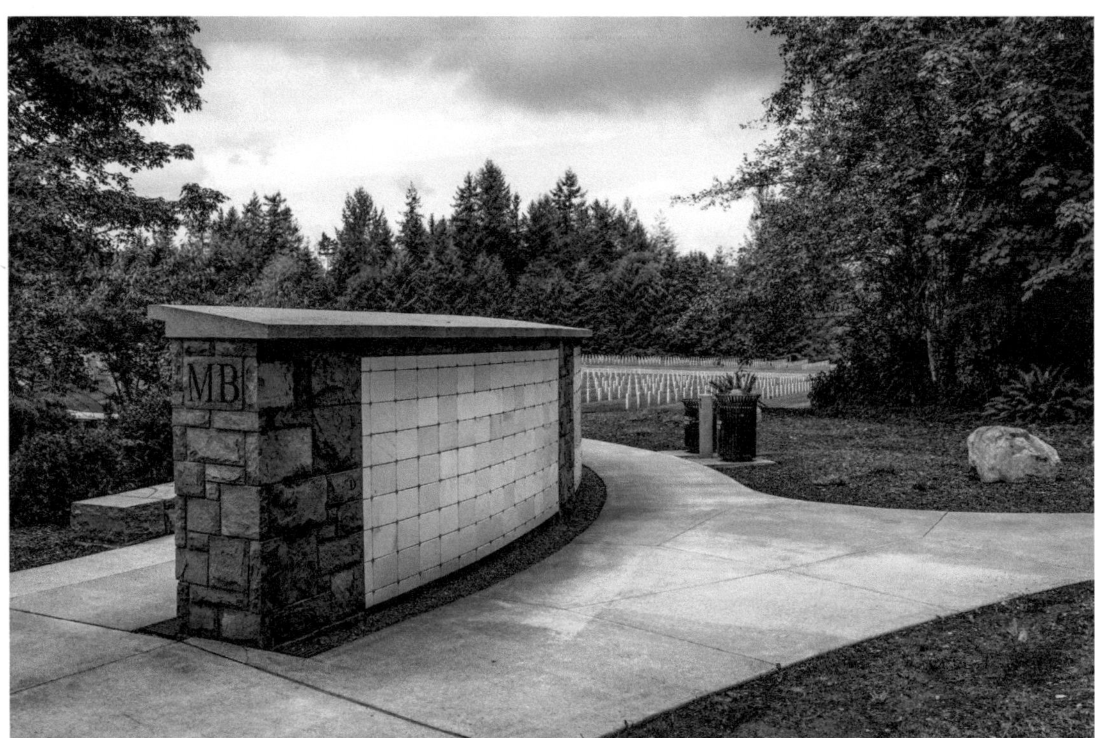

Tahoma National Cemetery (established in 1994), Kent, Washington, 2019.

nation.[2] But it is also a place made of human remains. The soil is rich, and though my aim here is not to excavate the metaphysics of burial and remembrance, I want to point out—no, insist on recognizing—the presence of more than four million dead, too many for their memories to be overtaken by a single nation, their names and stories free to be spoken by other voices. In fact, one of the most radical features of the Civil War cemeteries is that the combatants were buried individually and, whenever possible, identified. So the War Department assumed the power to name, but with that power came a corresponding recognition of the dead, each one in turn. This was American democracy, the soldier's story finally written in earth.

The act of naming took place on flat surfaces, first wooden markers and then granite and marble headstones. The US Army was already in the practice of marking graves in cemeteries linked to frontier forts—using wooden headboards—but the war required a more durable, standardized approach to tracking the dead. The engraved names corresponded with registries of the Union dead that the War Department compiled and published (however incompletely) in "Rolls of Honor," while the headstones—ten inches wide and twelve inches above the ground—were systematically organized in archival fashion. The design of the headstones evolved over time. The face of the Union dead initially took the shape of a sunken shield, and though there were variations on this form, the headstones nearly always included a name (unless it was unknown), a number, and the soldier's home state. Around 1890, after the Spanish-American War, the letters "SP-AM" appeared on the headstones of veterans who fought in that conflict.

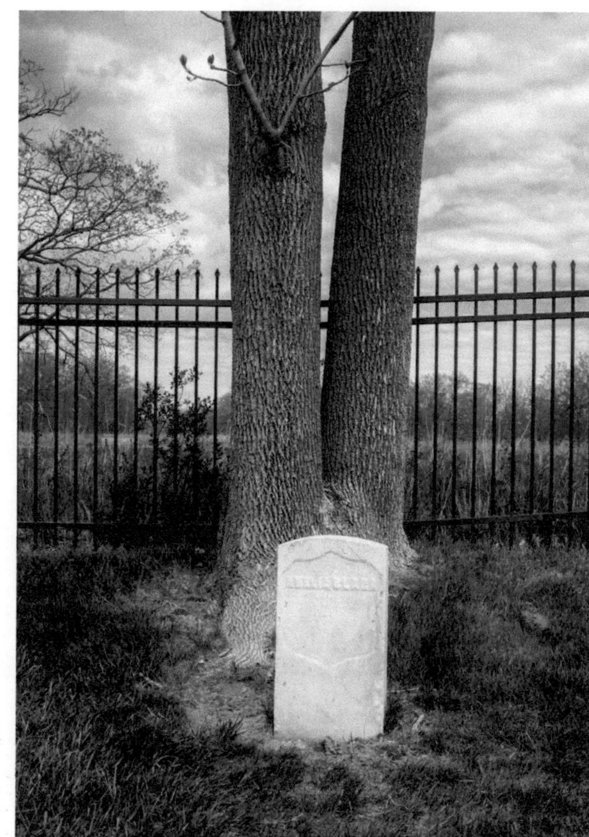

Fort Sheridan National Cemetery (established in 2019), Lake Forest, Illinois, 2021. For more than a century the burial ground was a post cemetery affiliated with Fort Sheridan and administered by the Department of the Army. In 2019, it was transferred to the National Cemetery Administration.

There was no need, no thought of designating the provenance of death during the Civil War—who knew there would be reason later to distinguish among conflicts—but, for every subsequent war, some government official has authorized the inscription of the relevant war: "Korea," "Vietnam," "Persian Gulf," and so forth.[3]

After World War I, veterans were allowed to display a religious emblem on their headstone, a Latin Cross or Star of David, and in 1951, the secretary of the army approved the use of a Buddhist icon. Today, veterans have almost one hundred Emblems of Belief to choose from, a selection that runs the gamut from Atheist and Landing Eagle to almost every faith tradition.[4] In addition to the individual's legal name, year of birth and death, service branch, and section or grave number—all required—the veteran may now choose to include (among other options) a personalized inscription such as "Gone but not forgotten" or "Loved by all." Depending on the cemetery, the hardware will be an upright headstone (in marble), a flat marker (in bronze, granite,

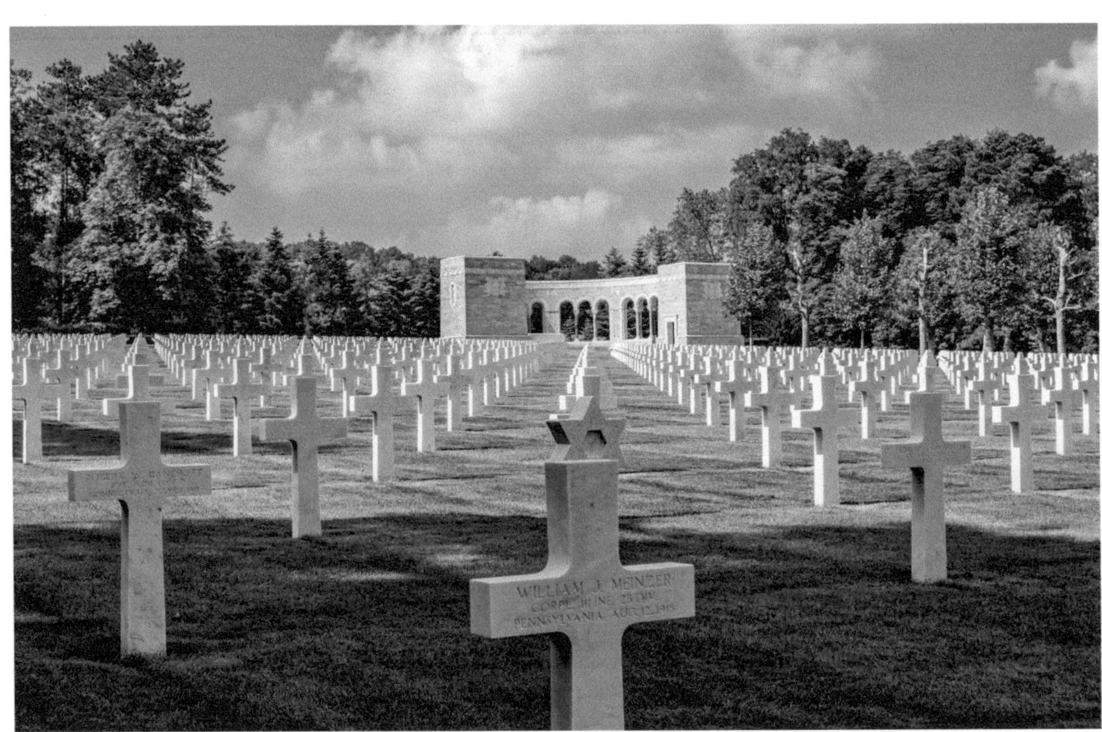

Oise-Aisne American Cemetery and Memorial (dedicated in 1937), the second-largest American World War I cemetery, Seringes-et-Nesles, France, 2016.

or marble), or a niche plaque (as on a columbarium). These displays are complementary to veterans (but not to spouses or dependents) and may even be used in private cemeteries.

The headstones, flat markers, and plaques with names of military personnel whose ashes have been scattered across a garden or placed in an ossuary are not so different from the memorials found in private cemeteries. But they read differently in a memorial landscape otherwise devoted to the ideals of the Republic, and some visitors (like me) may have difficulty translating some of the acronyms found on the headstones, especially the abbreviated ranks. Once the requisite information has been placed on the stone, there are only so many lines, so many characters, left to illuminate everything else. Epitaphs are not really history or even obituaries, and the pithiness required to mark and evoke a life in a national cemetery requires input from the state as well as the individual or family. It is a matter of coauthorship, and this sense of collective production applies to the life as well as the language on the headstones. And many of these lives were cut short. I doubt anyone has done a comparative analysis, but because a significant portion of the dead perished in war, the national cemeteries are more youthful places than private burial grounds.

Memory is a powerful but elusive force, and when I began this project—hoping to capture its imprint—I soon discovered what I would not be doing. I was at Cypress Hills in Brooklyn when a car drove up beside me and a man asked me where he could find the grave of one of the Medal of Honor recipients buried there. I did not know, and I realized I was more interested in the landscapes than the people buried in them. I can note here, as writers sometimes do, that to say more about those life histories would require that I write a different book. That is true, but the loss seems especially poignant, given my subject matter. And I wonder what I have given up in the trade. Then again, the act of remembering is the work of the cemeteries, and I most of all want to show how this work takes place. Still, that does not mean I did not pay attention to details; in fact, I often had a hard time pulling my camera away from individual headstones. One of my first shots was of "His Wife Helen," a grave plot at the back or top of Cypress Hills, with the cemetery rolling down before me. A couple weeks later, at Bath, I photographed several headstones adorned with stuffed animals and pumpkins (it was September), which friends and family had left to remember the deceased ("beloved husband and father"). This is one way of seeing history in these spaces: a haiku-like record of military service and personalized sentiments expanded and revised through mementos, the outrigging of memory and consciousness.

Over the course of my journey to visit all but a few of America's national cemeteries, I took pictures of many headstones, thinking of them as individual portraits or group shots when I photographed in clusters. I took them because I was drawn to how they looked in their place, pulling them into view not just because of their beauty (and I do find them beautiful) but also because of the presence they established on the landscape. That presence includes the words on the face, inscriptions that set one headstone apart from the other. That presence likewise embraces the texture of the stone, the light, trees, sky, weather, and all the other things that prompt us to take a picture, many of which cannot be explained. And there is history to be recovered from details on headstones—a partial history to be sure but accessible in bits through online finding aids.

So I close this book with a "Gallery of Honor," showing photos of fourteen headstones and evoking memories of those who served their country. Their lives—and the lives of more than four million other veterans buried in America's national cemeteries—continue to shape the ground beyond their names in a landscape whose end is nowhere in sight.[5]

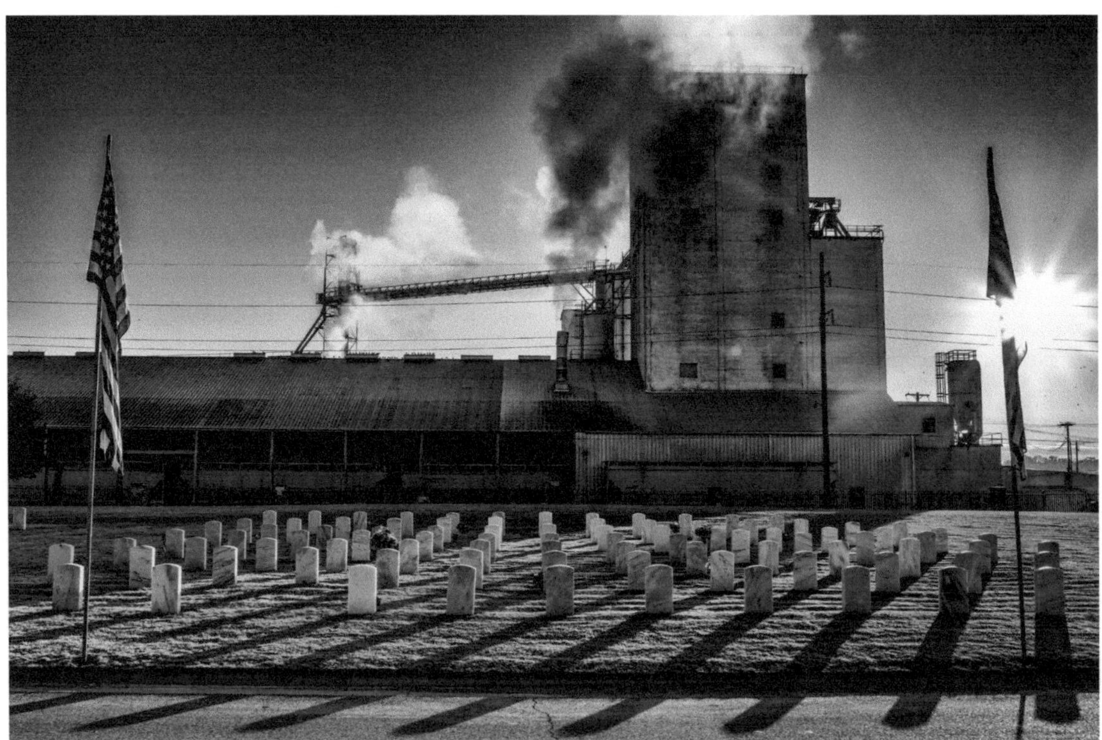

A feed mill adjacent to Fort Smith National Cemetery (established in 1867), Fort Smith, Arkansas, 2019.

Gallery of Honor

SELIGMAN B. AUSTRIAN—Meuse-Argonne American Cemetery, near Romagne-sous-Montfaucon, France: Plot B, Row 15, Grave 40, 2016.

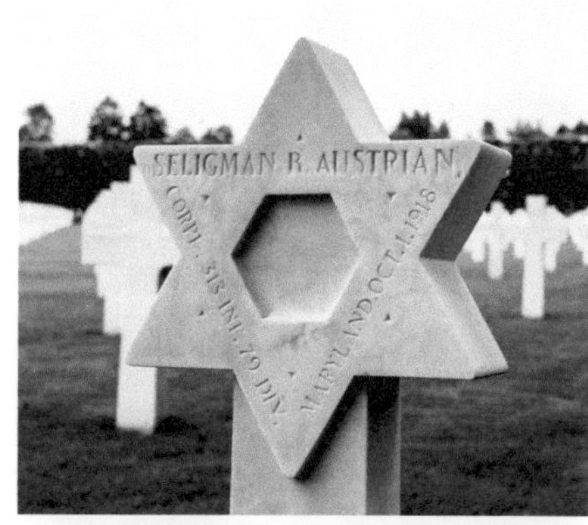

The headstone that the American Battle Monuments implanted in Romagne, France, says that Corporal Austrian, an infantryman, died on October 1, 1918, most likely during the Meuse offensive. His headstone, shaped as the Star of David, indicates that he was Jewish. Prior to the war, he was from Baltimore, Maryland, worked in insurance, and, before that, attended the Massachusetts Institute of Technology. He was single and thirty years old when he died from wounds.[1]

JOSE MARIA-RAUL CUPIS—Monte Calvario Veterans Cemetery (established in 2011), Tucson, Arizona, 2022.

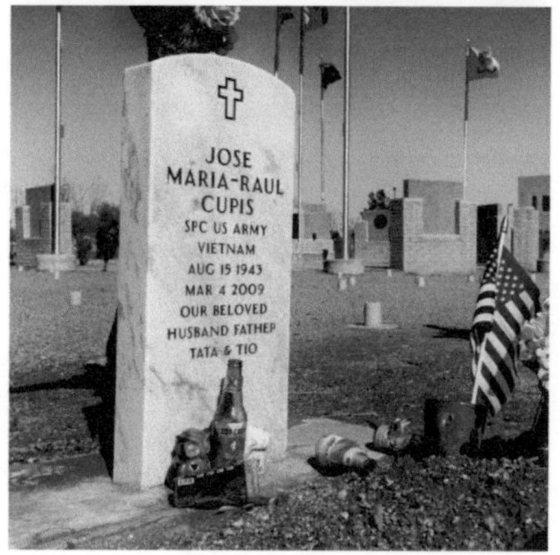

Born in Tucson on August 15, 1943, Jose Maria-Raul Cupis spent most of his adult life in his hometown, surrounded by a large, extended family. He served as a specialist in the army during the Vietnam War and, after the war, continued his military service by joining the US Army National Guard as a member of Arizona's Charlie Battery. He worked as a security guard at the Casino of the Sun, owned and operated by the Pascua Yaqui Tribe. Following his death on March 3, 2009, he was buried in Monte Calvario Veterans Cemetery in Tucson, along with other Yaqui-American veterans.[2]

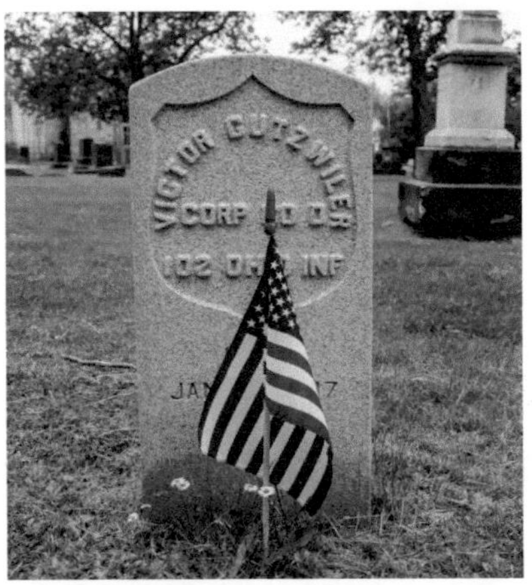

VICTOR GUTZWILER JR.—Soldiers' Lot in Woodland Cemetery (lot established in 1863), Cleveland, Ohio, 2018.

Born in 1844—the son of immigrants from France and Switzerland—Victor Gutzwiler Jr. served as a corporal in the 102nd Ohio Infantry Regiment, fighting for the Union for four months until he was discharged because of a disability. He died in 1897.[3]

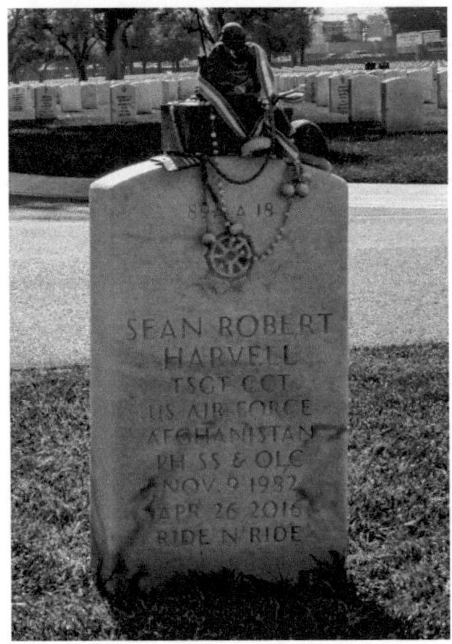

SEAN ROBERT HARVELL—Los Angeles National Cemetery, Los Angeles, California: Section 89S, Row A, Site 18, 2018.

Staff Sergeant Harvell served in the US Air Force and was awarded two Silver Stars for his courageous actions during the Global War on Terrorism, specifically in Afghanistan. After his fourth deployment, he moved back home to Long Beach and opened a motorcycle shop. On April 26, 2016, he drowned off Alamitos Beach, five years after his younger brother, Andrew, who likewise served in the air force, was shot down in Afghanistan.[4] He was thirty-tree. Sean and Andrew share a grave at Los Angeles National Cemetery.

JAMES R. HENDRIX—Florida National Cemetery, Bushnell, Florida: Section MOH, Site 1, 2018.

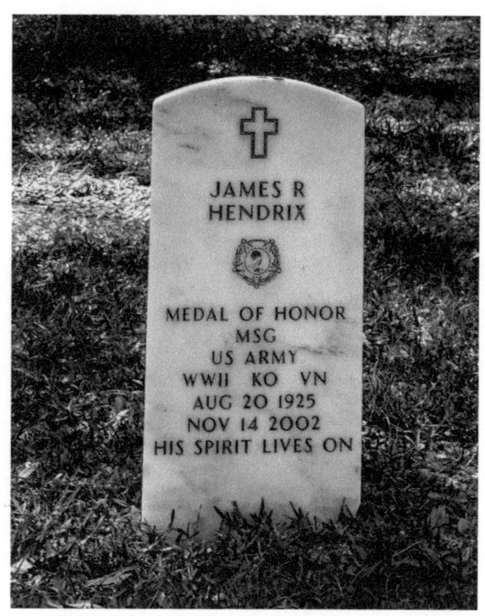

James R. Hendrix, a Medal of Honor recipient, earned front-page news during World War II when he rescued several of his fellow soldiers and captured a number of Germans in the Battle of the Bulge. Hendrix was a private in the army—the infantry—but later became a paratrooper. He served in the military until 1965, when he retired as a master sergeant. Born in rural Arkansas, the son of a sharecropper, he died in Davenport, Florida, at the age of seventy-seven.[5]

LEE SANFORD HULETT—Arlington National Cemetery, Arlington, Virginia: Section 8, Grave 5089-A, 2021.

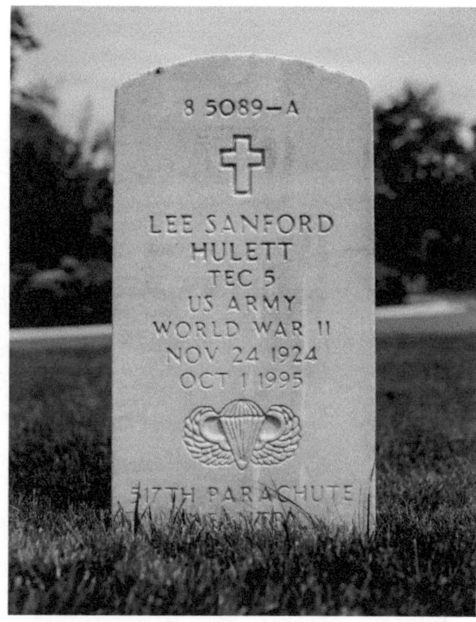

In October 1995, Lee S. Hulett was killed in Hanover, Pennsylvania, after his parachute failed to open following his fourth jump of the day. Hulett served with the 517th Parachute Infantry during World War II and continued to parachute in civilian life, performing 1,400 jumps by the time he died. After the war, he returned to Ohio to attend college and subsequently taught high school and sold insurance in Montgomery County, Maryland. He was seventy years old when he died.[6]

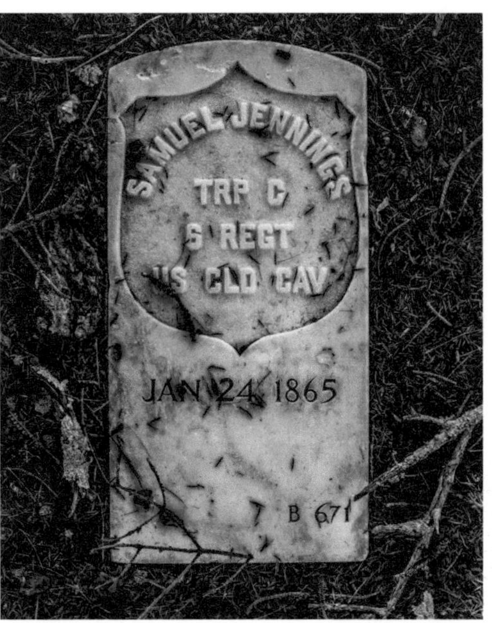

SAMUEL JENNINGS—Camp Nelson National Cemetery, Nicholasville, Kentucky: Section B, Site 671, 2019.

Samuel Jennings—"Sam" on the War Department's register of volunteers who died during the Civil War—was a private in Troop C, Sixth Regiment of the US Colored Cavalry. Jennings died of typhoid fever while at Camp Nelson, which served as a recruitment center for Black soldiers and included a large hospital.[7]

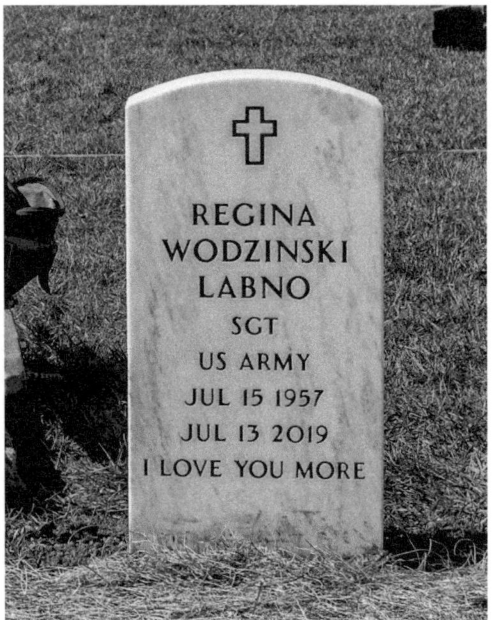

REGINA WODZINSKI LABNO—West Virginia National Cemetery (established in 1987), Grafton, West Virginia: Section 5, Site 1201, 2019.

Regina Wodzinski Labno was born in Scranton, Pennsylvania, in 1957 and died sixty-one years later in Clarksburg, West Virginia. She served for ten years in the US Army, reaching the rank of sergeant. After leaving the military, she made a home with her family in Buckhannon, West Virginia.[8]

ROGER H. LAROCQUE—Farmingdale Cemetery (established in 1987), Middlebury, Vermont, 2020.

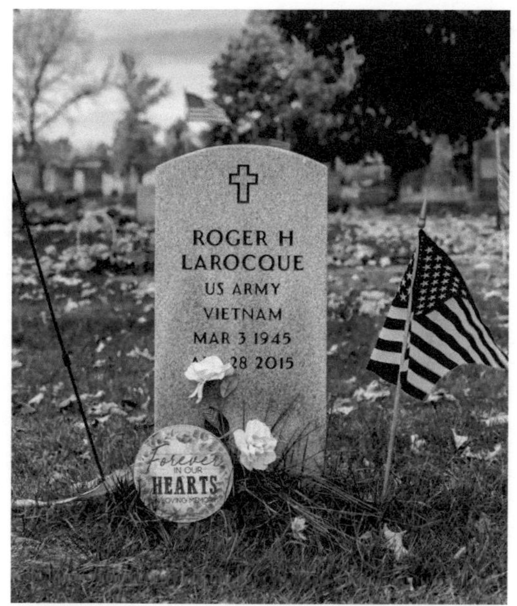

Born in 1945, Roger H. Larocque grew up on a family farm in Salisbury, Vermont, and was drafted into the US Army in 1968 to fight in the Vietnam War. After the war, he worked as a roofer and was employed by several local schools. He died in 2015 and is buried at a private cemetery in Middlebury, Vermont, in a grave marked by a headstone provided by the National Cemetery Administration.[9]

CHARLES GENTRY MARLIN SR.—Andersonville National Cemetery, Andersonville, Georgia: Section J, Site 248, 2017.

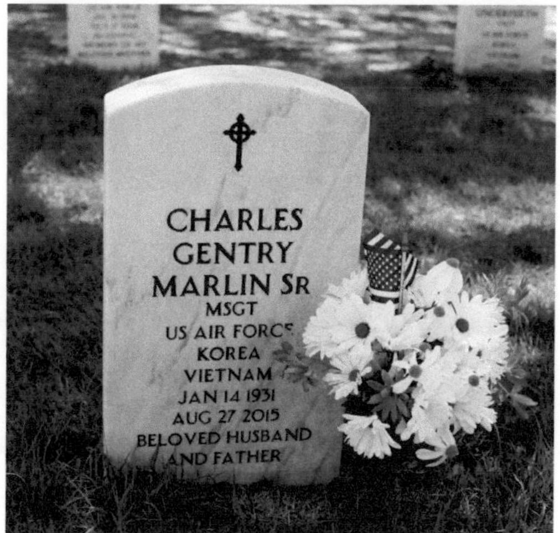

Charles Gentry Marlin Sr. was born in Franklin, Tennessee, in 1931 and worked as a radio operator in the US Air Force for twenty years, joining the military in 1948 and serving in both the Korean and Vietnam Wars. After retiring from the air force as a master sergeant, he worked as an avionics technician at Robins Air Force Base in Georgia, building electrical systems in aircraft. He and his family made their home in nearby Macon. When he died at the age of eighty-four, he was buried at Andersonville National Cemetery. His wife, Charlotte, is interred with him.[10]

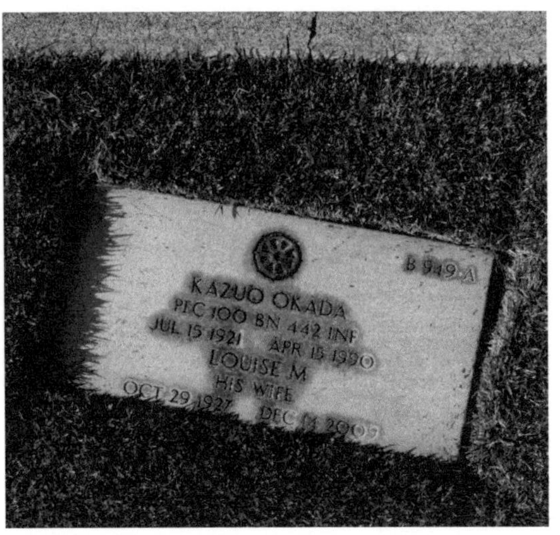

KAZUO OKADA—National Memorial Cemetery of the Pacific, Honolulu, Hawaii: Section B, Site 949-A, 2020.

Kazuo Okada was born in Hanapepe, Kauai, in 1921 and, during World War II, served as a private first class in the 100th Battalion, 442nd Infantry, a unit comprised of second-generation Japanese Americans (Nisei), many of them from Hawaii, who fought mostly in Italy and France. When he returned from the war, he pursued a career as a woodworker at the Barbers Point Naval Air Station in Honolulu. He died in 1990. His wife, Louise Mieko Kazuo, a native of Honolulu, worked as a produce clerk at a supermarket in the city and outlived Kazuo by nineteen years. They are buried together at the Punchbowl.[11]

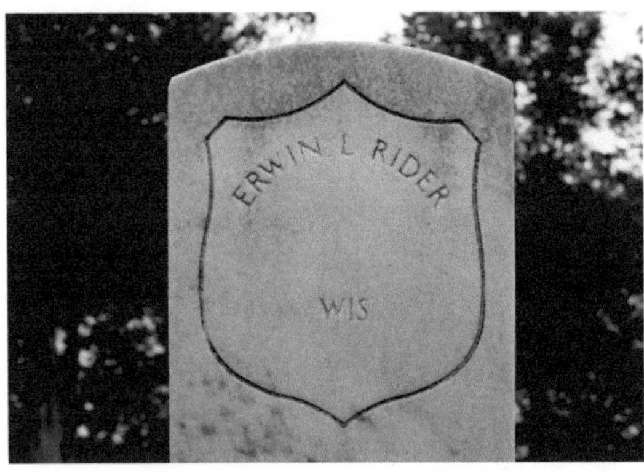

ERWIN L. RIDER—Shiloh National Military Park, Shiloh, Tennessee: Site 1814, 2017.

From Richfield, Wisconsin, Private Erwin L. Rider enlisted in the Sixteenth Wisconsin Volunteer Infantry Company on November 18, 1861, and was killed in combat at the Battle of Shiloh, at Pittsburg Landing, Tennessee, on April 6, 1862. Rider was a member of the colors guard and responsible for protecting the regimental banners and flag. His headstone at Shiloh is a cenotaph, not a grave marker, meaning that his remains may still be buried on the battlefield. Existing Civil War records do not indicate how old he was when he died, though his rank and role, as well as a surviving photograph (a carte-de-visite), suggest he was quite young.[12]

AUGUSTA GRACE SAUCER—Mountain Home National Cemetery (established in 1903), Johnson City, Tennessee: Section SS, Site 1070B, 2019.

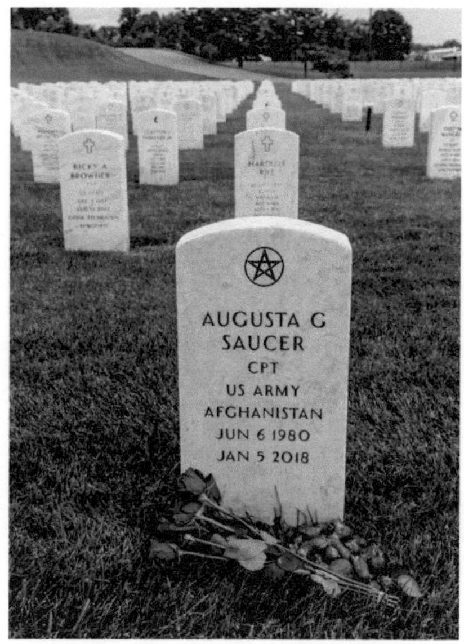

Augusta Grace Saucer was an engineer and captain in the US Army who served in Afghanistan with the 864th Engineer Battalion. After leaving the military, she moved to Tennessee, where she lived with her husband and pursued a career in mental health care as a social worker.[13] She died in 2018 at the age of thirty-seven.

ERNEST C. SYKES—Hampton National Cemetery (established in 1898), Hampton, Virginia: Section D, 3190A, 2019.

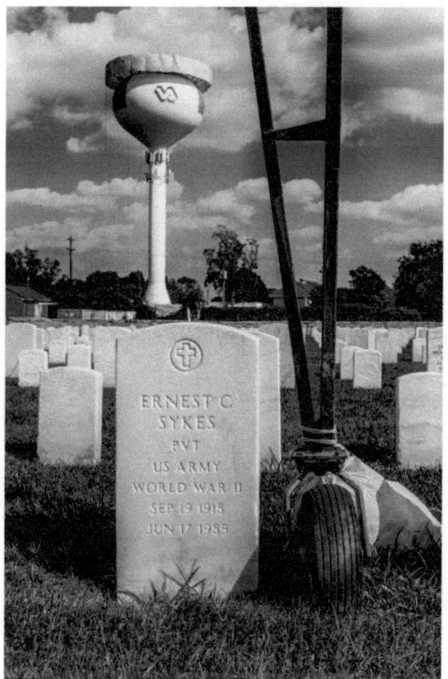

Ernest C. Sykes was born and raised in Boston, Massachusetts, and worked as a cook after graduating from high school. In the fall of 1942, at the age of twenty-four, he enlisted in the US Army and served during World War II. Sometime after the war, he settled in Newport News, Virginia, and made his living as a hospital attendant until he died in 1985. His wife, Virginia, is also buried at Hampton National Cemetery (Section D-H, Site 3261A).[14]

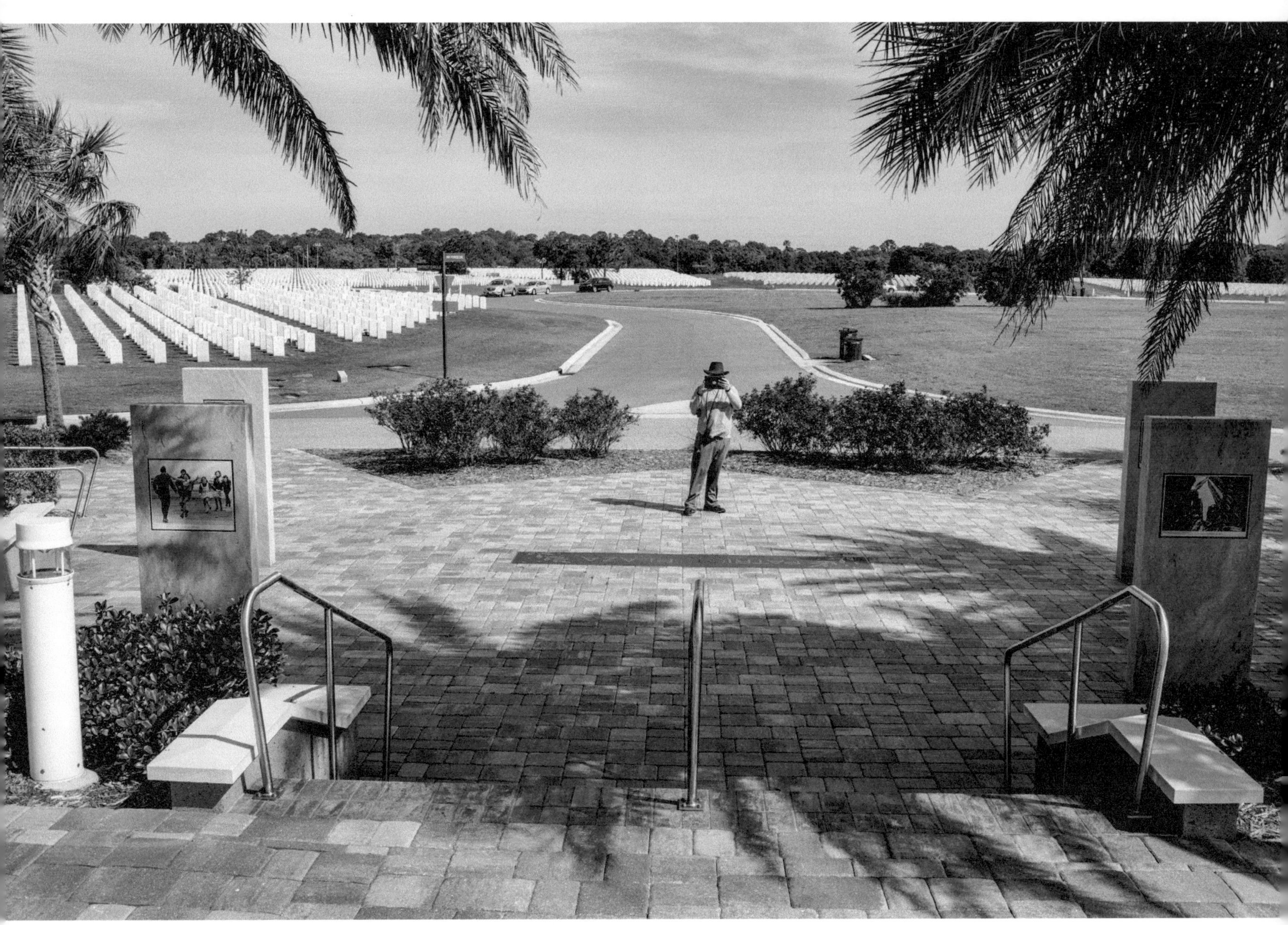

Baird Spears, the author's son, takes a picture of Patriot Plaza, a 2,800-seat ceremonial amphitheater at Sarasota National Cemetery (established in 2009), Sarasota, Florida, 2019.

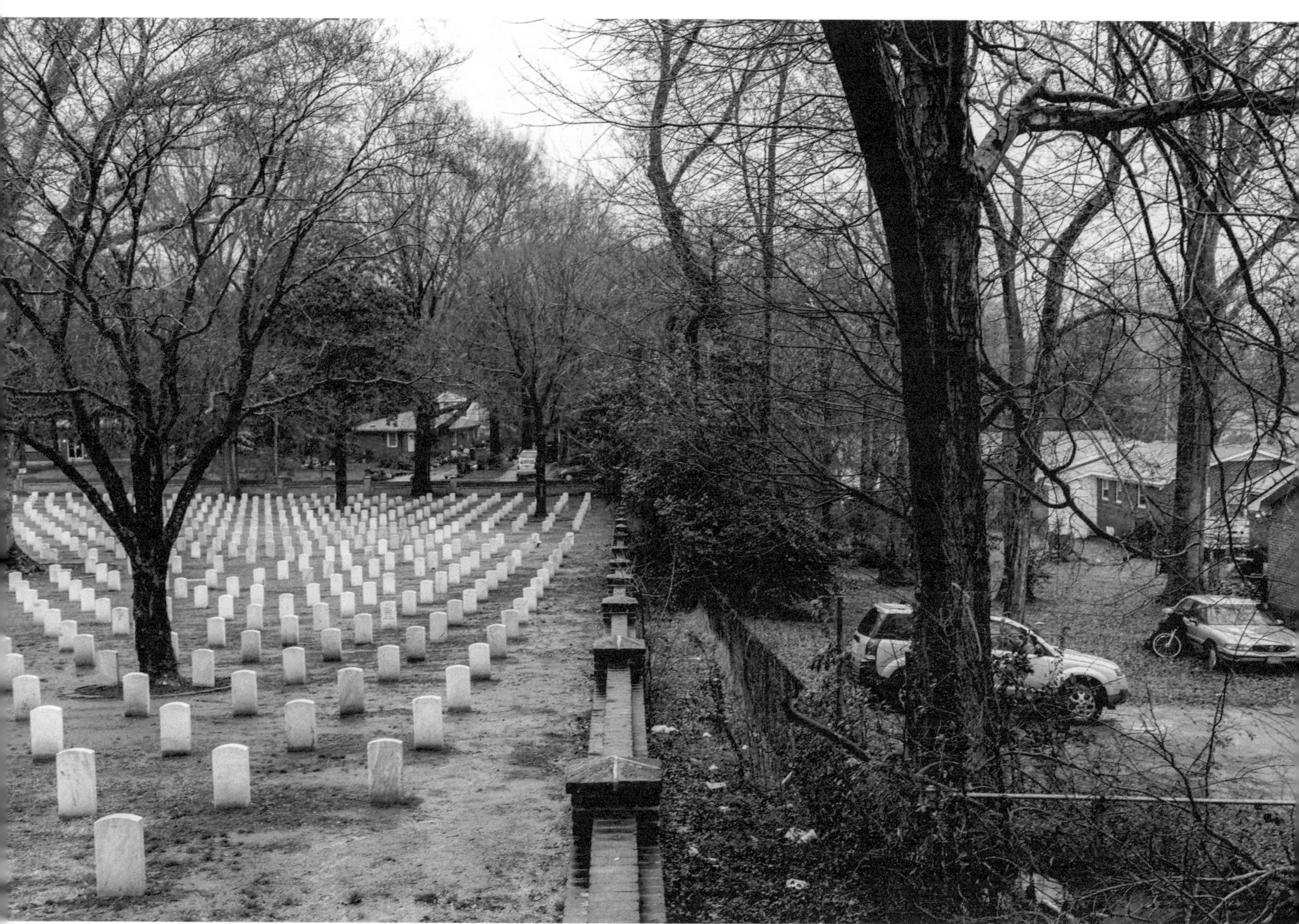

Raleigh National Cemetery (established in 1865), Raleigh, North Carolina, 2019.

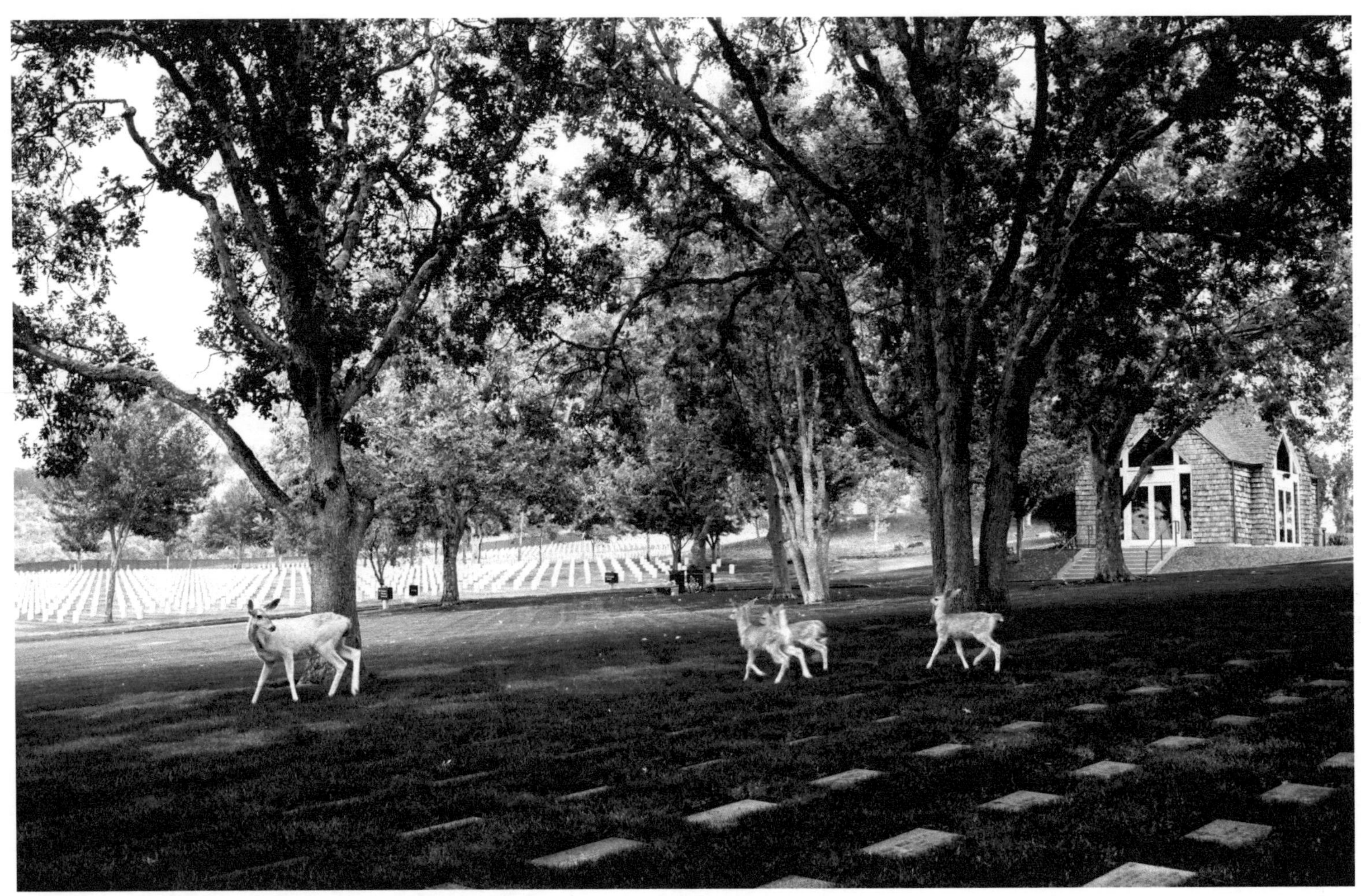

Eagle Point National Cemetery (established in 1952), Eagle Point, Oregon, 2019.

Acknowledgments

This book is the culmination of many journeys, and I appreciate the input and support I received along the way from many friends, especially Katy Smith Abbott, Febe Armanios, Bill Brooks, Pieter Broucke, Deb Evans, Kirsten Hoving, Matt Jennings, Bill Koulopoulos, David Leviatin, Peter Lourie, Doug Mills, and Jamie Northrup. Particular thanks go to Michael Eastman, Tim Gilfoyle, John Huddleston, Susan Schulten, and Allyson Torrisi, who offered important assistance at various points in the book's development. Elliott Gorn and the late Matthew Pacholec read earlier versions of the manuscript, and the book is better for their insights and suggestions. As they have in the past, Nancy and Liza Spears helped improve my prose. I also want to thank the reviewers who read the manuscript and offered suggestions that enhanced the book. One of these readers, Steven Trout, edits the series this volume is now a part of, and it has been a pleasure working with him, editor-in-chief Dan Waterman, and the entire team at the University of Alabama Press.

George F. Thompson played a key role in the selection and sequencing of the photographs. He also read the manuscript numerous times, providing valuable editorial oversight along the way. I am likewise grateful for George's leadership as founder and director of the Center for the Study of Place since 1990 (known as the Center for American Places before February 2007), through which projects like this see the light of day. Thanks, also, to Mikki Soroczak, who helped prepare the manuscript for publication.

I could not have undertaken this project without the support of Middlebury College, whose generous funding of research opportunities enables faculty to pursue their intellectual and creative interests beyond Vermont. I particularly thank Jim Ralph, Dean of the Faculty, for his efforts in coordinating this support.

Final thanks go to my family, especially Nancy Spears, whose love and tolerance made room for this book. Baird Spears, Liza Spears, and Straker Carryer were excellent fellow travelers and continue to help me see the wider world.

Notes

Foreword

1. As reported in "Washington Letter," *Wilmington Morning Star*, June 6, 1868, 2.

2. William A. Blair, "Black Lives at Arlington National Cemetery: From Slavery to Segregation," *Southern Spaces*, April 2, 2019.

Introduction

1. See Roger Cohen, "Black Patriots Fought and Died in Europe, to Little Avail in U.S.," *New York Times*, March 1, 2021, A7.

2. "List of All VA Cemeteries," National Cemetery Administration (website), last updated March 28, 2024.

3. "Facts about the National Cemetery Administration," National Cemetery Administration (website), last updated March 6, 2023. On the reassignment of US Army post cemeteries, see the Department of Veterans Affairs' news release, "VA Completes Transfer of U.S. Army Cemeteries as Part of Government Reform and Reorganization Effort," in Southern Maryland Chronicle (website), October 9, 2020.

4. "About NCA," National Cemetery Administration (website), last updated November 20, 2023.

5. See the list at "National Register of Historic Places and Designated National Historic Landmarks," National Cemetery Administration (website), last updated December 15, 2023.

6. For chronological data I have relied on "Dates of Establishment: National Cemeteries & NCA Burial Sites," National Cemetery Administration (website), last updated November 2, 2023. Similar information regarding the founding dates of military cemeteries abroad is available on the American Battle Monuments Commission website.

7. And historians assert that well before 1619, "hundreds of thousands of Africans, both free and enslaved, aided the establishment and survival of colonies in the Americas and the New World. They also fought against European oppression and, in some instances, hindered the systemic spread of colonization." See Chrystal Ponti, "America's History of Slavery Began Long before Jamestown," History (website), August 14, 2019 (updated August 26, 2019).

8. For instance, see Edward Tabor Linenthal, *Sacred Ground: Americans and Their Battlefields* (Urbana: University of Illinois Press, 1991), especially 1–7; John Bodnar, *Remaking America: Public Memory, Commemoration,*

and Patriotism in the Twentieth Century (Princeton, NJ: Princeton University Press, 1992), "contested discourse" on 20.

Chapter 1

1. Atul Gawande addresses this reluctance in *Being Mortal: Medicine and What Matters in the End* (New York: Picador, 2014).

2. "Eligibility for Burial in a VA National Cemetery," US Department of Veterans Affairs (website), last updated June 7, 2023.

3. US Department of Veterans Affairs, "Department of Veterans Affairs FY 2018–2024 Strategic Plan," 14, archived at VA Plans, Budget, and Performance, US Department of Veterans Affairs (website), last updated November 23, 2020. For a state-by-state list of national cemeteries, see "List of All VA National Cemeteries," National Cemetery Administration (website), last updated April 19, 2024. On Arlington, see "The History of Arlington National Cemetery," Arlington National Cemetery (website).

4. Susie Linfield, *The Cruel Radiance: Photography and Political Violence* (Chicago: University of Chicago Press, 2010), 7–12.

5. Linfield, *Cruel Radiance*, xv.

6. US Congress, *Public Acts of the Thirty-Seventh Congress of the United States*, Session II, December 2, 1861–July 17, 1862, 596, Library of Congress (website).

7. Walker Percy, "The Loss of the Creature," in *The Message in the Bottle: How Queer Man Is, How Queer Language Is, and What One Has to Do with the Other* (New York: Farrar, Straus and Giroux, 1981), 47.

8. Percy, "Loss of the Creature," 58.

9. Walt Whitman, *Specimen Days*, in *The Portable Walt Whitman*, ed. Mark Van Doren (New York: Viking Press, 1974), 481 and 482.

10. Whitman, *Specimen Days*, 639.

Chapter 2

1. US Congress, *Public Acts of the Thirty-Seventh Congress of the United States*, Session II, December 2, 1861–July 17, 1862, 596, Library of Congress (website).

2. Drew Gilpin Faust, *This Republic of Suffering: Death and the American Civil War* (New York: Alfred A. Knopf, 2008), "most elaborate" on 219, "emergency circumstance" on 99–101. The original twelve cemeteries are Alexandria (VA), Annapolis (MD), Camp Butler (IL), Cypress Hills (NY), Danville (KY), Fort Scott (KS), Keokuk (IA), Loudon Park (MD), Mill Springs (KY), New Albany (IN), and Soldiers' Home (Washington, DC). Although Antietam and Philadelphia were once thought to be part of this group, according to the National Cemetery Administration, their inclusion seems to have been "a misinterpretation of the historical record." See the opening section in "Dates of Establishment: National Cemeteries & NCA Burial Sites," National Cemetery Administration (website), last updated November 2, 2023.

3. Minutes quoted in Charles W. Snell and Sharon A. Brown, *Antietam National Battlefield and National Cemetery, Sharpsburg, Maryland: An Administrative History* (Washington, DC: US Department of the Interior/National Park Service, 1986), 8.

4. A perch is a 16.5 x 16.5–foot Anglo-Saxon unit of measurement once used by surveyors and equal to 272 square feet (or 25.3 square meters).

5. Armando Petrucci, *Writing the Dead: Death and Writing Strategies in the Western Tradition*, trans. Michael Sullivan (Stanford, CA: Stanford University Press, 1996), 117; Thomas W. Laqueur, *The Work of the Dead: A Cultural History of Mortal Remains* (Princeton, NJ: Princeton University Press, 2015), 413–46.

6. Frederick Law Olmsted to Montgomery Cunningham Meigs, August 2, 1870, in *The Years of Olmsted, Vaux & Company 1865–1874*, ed. David Schuyler and Jane Turner Censer (Baltimore: Johns Hopkins University Press, 1992), vol. 5, 386–87. On the rural cemetery movement, see David Charles Sloane, *The Last Great Necessity: Cemeteries in American History* (Baltimore: Johns Hopkins University Press, 1991), especially 65–95.

Chapter 3

1. As quoted in James M. McPherson, *Battle Cry of Freedom: The Civil War Era* (New York: Oxford University Press, 1988), 402.

2. Drew Gilpin Faust, *This Republic of Suffering: Death and the American Civil War* (New York: Alfred A. Knopf, 2008), 219–20.

3. Here and in subsequent references to Whitman's report, I quote from "The Report of Lt. Col. E. B. Whitman, Superintendent of National Cemeteries, Dept. of the Cumberland, Louisville, KY" (May 10, 1869), Box 1, Records of the Office of the Quartermaster General Cemeterial, Other Records, 1828–1929, RG 92, National Archives, Washington, DC.

4. Colonel Marshall I. Ludington to Maj. General M. C. Meigs, Quartermaster General (September 21, 1866), 562, Letters Sent by the Quartermaster Relating to Cemeteries, 1867, RG 92, National Archives, Washington DC.

5. Michael Haines, "Life Expectancy," in *The Oxford Companion to United States History*, ed. Paul S. Boyer (New York: Oxford University Press, 2001), 444–45.

6. Lonnie R. Speer, *Portals to Hell: Military Prisons of the Civil War* (Mechanicsburg, PA: Stackpole Books, 1997), 276.

7. Michael E. Ruane, "Bones of Civil War Dead Found on a Battlefield Tell Their Horror Stories," *Retropolis* (blog), *Washington Post* (website), June 20, 2018.

8. "Hazen Brigade Monument," National Park Service (website), last updated April 5, 2024.

9. For instance, see Elizabeth Lesser, *Broken Open: How Difficult Times Can Help Us Grow* (New York: Villard, 2004).

10. David W. Blight, *American Oracle: The Civil War in the Civil Rights Era* (Cambridge, MA: Harvard University Press, 2013), 26.

Chapter 4

1. "An Interview with Walker Evans: 'The Thing Itself Is Such a Secret and So Unapproachable' (1974)," American Suburb X (website), October 4, 2011. The interview was originally published in the *Yale Alumni Magazine* in February 1974.

2. Ana Pacheco, "Fiesta de Santa Fe: A Celebration of Faith," *Santa Fe New Mexican*, September 4, 2016; Santa Fe National Cemetery, National Cemetery Administration (website), last updated October 13, 2023.

3. As quoted in Robert Macfarlane, *The Old Ways: A Journey on Foot* (New York: Viking, 2012), 25.

4. Thomas W. Laqueur, *The Work of the Dead: A Cultural History of Mortal Remains* (Princeton, NJ: Princeton University Press, 2015), 1.

5. David Gunter, "Cemetery Tales: The Odd Sandstone Tombstone in the Santa Fe National Cemetery," *Everyday Knosticism* (blog), April 26, 2018 (updated April 27, 2018).

Chapter 5

1. Robert Penn Warren, "The South: Distance and Change," interview by Lous D. Rubin Jr., in *Talking With Robert Penn Warren*, ed. Floyd C. Watkins, John T. Hiers, and Mary Louise Weaks (Athens: University of Georgia Press, 1990), 273.

2. National Cemetery Administration, *Federal Stewardship of Confederate Dead* (Washington DC: US Department of Veterans Affairs, 2016), 24–25, 84–85, and 156.

3. National Cemetery Administration, *Federal Stewardship of Confederate Dead*, 12–14.

4. A series of court rulings established this outcome. See John R. Neff, *Honoring the Civil War Dead: Commemoration and the Problem of Reconciliation* (Lawrence: University Press of Kansas, 2005), 240.

5. McKinley quoted in Neff, *Honoring the Civil War Dead*, 222; William Blair, *Contesting the Memory of the Civil War in the South, 1865–1914* (Chapel Hill: University of North Carolina Press, 2004), 188–90; National Cemetery Administration, *Federal Stewardship of Confederate Dead*, "who died in federal prisons" on 3.

6. David W. Blight, *Race and Reunion: The Civil War in American Memory* (Cambridge, MA: Harvard University Press, 2001), especially 350–52; Neff, *Honoring the Civil War Dead*, 240.

7. On this topic and the persistence of Lost Cause ideology, see Clint Smith, *How the Word Is Passed: A Reckoning with the History of Slavery across America* (New York: Back Bay Books, 2021), 118–72. Smith, who is Black, describes his visit to Blandford Cemetery in Petersburg, Virginia (a Confederate cemetery) and his encounter with white southerners at a Memorial Day event sponsored by the Sons of Confederate Veterans.

8. Jim Salter, "Government Spends Millions to Guard Confederate Cemeteries," AP News (website), October 15, 2018.

9. Steve Pokin, "Pokin Around: Out-of-State Security Safeguards Confederate Monument at Springfield Cemetery," *Springfield News-Leader*, August 29, 2017.

10. "Confederate Symbols: Relation to Federal Lands and Programs," Congressional Research Service (website), updated September 20, 2017.

11. James M. McPherson, *Battle Cry of Freedom: The Civil War Era* (New York: Oxford University Press, 1988), 293.

12. Karla Ward and Beth Musgrave, "Confederate Statues Quietly Moved to Lexington Cemetery," *Lexington Herald-Leader*, July 24, 2018.

Chapter 6

1. Vikaas Shanker, "Ceremony in Santa Nella Honors Veterans," *Modesto Bee*, May 29, 2016.

2. "Rostrum," noun, Oxford English Dictionary (website).

3. Micki McElya, *The Politics of Mourning: Death and Honor in Arlington National Cemetery* (Cambridge, MA: Harvard University Press, 2016), 139.

4. National Park Service, US Department of the Interior, "Historic American Landscapes Survey, National Cemeteries, Rostrums, HALS DC-47" (Washington, DC: US Department of the Interior, 2013), 2, archived at Rostrums in National Cemeteries, National Cemetery Administration (website), last updated April 18, 2024.

5. National Park Service, "Historic American Landscapes Survey," 51–62.

6. David W. Blight, *Race and Reunion: The Civil War in American Memory* (Cambridge, MA: Harvard University Press, 2001), 68–71, "founded" and "ritual" on 71.

7. Annette Gordon-Reed, *On Juneteenth* (New York: W. W. Norton, 2021), "sense of promise" on 134.

8. *Republican Banner*, May 31, 1871.

9. National Park Service, "Historic American Landscapes Survey," 12–13, "free speech" on 13.

10. Carolyn E. Janney, *Remembering the Civil War: Reunion and the Limits of Reconciliation* (Chapel Hill: University of North Carolina Press, 2013), 332n10.

11. *Pittsburgh Daily Commercial*, May 31, 1875; *Moline Review*, June 4, 1875.

12. Willam A. Blair, *Contesting the Memory of the Civil War in the South, 1865–1914* (Chapel Hill: University of North Carolina Press, 2004), 75–76.

13. Janney, *Remembering the Civil War*, 91–91; Donald C. Pfanz, *Where Valor Proudly Sleeps: A History of Fredericksburg National Cemetery, 1866–1933* (Carbondale: Southern Illinois University Press, 2018), 167.

14. Pfanz, *Where Valor Proudly Sleeps*, 169. These larger trends are described in Blight, *Race and Reunion*; Blair, *Contesting the Memory*; John R. Neff, *Honoring the Civil War Dead: Commemoration and the Problem of Reconciliation* (Lawrence: University Press of Kansas, 2005); Janney, *Remembering the Civil War*.

15. David W. Blight, *Beyond the Battlefield: Race, Memory, and the American Civil War* (Amherst: University of Massachusetts Press, 2002), 93–119.

16. Frederick Douglass, "Address at the Grave of the Unknown Dead," Arlington, Virginia, May 30, 1871, Frederick Douglass Papers, Library of Congress (website).

17. McElya, *Politics of Mourning*, 103 and 126.

18. Drew Gilpin Faust, *This Republic of Suffering: Death and the American Civil War* (New York: Alfred A. Knopf, 2008), 236.

19. "Buffalo Soldiers," Charles Young Buffalo Soldiers National Monument Ohio, National Park Service (website), last updated January 5, 2023; Walter Johnson, *The Broken Heart of America: St. Louis and the Violent History of the United States* (New York: Basic Books, 2020), 166–67.

20. *Sacramento Bee*, April 23, 1947; *Bristol Herald Courier*, April 27,1947; Morris J. MacGregor Jr., *Integration of the Armed Forces 1940–1965* (Washington, DC: Center of Military History, US Army, 2001), 224–26.

21. Karl Puckett, "'It's Beautiful.' But Time Is Catching Up 158-Year-Old Beaufort National Cemetery," *Island Packet* (website), November 11, 2021; Alexandria National Cemetery, Louisiana, National Cemetery Administration (website), last updated March 26, 2024; Beaufort National Cemetery, National Cemetery Administration (website), last updated November 9; 2023; "U.S. Colored Troops Burials," Center for Civil War Research (website), University of Mississippi, accessed August 10, 2020.

22. Nikole Hannah-Jones, "Democracy," in *The 1619 Project*, ed. Nikole Hannah-Jones, Caitlin Roper, Ilena Silverman, and Jake Silverstein (New York: One World, 2021), 33.

23. In the title of his book, Philip Dray echoes the phrase that newspapers sometimes used to identify those responsible for lynchings: *At the Hands of Persons Unknown: The Lynching of Black America* (New York: Random House, 2002).

24. James H. Cone, *The Cross and the Lynching Tree* (Maryknoll, NY: Orbis Books, 2001). On truth and reconciliation, see Sherrilyn A. Ifill, *On the Courthouse Lawn: Confronting the Legacy of Lynching in the 21st Century* (Boston: Beacon Press, 2007), xxi–xxii and 124.

Chapter 7

1. Geoff Dyer, *The Missing of the Somme* (New York: Vintage, 1994), 14.

2. "Killed, wounded, and missing," Encyclopedia Brittanica (website); Birgit Görtz, "World War I Created New Culture of Mourning," interview with Jay Winter in Deutsche Welle (website), November 18, 2013. Jay Winter, *Remembering War: The Great War between Memory and History in the Twentieth Century* (New Haven: Yale University Press, 2006), 141–43; Gavin Stamp, *The Memorial to the Missing of the Somme* (London: Profile Books, 2016), 40–43.

3. As quoted in David Crane, *Empires of the Dead: How One Man's Vision Led to the Creation of WWI's War Graves* (London: William Collins, 2013), 109–10. Regarding Lutyens's role in establishing the design principles adopted by the Imperial War Graves Commission, also see Christopher Hussey, *The Life of Sir Edwin Lutyens* (London: Country Life, 1950), 372.

4. On Kipling see Stamp, *Memorial to the Missing of the Somme*, 78–79; David Gilmour, *The Long Recessional: The Imperial Life of Rudyard Kipling* (New York: Farrar, Straus and Giroux, 2002), 278–81

5. T. S. Eliot, "The Waste Land," in *T. S. Eliot: The Complete Poems and Plays 1909–1950* (New York: Harcourt, Brace & World, 1971), 46; Jay Winter, *Sites of Memory, Sites of Mourning: The Great War in European Cultural History* (Cambridge: Cambridge University Press, 1995), 5.

6. Stamp, *Memorial to the Missing of the Somme*, 98.

7. Dyer, *Missing of the Somme*, 13.

8. Dyer, *Missing of the Somme*, 3.

9. "Cemeteries & Memorials," American Battle Monuments Commission (website); "About Us," American Battle Monuments Commission (website). The first web page includes the reference to "shrines."

10. Jeffrey Goldberg, "Trump: Americans Who Died in War are 'Losers' and 'Suckers,'" *Atlantic*, September 3, 2020.

11. US Congress, House of Representatives, Committee on Foreign Affairs, *American Battle Monuments Commission: Hearings Before the Committee on Foreign Affairs, House of Representatives, Sixty-Seventh Congress, Second and Third Sessions, On H. R. 9634 and H. R. 10801, for the Creation of an American Battle Monuments Commission to Erect Suitable Memorials Commemorating the Services of the American Soldier in Europe, March 15–20, November 28, December 7–9, 1922* (Washington, DC: Government Printing Office, 1922), 1, 7–8, 18–21, and 25–27. On the development of Gettysburg as a military park, see Jim Weeks, *Gettysburg: Memory, Market, and an American Shrine* (Princeton, NJ: Princeton University Press, 2003), especially 60–66, 116–17.

On how Gettysburg evolved as a place of memory, see Brian Black, *Gettysburg Contested: 150 Years of Preserving America's Cherished Landscape* (Staunton, VA: George F. Thompson Publishing, 2019).

12. Angelique Chrisafis, "'The Real Misery Is in the Countryside': Support for Le Pen Surges in Rural France," *Guardian* (website), April 21, 2017.

13. Vincent Scully, "The Terrible Art of Designing a War Memorial," *New York Times*, July 14, 1991, Section 2, 28. Winter likewise disagrees with Scully, and I have benefited from his discussion of Lutyens in developing my own comments. See Winter, *Sites of Memory*, 105–7.

14. Walker Blaine Beale was the grandson of James G. Blaine, the Republican politician from Maine who ran for president in 1884. See "Walker Blaine Beale," Honor States (website), accessed April 11, 2024.

15. John J. Pershing's cable to John Russell Pope (June 3, 1931) and John Russell Pope to John J. Pershing (June 9, 1931), both in Box 18, WWI Monument and Memorial Files, RG 117, Records of the American Battle Monuments Commission, National Archives, College Park, Maryland (hereafter referred to as RG 117).

16. For a discussion of how the United States marked its participation in the war, see Timothy B. Spears, "Stone Truths: American Memorial Landscapes of World War I," *Journal of Military History* 85, no. 2 (April 2021): 342–68.

17. "Salient," adj. and noun, Oxford English Dictionary (website).

18. Samuel Parker to ABMC (October 10, 1928), Box 188, Correspondence with Former Division Officers, RG 117.

19. On Cret, see Witold Rybczynski, "The Late, Great Paul Cret," *New York Times Style Magazine* (website), October 21, 2014; Paul P. Cret to X. H. Price (December 27, 1929), Box 11, WWI Monument and Memorial Files, RG 117.

20. On the integration of ABMC cemeteries, see V. William Balthrop and Carole Blair, "ISSA Proceedings 2014—Controversy, Racial Equality, and World War I, Cemeteries in Europe," Rozenberg Quarterly (website), 2014, accessed April 11, 2024.

Chapter 8

1. Tom Brokaw, *The Greatest Generation* (New York: Random House, 1998), 17 and 18. The full title of Ambrose's book is *Band of Brothers: E Company, 506th Regiment, 101st Airborne from Normandy to Hitler's Eagle's Nest* (New York: Simon & Schuster, 1992).

2. Michael Sledge, *Soldier Dead: How We Recover, Identify, Bury, and Honor Our Military Fallen* (New York: Columbia University Press, 2005), 78 and 140–43; Yochi J. Dreazen and Gary Fields, "How We Bury the War Dead," *Wall Street Journal*, May 29, 2010, W.3.

3. Critiques of these bombing campaigns include John Hersey, *Hiroshima* (New York: Alfred A. Knopf, 1946); Leslie M. M. Blume, *Fallout: The Hiroshima Cover-up and the Reporter Who Revealed It to the World* (New York: Simon Schuster, 2020); A. J. Grayling, *Among the Dead Cities: The History and Moral Legacy of the WWII Bombing of Civilians in Germany and Japan* (New York: Walker, 2006), with a discussion of just war theory on 210–13; Elizabeth D. Samet, *Looking for the Good War: American Amnesia and the Violent Pursuit of Happiness* (New York: Farrar, Straus and Giroux, 2021), especially 25–91. The British Broadcasting Corporation offers a primer on just war theory at "Just War—Introduction," BBC (website), accessed April 18,

2024; Paul Fussell, *Wartime: Understanding and Behavior in the Second World War* (New York: Oxford University Press, 1989), "stupid and sadistic" on 142.

4. John Bodnar discusses American ambivalence about commemorating patriotic ideals in *The "Good War" in Modern Memory* (Baltimore: Johns Hopkins University Press, 2010), 1–3, 100–8, 116–17, and 128–29; E. B. Sledge, *With the Old Breed at Peleliu and Okinawa* (New York: Ballantine Books, 1981), 315. The soldier's view of the war is also reflected in Studs Terkel, *"The Good War": An Oral History of World War Two* (New York: Pantheon Books, 1984).

5. "Pearl Harbor Veteran's Interment to Be Last on Sunken Arizona," NBC News (website), December 6, 2019; "USS Arizona Interments," Pearl Harbor National Memorial, National Park Service (website), last updated July 20, 2020.

6. Benedict Anderson, *Imagined Communities: Reflections on the Origin and Spread of Nationalism* (New York: Verso, 1983), 9.

7. Doug Carlson, *Punchbowl: The National Memorial Cemetery of the Pacific* (Honolulu: Island Heritage, 1982).

8. Kathy E. Ferguson and Phyllis Turnbull, "Narratives of History, Nature, and Death at the National Memorial Cemetery of the Pacific," *Frontiers* 16, no. 2/3 (1996): 1–23; R. D. K. Herman, "The Dread Taboo, Human Sacrifice, and Pearl Harbor," *Contemporary Pacific* 8, no. 1 (Spring 1996): 81–126.

9. American Battle Monuments Commission, *Honolulu Memorial: National Memorial of the Pacific, Honolulu, Hawaii, West Coast Memorial—East Coast Memorial* (Washington, DC: American Battle Monuments Commission, 2009); "Secretary Cleland Shares Details with President Obama on Vietnam Battle Maps," American Battle Monuments Commission (website), February 21, 2012; John Canaday, "Our National Pride: The World's Worst Sculpture," *New York Times*, July 25, 1965, Section 2, 10.

10. "Honolulu Memorial," American Battle Monuments Commission (website); National Park Service, US Department of the Interior, National Register of Historic Places Registration Form, "National Memorial Cemetery of the Pacific" (certified June 18, 2014), 15, archived at National Register of Historic Places and Designated National Historic Landmarks, National Cemetery Administration (website), last updated May 2, 2024. Details on interment availability (e.g. "casketed remains") at "National Memorial Cemetery of the Pacific," National Cemetery Administration (website), last updated December 11, 2023.

11. For the tally of Punchbowl visitors see "National Memorial Cemetery of the Pacific." On the national cemetery system's growth between 1930 and 1950, see National Park Service, US Department of the Interior, National Register of Historic Places Multiple Property Documentation Form, "Inter-World War National Cemeteries, 1934–1939" (certified March 7, 2016), 9–18, archived at National Register of Historic Places and Designated National Historic Landmarks, National Cemetery Administration (website), last updated May 2, 2024.

12. National Park Service, "Inter-World War National Cemeteries."

13. Casualty estimates found at "Civil War Casualties," American Battlefield Trust (website), November 16, 2012 (updated September 15, 2023); National Park Service, "Inter-World War National Cemeteries," 17.

14. Andrew J. Bacevich, *The New American Militarism: How Americans Are Seduced by War* (New York: Oxford University Press, 2005), 97–99, "demolished" on 99, "myth" on 97, "imperial policing" on 98.

15. "Welcome Center" and "Arlington National Cemetery: Historical Expansion," Arlington National Cemetery (website).

16. "Memorial Amphitheater," Arlington National Cemetery (website); Robert M. Poole, *On Hallowed Ground: The Story of Arlington National Cemetery* (New York: Walker, 2009), 226–27.

17. Poole, *On Hallowed Ground*, 93–99; "Arlington House, The Robert E. Lee Memorial," Arlington National Cemetery (website).

18. Brian W. Everstine, "Arlington's Southern Expansion," *Air Force Magazine* 102, no. 6 (July/August 2019): 36–40; "Establishing Eligibility," Arlington National Cemetery (website); Leo Shane III, "As Space Dwindles, Final Rules on Burial Eligibility for Arlington Cemetery Expected This Fall," Military Times (website), May 5, 2021.

19. Poole, *On Hallowed Ground*, 71–73; Micki McElya, *The Politics of Mourning: Death and Honor in Arlington National Cemetery* (Cambridge, MA: Harvard University Press, 2016), 96 and 102.

20. The term "sites of memory" comes from Pierre Nora, "Between Memory and History: Les Lieux de Mémoire," *Representations*, no. 26, Special Issue: Memory and Counter-Memory (Spring 1989): 7.

21. On controversial monuments, see Keith Lowe, *Prisoners of History: What Monuments to World War II Tell Us about Our History and Ourselves* (New York: St. Martin's Press, 2020); Erin L. Thompson, *Smashing Statues: The Rise and Fall of America's Public Monuments* (New York: W. W. Norton, 2022); "Presidential Initiatives: The Monuments Project," Mellon Foundation (website), accessed April 14, 2024; Erika Doss, *Memorial Mania: Public Feeling in America* (Chicago: University of Chicago Press, 2010), "obsession" on 2, 46–48. Studies that highlight the challenges of telling a unified narrative about US history in public installations include Roger C. Aden, *Upon the Ruins of History: Slavery, the President's House at Independence National Historical Park, and Public Memory* (Philadelphia: Temple University Press, 2015); Dell Upton, *What Can and Can't Be Said: Race, Uplift, and Monument Building in the Contemporary South* (New Haven, CT: Yale University Press, 2015); Clint Smith, *How the Word Is Passed: A Reckoning with the History of Slavery across America* (New York: Back Bay Books, 2021).

22. John Bodnar, "Pierre Nora, National Memory, and Democracy: A Review," *Journal of American History* 87, no. 3 (December 2000): 952.

Chapter 9

1. Jason De León, *The Land of Open Graves: Living and Dying on the Migrant Trail* (Berkeley: University of California Press, 2015), 62–82. On animals and their ways of dying, see Bernd Heinrich, *Life Everlasting: The Animal Way of Death* (New York: Mariner Books, 2012).

2. Mitford updated her 1963 account in *The American Way of Death Revisited* (New York: Vintage, 1998). For a more recent discussion of mortuary practices and how people are drawn to participate in funerary culture, see Caitlin Doughty, *From Here to Eternity: Traveling the World to Find the Good Death* (New York: W. W. Norton, 2017).

3. Brian Black describes this process in *Gettysburg Contested: 150 Years of Preserving America's Cherished Landscape* (Staunton, VA: George F. Thompson Publishing, 2019).

4. Thomas W. Laqueur, *The Work of the Dead: A Cultural History of Mortal Remains* (Princeton, NJ: Princeton University Press, 2015), 133–37 and 211–361, "luxuriantly protean space" and "a historicist jumble" on 212. Laqueur points out (287) that John Louden, one of the first designers of cemeteries in Britain, coined the term "landscape architecture."

5. Aaron Sachs, *Arcadian America: The Death and Life of an Environmental Tradition* (New Haven, CT : Yale University Press, 2013), 19–6l, on "repose," see 21–22; quoting historian David Schuyler, Sachs notes (38) that rural cemeteries are "didactic landscapes." On nature's alluring effects, see John Dixon Hunt, "'Come into the Garden, Maud': Garden Art as a Privileged Mode of Commemoration and Identity," in *Places of Commemoration: Search for Identity and Landscape Design*, ed. Joachim Wolschke-Bulmahn (Washington, DC: Dumbarton Oaks Research Library and Collection, 2001), 15–17.

6. The National Cemetery of Arizona was established as a state veterans' cemetery in 1978 and moved into the federal system in 1989.

7. Mike Yessis, "These Five 'Witness Trees' Were Present at Key Moments in America's History," *Smithsonian Magazine* (website), August 25, 2017; Elizabeth Redden, "Managing the Trees of Arlington Cemetery," *Orion Magazine* (website), March/April 2008.

8. On restoring the body, see Thomas Lynch, *The Undertaking: Life Studies from the Dismal Trade* (New York: W. W. Norton, 1997), 22–25. Charles Watkins discusses pollarding in *Trees, Woods and Forests: A Social and Cultural History* (London: Reaktion Books, 2014), 115–39.

9. Sara Amy Leach, "Design History of National Cemeteries," National Park Service (website), last updated July 12, 2023. This overview is adapted from an article Leach wrote for the National Park Service called "Designing the First National Cemeteries."

10. Michael Ragon, *The Space of Death: A Study of Funerary Architecture, Decoration, and Urbanism*, trans. Alan Sheridan (Charlottesville: University of Virginia Press, 1983), 114–15.

11. Gaston Bachelard, *The Poetics of Space*, trans. Maria Jolas (1994; Boston: Beacon Press, 1958), 202, xv, and xxxv.

12. Jeffrey K. Olick, Vered Vinitzky-Seroussi, and Daniel Levy, "Introduction," in *The Collective Memory Reader*, ed. Jeffrey K. Olick, Vered Vinitzky-Seroussi, and Daniel Levy (New York: Oxford University Press, 2011), 36–39.

13. Sarah E. Wagner, *What Remains: Bringing America's Missing Home from the Vietnam War* (Cambridge, MA: Harvard University Press, 2019), "exceptional care" on 53.

14. Michael A. Stern refers to "corporate pastoralism" and discusses the anonymous nature of the newer cemeteries in "The National Cemetery System: Politics, Place, and Contemporary Cemetery Design," in Wolschke-Bulmahn, *Places of Commemoration*, 114 and 117–21; National Park Service, US Department of the Interior, National Register of Historic Places Multiple Property Documentation Form, "Inter-World War National Cemeteries, 1934–1939" (certified March 7, 2016), 25, archived at National Register of Historic Places and Designated National Historic Landmarks, National Cemetery Administration (website), last updated May 2, 2024.

15. Jay Winter, *War Beyond Words: Languages of Remembrance from the Great War to the Present* (Cambridge: Cambridge University Press, 2017), 144.

16. Lisa Tonneson-McCorkell, "The National Cemetery: A Journey through Design," LA Group (website), October 26, 2017.

17. Office of Construction & Facilities Management, Office of Facilities Planning, Department of Veterans Affairs, *National Cemetery Administration Design Guide* (Washington, DC: Department of Veterans Affairs, 2024), 2–18 (on committal shelters) and 2–20 (on the importance of the flag).

18. Patrick J. Kelly, *Creating a National Home: Building the Veterans' Welfare State 1860–1900* (Cambridge, MA: Harvard University Press, 1997), 2, 105–8.

19. On belief and imagined selves, see Stanley Cavell, *Conditions Handsome and Unhandsome: The Constitution of Emersonian Perfectionism* (Chicago: University of Chicago Press, 1990), 6–12; Mia Bay, *Traveling Black: A Story of Race and Resistance* (Cambridge, MA: Harvard University Press, 2021).

20. Katherine Verdery, *The Political Lives of Dead Bodies: Reburial and Postsocialist Change* (New York: Columbia University Press, 1999), "dead-body politics" on 3, 27–33, and 39–47.

Chapter 10

1. With the passage of the National Cemetery Expansion Act of 2003, Congress directed the Department of Veterans Affairs to establish six new national cemeteries in areas with at least 170,000 residents not currently served by burial locations for veterans.

2. George Yancy, "Facing the Fact of My Death," *The Stone* (blog), New York Times (website), February 3, 2020; Mark Ralkowski, "Being-toward-Death," in *50 Concepts for a Critical Phenomenology*, ed. Gail Weiss, Ann V. Murphy, and Gayle Salamon (Evanston: Northwestern University Press, 2020), 39–45.

3. Amanda Barroso, "The Changing Profile of the U.S. Military: Smaller in Size, More Diverse, More Women in Leadership," Pew Research Center (website), September 10, 2019; "Demographics of the U. S. Military," Council on Foreign Relations (website), updated July 13, 2020; "Department of Defense Releases Annual Demographics Report—Upward Trend in Number of Women Continues," US Department of Defense (website), December 14, 2022; Katherine Schaeffer, "The Changing Face of America's Veteran Population," Pew Research Center (website), April 5, 2021 (updated November 8, 2023).

4. For instance, see Charles C. Moskos and John Sibley Butler, *All That We Can Be: Black Leadership and Racial Integration the Army Way* (New York: Basic Books, 1996), especially 4–5, 63–64, and 132–33.

5. Helene Cooper, "Black Troops Fight at the Front, but Rarely Get Jobs at the Top," *New York Times*, May 25, 2020, Section A, 1. On extremists in the military, see Kathleen Belew, *Bring the War Home: The White Power Movement and Paramilitary America* (Cambridge, MA: Harvard University Press, 2018). For a historical critique of racism in the military, see Ty Seidule, *Robert E. Lee and Me: A Southerner's Reckoning with the Myth of the Lost Cause* (New York: St. Martin's Press, 2021).

6. Walter Johnson, *The Broken Heart of America: St. Louis and the Violent History of the United States* (New York: Basic Books, 2020), especially 1–71.

7. Monro MacCloskey, *Hallowed Ground: Our National Cemeteries* (New York: Richard Rosen Press, 1968), "honorably discharged" on 42, "late war" on 41–43.

8. Chris Hawley, "US Heroes Are Villains at Cemetery in Mexico," Banderas News (website), May 2007.

9. "Mexico City National Cemetery, Mexico City, Mexico," Interment.Net (website), September 19, 1999 (updated November 15, 2019).

10. "1955: Ceremony Planned for Colonel Bliss; Body Is Found," *Tales From the Morgue* (blog), *El Paso Times* (website), October 23, 2012. This story was republished from the November 11, 1955, issue of the newspaper.

11. Lindsey Anderson, "Storms Go Easy on Fort Bliss National Cemetery," *El Paso Times*, August 5, 2015.

12. National Park Service, US Department of the Interior, National Register of Historic Places Registration

Form, "Fort Bliss National Cemetery" (certified March 8, 2016), Section 8, 15–16, archived at National Register of Historic Places and Designated National Historic Landmarks, National Cemetery Administration (website), last updated May 2, 2024.

13. "Buffalo Soldiers, Buried at Ft. Bayard, New Mexico," New Mexico Genealogy (website), accessed March 3, 2021.

14. Danny Udero, "Fort Bayard Has Had a Rich and Diverse History," azcentral (website), February 27, 2017.

15. Augusta Stevenson, *Kit Carson: Boy Trapper* (Indianapolis: Bobbs-Merrill, 1945).

16. John Berger, *Ways of Seeing* (London: Penguin, 1972), 8. For a recent critique of the frontier, see Greg Grandin, *The End of the Myth: From the Frontier to the Border Wall in the Mind of America* (New York: Metropolitan Books, 2019). On the "sense of the tragic" in history, see Czeslaw Milosz, "Tiger," in *To Begin Where I Am: Selected Essays* (New York: Farrar, Straus and Giroux, 2001), 147.

17. "Fort McPherson," Explore Nebraska History (website), accessed May 2, 2024; Fort McPherson National Cemetery, National Cemetery Administration (website), last updated December 5, 2023; Kamie Stephen, "Fort McPherson Provides Options for Veteran Burial," *North Platte Telegraph* (website), November 7, 2015 (updated August 10, 2020).

18. Sitka Historic Preservation Commission, *Sitka Historic Preservation Plan: A Guide for Cultural Preservation, Protection, and Advocacy* (Sitka, AK: City and Borough of Sitka, 2017). On Sitka National Cemetery and the growth of empire, see Shannon Bontrager, *Death at the Edges of Empire: Fallen Soldiers, Cultural Memory, and the Making of an American Nation,1863–1921* (Lincoln: University of Nebraska Press, 2020), 70–74.

Coda

1. Jasper Craven, "On Memorial Day, the Veterans Who Bury Their Own," *New York Times*, May 31, 2021, Sec A, 19.

2. David Charles Sloane, *The Last Great Necessity: Cemeteries in American History* (Baltimore: Johns Hopkins University Press, 1991), 112–15.

3. "History of Government-Furnished Headstones and Markers," National Cemetery Administration (website), updated December 22, 2023; Mark C. Mollan, "Honoring Our War Dead: The Evolution of the Government Policy on Headstones for Fallen Soldiers and Sailors," *Prologue Magazine* 35, no. 1 (Spring 2003): 56–65.

4. "Emblems of Belief," National Cemetery Administration (website), last updated February 15, 2023; "Headstones, Markers, and Medallions," National Cemetery Administration (website), last updated September 9, 2022; "Government Headstones and Markers FAQs," US Department of Veterans Affairs (website), last updated March 19, 2021; "Types of Headstones, Markers, and Medallions," National Cemetery Administration (website), last updated December 11, 2023.

5. In compiling these thumbnail portraits, I have relied on various online resources, including genealogical sites such as Ancestry.com.

Gallery of Honor

1. Biographical information archived at Ancestry.com (website), accessed September 16, 2022.

2. "Jose Raul Cupis," Legacy.com (website), accessed April 24, 2022; "Pascua Yaqui Tribal Base Roll of

September 18, 1980," *Federal Register* 49, no. 97, May 17, 1984, Membership Criteria and Requirements, Pascua Yaqui Tribe (website), accessed April 25, 2022.

3. "Victor Gutzwiler," American Civil War Research Database (website), accessed November 23, 2022; "Hancock County, Ohio Biographies," Genealogy Trails (website), accessed November 23, 2022.

4. "Sean R. Harvell," The Hall of Valor Project (website), accessed June 20, 2021; Greg Yee, "Roughly 300 Gather to Remember Sean Harvell, Decorated Veteran Who Drowned off Alamitos Beach," *Press-Telegram* (website), May 6, 2016 (updated September 1, 2017).

5. Richard Goldstein, "James R. Hendrix, War Hero, Dies at 77," *New York Times*, November 21, 2002, Sec A, 35.

6. Alisa Samuels, "Skydiver's Family Remembers His Love of Risk," *Baltimore Sun* (website), October 3, 1995 (updated October 23, 2018).

7. Biographical information archived at Ancestry.com (website), accessed June 21, 2022.

8. "Obituary of Regina Wodzinski Labno," Poling St. Clair Funeral Home and Crematory (website), accessed April 12, 2024.

9. "Roger H. Larocque Obituary," Sanderson Funeral Home (website), accessed April 18, 2024.

10. "Master Sergeant Charles Gentry Marlin (Ret.) Obituary," Legacy.com (website), accessed April 12, 2024.

11. "Asian-Pacific Americans in the U.S. Army, 100th Battalion, 442d Infantry," US Army Center of Military History (website), prepared December 29, 1995; *Honolulu Advertiser*, April 20, 1990; *Honolulu Star Bulletin*, January 6, 2010.

12. Bev Hetzel (compiler), "Wisconsin Soldiers Deaths at Shiloh, Tennessee," Wisconsin Genealogy Trails (website), accessed April 18, 2024; Jim Miller, "Color Bearers of the 16th Wisconsin Infantry: Shiloh National Cemetery," *Civil War Notebook* (blog), August 24, 2012; "The 16th Wisconsin at Shiloh," CivilWarTalk (website), March 24, 2020; "Photo Record, Erwin L. Rider," Wisconsin Veterans Museum (website), accessed April 18, 2024.

13. "Augusta Grace Derrick Saucer," *Johnson City Press* (website), January 9, 2018 (updated July 6, 2020).

14. Biographical information archived at Ancestry.com (website), accessed April 25, 2022.

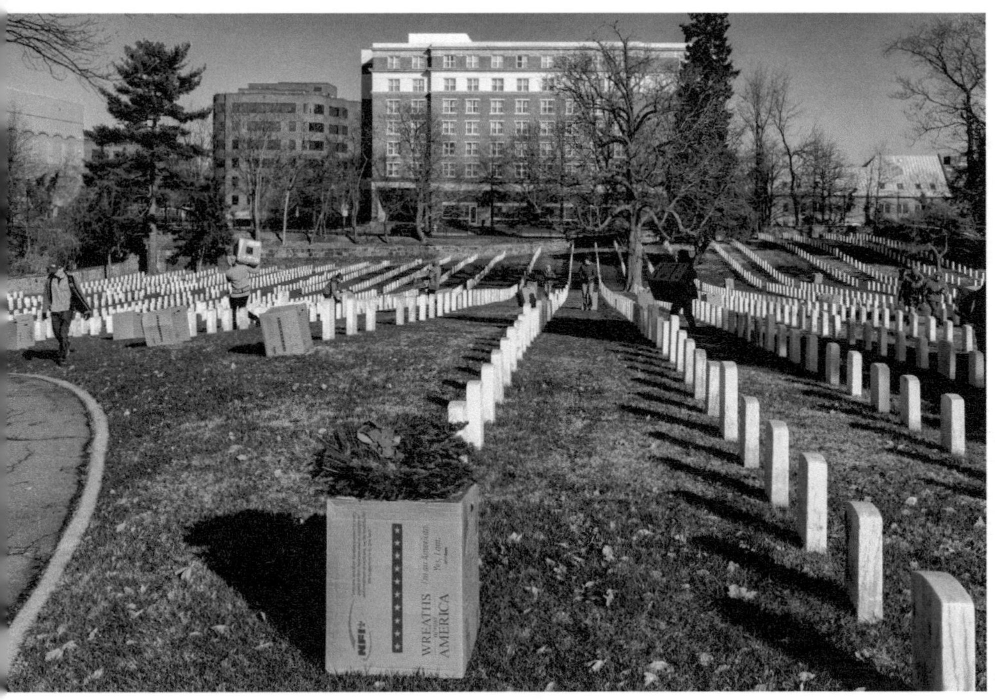

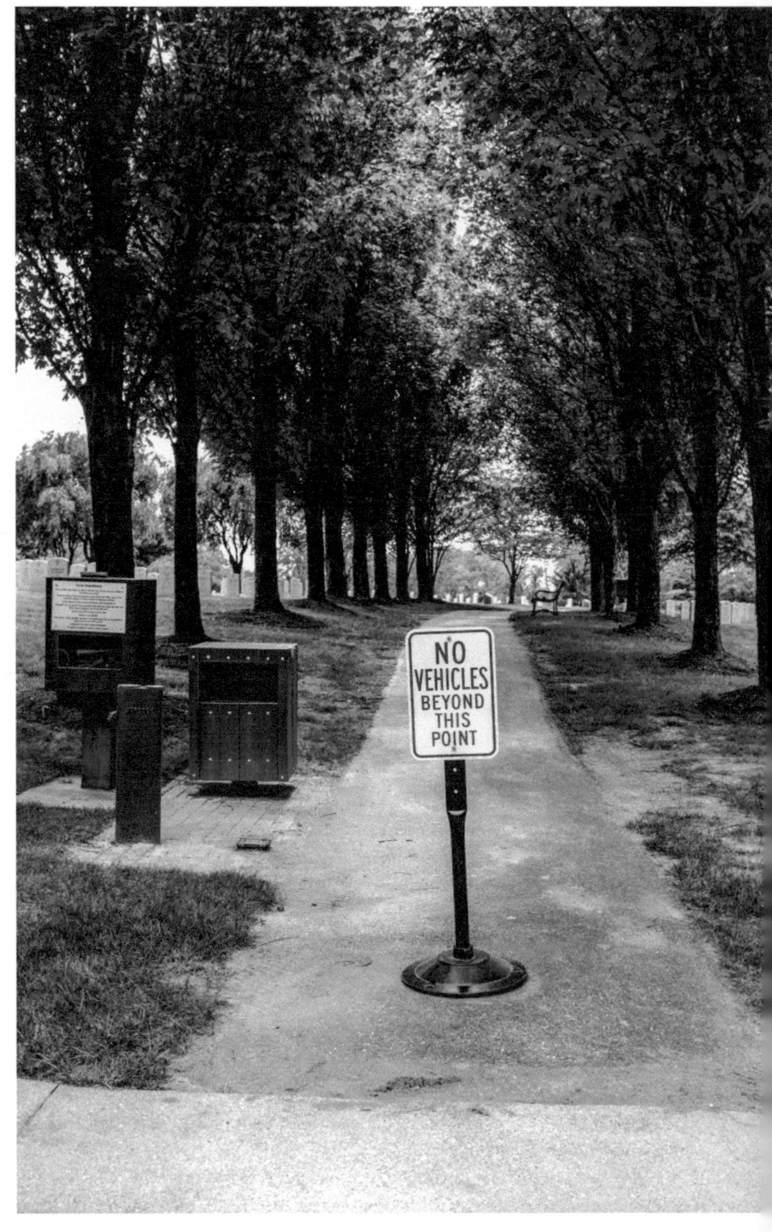

(*Above*) Alexandria National Cemetery (established in 1862), Alexandria, Virginia, 2017. Laying holiday wreaths at each of the more than 4,000 headstones. Volunteers annually donate more than 78,000 hours of service at America's 155 national cemeteries.

(*Right*) Indiantown Gap National Cemetery (established in 1976), Annville, Pennsylvania, 2019.

Suggested Readings

Websites

There is a wealth of information online about the national cemeteries, much of it provided by the federal government. The best source is the National Cemetery Administration's official website, which details the cemeteries' ongoing operations and includes materials related to their mission and history. The National Park Service also hosts websites devoted to cemeteries established during the Civil War era, and Arlington National Cemetery maintains its own extensive site illuminating the purpose and history of that important memorial landscape. Similarly, the American Battle Monuments Commission has a robust online presence, and the ABMC website is an important destination for anyone who wants to learn about American military cemeteries abroad.

In maintaining these websites, the federal government is engaged in first-rate public history. At the same time, the National Cemetery Administration and Arlington National Cemetery websites are interactive platforms that provide real-time information on a range of topics, from interment policies to funeral schedules to grave locations. Their educational orientation is always in service to their primary institutional commitment, which is to honor the service and sacrifice of American military personnel.

Books

Among the books describing the national cemetery system, Dean W. Holt's *American Military Cemeteries: A Comprehensive Illustrated Guide to the Hallowed Grounds of the United States* (Jefferson, NC: McFarland, 1992) and Monro MacCloskey's *Hallowed Ground: Our National Cemeteries* (New York: Richard Rosen Press, 1968) are especially useful.

Anyone interested in the creation of the national cemeteries should begin with Drew Gilpin Faust's outstanding history, *This Republic of Suffering: Death and the American Civil War* (New York: Alfred A. Knopf, 2008). Other important books on the Civil War and memorial culture—and cemeteries in particular—include David W. Blight, *Race and Reunion: The Civil War in American Memory* (Cambridge, MA: Harvard University Press, 2001); William Blair, *Contesting the Memory of the Civil War in the South, 1865–1914* (Chapel Hill: University of North Carolina Press, 2004); John R. Neff, *Honoring the Civil War Dead: Commemoration and the Problem of Reconciliation* (Lawrence: University Press of Kansas, 2005); Carolyn E. Janney, *Remembering the Civil War: Reunion and the Limits of Reconciliation* (Chapel Hill: University of North Carolina Press, 2013); and Brian Matthew Jordan and Jonathan W. White, eds., *Final Resting Places: Reflections on the Meaning of Civil War Graves* (Athens: University of Georgia Press, 2023).

Related studies that offer insightful analyses of how the United States honors its military dead include G. Kurt Piehler, *Remembering War the American Way* (Washington, DC: Smithsonian Books, 1995); Michael Sledge, *Soldier Dead: How We Recover, Identify, Bury & Honor Our Military Dead* (New York: Columbia University Press, 2005); Robert M. Poole, *On Hallowed Ground: The Story of Arlington Cemetery* (New York: Walker, 2009); and Micki McElya, *The Politics of Mourning: Death and Honor in Arlington Cemetery* (Cambridge, MA: Harvard University Press, 2016).

The mission of the American Battle Monuments Commission is the subject of several books that highlight American memorial sites abroad, along with related diplomatic efforts. For instance, see Ron Theodore Robin, *Enclaves of America: The Rhetoric of American Political Architecture Abroad, 1900–1965* (Princeton, NJ: Princeton University Press, 1992); Thomas H. Conner, *War and Remembrance: The Story of the American Battle Monuments Commission* (Lexington: University of Kentucky Press, 2018); Kate Clarke Lemay, *Triumph of the Dead: American World War II Cemeteries, Monuments, and Diplomacy in France* (Tuscaloosa: University of Alabama Press, 2018); and American Battle Monuments Commission, *Time Will Not Dim: American Battle Monuments Commission, A Century of Service, 1923–2023* (Arlington, VA: American Battle Monuments Commission, 2023).

Beyond the American context, the scholarship on war and remembrance is deep and rich. Jay Winter's work, beginning with *Sites of Memory, Sites of Mourning: The Great War in European Cultural History* (Cambridge: Cambridge University Press, 1995), provides an essential map for understanding the impact of World War I on modern thought and culture. And Thomas W. Laqueur's *The Work of the Dead: A Cultural History of Mortal Remains* (Princeton, NJ: Princeton University Press, 2015), a magisterial study of how Westerners have engaged the dead, also focuses on war (in particular, World War I) and memorial culture.

For a general overview of cemeteries in US history, the classic work remains David Charles Sloane's *The Last Great Necessity: Cemeteries in American History* (Baltimore: Johns Hopkins University Press, 1991). See, also, Sloane's *Is the Cemetery Dead?* (Chicago: University of Chicago Press, 2018). For pivotal books in memory studies that emphasize the relation between landscape and loss, a good starting point is Kenneth E. Foote's *Shadowed Ground: America's Landscapes of Violence and Tragedy* (Austin: University of Texas Press, 1997).

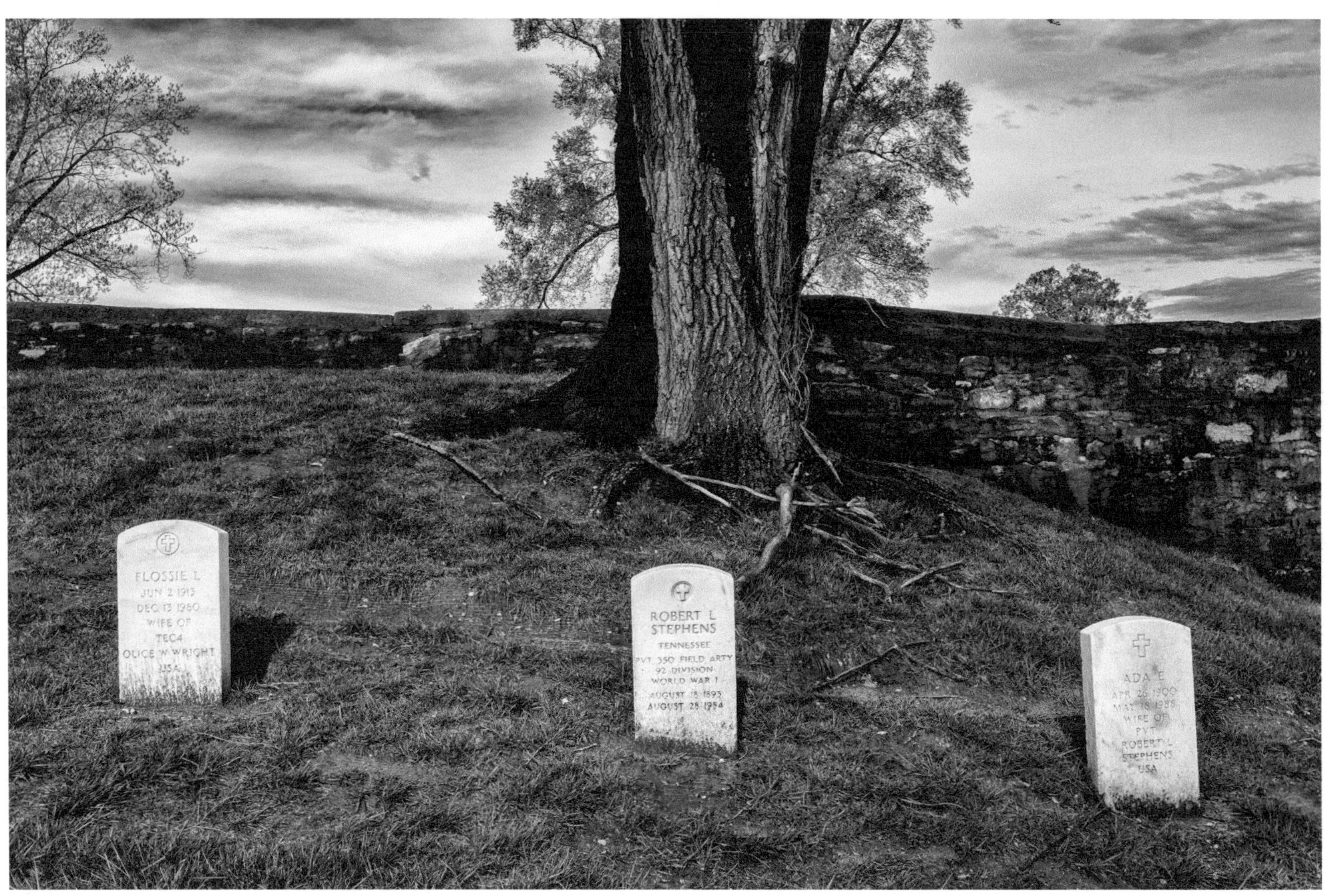

Jefferson Barracks National Cemetery (established in 1863), St. Louis, Missouri, 2018.

Index